HOW TO USE THIS BOOK

Chapter 1

24 Absolute Patterns in

Writing & Language Section

The entire Writing and Language Section uses these patterns.

CollegeBoard SAT creates the questions based on these patterns.

Instead of solving each individual question endlessly without knowing the patterns and logic, assume that each question is made of a unique formula.

Memorize 24 patterns in this chapter and check to see if you are following the patterns.

Practice until every pattern becomes natural to you.

To obtain a <u>free</u> Collegeboard Official SAT reading test analyzed by the patterns, please send a simple email request: satvancouver@gmail.com

24 Absolute Patterns in Writing & Language Section

1 Adding, Revising, Deleting, Retaining Information

1▶ This most commonly found pattern typically contains phrases such as 'If the author…'deleted / wish to add / support / would lose…"

2▶ The multiple choices normally carries 'YES', 'NO' or 'Keep', 'Delete'.

3▶ You bet it sounds jubilant and logical but don't ride on a new horse while racing on the track!

4▶ Please do not choose any new information including pronouns like "He" or "They."

5▶ Any new information that steers the flows of a sentence, a paragraph, or a passage is automatically incorrect.

How to use this book

Chapter 2.

Twelve Writing and Language Tests

12 Writing Tests in this book are designed with the same level of difficulties and methodologies as used in the real SAT.

Writing and Language Test 1
35 MINUTES, 44 QUESTIONS

Each passage below is accompanied by a number of questions. For some questions, you will consider how the passage might be revised to improve the expression of ideas. For other questions, you will consider how the passage might be edited to correct errors in sentence structure, usage, or punctuation. A passage or a question may be accompanied by one or more graphics (such as a table or graph) that you will consider as you make revising and editing decisions.

Questions 1-12 are based on the following passage

Global Warning

Harvard University The Crimson
 Reprinted with permission

Just when I was starting to get used to the passionate debates [1] characterize meals in Annenberg, a recent dinner conversation threw me a curveball. Last week, I had the unique—and frustrating—privilege of dining with the last individual on earth who does not believe in global warming.

Or so I thought. Further research indicates that my

1

A) that characterize
B) ,which characterizes
C) characterizes
D) characterized

2

At this point, the author is considering adding the sentence below.

   Within the scientific community, this statistic is
   only three percent.

Should the author add this sentence here?

A) Yes, because it contrasts the views between the public and scientists
B) Yes, because it shows lack of interest in global warming among scientists
C) No, because scientists' view deviates from the

CONTINUE ⇒

HOW TO USE THIS BOOK
12 Writing & Language Tests Absolute Pattern Analysis

Test 1 Writing Section Patterns

Q1. Absolute Pattern 12: Modifier (Placement) Error

Just when I was starting to get used to the passionate **debates [1]** _characterize_ meals in Annenberg, a recent dinner conversation threw me a curveball. Last week,

√	**A) that characterize**	A) 1>"that characterize meals in Annenberg" describes "debates" as the adjective modifier.
	B) , which characterizes	2> Because "debates" is plural, the plural verb "characterize" should be used.
	C) characterizes	B) modifies the "debates" but uses the singular verb "characterizes"
	D) characterized	C), D) are regular verbs, not a modifier.

Q2. Absolute Pattern 1: Adding, Revising, Deleting, Retaining Information

about 11 percent of Americans still think that global warming "will never happen." [2] Within the scientific community, this statistic is only three percent.

√	**A) Yes, because it contrasts the views between the public and scientists**
	B) Yes, because it shows lack of interest in global warming among scientists
	C) No, because scientists' view deviates from the main focus of the paragraph
	D) No, because 3 percent is too insignificant to emphasize the author's view.

A) The author brings up the scientists' view to show 97% of them believe the global warming.

B) The sentence "~among scientists" should change to "~among the public"

C) The author wants to elaborate her thought about global warming based on the scientific justification and therefore "scientists" does not deviates, but emphasizes her belief.

D) is opposite, 3% is very significant because it means 97% believes the global warming.

HOW TO USE THIS BOOK

Chapter 3.

College Board PSAT Writing Section Absolute Pattern Analysis

To download the test, please visit:
https://collegereadiness.collegeboard.org/pdf/psat-nmsqt-practice-test-1.pdf

	Q3. Absolute Pattern 21: Subject-Verb, Pronoun, Noun Agreement	
	Passage keywords: American (singular)	
	A) spend	C) The singular verb in the adjective clause
	B) have spent	1> "the average American spend" modifies (or supports) the subject "The hours", serving as an adjective clause.
√	**C) spends**	2> Even though it is in the middle of the sentence working as an adjective for the main subject, 3> it still needs to follow the subject-verb agreement.
	D) are spent	4> "the average American" is singular (the singular subject in the adjective clause).
		5> Therefore, the verb "spend" should be "spends." (the singular verb in the adjective clause)
		A) Plural B) The present perfect D) Passive

	Q20. Absolute Pattern 16: Precision, Concision, Style	
	Passage keywords: farmers, resorted (A complete sentence)	
	A) crops; when, being	C) 1> Always choose the most concise sentence from the options.
	B) crops, this is	2> The most concise sentence means having no conjunction or dependent clause without losing the original meaning.
√	**C) crops, an expensive**	3> This is called simplification rule"
	D) crops; an expensive	4> The option that usually starts with "an" is the answer under the simplification pattern.

(A) has several errors:

1> a semicolon should carry a dependent clause, which is not applied in this question.

2> the subordinating conjunction 'when' cannot be used together with the semicolon.

3> the usage of 'being' suddenly changes the active voice into the passive within one sentence.

(B) 1> Comma splice 2> "this is" is ambiguous. (D) Semicolon error

HOW TO USE THIS BOOK

Chapter 3.

College Board SAT Writing Section Absolute Pattern Analysis

To download the test, please visit:
https://collegereadiness.collegeboard.org/pdf/sat-practice-test-1.pdf

Q6. Absolute Pattern 1: Adding, Revising, Deleting, Retaining Information	
Passage keywords: Though, these, methods, well worth effort (Positive)	
A) Yes, not provide	The topic sentence should remain definitely.
B) Yes, fails	Therefore, the answer should be either (C) or (D).
C) No, how, can be disposed	(C) The description is based on the previous paragraph.
√ **D) No, benefits**	(D) The description is based on the paragraph where the topic sentence belongs to. Therefore, the answer should be (D)

Q11. Absolute Pattern 7: Conjunction Error	
Passage keywords: Because	
A) therefore farmers	B) Two clauses require only one conjunction.
√ **B) ,farmers**	1> "Because" is a subordinating conjunction or simply a conjunction. 2> "therefore" is a conjunctive adverb. or simply a conjunction.
C) ,so farmers	3> Having two conjunctions (because, therefore) in two clauses, this sentence technically has no completely independent main clause but two subordinating clauses.
D) :farmers	4> Therefore, the answer should be the one that has no conjunction. A) "therefore" and C) "so" are conjunctions (conjunctive adverbs) D) a colon also must be carried by an independent clause, which is disabled by placing the colon.

HOW TO USE THIS BOOK

Chapter 4.

70 Rules for the Sentence-Error Questions

To optimize your success in Writing & Language Test and minimize surprise by making all the questions ABSOLUTELY predictable, following 70 Rules for the sentence-error questions will change the way you react to each sentence-error questions.

Question 1

For decades the paleontologists had assumed that the Ice Age killed the dinosaurs, <u>and their views changed</u> quickly when the massive meteorite crater was found in Yucatan.

A) NO CHANGE
B) but their views had changed
C) however, their views changed
D) but their views changed

Rule #1	"But" is used to Contrast Idea. "And" is used to shore up Idea.
Hint: Conjunction	The correct answer is D.

Use the conjunction 'but' to cancel out the previous sentence when two contrasting ideas are presented.

Option A):

1> The keywords "views changed quickly"

2> Two clauses between "and" are conflicting each other.

3> This is called "Misused AND"

Option B) is incorrect because "had changed" (the past perfect)" means that their views had changed before the crater was found, an impossible situation.

Option C) is incorrect because 'however' requires a semicolon (; however,)

All inquiries should be addressed to:
Rockridge edu. enterprise & services inc.
869 SEYMOUR BLVD. NORTH VANCOUVER B.C. CANADA V7J 2J7
satvancouver@gmail.com

CONTENTS

CONTENTS

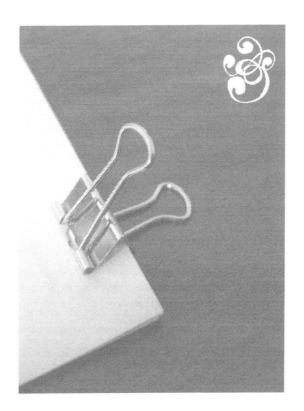

Chapter 1

24 ABSOLUTE PATTERNS
FOR
THE WRITING & LANGUAGE TEST

Chapter 1

24 Absolute Patterns for the Writing & Language Test

The entire Writing and Language Section uses these patterns.

CollegeBoard SAT creates the questions based on these patterns.

Instead of solving each individual question endlessly without knowing the patterns and logic, assume that each question is made of a unique formula. Memorize the 24 patterns in this chapter and check each time to see if you are following the patterns. Practice until every pattern becomes natural to you.

24 Absolute Patterns in Writing & Language Section

1 │ Adding, Revising, Deleting, Retaining Information

1▶ This most commonly found pattern typically contains phrases such as 'If the author…'deleted / wish to add / support / would lose…"

2▶ The multiple choices normally carries 'YES', 'NO' or 'Keep', 'Delete'.

3▶ You bet it sounds jubilant and logical but don't ride on a new horse while racing on the track!

4▶ Please do not choose any new information including pronouns like "He" or "They."

5▶ Any new information that steers the flows of a sentence, a paragraph, or a passage is automatically disqualified.

2 │ Cause-Effect Relations

1▶ This question presents the cause-effect relations, in which you should find the subordinating conjunctions such as 'because' 'if' 'so' or adverb like 'as a result', 'consequently', etc.

2▶ Please be careful there's no stunning corner that distinguishes between cause and effect.

3▶ They are look alike!

4▶ The cause-effect context you're staring at quietly switches the conjunctions, pulls one off, or put up two conjunctions instead of one, such as switching the causative conjunction "because" to the effects-adverb "as a result", or switching the present tense "results in" to past tense "resulted by" that only to divert your attention and make you desperate to figuring out the difference between "in" and "by", which are both acceptable.

3 │ Colloquialism (Nonstandard Language)

1▶ Colloquialism asks whether the word or phrase is following the formal written language.

2▶ Any option with the informal casual language such as 'thing' or 'plus' is considered to be incorrect.

24 Absolute Patterns in Writing & Language Section

4 Comparison

1 ▶ Comparison pattern asks the broad range of comparisons such as comparing the subjects, adjective, pronoun, phrase, or clause. "Apple to Apple."

2 ▶ When things are being compared, it should maintain the exactly same parallel structure.

3 ▶ The most typical question in this pattern employs a correlative conjunction such as "not only ~but also."

4 ▶ If a question underlines the former portion of the conjunction, it becomes relatively easy. However, if the former is missing, while the latter one appears, it won't be a piece of cake.

5 Comma Splice Error

1 ▶ Comma splice appears when two independent sentences (clauses) are not joined by a conjunction.

2 ▶ It is relatively easy to identify the error if there is no conjunction at all.

3 ▶ Ironically, however, it becomes more complex when more than one conjunction appears in two clauses. You should have only one conjunction to combine two clauses.

6 Confusing Words

This pattern asks the frequently confusing words (e.g., 'complement' and 'compliment')

24 Absolute Patterns in Writing & Language Section

7 | Conjunction Error

1 ▶ There are three types of conjunctions: coordinating, subordinating, and correlative conjunction.

2 ▶ A conjunction connects two clauses.

3 ▶ Typical questions related with this pattern are a question asking: (1) whether the text is a clause or a phrase—a phrase should not be connected to a conjunction. (2) whether the type of conjunction is properly used.

Three types of conjunctions are summarized in page 46.

8 | Double Negative Error

1 ▶ Double negative pattern appears less frequently.

2 ▶ Double negatives usually carry a negative adverb such as 'hardly, rarely, or seldom'

3 ▶ But more often, a negative noun or verb such as "decrease" or "detract" is combined with a negative adverb such as "least"

9 | Informational Graphs

1 ▶ Informational graph questions can be subcategorized into two types: (1) Independent questions that you don't need the passage for review, and (2) Integrated questions that require information from the passage.

2 ▶ The former appears more frequently (Two informational graph questions in writing section in the SAT Official Test in the Appendix A are independent question that actually didn't require the reading resources.

3 ▶ In which case, you really do not have to waste your time peeking on the reading passage, even though the question indiscriminately asks you to read the passage to solve the problem. This is what everyone in the College Board knows, except you.

24 Absolute Patterns in Writing & Language Section

10 Logical Expression

1 ▶ This pattern borrows the word-in-context technique in the reading passage.

2 ▶ Unlike that of reading section that focuses more on distinguishing literal meaning from figurative or relying on complex vocabularies, the logical expression in writing section more often comes with the rules of syntax such as adjective, adverb, noun, and verb usage—if not the entire phrase or clause.

11 Logical Sequence

1 ▶ This pattern is about identifying the best placement for a given sentence, phrase, or word.

2 ▶ The multiple choices in a logical sequence question normally carry the words such as (A) 'before sentence 1', (D) 'after sentence 4.'

3 ▶ One trick to find the best sequence (the answer) is to review the sentences from backward. (I know it will be uncomfortable at first like wearing a brand new underwear. Here's a couple of steps:
(1) Find your best choice by using your own method.
(2) Try to read your best choice from backward order (from bottom to top), so that you can read from the conclusion that you believe it is.
Identifying the conclusion is always easier than identifying the introduction.

12 Modifier (Placement) Error

1 ▶ A modifier must be placed immediately next to the main element that it intends to describe.

2 ▶ It should not be located adjacently.

3 ▶ To illustrate, if a modifying phrase appears at the beginning of the sentence to describe the main clause, the subject in the main clause has to be the direct agent of the modifier.
please consider the following sentence: "Known as the great writer in U.S., *the brilliant skills of Mark Twain* are not from his education, but from intuition."

4 ▶ The modifier "the great writer" must describe a human (Mark Twain) not "the brilliant skills"
The correct answer for this dangling modifier error should be "*Mark Twain* developed his brilliant skills not from the education, but from intuition."

24 Absolute Patterns in Writing & Language Section

13 Parallel Structure

1▶ You should find if there's any inappropriate shift in a parallel construction.

2▶ The parallelism error occurs from a simple adjective-noun combination, or complex abbreviated form of phrase to an unparalleled tense.

Ex) "The population of Kentucky is smaller than California" is a flawed sentence because it compares the "population" to "California."

Here's another example: "Traffic accidents occur most frequently in New York than any other cities except in Seattle." This sentence is defective too. "in Seattle" has to be "Seattle" because it is no longer comparing Seattle to accidents in New York anymore. It compares to any other cities.

14 Possessive Determiners and Possessive Noun Error

1▶ This pattern asks the possessive determiners ("its," "his," "their"), contractions ("we're," "you're,"), and adverbs ("there")

2▶ The possessive of a singular noun is formed by adding an apostrophe and s.

15 Prepositional Idiom

Idiom and prepositional idiom pattern asks the correct usage of preposition.

24 Absolute Patterns in Writing & Language Section

16 Precision, Concision, Style

1▶ This pattern asks the most appropriate and economic way of expression

2▶ Ether too choppy or unreasonably detailed and separated clause by using a conjunction or punctuation is considered to be incorrect.

3▶ As long as it puts all the information together into an ideal and smooth one sentence, the shorter choice is always the better, which means the concise sentence shouldn't contain conjunction or dependent clause.

4▶ The redundancy should be the number one culprit to blame in the incorrect options.

17 Pronoun Error

1▶ Pronoun error asks whether the sentence inappropriately changes pronoun (e.g., from 'there' to 'their', or 'he' to 'they').

2▶ This pattern also put an ambiguous pronoun on the table. As an example, please consider the following sentence: "While Jason and John were walking, he hit him." The second pronoun must be identified.

18 Punctuation Error

Punctuation pattern mainly asks if the punctuation usage (e.g., colon, semicolon, dashes, super comma, a pair of commas) correctly represents the sentence.

24 Absolute Patterns in Writing & Language Section

19 Redundant Error

1 ▶ The redundant error can be easily identified when redundancy—in either meaning or word—is made within a short proximity.

2 ▶ The more complex form can be created using an unnecessary modifier that repeats the meaning of the main clause or vise versa.

20 Restrictive Modifier (Essential Information)

1 ▶ Essential information should be free from commas, dashes, or parentheses that separate the essential information from the main clause.

2 ▶ You should identify whether the modifier is restrictive (essential information) or nonrestrictive (inessential information).

3 ▶ To do that, imagine whether the question sentence can stand alone without the word, the phrase, or the clause offset by a pair of commas, dashes, or parenthesis. If the sentence delivers sufficient information, it is non-restrictive modifier and therefore should be offset by the punctuation.

4 ▶ If, however, the question sentence becomes ambiguous without the word, the phrase, or the clause, then it is considered to be the restrictive modifier and should not be offset by the punctuation.

21 Subject-Verb, Pronoun, Noun Agreement

1 ▶ Independent sentence must have the essential elements: subject and verb.

2 ▶ This pattern frequently asks a missing verb, some disagreement between a singular/plural pronoun, or numbers in noun and verb.

24 Absolute Patterns in Writing & Language Section

22 Nonrestrictive Modifier (Inessential Information)

Nonrestrictive modifier (inessential information) should be offset by a pair of commas, dashes, or parentheses to separate it from the main clause.

23 Transition Words/Phrase for Supporting Detail, Contrast, and Consequence

1 ▶ Transition words/phrase focus on words and phrases that support, contrast, or produce consequence.
   (e.g., 'for example' for supporting detail; 'As a result' for the consequence)

2 ▶ It is easier to find the most logical and smooth connector between two clauses.

3 ▶ However, it is harder to identify and remove an unclear transition word that shouldn't be there.
   Imagine an example sentence is followed by another example sentence connected by "for example"

24 Verb Tense/Voice Error

1 ▶ Verb tense question asks whether the sentence inappropriately changes the tense (e.g., from past to past perfect).

2 ▶ Voice question asks whether the sentence inappropriately changes voice (e.g., from active to passive).

24 Absolute Patterns in Writing Summary

Absolute Pattern 1: Adding, Revising, Deleting, Retaining Information

Absolute Pattern 2: Cause-Effect Relations

Absolute Pattern 3: Colloquialism (Nonstandard Language)

Absolute Pattern 4: Comparison

Absolute Pattern 5: Comma Splice Error

Absolute Pattern 6: Confusing Words

Absolute Pattern 7: Conjunction Error

Absolute Pattern 8: Double Negative Error

Absolute Pattern 9: Informational Graphs

Absolute Pattern 10: Logical Expression

Absolute Pattern 11: Logical Sequence

Absolute Pattern 12: Modifier (Placement) Error

Absolute Pattern 13: Parallel Structure

Absolute Pattern 14: Possessive Determiners and Possessive Noun Error

Absolute Pattern 15: Prepositional Idiom

Absolute Pattern 16: Precision, Concision, Style

Absolute Pattern 17: Pronoun Error

Absolute Pattern 18: Punctuation Error

Absolute Pattern 19: Redundant Error

Absolute Pattern 20: Restrictive Modifier (Essential Information)

Absolute Pattern 21: Subject-Verb, Pronoun, Noun Agreement

Absolute Pattern 22: Nonrestrictive Modifier (Inessential Information)

Absolute Pattern 23: Transitions (Supporting Detail, Contrast, and Consequence)

Absolute Pattern 24: Verb Tense/Voice Error

Types of conjunctions

Coordinating Conjunction   And, But, For, Or, Yet, So, Nor (FANBOYS)

Subordinating Conjunction					
As soon as	Even if	Since	until	Wherever	Whether
As	How	So that	unless	when	Once
As far as	If	Supposing	Because	Although	While
After	In that	Though	before	No matter what	Provided
As if	In case				

Correlative Conjunction			
neither… nor	either… or	not only… but also	both… and
so… as	whether… or		

Conjunctive Adverb				
as a result	for example	however	incidentally	likewise
after all	furthermore	otherwise	in fact	meanwhile
consequently	hence	indeed	instead	in addition
finally	thus	still	therefore	on the other hand

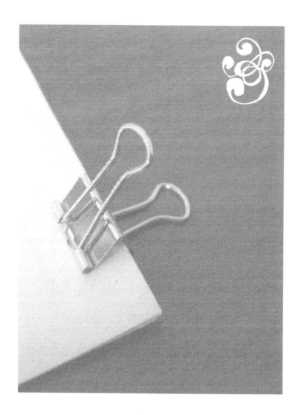

Chapter 2

12 WRITING & LANGUAGE TESTS WITH THE ABSOLUTE PATTERNS

SAT
Writing and Language
Test 1

ALL THE LOGIC AND RULES
BEHIND THE EVERY SINGLE
SAT QUESTION

Writing and Language Test 1
35 MINUTES, 44 QUESTIONS

Each passage below is accompanied by a number of questions. For some questions, you will consider how the passage might be revised to improve the expression of ideas. For other questions, you will consider how the passage might be edited to correct errors in sentence structure, usage, or punctuation. A passage or a question may be accompanied by one or more graphics (such as a table or graph) that you will consider as you make revising and editing decisions.

Question 1-11 is based on the following passage.

An Imperfect Necessity
© Harvard university, The crimson
Reprinted with Permission

When it comes to the standardized college admissions tests [1] like the SAT and ACT, there's a lot to gripe about. Beyond bringing additional stress to the admissions process, [2] there is a unclear problem that standardized tests are really fair or measure actual aptitude. Indeed, studies [3] have shown that standardized test scores are less effective than things like high school grades at predicting academic performance in college, are correlated with the socioeconomic status of test takers, and [4] have also shown that they are subjective to the influence of coaching and private tutoring, luxuries only available to those who can afford them.

1
(A) for example,
B) as
C) like
D) with

2
(A) NO CHANGE
B) will be unclear
C) it is unclear
D) there is a unclear matter for this issue

3
Which of the following choices would be LEAST likely be used?
(A) have suggested that
B) have analyzed that
C) revealed that
D) inspected that

4
A) NO CHANGE
(B) are subject to
C) is subject to
D) were subject to

CONTINUE

2   2

[5] <u>Despite in spite of</u> many flaws, standardized tests are a necessary convenience for many schools,

[6] <u>serving as a coarse method of comparison between the tens of thousands of applicants a school may consider every year.</u>

[7] ①The good news is that debate about the importance of standardized testing in college admissions finally seems to be spreading to those with the power to reform the system. ②Steps should be taken to ameliorate the importance of these tests, but getting rid of them is unfortunately not a viable option. ③And NACAC is taking action—it formed a Commission on the Use of Standardized Tests in Undergraduate Admission, chaired by Harvard Dean of Admissions William R. Fitzsimmons '67, which will issue a report next year. ④Indeed, at the National Association for College Admissions Counseling (NACAC) Conference held last week, discussion about the importance of standardized testing took the limelight. The Commission's report is expected to address the [8] <u>effect</u> of test preparation

---

5

A) NO CHANGE
B) Despite there are
C) However,
D) Despite there

6

The writer is thinking of removing the underlined portion of the sentence. If the writer were to delete, the passage would most likely lose (consider comma is replaced a with period):

A) the emphasis on its necessity to maintain college course
B) the emphasis on its necessity to measure applicants' aptitudes
C) the extended explanation for the defects of the test systems
D) information that benefits the number of applicants

7

What is the most logical sequence of the sentences in this paragraph?
A) 1-2-3-4
B) 2-1-4-3
C) 1-3-2-4
D) 4-3-2-1

8

A) NO CHANGE
B) impact
C) affect
D) perfect

CONTINUE ➤

2

2

on student performance, test biases, [9] but the possible advantages of using subject tests over the SAT.

In addition, the Commission will also propose recommendations to college admissions officers and high school counselors on how they should view standardized tests, in light of the tests' potential weaknesses.

These efforts are commendable, because identifying where the SAT falls short will [10] decrease admissions officers' awareness of the test's limitations, but also encourage the development of more reliable and more equitable methods of evaluation.

In the current admissions [11] system, however, standardized tests will continue to serve a useful role for many colleges.

Scores, although limited in their predictive power, still provide a nationally standardized

[12] benchmark against which admissions officers may quickly garner a rough idea of an applicant's comparative academic ability.

9

A) NO CHANGE
B) and possibly the advantages that benefit for
C) and the advantages of
D) with the possible benefits for advantages of

10

A) NO CHANGE
B) not only decrease
C) increase
D) not only increase

11

A) NO CHANGE
B) system; however,
C) system however,
D) system however

12

Which of the following alternatives would NOT be appropriate?
A) benchmark, with which
B) benchmark, by which
C) benchmark, based upon which
D) benchmark, to which

CONTINUE

2   2

Questions 13-23 are based on the following passages

Artificial Intelligence in Aviation Industry

[13] The Air Operations Division (AOD) uses AI for the rule based expert systems.

The AOD has used artificial intelligence for surrogate operators for combat and training simulators, mission management aids, support systems for tactical decision making, and post processing of the simulator data into symbolic summaries.

The use of artificial intelligence in simulators [14] is proving to be very useful in its utilization for the AOD. Airplane simulators are using artificial intelligence in order to process the data taken from simulated flights. [15]

The computers are able to come up with the best strategic combat plan.

13

Which of the following alternatives would NOT be appropriate?
A) The Air Operations Division (AOD)
B) The Air Operations Division—AOD—
C) The Air Operations Division, AOD,
D) The Air Operations Division—AOD

14

A) NO CHANGE
B) is very useful
C) are very useful
D) are very useful when considering their wide applications

15

At this point, the writer is considering adding the following information.

    Other than simulated flying, there is also simulated aircraft warfare.

Should the writer make this addition?
A) Yes, because it explains the importance of aircraft in modern warfare
B) Yes, because it helps the coherence of the essay
C) No, because it interrupts the paragraph
D) No, because it is mentioned in both previous and the following sentences

CONTINUE ➡

2

2

The artificial intelligent programs can sort the information and provide the pilot with the best possible maneuvers. Multiple aircrafts are needed to get good approximations for some calculations so computer simulated pilots can gather data.[16]

These computer simulated pilots are also used to train future air traffic controllers.

The system used by the AOD in order to measure performance is the Interactive Fault Diagnosis and Isolation System, or IFDIS. The performance system [17] was also used to replace specialized workers. The system allows the regular workers to communicate with the system analyzing staff and avoid mistakes, miscalculations, [18] or help access dialogue with the system analysts.

[19] Artificial intelligence in speech recognition software is also being used by AOD. The air traffic controllers give directions to the artificial pilots and the AOD wants to the pilots to respond to the ATC's with simple responses. The programs that incorporate the speech software must be trained, which means they use neural networks.

16

At this point, the writer is considering deleting the underlined sentence. Should the writer make this deletion?

A) Yes, because it merely repeats the previous information

B) Yes, albeit additional information, current technology has yet reached to this level

C) No, because it supports the previous sentence

D) No, because it reveals superiority of AI to human

17

A) NO CHANGE

B) is

C) has

D) have

18

A) NO CHANGE

B) or set up the meeting with the staff

C) or help communication with the workers

D) Delete, and ends the sentence by replacing the comma with period

19

A) NO CHANGE

B) The AOD also uses artificial intelligence in speech recognition software.

C) Artificial Intelligence uses speech recognition software made by AOD

D) Speech recognition software is also one of the artificial intelligence used by AOD

CONTINUE

2   **2**

The program Verbex 7000 is still a very early program that has plenty of room for improvement. The improvements are imperative, [20] so ATCs use very specific dialog and the software needs to be able to communicate correctly and promptly every time. [21] This program allows the designers to focus more on the design itself and less on the design process. The software also allows the user to focus less on the software tools. The AIDA uses rule based systems to compute its data.

In 2003, NASA's Dryden Flight Research Center, and many other companies, created software that could enable a damaged aircraft to continue to flight until a safe landing zone can be reached. The software compensates for all the damaged components by relying on the undamaged components. The neural network used in the software proves to be so effective [22] and marks a triumph for artificial intelligence

20

A) NO CHANGE
B) because
C) and
D) but

21

Which of the following items would be the best topic sentence of this paragraph?
A) The applications of AI in industry is virtually unlimited
B) The Artificial Intelligence supported Design of Aircraft, or AIDA, is used to help designers in the process of creating conceptual designs of aircraft.
C) The AOD is now seeking some profitable business model other than training using AI.
D) The main issues challenging the AOD is the Artificial Intelligence supported Design of Aircraft (AIDA)

22

A) NO CHANGE
B) , which
C) that
D) as

CONTINUE

2 **2**

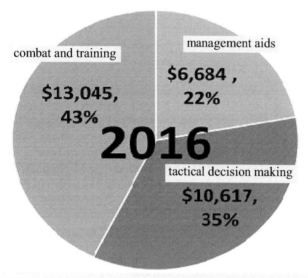

US government fund spent on AI in The Air Operations Division in 2016 (*US million dollars)

Which item best supports the pie chart?

A) Human operation takes up greater responsibility on management aids than other sectors

B) Tactical decision making takes up almost half of the funding in AI

C) Combat and training proves to be the most difficult sector to employ AI technology

D) The timing of the pie chart suggests AI in AOD is not yet at the full-fledged stage.

CONTINUE

2   2

Questions 24-33 are based on the following passages

Sea Otter Conservation

Modern efforts in sea otter conservation [24] that began in the early 19th century, when the sea otter was nearly extinct due to large-scale commercial hunting.

The sea otter was once abundant in a wide arc across the North Pacific ocean, from northern Japan to Alaska to Mexico. By 1911, hunting for the animal's luxurious fur [25] reduced the sea otter population to [26] less than 2000 individuals in the most remote and inaccessible parts of its range.

During the 20th century, sea otter populations recovered from remnant populations in the far east of Russia, western Alaska, and California.

Beginning in the 1960s, efforts to [27] transplant sea otters to previously populated areas were also successful in restoring sea otters to other parts of the west coast of North America

24

A) NO CHANGE
B) began in the early 19th century
C) has begun in the early 19th century
D) that has begun in the early 19th century

25

A) NO CHANGE
B) has reduced
C) had reduced
D) was reduced

26

A) NO CHANGE
B) fewer
C) smaller
D) more

27

A) NO CHANGE
B) transpire
C) translocate
D) transgender

CONTINUE

2

. [28] Although, sea otter populations' relocation into a new habitat was daunting in the beginning ⊡ due to ecological concerns and environmental concerns ⊡ such as the inevitable competition for food with indigent animals in the area, or endemic diseases brought by the sea otters into the new habitat,

efforts from volunteers, ecologists, and environmental organizations rapidly stabilized the issues. ⊡ Sea otters' amiable physical characteristics often attract people's attention. ⊡ Populations in some areas are now thriving,

[29] with the recovery of the sea otter is considered one of the greatest successes in marine conservation.

In two important parts of its range, however, sea otter populations have recently declined or have plateaued at depressed levels. In the Aleutian Islands, a massive and unexpected disappearance of sea

otters has occurred in recent decades. [30] However, the cause of the decline is not known, although the observed pattern of disappearances is consistent with a rise in orca predation. Sea otters give live birth.

In the 1990s, California's sea otter population stopped growing for reasons that are probably

different from the difficulties facing Alaska's otters.

28

Which of the following sentences of this paragraph is LEAST relevant to the main focus of the essay and therefore should be deleted?

A) Statement ⊡

B) Statement ⊡

C) Statement ⊡

D) Statement ⊡

29

A) NO CHANGE

B) together with

C) and

D) likewise

30

A) NO CHANGE

B) The cause of the decline is not known,

C) The cause of the declines, however, are not known,

D) Due to the fact that the cause of the decline is not known,

CONTINUE

2   **2**

A high prevalence of infectious disease in juveniles and adults has been found to cause many sea otter deaths; however, it is not known why [31] California sea otters would be more vulnerable to disease than populations elsewhere. Other threats to sea otters are well-known. In particular, sea otters are highly [32] vulnerable to oil spills, and a major spill can rapidly kill thousands of the animals. The IUCN lists the sea otter as an endangered species.

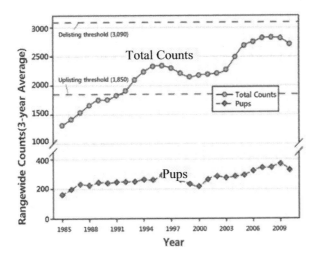

31

Which of the following alternatives would NOT be appropriate?
A) California should not be the suitable habitat for sea otters
B) California sea otters disappeared suddenly
C) California provides the most suitable habitat while other areas cannot
D) California sea otters are not as robust as other sea otters in other regions

32

Which of the following words would NOT be appropriate to use?
A) sensitive
B) unresponsive
C) susceptible
D) open

33

Please refer to the information in the graph to choose the best answer.
A) The number of pups controls the number of total sea otters
B) Total counts decline in 2000 reflects pups decline in the same year
C) After 2009, pups population started to increase
D) Total counts of sea otters have been relatively more stable than pups between 1985 and 2009.

CONTINUE ➡

2   2

Question 34-44 are based on the following passages

Genesis of the Airflow project

The basis for the Chrysler Airflow was rooted in Chrysler Engineering's Carl Breer's curiosity about how forms affected their movement through the environment. According to Chrysler, Breer's quest was started [34] while watching geese travel through the air [35] in a "V" flight pattern.

Another source lists Breer as watching military planes on their practice maneuvers, while still other sources attach the genesis of the project to Breer's interest [36] in lighter than air's airships and how their shapes helped them move through the atmosphere. One day, Breer along with fellow Chrysler engineers Fred Zeder and Owen Skelton [37] were conducting a series of wind tunnel test, with the cooperation of Orville Wright, to study which forms were [38] better effective shape created by nature that could suit an automobile.

34

A) NO CHANGE
B) while he was watching geese travel
C) while people were watching geese travel,
D) while geese travel

35

At this point, the author wishes to delete the underlined phrase. Should the author proceeds to delete it or not?

A) keep, because it helps visualize the pattern
B) Keep, because it suggests Breer's in-depth knowledge about geese
C) delete, because the phrase is stated elsewhere
D) delete, because "V" pattern is a subjective analysis

36

A) NO CHANGE
B) in lighter-than-air airships
C) in lighter than air airships
D) in lighter-then-air airships

37

A) NO CHANGE
B) was conducting
C) had conducted
D) has conducted

38

A) NO CHANGE
B) the most
C) most
D) the more

CONTINUE

2

2

Chrysler built a wind tunnel at the Highland Park site [39]

and tested at least 50 scale models by April 1930.Their engineers found that then-current two-box automobile design was so aerodynamically inefficient, that it was actually more efficient turned around backwards. Applying what they had learned about shape, the engineers also began looking into ways that a car could be built, which also used monocoque (<u>unibody</u>) construction to both strengthen the construction (the strengthening was used in a publicity reel) of the car while reducing its overall drag, and thus increasing the power-to-drag ratio as the lighter, more streamlined body allowed air to flow around it instead of being caught through upright forms, such as radiator grilles, headlights and windshields Traditional automobiles of the day were the typical two-box design, [40] <u>with about 65% of the weight over the rear wheels.</u> When loaded with passengers, the weight distribution tended to become further imbalanced, rising to 75% or more over the rear wheels, resulting in unsafe handling characteristics on slippery roads. Spring rates in the rear of traditional vehicles were, therefore, necessarily higher, and passengers were subjected to a harsher ride.

39

At this point, the writer is considering adding the sentence below.

,where Breer spent his youth with his siblings who were interested in science,

Should this addition be allowed?

A) Yes, because it supplies additional information regarding Breer's early interest in his career

B) Yes, because it explains Breer's hometown briefly.

C) No, because it interrupts the discussion of wind tunnel test

D) No, because the following sentence contradicts it.

40

Which of the following sentences is LEAST applicable to the previous sentence?

A) with about 65% of the weight over the rear wheels.

B) allotting about 65% of the weight over the rear wheels.

C) with which about 65% of the weight over the rear wheels.

D) based upon which about 65% of the weight could go over the rear wheels.

CONTINUE

2   **2**

The car's grille work cascaded forward and downward [41] forming a waterfall look where other makes featured fairly the running surface of the tire tread. [42] Therefore, in the rear, Airflows encased the rear wheels through the use of fender skirts.

Instead of a flat panel of glass, the windshield comprised two sheets of glass that formed a raked "vee" both side to side, and top to bottom. Passengers were carried in a full steel body (at a time when automakers like General Motors,

Ford and even Chrysler itself continued to use wood structural framing members in their car bodies) that rested between the wheels instead of upon them. The front seat was wider than in other cars and the rear seat was deeper. Overall, the car possessed a better power-to-weight ratio, and its

[43] structural integrity was stronger than other

[44] like models of the day.

41

At this point, the author wishes to delete the underlined phrase. Should the author proceeds to delete it or not?

A) keep, because it helps compare with other makes

B) Keep, because it suggests a waterfall inspired engineers' design

C) delete, because the design was not exactly like a waterfall

D) delete, because the earlier phrase already mentioned about a visual effect

42

A) NO CHANGE

B) In the rear,

C) However, in the rear

D) On the other hand, in the rear part

43

A) NO CHANGE

B) structure and integrity

C) structure integrity

D) structuring integrity

44

Which of the following alternatives would NOT be appropriate to use?

A) compatible

B) delete the word "like"

C) matching

D) assimilated

TEST 1

WRITING ABSOLUTE PATTERNS

TEST 1

WRITING AND LANGUAGE SECTION PATTERN ANALYSIS

	Q1. Absolute Pattern 15: Prepositional Idiom	
	When it comes to the standardized college admissions tests [1] <u>like</u> the SAT and ACT, there's a lot to gripe about.	
	A) for example,	"like" is a preposition that compares two or more entities with the similar characteristics.
	B) as	
√	**C) like**	A) "for example" usually carries a clause, supporting the previous sentence.
	D) with	B) The preposition 'as' is not used as a comparison. It means the same degree as another. (e.g., I am free as a bird.)

	Q2. Absolute Pattern 21: Subject-Verb, Pronoun, Noun Agreement	
	Beyond bringing additional stress to the admissions process, [2] <u>there is unclear problem</u> that standardized tests are really fair or measure actual aptitude.	
	A) NO CHANGE	"Beyond bringing additional stress to the admissions process," requires the main clause with the subject and the verb.
	B) will be unclear	
√	**C) it is unclear**	A) "there" as a subject is normally used when the real subject is too long such as "To-infinitive clause" or "That clause." e.g., There are some difficulties to get over with the obstacles. There are some difficulties that we need to get over with.
	D) there is an unclear matter for this issue	B) has no subjects and uses the future tense.

Q3. Absolute Pattern 10: Logical Expression

Indeed, studies [3] have shown that standardized test scores are less effective than things like high school grades at predicting academic performance in college,

	A) have suggested that	'suggested,' 'analyzed,' 'revealed' are all synonyms or similar perception.
	B) have analyzed that	D) Studies can't be inspected.
	C) revealed that	
√	**D) inspected that**	

Q4. Absolute Pattern 13: Parallel Structure

Indeed, studies have shown that standardized test scores *are less effective* than things like high school grades at predicting academic performance in college, *are correlated with* the socioeconomic status of test takers, *and* [4] have also shown that they are subjective to the influence of coaching and private tutoring, luxuries only available to those who can afford them.

	A) NO CHANGE	"**are** less effective…", "**are** correlated with….", and "**are** subject to…"
√	**B) are subject to**	The parallel structure must be maintained after the conjunction "and."
	C) is subject to	
	D) were subject to	

Q5. Absolute Pattern 23: Transitions (Supporting Detail, Contrast, and Consequence)

[5] Despite in spite of many flaws, standardized tests are a necessary convenience for many schools

	A) NO CHANGE	D) uses the preposition "Despite" plus the phrase, not a clause.
	B) Despite there are	1>"Despite" and "in spite of" are synonyms, thus one of which should be removed. Therefore, (A) is incorrect
	C) However,	2> "Despite" is a preposition, so it carries a phrase, not a clause with a verb. Therefore, (B) is incorrect.
√	**D) Despite there**	C) changes the original meaning. The author wants to put a concessional transition, 'despite,'

Q6. Absolute Pattern 1: Adding, Revising, Deleting, Retaining Information

Despite their many flaws, standardized tests are a necessary convenience for many schools, [6] serving as a coarse method of comparison between the tens of thousands of applicants a school may consider every year.

	A) the emphasis on its necessity to maintain college course
✓	**B) the emphasis on its necessity to measure applicants' aptitudes**
	C) the extended explanation for the defects of the test systems
	D) information that benefits the number of applicants

1> The phrase "Despite their many flaws" signals that a concessional clause is following.

2> The concessional clause—as a countermeasure—justifies the "flaws" or necessitates of the test.

A) is new information. New information is always incorrect.

C) is opposite perception

D) is new information and positive, which is opposite to the passage's concessional tone.

Q7. Absolute Pattern 11: Logical Sequence

[2] **Steps should be taken** to ameliorate the importance of these tests, but getting rid of them is unfortunately not a viable option. [1] **The good news is** that debate about the importance of standardized testing in college admissions finally seems to be spreading to those with the power to reform the system. [4] Indeed, at the **National Association for College Admissions Counseling (NACAC) Conference** held last week, discussion about the importance of standardized testing took the limelight. [3] **And NACAC is taking action**—it formed a Commission on the Use of Standardized Tests in Undergraduate Admission, chaired by Harvard Dean of Admissions William R. Fitzsimmons '67, which will issue a report next year.

	A) 1-2-3-4	A), C)
✓	**B) 2-1-4-3**	[3] has to be placed after [4] because the author has to explain the acronym for NACAC first.
	C) 1-3-2-4	
	D) 4-3-2-1	D) Because NACAC is an example, [4] can't be the topic sentence.

Q8. Absolute Pattern 6: Confusing Words

The Commission's report is expected to address the [8] <u>effect</u> of [9] <u>test preparation on student performance, test biases, and the possible advantages of using subject tests over the SAT.</u>

√	A) NO CHANGE	The sentence requires a noun. "effect" is a noun.
	B) impact	too strong as its meaning conjures up a strong physical collision.
	C) affect	"affect" is used as a verb.
	D) perfect	adjective

Q9. Absolute Pattern 16: Precision, Concision, Style

The Commission's report is expected to address the <u>effect</u> of test preparation on student performance, test biases,[9] <u>but the possible advantages of</u> using subject tests over the SAT.

A) NO CHANGE	C) is most concise and precise, while maintaining the parallel structure.
B) and possibly the advantages that benefit for	
√ C) and the advantages of	A) "but" cancels out the previous sentence.
D) with the possible benefits for advantages of	B), D) "advantages" and benefit" are synonyms, causing a redundant error.

Q10. Absolute Pattern 23: Transitions (Supporting Detail, Contrast, and Consequence)

These efforts are commendable, because identifying where the SAT falls short will [10] <u>decrease</u> admissions officers' awareness of the test's limitations, **but also encourage**

A) NO CHANGE	1> The sentence should use the verb 'increase' NOT 'decrease'.
B) not only decrease	2> The proper idiom "not only ~ but also" clause is needed since the sentence ends with "but also."
C) increase	
√ D) not only increase	

Q11. Absolute Pattern 18: Punctuation Error

In the current admissions [11] <u>system, however, standardized</u> tests will continue to serve a useful role for many colleges.

√	A) NO CHANGE	When conjunctive adverb 'however' is interjected in the middle of a sentence, it must be offset by a pair of commas.
	B) system; however,	
	C) system however,	
	D) system however	

Q12. Absolute Pattern 15: Prepositional Idiom

Scores, although limited in their predictive power, still provide a nationally standardized [12] <u>benchmark against which</u> admissions officers may quickly garner a rough idea of an applicant's comparative academic ability.

	A) with which	means 'with this benchmark'
	B) benchmark, by which	means 'by this benchmark'
	C) benchmark, based upon	means 'based upon this benchmark'
√	D) benchmark, to which	Preposition 'to' is used to express motion moving forward, which is not suitable in this sentence.

Q13. Absolute Pattern 18: Punctuation Error

[13] <u>The Air Operations Division (AOD)</u> uses AI for the rule based expert systems. The AOD has used artificial intelligence for surrogate operators for combat and training simulators,

	A) The Air Operations Division (AOD)	1> A single dash makes the main sentence incomplete because.
	B) The Air Operations Division—AOD—	2> it physically severs the subject from the verb.
	C) The Air Operations Division, AOD,	3> "AOD" should be offset by a pair of dashes like (B) to separate AOD from the main sentence.
√	D) The Air Operations Division—AOD	4> A pair of parenthesis in (A) and a pair of commas in (C) function the same way as double-dashes in (B)

Q14. Absolute Pattern 16: Precision, Concision, Style

The **use** of artificial intelligence in simulators [14] <u>is proving to be very useful in its utilization</u> for the AOD.

	A) NO CHANGE	B) The sentence is succinct and precise.
√	**B) is very useful**	A) (1) "useful" and "utilization" are synonym, causing redundancy. (2) "proving to be" is unnecessary.
	C) are very useful	C), D) The subject is "use" that requires the singular verb "is", not "are," the plural.
	D) are very useful when considering their wide applications	D) is wordy

Q15. Absolute Pattern 1: Adding, Revising, Deleting, Retaining Information

[15] The computers are able to come up with the best strategic combat plan.	
	A) Yes, because it explains the importance of Aircraft in modern warfare
√	**B) Yes, because it helps the coherence of the essay**
	C) No, because it interrupts the paragraph
	D) No, because it is mentioned in both previous and the following sentences

This additional sentence is needed. The following sentences discuss air combat and pilots; thus, this sentence could be the topic sentence.

A) is not related issue. The statement in (A) discusses real aircraft, not a simulation, which is the main theme of the passage.

C) is opposite to the answer. It helps, instead of interrupting the paragraph.

D) This specific topic sentence does not appear anywhere else.

Q16. Absolute Pattern 1: Adding, Revising, Deleting, Retaining Information

Multiple aircrafts are needed to get good approximations for some calculations so computer simulated pilots can gather data.[16]

	A)	Yes, because it merely repeats the previous information
	B)	Yes, albeit additional information, current technology has yet reached to this level
√	**C)**	**No, because it supports the previous sentence.**
	D)	No, because it reveals superiority of AI to human

The previous sentence and this sentence are organically related to each other by further describing how AI application data are processed.

A) is incorrect because the sentence is not repeating but only gives more details to the previous information

B), D) are not only unrelated issues, but also not mentioned anywhere in the passage.

Q17. Absolute Pattern 24: Verb Tense / Voice Error

The performance system [17] was also used to replace specialized workers.

	A) NO CHANGE	The demonstrative statement uses the simple present tense.
√	**B) is**	A) 'was' is the simple past tense
	C) has	C) 'has' is the present perfect tense
	D) have	D) 'have' is the present perfect, plural

Q18. Absolute Pattern 1: Adding, Revising, Deleting, Retaining Information

The system allows the regular workers to communicate with the system analyzing staff and avoid mistakes, miscalculations, [18] or help access dialogue with the system analysts.

	A) NO CHANGE	1> The underlined portion has to be deleted because it repeats the previous statement.
	B) or set up the meeting with the staff	2> In fact, A), C) are very similar to the original sentence, but much less descriptive.
	C) or help communication with the workers	3> Therefore, there is no reason to add
√	**D) Delete**	B) is too extreme.

Q19. Absolute Pattern 16: Precision, Concision, Style

[19] Artificial intelligence in speech recognition software is also being used by AOD.

	A) NO CHANGE
√	**B) The AOD also uses artificial intelligence in speech recognition software.**
	C) Artificial Intelligence uses speech recognition software made by AOD
	D) Speech recognition software is also one of the artificial intelligence used by AOD

B) is active voice, making the sentence more direct and succinct.

A) The original sentence is passive. The application of passive voice is very limited. For instance, when an object is more important than a subject or when an agent "by" plays a significant role. Other than these situations, changing the active voice to the passive is not commendable.

C), D) changed the meaning

Q20. Absolute Pattern 2: Cause-Effect Relations

The improvements are imperative, [20] so ATCs use very specific dialog and the software needs to be able to communicate correctly and promptly every time.

	A) NO CHANGE	1> The meaning "imperative" implies the premise clause should follow.
√	**B) because**	2> Therefore, it should be linked to "because"
	C) and	A) "so" is used for the consequence.
	D) but	

Q21. Absolute Pattern 1: Adding, Revising, Deleting, Retaining Information

[21]This program allows the designers to focus more on the design itself and less on the design process. The software also allows the user to focus less on the software tools.

	A) The applications of AI in industry is virtually unlimited
√	**B) The Artificial Intelligence supported Design of Aircraft, or AIDA, is used to help designers in the process of creating conceptual designs of aircraft**
	C) The AOD is now seeking some profitable business model other than training using AI.
	D) The main issues challenging the AOD is the Artificial Intelligence supported Design of Aircraft (AIDA)

B) is the right topic sentence for this paragraph as it now discusses AIDA and its application.

A) The paragraph focuses on AIDA, not unlimited industries.

A) and C) Both statements do not focus on AIDA.

D) Unlike the positive tone of the paragraph, the statement is negative.

Q22. Absolute Pattern 2: Cause-Effect Relations

The neural network used in the software proves to be **so effective** [22] and marks a triumph for artificial intelligence

	A) NO CHANGE	"So-that" clause
	B) , which	1> The sentence focuses on a cause-effect situation, not a paralleling situation as used in (A).
√	**C) that**	
	D) as	B) is too vague.
		D) "so-as" is used for a phrasal connection, not a clause.

Q23. Absolute Pattern 9: Informational Graphs

1> management aids take up the lowest AI funding, which implies that
2> the differences should be largely responsible for the human operation.

√	**A) Human operation takes up greater responsibility on management aids than other sectors**
	B) Tactical decision making takes up almost half of funding in AI
	C) Combat and training proves to be the most difficult sector to employ AI technology
	D) Timing of the pie chart suggests AI in AOD is not yet at the full-fledged stage.

B) should be changed to "Combat and training"

C) At least from the funding size prospect, the statement is opposite

D) is not known fact

Q24. Absolute Pattern 24: Verb Tense / Voice Error

Modern efforts in sea otter conservation [24] **that** began in the early 19th century, when the sea otter was nearly extinct due to large-scale commercial hunting.

	A) NO CHANGE	1> "In the early 19th century" must use the simple past tense.
√	**B) began in the early 19th century**	2> When the time adverbial phrase indicates a specific time in the past such as "the last Thanksgiving", the simple past tense must be used.
	C) has begun in the early 19th century	
	D) that has begun in the early 19th century	A), D) 'that' in the underlined portion blocks the primary verb "began" from the subject. Therefore, "that" should be removed. C), D) are present perfect tense.

Q25. Absolute Pattern 24: Verb Tense / Voice Error

The sea otter **was** once abundant in a wide arc across the North Pacific ocean, from northern Japan to Alaska to Mexico. **By 1911**, hunting for the animal's luxurious fur [25] reduced the sea otter population

	A) NO CHANGE	1> Preposition 'By' plus time adverbial phrase indicates the completion of the activity.
	B) has reduced	2> Therefore, the verb should be the (present, past, or future) perfect tense.
√	**C) had reduced**	A) is the simple past tense
	D) was reduced	B) 'By 1911' isn't present. "has reduced" is the present perfect.
		D) is the passive voice.

Q26. Absolute Pattern 4: Comparison

By 1911, hunting for the animal's luxurious fur had reduced the sea otter population to [26] less than 2000 individuals in the most remote and inaccessible parts of its range.

	A) NO CHANGE	"2000" is a numeric value. Therefore, the proper determiner must be fewer.
√	**B) fewer**	A) 'less than' and C) 'smaller than' are determiners for amount.
	C) smaller	D) the sentence requires the negative, not the positive determiner.
	D) more	

Q27. Absolute Pattern 6: Confusing Words

Beginning in the 1960s, efforts to [27] transplant sea otters to previously populated areas were also successful in restoring sea otters to other parts of the west coast of North America.

	A) NO CHANGE	transplant means a plant that has been uprooted and replanted
	B) transpire	transpire means giving off water vapor
√	**C) translocate**	translocate means moving something from one location to another
	D) transgender	transgender means change of gender

Q28. Absolute Pattern 1: Adding, Revising, Deleting, Retaining Information

Although, sea otter populations' relocation into a new habitat was daunting in the beginning <1> due to ecological concerns and environmental concerns <2> such as the inevitable competition for food with indigent animals in the area, or endemic diseases brought by the sea otters into the new habitat, efforts from volunteers, ecologists, and environmental organizations rapidly stabilized the issues.
<3> Sea otters' amiable physical characteristics often attract people's attention.
<4> Populations in some areas are now thriving,

	A) Statement 1	A), B), and D) all describe the Sea otter's population decrease.
	B) Statement 2	"Sea otters' amiable physical characteristics" has nothing to do with its scientific research concerning the population decrease.
√	**C) Statement 3**	
	D) Statement 4	

Q29. Absolute Pattern 7: Conjunction Error

Populations in some areas are now thriving, [29] <u>with</u> the recovery of the sea otter **is considered** one of the greatest successes in marine conservation.

	A) NO CHANGE	1> A), and B) are prepositions that can't link a clause.
	B) together with	2> The verb "is considered" indicates that the clause should be linked with a conjunction, not a preposition.
√	**C) and**	
	D) likewise	D) "likewise" is an adverb, not a conjunction. Is it? No, It is not okay to use "likewise" instead of conjunction "and"

Q30. Absolute Pattern 7: Conjunction Error

[30] <u>However, the cause of the decline is not known,</u> **although** the observed PATTERN of disappearances is consistent with a rise in orca predation.

	A) NO CHANGE	1> Both 'however' and 'although' are subordinating clauses,
√	**B) The cause of the decline is not known,**	2> which means there's no main sentence here. 3> Therefore, either "however" or "although" must be removed.
	C) The cause of the declines ,however, are not known,	4> So that it can create one subordinating clause plus one main clause.
	D) Due to the fact that the cause of the decline is not known,	C), D) are incorrect for the same reasoning as A)

Q31. Absolute Pattern 1: Adding, Revising, Deleting, Retaining Information

A high prevalence of infectious disease in juveniles and adults has been found to cause many sea otter deaths; however, it is not known why [31] <u>California sea otters would be more vulnerable to disease than populations elsewhere.</u>

	A) California should not be the suitable habitat for sea otters
	B) California sea otters disappeared suddenly
√	**C) California provides the most suitable habitat while other areas cannot**
	D) California sea otters are not as robust as other sea otters in other regions

The reading passage states that California sea otters would be more vulnerable to disease. (Negative)
C) is positive therefore the direct opposite from the main issue of this paragraph.

A), B), and D) are negative as they partially express the concern about the sea otters' vulnerability.

Q32. Absolute Pattern 10: Logical Expression

Other threats to sea otters are well-known. In particular, sea otters are highly [32] <u>vulnerable</u> to oil spills, and a major spill can rapidly kill thousands of the animals. The IUCN lists the sea otter as an endangered species.

	A) sensitive	1> "unresponsive" to oil spills is positive characteristic that does not agree with the negative tone in the sentence.
√	**B) unresponsive**	
	C) susceptible	A), C), and D) are all negative words that fit well in the sentence context.
	D) open	D) "open" means penetrable.

Q33. Absolute Pattern 9: Informational Graphs

	A) The number of pups controls the number of total sea otters
√	**B) Total counts decline in 2000 reflects pups decline in the same year**
	C) After 2009, pups population started to increase
	D) Total counts of sea otters have been relatively more stable than pups between 1985 and 2009

B) The graph shows that both groups experienced a decrease in the year 2000.

A) 1> The graph does not show that pups control the number of total sea otters.

   2> Bigger curves in total counts reflect some factors other than pups control the total counts.

C) It is opposite. Pups started to decrease.

D) It is opposite. The graph shows that pups have been relatively more stable

Q34. Absolute Pattern 12: Modifier (Placement) Error

According to Chrysler, Breer's quest was started [34] <u>while watching geese travel</u> through the air <u>in a "V" flight PATTERN</u>.

	A) NO CHANGE	1> **quest** is the main subject, not Breer.
√	**B) while he was watching geese travel**	2> 'quest' can't watch geese travel. 3> Because the original sentence does not include "Breer", we should add one next to "while."
	C) while people were watching geese travel,	
	D) while geese travel	C), D) both provide the incorrect subjects "people" and "geese."

Q35. Absolute Pattern 1: Adding, Revising, Deleting, Retaining Information

According to Chrysler, Breer's quest was started while he was watching geese travel through the air [35] in a "V" flight PATTERN.

√	A) keep, because it helps visualize the PATTERN
	B) Keep, because it suggests Breer's in-depth knowledge about geese
	C) delete, because the phrase is stated elsewhere
	D) delete, because "V" PATTERN is a subjective analysis

The sentence cannot be removed because it helps visualize how geese travel, through which the design PATTERN was created.

B) Knowing about geese was not Breer's concern, but their flying PATTERN was.

C) The phrase is not stated elsewhere

D) 'V' PATTERN is an objective analysis.

Q36. Absolute Pattern 18: Punctuation Error

Another source lists Breer as watching military planes on their practice maneuvers, while still other sources attach the genesis of the project to Breer's interest [36] in lighter than air's airships and how their shapes helped them move through the atmosphere.

	A) NO CHANGE	1> "lighter than air" is used as a single adjective.
√	B) in lighter-than-air airships	2> When a group of words is used as a single adjective to describe the following noun, they have to be hyphenated.
	C) in lighter than air airships	
	D) in lighter-then-air airships	D) 'then' should be changed to 'than'

Q37. Absolute Pattern 21: Subject-Verb, Pronoun, Noun Agreement

[37] One day, Breer **along with** fellow Chrysler engineers Fred Zeder and Owen Skelton <u>were conducting</u> a series of wind tunnel test, with the cooperation of Orville Wright, to study which forms were the most

	A) NO CHANGE	1> The phrase that comes after "along with" is not part of the subject
√	**B) was conducting**	2> Because "along with" is an adverb, not a conjunction,
		3> So, the subject is singular "Breer", not "Breer *along with* fellow Chrysler
	C) had conducted	engineers Fred Zeder and Owen Skelton."
	D) has conducted	4> Therefore, the verb should be singular.
		C) "One day" indicates the past occurrence," which requires the simple past, not the past perfect nor D) present.

Q38. Absolute Pattern 4: Comparison

to study which forms were [38] <u>better</u> effective shape created by nature that could suit an automobile.

	A) NO CHANGE	1> The description doesn't specify any comparison between two things.
√	**B) the most**	2> Therefore, A) and D) are incorrect because they are used only for a comparison.
	C) most	C) "The" definite article should be placed before "most" to make the superlative.
	D) the more	

Q39. Absolute Pattern 1: Adding, Revising, Deleting, Retaining Information

Chrysler built a wind tunnel at the Highland Park site [39]<u>where Breer spent his youth with his siblings who were interested in science</u> and tested at least 50 scale models by April 1930.

	A) Yes, because it supplies additional information regarding Breer's early interest in his career
	B) Yes, because it explains Breer's hometown briefly.
√	**C) No, because it interrupts the discussion of wind tunnel test**
	D) No, because the following sentence contradicts it.

A) "Siblings" is new idea and should not be brought into the sentence discussing the wind tunnel test.

B) Breer's siblings or hometown are not previously mentioned.

D) The following sentence continues the main issue about wind tunnel test.

Q40. Absolute Pattern 10: Logical Expression

Traditional automobiles of the day were the typical two-box design, [40] <u>with about 65% of the weight over the rear wheels.</u>

	A) with about 65% of the weight over the rear wheels.	1> "with which" in (C) requires a clause just like D) "based upon which."
	B) allotting about 65% of the weight over the rear wheels.	2> However, (C) has no verb, while using the conjunction "which" as if it is a clause.
√	**C) with which about 65% of the weight over the rear wheels.**	D) 'based upon which' is a conjunctive adverb that connects well with the following clause.
	D) based upon which about 65% of the weight could go over the rear wheels.	

Q41. Absolute Pattern 1: Adding, Revising, Deleting, Retaining Information

The car's grille work cascaded forward and downward [41] <u>forming a waterfall look</u> where other makes featured fairly the running surface of the tire tread.

	A) keep, because it helps compare with other makes
√	**B) Keep, because it suggests a waterfall inspired engineers' design**
	C) delete, because the design was not exactly like a waterfall
	D) delete, because the earlier phrase already mentioned about a visual effect

1> The clause must be kept because "forming a look" implies how the engineers obtained the design concept.

A) "The car's grille", not "a waterfall", is compared with other makes. Therefore, (A) is an unrelated issue with other makes.

C) deviates from the question. It does not ask the exactness of the design.

D) Although the similar visual effect was mentioned earlier, that was a different object.

Q42. Absolute Pattern 1: Adding, Revising, Deleting, Retaining Information

[42] <u>Therefore, in the rear,</u> Airflows encased the rear wheels through the use of fender skirts.

	A) NO CHANGE	1> The previous sentence discusses "The car's grille..."
√	**B) In the rear,**	2> This sentence discusses the fender skirts on the rear of the vehicle.
		3> Because two sentences are different issues, "Therefore" can't be used.
	C) However, in the rear	
	D) On the other hand, in the rear part	A), B), D) are all conjunctive adverbs that connect the previous information.

Q43. Absolute Pattern 10: Logical Expression

Overall, the car possessed a better power-to-weight ratio, and its [43]<u>structural integrity</u> was stronger than other [44] <u>like</u> models of the day.

√	**A) NO CHANGE**	'Integrity' is a noun. Using an adjective before noun is most desirable.
	B) structure and integrity	B) changes the meaning
	C) structure integrity	C) "structure" and "integrity" are two independent nouns and can't be linked to each other
	D) structuring integrity	D) 'structuring' is participle like someone is structuring integrity.

Q44. Absolute Pattern 6: Confusing Words

Overall, the car possessed a better power-to-weight ratio, and its structural integrity was stronger than other [44] <u>like</u> models of the day.

	A) compatible	Assimilate means to become a member of a group.
	B) delete the word "like"	
	C) matching	A), B), and C): all the other choices work fine with the noun "models"
√	**D) assimilated**	without changing the meaning 'like'

SAT
Writing and Language
Test 2

ALL THE LOGIC AND RULES

BEHIND THE EVERY SINGLE

SAT QUESTION

Writing and Language Test 2
35 MINUTES, 44 QUEST IONS

Each passage below is accompanied by a number of questions. For some questions, you will consider how the passage might be revised to improve the expression of ideas. For other questions, you will consider how the passage might be edited to correct errors in sentence structure, usage, or punctuation.
A passage or a question may be accompanied by one or more graphics (such as a table or graph) that you will consider as you make revising and editing decisions.

Questions 1-12 are based on the following passages

Press the On Button

Harvard University © The Harvard Crimson
Reproduced with permission

Privacy in our society is clearly [1] diminishing: we carry devices everywhere we go so that people can reach us, the credit cards we use let any corporation view our purchases, and the Internet has allowed an unprecedented level of information to be [2] publicly available.
While this trend can be troubling, simple-minded reactions are not warranted.

[3] Unfortunately, this is exactly what happened in the Cambridge City Council on Wednesday when, following protests from many fearful and disgruntled citizens, the body voted to keep surveillance cameras already installed in the city turned off,
[4] cited their possible contribution to the erosion of civil liberties.

1

Which of the following choices would be LEAST likely be used?
A) diminishing.
B) diminishing,
C) diminishing;
D) diminishing as

2

A) NO CHANGE
B) promoted
C) advertised
D) publicized

3

A) NO CHANGE
B) Although,
C) With all due respect
D) Granted,

4

A) NO CHANGE
B) citing
C) was cited
D) had cited

CONTINUE ➡

2   2

This move by the council was an overreaction in light of the surveillance program's scope, purpose, and prior history.

[5] The fund was made by a grant from the Department of Homeland Security, a mere eight cameras were installed around Cambridge in 2008 to aid firefighters and other evacuation personnel in the event of an emergency. For a sizeable community like Cambridge, the cameras' potential to be life-saving in dire circumstances greatly [6] overwhelm their minimal impact on privacy.

   Most of those in opposition to the use of these cameras at the city council meeting did not have a problem with the standard function of the cameras in emergency situations [7] and were more concerned about the possibility of exploitation. But [8] as much as these cameras may conjure up images of an Orwellian nightmare with the government watching our every move, they add no more cause for alarm than cameras installed on highways to monitor speed limits or in stores to monitor shoplifting. Boston has installed over 100 similar cameras already and has seen no problem in surveillance-related abuse.

[9] While the installation process was not particularly transparent,

5

A) NO CHANGE
B) Fund made by
C) There was the fund by
D) Funding

6

A) NO CHANGE
B) outweighs
C) outperform
D) outweight

7

A) NO CHANGE
B) so
C) but
D) however

8

A) NO CHANGE
B) as far as
C) as long as
D) as soon as

9

A) NO CHANGE
B) However,
C) Moreover,
D) Because

CONTINUE

with most of it taking place without the involvement of the Cambridge City Council, disallowing these cameras is [10] not necessary, rash, and wasteful. Like any newly instituted system, the cameras should be allowed a trial period with evaluation and feedback. Just as nearby Brookline agreed to activate the cameras and use them on a trial basis, Cambridge should observe the impact of cameras before making its decision. It is a city's obligation to protect and assist its residents in a time of emergency, and blocking a possible rescue due to unfounded fears of the government being able to view a public street shows little perspective. [11]

Hopefully Cambridge residents will not have to wait for an accident to ensue for us to learn this.

U.S. citizen's view on CCTV

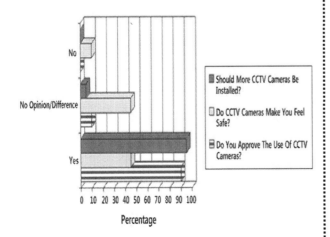

Percentage

Source: Modern Security Systems of England, 1995

10

A) NO CHANGE
B) unnecessary, rash, and wasteful.
C) unnecessarily rash and wasteful.
D) unnecessary, but rash and wasteful.

11

At this point, the writer is considering adding the following information.

Eight cameras will not mark the end of our First Amendment rights.

Should the writer make this addition?

A) Yes, because it sarcastically criticizes the groundless fears
B) Yes, because it explains higher law can dismiss the subordinate law
C) No, because First Amendment does not specify camera installation regulations
D) No, because it undermines the author's arguments

12

Which of the following choices meets the author's opinion?

A) Should More CCTV be installed? YES
B) Do CCTV make you feel Safe? No
C) Do you Approve the use of CCTV? No
D) Privacy is more important than safety. Yes

CONTINUE

2   2

Questions 13-23 are based on the following passages

Maintenance Engineering

{ 1 }

Maintenance Engineering is the discipline and profession of applying engineering concepts to the optimization of equipment, procedures, and departmental budgets to achieve better [13] maintenance, reliability, and availability of equipment. Since the Industrial Revolution, devices, equipment, machinery and structures have grown increasingly [14] complex, requiring a host of personnel, vocations and related systems needed to maintain them.

{ 2 }

Prior to 2006, the US [15] spent every single year approximately US$300 billion annually on plant maintenance and operations alone. Maintenance is to ensure a unit is fit for purpose, with maximum availability at minimum costs.

{ 3 }

[16] A Maintenance Engineer should possess significant knowledge of statistics, probability and logistics, and additionally in the fundamentals of the operation of the equipment and machinery he or she is responsible for.

13
A) NO CHANGE
B) maintainability, reliability, and availability
C) maintenance, reliance, and available
D) reliable as well as available maintenance

14
A) complex, requiring
B) complex, which requires
C) complex requiring
D) complex that require

15
A) NO CHANGE
B) spent about
C) spent throughout the year approximately
D) was spending about

16
At this point, the writer is considering adding the following sentence
  A person practicing Maintenance Engineering is known as a Maintenance Engineer.
Should the writer make this addition?
A) Yes, because it works as the topic sentence in this paragraph
B) Yes, because the role of Maintenance Engineer is the central claim of this passage
C) No, because it distracts from the main concern in this paragraph
D) No, because the following sentence already briefly introduces the Maintenance Engineer

CONTINUE

2

2

A Maintenance Engineer shall also possess high interpersonal, communication, management skills and ability to make quick decisions.

Institutions across the world [17] have recognized the need for Maintenance Engineering.

[18] Maintenance Engineers usually hold a degree in Mechanical Engineering, Industrial Engineering, or other Engineering Disciplines. In recent years specialized degree in master courses [19] have developed.

{ 4 }

MRO may be defined as, "All actions which have the objective of retaining or restoring an components, line, or heavy item in or to a state in which it can perform its required function. The actions include the combination of all technical and corresponding [20] administrative, managerial, and supervision actions.

17

A) NO CHANGE
B) has recognized
C) recognized
D) is recognized

18

At this point, the writer is considering deleting the underlined portion of the sentence.

Should the writer make this deletion?

A) Yes, because the paragraph is about to focus on MRO

B) Yes, because work experience is more important than the college degree to become a Maintenance Engineer

C) No, because it shows how sophisticated the profession is

D) No, because it shows the requirements for the educational background

19

A) NO CHANGE
B) has developed
C) had developed
D) are going to be developed and launched

20

A) NO CHANGE
B) administrative, management, and supervision
C) administration, management, and supervisory
D) administrative, managerial, and supervisory

CONTINUE ➡

2 | | **2**

[21] <u>The theory also represents</u> a closed loop supply chain and usually has the scope of maintenance, repair or overhaul of the product. The latter criteria [22] <u>is an open loop supply chain and is</u> typified by refurbishment and remanufacture.

Airline Expectations of MRO Technology

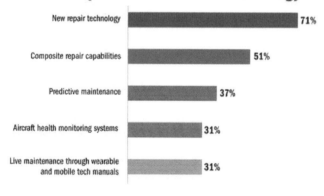

New repair technology	71%
Composite repair capabilities	51%
Predictive maintenance	37%
Aircraft health monitoring systems	31%
Live maintenance through wearable and mobile tech manuals	31%

21

A) NO CHANGE
B) MRO also represents
C) They also represent
D) It has also represented

22

A) NO CHANGE
B) are an open loop supply chain but is
C) is an open loop supply chain but is
D) are an open loop supply chain and are

23

Which paragraph in the passage best represents the chart?

A) Paragraph {1}
B) Paragraph {2}
C) Paragraph {3}
D) Paragraph {4}

CONTINUE

2   2

Questions 24-34 are based on the following passages

Equipment of the painter

Where our painters [24] have chosen wood or
canvas as a ground, the Chinese have employed silk
or paper.

While our art recognizes that drawing itself, quite
apart from painting, [25] sufficient objective,
drawing and painting have always been closely
intermingled in the Far East. While the mediums
used in Europe for painting in color, distemper,
tempera and oil, led to an exact study of form, the
colors employed by the Orientals--at times brilliant,
at times subdued with an almost studied
restraint--preserved a singular fluidity and lent
themselves to undefined evanescence which gave
them a [26] surprising charm. The early paintings
were generally done on cotton, coarse silk or paper.
In the eighteenth century, under the Tang dynasty,
the use of finer silk began [27] in the period from
1701 to 1799. The dressing was removed with
boiling water, the silk was then sized and smoothed
with a paddle. The use of silken fabric of the finest
weave, prepared with a thick sizing, [28] became
general during the Sung dynasty.

24
A) NO CHANGE
B) chose
C) had chosen
D) were chosen

25
A) NO CHANGE
B) is sufficiently objective,
C) is sufficient enough and objective,
D) is sufficient enough to be objective,

26
A) NO CHANGE
B) surprisingly
C) surprising with
D) surprising that brings

27
A) NO CHANGE
B) from 1701 to 1799
C) between the year 1701 and 1799
D) delete the underlined portion

28
A) NO CHANGE
B) become general skill
C) had been general skill
D) were skill

CONTINUE ➤

2 2

Papers were made of vegetable fibers, principally of bamboo.

[29] Being prepared, as was the silk, they became practically indestructible with a sizing of alum. Upon these silks and papers the painter worked with brush and Chinese ink color being introduced with more or less freedom or restraint.

The brushes are of different types. Each position of the brush conforms to a specific quality of the line, either sharp and precise or broad and quivering, the ink spreading in strong touches or thinning to delicate shades.

The colors are simple [30] without complexity. Chinese painters have always avoided mixing colors as far as possible. From malachite, they obtained several shades of green, from cinnabar or sulphide of mercury, a number of reds. They knew also how to combine mercury, sulphur and potash to produce vermilion.

The different shades of [31] ink of Chinese add gold. It is a very different composition [32] from Western countries.

29

Which choice most effectively combines the underlined sentences ?

A) NO CHANGE

B) Being prepared, as did the silk, they became practically indestructible

C) Being prepared with silk, they became practically indestructible

D) They became practically indestructible like silk when they were prepared

30

Which choice provides the additional information that best supports the previous portion and the following sentence?

A) NO CHANGE

B) from mineral or vegetable origin

C) using only a few hues

D) following the custom

31

A) NO CHANGE

B) Chinese's ink

C) ink made in China

D) Chinese ink

32

A) NO CHANGE

B) from that of Western countries

C) than that of Western countries

D) from Western countries

CONTINUE ►

2   2

[33] ① Other ingredients may be added to produce sheen or a dead finish. ② It is a solid made of soot obtained by burning certain plants, which is then combined with glue or oil and molded into a cake and dried. ③ The cake is moistened and rubbed on a slab, and the ink thus obtained must be used in a special way and with special care to produce the full effect. ④ For storage, it improves with age if properly kept.

[34] ① The brush-stroke in the painting of the Far East is of supreme importance. ② My mother used to attend the local Chinese choreography class where she learned how to use brush and cake paint. ③ We know that this could not be otherwise if we recall that the characters in Chinese writing are ideographs, not actually written, but rather drawn. ④ The stroke is not a mere formal, lifeless sign. It is an expression in which is reflected the beauty of the thought that inspired it as well as the quality of the soul of him who gives it form.

33

What is the most logical sequence of the sentences of this paragraph ?
A) 1-2-3-4
B) 2-1-4-3
C) 4-3-2-1
D) 1-3-2-4

34

Which sentence is LEAST related with other sentences of this paragraph ?
A) 1
B) 2
C) 3
D) 4

CONTINUE

2   **2**

Question 35-44 are based on the following passages

Deep blue sea

The deep sea typically has [35] a sparser fauna dominated by tiny worms and crustaceans, with an even sparser distribution of larger animals (36), and near hydrothermal vents, arears of the ocean where warm water emerges from subterranean sources, live remarkable densities of huge clams, blind crabs, and fish.

Most deep-sea faunas rely for food on particular matter, ultimately derived from photosynthesis, falling from above.

(37) The food supplies necessary to sustain the large vent communities, however, must be many times the ordinary fallout.

The first reports [38] described vent faunas proposed two possible sources of nutrition: bacterial chemosynthesis, production of food by bacteria using energy derived from chemical changes, and advection, the drifting of food materials is from surrounding regions.

35

A) NO CHANGE
B) a sparse
C) the sparest
D) the more sparse

36

A) NO CHANGE
B) ;however,
C) ;nonetheless,
D) ;in the meantime,

37

At this point, the author wishes to delete the underlined sentence. Should the author proceed to delete it or not?

A) Keep, because it helps readers understand the quality of food sources faunas require
B) Keep, because it suggests the quantity of food required to feed faunas
C) Delete, because the sentence should focus on identifying the particular matter.
D) Delete, because the following sentences rely more on flora than fauna.

38

A) NO CHANGE
B) have described
C) describing
D) were described

CONTINUE ➡

2   2

Later, evidence in support of the idea of intense local chemosynthesis was accumulated: hydrogen sulfide was found in vent water; vent-site bacteria [39] were found to be [40] capable with chemosynthesis; and extremely large concentrations of them were found in samples of [41] vent water thought to be pure. This final observation seemed decisive. If such an astonishing concentration of organisms [42] were typical of vent outflow, then food within the vent would dwarf any contribution from advection.

39

A) NO CHANGE
B) was
C) are
D) is

40

A) NO CHANGE
B) capable of
C) able to
D) available to

41

Which choice would NOT be applicable in the sentence ?
A) vent water seemingly without organism
B) vent water, which was originally considered to be pure
C) pure vent water
D) water believed to be devoid of matters in vent

42

A) NO CHANGE
B) was
C) had been
D) would be

CONTINUE ➤

2

2

Hence, the widely quoted conclusion was reached that bacterial chemosynthesis provides the foundation for hydrothermal-vent food [43] chains—an exciting prospect because no other communities on earth are independent of photosynthesis. [44]

43

Which of the following choices would NOT be acceptable?

A) chains—an exciting
B) chains, an exciting
C) chains; an exciting
D) chains: an exciting

44

At this point, the writer is considering to add the sentence below.

This suggests that bacterial chemosynthesis is not a sufficient source of nutrition for these creatures.

Should this addition be allowed?

A) Yes, because it reminds the reader another source of nutrition: advection

B) Yes, because it explains that bacterial chemosynthesis is not sufficient source of nutrition

C) No, because it contradicts to the description in the previous paragraph

D) No, because it should now focus on why no other communities on earth are independent.

TEST 2

WRITING ABSOLUTE PATTERNS

TEST 2

WRITING AND LANGUAGE SECTION PATTERN ANALYSIS

Q1. Absolute Pattern 18: Punctuation Error

Privacy in our society is clearly [1] <u>diminishing: we </u>carry devices everywhere we go

	A) diminishing. We	B) is comma splice error.
√	**B) diminishing, we**	A) starting as a new independent sentence shouldn't be a problem.
	C) diminishing; we	C) The semicolon functions as a conjunction describing the cause-effect
	D) diminishing as we	D) "as" is used as a conjunction for the cause-effect.

Q2. Absolute Pattern 10: Logical Expression

and the Internet has allowed an unprecedented level of information to be [2] <u>publicly available.</u>

√	**A) NO CHANGE**	<u>publicly available</u> means to be known to the public
	B) promoted	B), C) are Unrelated Word Usage
	C) advertised	
	D) publicized	It mainly means a type of book or materials to be printed out.

Q3. Absolute Pattern 23: Transitions (Supporting Detail, Contrast, and Consequence)

[3] <u>Unfortunately,</u> this is exactly what happened in the Cambridge City Council on Wednesday when, following protests from many fearful and disgruntled citizens, the body voted to keep surveillance cameras already installed in the city turned off, citing their possible contribution to the erosion of civil liberties.

√	**A) NO CHANGE**	A) The following sentence further elaborates the unfortunate incident on Wednesday.
	B) Although,	B), C), D)
	C) With all due respect	1> "Although" is used for a concessional tone, in which the author suggests a different view while accepting the previous statement.
	D) Granted,	2>That is, the author uses these words when he wants to balance between "privacy" and "safety."
		3> The author is adamant supporter for safety.

Q4. Absolute Pattern 12: Modifier (Placement) Error

on Wednesday when, following protests from many fearful and disgruntled citizens, **the body voted** to keep surveillance cameras already installed in the city turned off, [4] <u>cited</u> their possible contribution to the erosion of civil liberties.

	A) NO CHANGE	1> "the body voted" is the main clause with the subject and the verb.
✓	**B) citing**	2> Therefore, there shouldn't be another verb after the comma.
		3> Choices A), C), and D) are all verbs
	C) was cited	B) creates a modifying phrase to describe the reason and situation
	D) had cited	mentioned in the main clause.

Q5. Absolute Pattern 1: Adding, Revising, Deleting, Retaining Information

[5] <u>The fund was made by</u> a grant from the Department of Homeland Security, **a mere eight cameras were installed** around Cambridge in 2008 to aid firefighters and other evacuation personnel in the event of an emergency.

	A) NO CHANGE	1> "a mere eight cameras were installed" is the main clause.
✓	**B) Fund made by**	2> The comma before the main clause indicates the previous portion of the sentence should be the modifying phrase, neither a sentence nor clause.
	C) There was the fund by	A) and C) both are independent sentences, making a comma splice error.
	D) Funding	D) "funding a grant" changes the meaning and also the subject "a mere eight cameras" can't fund by themselves.

Q6. Absolute Pattern 6: Confusing Words

the cameras' potential to be life-saving in dire circumstances greatly [6] <u>overwhelm</u> their minimal impact on privacy.

	A) NO CHANGE	1> The sentence compares "the cameras' potential" with "their minimal impact on privacy."
✓	**B) outweighs**	2> "outweigh" expresses this comparison.
	C) outperform	A) and C) are too extreme.
	D) outweight	D) is a noun.

Q7. Absolute Pattern 7: Conjunction Error

Most of those in opposition to the use of these cameras at the city council meeting **did not have a problem** with the standard function of the cameras in emergency situations [7] <u>and</u> were more concerned about the possibility of exploitation

	A) NO CHANGE	1> "did not have a problem" reveals that the cameras' functionality is mischaracterized, therefore denying the claim.
	B) so	2> The conjunction "but" is the best answer to cancel out the preceding sentence while supporting the following clause.
√	**C) but**	A), B) are used in a parallel situation.
	D) however	D) "however" requires a semicolon in the front.

Q8. Absolute Pattern 4: Comparison

But [8] <u>as much as</u> these cameras may conjure up images of an Orwellian nightmare with the government watching our every move, **they add no more** cause for alarm than cameras installed on highways to monitor speed limits or in stores to monitor shoplifting.

√	**A) NO CHANGE**	The main clause "<u>they add no more</u>" can be paired with 'as much as' for coherence.
	B) as far as	
	C) as long as	
	D) as soon as	

Q9. Absolute Pattern 23: Transitions (Supporting Detail, Contrast, and Consequence)

[9] <u>While</u> the installation process was not particularly transparent, with most of it taking place without the involvement of the Cambridge City Council, **disallowing these cameras is [10]** <u>unnecessary</u>, rash, and wasteful.

√	**A) NO CHANGE**	1> "While", meaning "in spite of the fact that", leads to the concessional tone in the main clause.
	B) However,	2> "unnecessary, rash, and wasteful." emphasize the author's moderate (concessional) tone.
	C) Moreover,	B) 'However' is used to cancel out the sentence
	D) Because	C) 'Moreover' means 'in addition to'
		D) 'Because' is used when a clear cause-and-effect situation exists.

Q10. Absolute Pattern 10: Logical Expression

While the installation process was not particularly transparent, with most of it taking place without the involvement of the Cambridge City Council, disallowing these cameras is [10] not necessary, rash, and wasteful.

	A) NO CHANGE	1> Writing "not necessary, rash, and wasteful" instead of "unnecessary, rash, and wasteful" can be misunderstood as "not necessary, not rash, and not wasteful."
√	**B) unnecessary, rash, and wasteful.**	
	C) unnecessarily rash and wasteful.	C) also changes the meaning as if it sounds cameras need to be uninstalled anyway.
	D) unnecessary, but rash and wasteful.	D) "but" can't be used for the parallel structure.

Q11. Absolute Pattern 1: Adding, Revising, Deleting, Retaining Information

It is a city's obligation to protect and assist its residents in a time of emergency, and blocking a possible rescue **due to unfounded fears of the government being able to view a public street shows little perspective.** [11] Eight cameras will not mark the end of our First Amendment rights.

√	**A) Yes, because it sarcastically criticizes the groundless fears**
	B) Yes, because it explains higher law can dismiss the subordinate law
	C) No, because First Amendment does not specify camera installation regulations
	D) No, because it undermines the author's arguments

1> The author criticizes that the decision made was based on "unfounded fears"

2> In order to emphasize his argument, the author employs "First Amendment rights," tinged with humor that sarcastically criticizes the "unfounded fears."

D) It has no evidence that it undermines the author's argument but the author strengthens his arguments in twisted sarcasm.

Q12. Absolute Pattern 9: Informational Graphs

Which of the following choices meets with the author's opinion?

√	**A) Should More CCTV be installed? YES**	**A) would be the author's answer.**
	B) Do CCTV make you feel Safe? No	The author would say Yes
	C) Do you Approve the use of CCTV? No	The author would say Yes
	D) Privacy is more important than safety. Yes	The author would say No.

Q13. Absolute Pattern 13: Parallel Structure

Maintenance Engineering is the discipline and profession of applying engineering concepts to the optimization of equipment, procedures, and departmental budgets to achieve better [13] maintenance, reliability, and availability of equipment.

	A) NO CHANGE	B) uses the list of words coherently.
√	B) maintain**ability**, reli**ability**, and avail**ability** of equipment	A) Although both maintenance and maintainability are nouns, the word containing 'ability' follow the coherence,
	C) maintenance, reliance, and available of equipment	C) noun, noun, adjective sequence violates the parallel structure.
	D) reliable as well as available maintenance of equipment	D) changes the meaning.

Q14.   Absolute Pattern 22: Nonrestrictive Modifier (Inessential Information)

Since the Industrial Revolution, devices, equipment, machinery and structures have grown increasingly [14]complex, requiring a host of personnel, vocations and related systems needed to maintain them.

√	A) complex, requiring	1> Nonrestrictive modifier (inessential information) must be separated from the main clause by a comma.
	B) complex, which requires	2> Using a comma, it indicates that this phrase modifies the primary subjects "devices, equip., mach., and structures."
	C) complex requiring	Choice B and D are incorrect because it is unclear exactly what
	D) complex that require	"which" and "that" refer to.

Q15. Absolute Pattern 19: Redundant Error

Prior to 2006, the US [15] spent **every single year** approximately US$300 billion *annually* on plant maintenance and operations alone.

	A) NO CHANGE	"every single year" in (A) and "throughout the year" in (C) are synonyms to "annually."
√	B) spent about	
	C) spent throughout the year approximately	
	D) was spending about	D) progressive tense can't be used in a specific point in time in the past or "2006."

Q16. Absolute Pattern 1: Adding, Revising, Deleting, Retaining Information

A person practicing Maintenance Engineering is known as a Maintenance Engineer.[16] A Maintenance Engineer should possess significant knowledge of statistics, probability and logistics, and additionally in the fundamentals of the operation of the equipment and machinery he or she is responsible for.

√	A) **Yes, because it works as the topic sentence of this paragraph**
	B) Yes, because the role of Maintenance Engineer is the central claim of this passage
	C) No, because it distracts from the main concern of this paragraph
	D) No, because the following sentence already briefly introduces the Maintenance Engineer

The author should use this sentence as the topic because defining the term Maintenance Engineer smoothly pulls the following sentences of this paragraph that describes the knowledge and experience required to become a maintenance engineer.

B) is not mentioned anywhere else. Becoming Maintenance Engineer belongs to this paragraph only.

C) is the opposite. It summarizes the main issue as the topic sentence

D) The following sentence further elaborates the topic sentence.

Q17. Absolute Pattern 24: Verb Tense / Voice Error

Institutions across the world [17] have recognized the need for Maintenance Engineering.

√	A) NO CHANGE	1> This is the demonstrative statement, which requires the simple present tense.
	B) has recognized	2> The following sentences also use the present tense as the above evidence.
	C) recognized	3> The primary subject' institutions' is plural, requiring a plural verb.
	D) is recognized	B), D) are singular verbs
		C) 'recognized' is the past tense.
		D) is also passive

Q18. Absolute Pattern 1: Adding, Revising, Deleting, Retaining Information

[18] Maintenance Engineers usually hold a degree in Mechanical Engineering, Industrial Engineering, or other Engineering Disciplines. In recent years specialized degree in master courses [19] have developed.

	A) Yes, because the paragraph is about to focus on MRO
	B) Yes, because work experience is more important than the college degree to become a Maintenance Engineer
	C) No, because it shows how sophisticated the profession is
√	**D) No, because it shows the educational background requirements**

The former and the latter parts that surround the question sentence discuss the engineering degrees.

Therefore, the sentence is related to each other and should not be deleted.

A) starts from the next paragraph.

B) is inconsistent with the question because the paragraph does not compare education with any other

    information including "the importance of work experience"

C) The professional sophistication is not the main concern of this paragraph.

Q19. Absolute Pattern 24: Verb Tense / Voice Error

In recent years specialized degree in master courses [19] have developed.

	A) NO CHANGE	1> Time adverbial phrase "In recent year" indicates the present perfect tense should be used.
√	**B) has developed**	2> The subject "degree" requires a singular verb.
	C) had developed	A) 'have' is plural
	D) are going to be developed and launched	C) is the past perfect tense D) is the future tense.

Q20. Absolute Pattern 13: Parallel Structure

The actions include the combination of all technical and corresponding [20] administrative, managerial, and supervision actions."

	A) NO CHANGE	A) adjective, adjective, noun
	B) administrative, management, and supervision	B) adjective, noun, noun
		C) noun, noun, adjective
	C) administration, management, and supervisory	D) **adjective, adjective, adjective maintain the paralleling structure.**
√	**D) administrative, managerial, and supervisory**	

Q21. Absolute Pattern 17: Pronoun Error

[21] The theory also represents a closed loop supply chain and usually has the scope of maintenance, repair or overhaul of the product.

	A) NO CHANGE	1> The new paragraph cannot start with the pronoun as in C) and D)
√	**B) MRO also represents**	2> MRO is more closely defined as the professional skills or technology rather than a theory as described throughout the passage.
	C) They also represent	3> Based on the tense applied throughout the passage and the type of the passage, the tense should be the simple present tense.
	D) It has also represented	
		D) uses the present perfect tense, which disrupts the tense parallelism.

Q22. Absolute Pattern 21: Subject-Verb, Pronoun, Noun Agreement

The latter **criteria** [22] is an open loop supply chain and is typified by refurbishment and remanufacture.

	A) NO CHANGE	1> The subject "criteria" is plural (criterion is singular)
	B) are an open loop supply chain but is	2> Therefore, choices A), B), and C) that use "is" as the verb are all incorrect.
	C) is an open loop supply chain but is	Additionally, (B) and (C) use the conjunction "but"
√	**D) are an open loop supply chain and are**	In this case, two sentences are paralleling and "but" shouldn't be used.

Q23. Absolute Pattern 9: Informational Graphs

Which paragraph in the passage best represents the chart?

	A) Paragraph {1}	Paragraph 1 introduces the concept of Maintenance Engineering.
	B) Paragraph {2}	Paragraph 2 illustrates the historical overview.
	C) Paragraph {3}	Paragraph 3 discusses the requirements of becoming the maintenance engineer
√	**D) Paragraph {4}**	Paragraph 4 initiates MRO and its practical applications that go beyond the theoretical presentations discussed so far. Therefore, the graph should best fit in paragraph 4.

Q24. Absolute Pattern 24: Verb Tense / Voice Error

Where our painters [24] have chosen wood or canvas as a ground, the Chinese **have employed** silk or paper.

✓ A) NO CHANGE	1> The following main clause (the Chinese have employed…) uses the present perfect;
B) chose	2> therefore, the same tense should be maintained in the preceding subordinating clause.
C) had chosen	
D) were chosen	B) is past tense C) is the past perfect tense D) is a passive past tense.

Q25. Absolute Pattern 19: Redundant Error

While our art recognizes that drawing itself, quite apart from painting, [25] sufficient objective,

A) NO CHANGE	A) has no verb
✓ **B) is sufficiently objective,**	C) and D) "sufficient" and "enough" are synonyms.
C) is sufficient enough and objective,	
D) is sufficient enough to be objective,	

Q26. Absolute Pattern 10: Logical Expression

the colors employed by the Orientals--at times brilliant, at times subdued with an almost studied restraint--preserved a singular fluidity and lent themselves to undefined evanescence which gave them a [26] surprising charm.

✓ A) NO CHANGE	1> The indefinite article "a" indicates the noun object is following.
B) surprisingly	2> "charm" is, therefore, a noun.
C) surprising with	3> The adjective "surprising" should then be used in front of the noun "charm." "a surprising charm"
D) surprising that brings	B) The adverb "surprisingly" can't modify a noun.
	C), D) are wordy.

Q27. Absolute Pattern 19: Redundant Error

In the **eighteenth century**, under the Tang dynasty, the use of finer silk began [27] in the period from 1701 to 1799.

	A) NO CHANGE	1> "eighteen century" refers to the period between 1701 and 1799.
	B) from 1701 to 1799	2> Therefore, The underlined portion should be deleted.
	C) between the year 1701 and 1799	
√	**D) delete the underlined portion**	

Q28. Absolute Pattern 10: Logical Expression

The use *of silken fabric of the finest weave,* prepared with a thick sizing, [28] became general during the Sung dynasty.

√	**A) NO CHANGE**	1> The main subject is "The use", not people.
	B) become general skill	2> That is, "use" can't be "skillful"
	C) had been general skill	3> Therefore, (B), (C), and (D) are all incorrect.
	D) were skill	

Q29. Absolute Pattern 12: Modifier (Placement) Error

[29] Being prepared, as was the silk, they became practically indestructible with a sizing of alum.	
√	**A) NO CHANGE**
	B) Being prepared, as did the silk, they became practically indestructible.
	C) Being prepared with the silk, they became practically indestructible.
	D) They became practically indestructible like silk when they were prepared

The original sentence was "(When they were) **being prepared as the silk was** (being prepared), **they became practically indestructible** with a sizing of alum. "

B) "as did" should change to "as was"

C) "with the silk" changes the original meaning.

D) "indestructible like silk" changes the original meaning.

Q30. Absolute Pattern 1: Adding, Revising, Deleting, Retaining Information

The colors **are simple** [30] without complexity. Chinese painters have always avoided mixing colors as far as possible. From malachite, they obtained several shades of green, from cinnabar or sulphide of mercury, a number of reds.

	A) NO CHANGE	1> The previous portion of the sentence discusses "colors"
√	**B) from mineral or vegetable origin**	2> The following sentence discusses the nature of the colors.
	C) using only a few hues	3> Therefore, (B) is the best answer "simple" and "without complexity" in (A) or "a few hues" in (C) are synonyms
	D) following the custom	(D) is not a related issue.

Q31. Absolute Pattern 14: Possessive Determiners and Possessive Noun Error

The different shades of [31] ink of Chinese add gold

	A) NO CHANGE	1> "Chinese ink" is used as a compound noun
	B) Chinese's ink	2> Therefore, it is wrong to use a possessive determiner such as "of" as in (A) or "apostrophe s" as in (B)
	C) ink made in China	(C) changes the meaning
√	**D) Chinese ink**	

Q32. Absolute Pattern 4: Comparison

It is a very different composition [32] from Western countries.

	A) NO CHANGE	1> "It" refers to the "composition drawn by Chinese ink"
√	**B) from that of Western countries**	2> The correct comparison should be "The composition drawn by Chinese ink" to "the composition drawn by Western ink", not "Western countries."
	C) than that of Western countries	
	D) from Western countries	3> Therefore, A), D) are incorrect. C) is an idiomatic error. The correct idiom is different ~ from'.

Q33. Absolute Pattern 11: Logical Sequence

[2] **Other ingredients** may be added to produce sheen or a dead finish.

[1] It is a solid made of soot obtained by burning certain plants, which is then combined with glue or oil and **molded into a cake and dried**.

[4] **The cake is moistened** and rubbed on a slab, and the ink thus obtained must be used in a special way and **with special care to produce the full effect**.

[3] For storage, **it improves with age if properly kept.**

	A) 1-2-3-4	1> "molded into a cake and dried" in sentence [1] and "The cake is moistened" in sentence [4] can not be separated.
√	**B) 2-1-4-3**	2> Therefore, the answer is (B).
	C) 4-3-2-1	OR
	D) 1-3-2-4	3> "For storage" should be mentioned in the last sentence.

Q34. Absolute Pattern 1: Adding, Revising, Deleting, Retaining Information

[34] ①**The brush-stroke** in the painting of the Far East is of supreme importance.

② **My mother** used to attend the local Chinese choreography class where she learned how to use brush and cake paint.

③ We know that this could not be otherwise if we recall that the characters in Chinese writing are ideographs, not actually written, but **rather drawn**.

④ **The stroke** is not a mere formal, lifeless sign. It is an expression in which is reflected the beauty of the thought that inspired it as well as the quality of the soul of him who gives it form.

	A) 1	A), C), D) all discuss the brush-stroke in Chinese painting.
√	**B) 2**	
	C) 3	
	D) 4	

Q35. Absolute Pattern 4: Comparison

The deep sea typically has (35) **a sparser** fauna dominated by tiny worms and crustaceans, with **an even sparser** distribution of larger animals.

	A) NO CHANGE	1> "even sparser" in the following phrase indicates the degree has increased and the comparison is being made.
√	**B) a sparse**	2> Therefore, the sentence should start from "a sparse"
	C) the sparest	C) is the superlative
	D) the more sparse	D) "sparse" is one syllable. An adjective with less than two syllables should use "~ er", not "more" (e.g., cheaper, not more cheap)

Q36. Absolute Pattern 23: Transitions (Supporting Detail, Contrast, and Consequence)

The deep sea typically has a sparse fauna dominated by tiny worms and crustaceans, with **an even sparser** distribution of larger animals (36), and near hydrothermal vents, arears of the ocean where warm water emerges from subterranean sources, **live remarkable densities of huge clams**, blind crabs, and fish.

	A) NO CHANGE	1> The main clause starts with the negative tone "sparse, even sparser..."
√	**B) ;however,**	2> The dependent clause after "and" shifts its tone to positive "live remarkable..."
	C) ;nonetheless,	A) "and" is used in a parallel structure.
	D) ;in the meantime,	C) is used in a concessional transition between sentences to show an alternative or different view.
		D) is used to change the subject being discussed.

Q37. Absolute Pattern 1: Adding, Revising, Deleting, Retaining Information

Most deep-sea faunas rely for food on particular matter, **ultimately derived from photosynthesis**, falling from above. (37) The food supplies necessary to sustain the large vent communities, however, must be many times the ordinary fallout.

	A) Keep, because it helps readers understand the **quality of food** sources faunas require
√	B) Keep, because it suggests the quantity of food required to feed faunas
	C) Delete, because the sentence should focus on **identifying the particular matter**.
	D) Delete, because the following sentences rely more on flora than fauna.

(A) "must be many times" indicates quantity, not quality.

(C) "ultimately derived from photosynthesis" indicates what basically the particular matter is.

The main focus is how the deep sea fauna feed on themselves and where they find food, not

identifying a particular matter.

(D) The following sentences continue discussing fauna, not flora.

Q38. Absolute Pattern 12: Modifier (Placement) Error

The first reports [38] described vent faunas **proposed** two possible sources of nutrition

	A) NO CHANGE	1> "proposed" is the main verb
	B) have described	2> "describing vent faunas" works as an adjective to modify the subject "The first reports."
√	C) describing	3> All the remaining options are verbs.
	D) were described	

Q39. Absolute Pattern 21: Subject-Verb, Pronoun, Noun Agreement

vent-site **bacteria** [39] were found to be [40]capable with chemosynthesis;

√	A) NO CHANGE	Bacteria is a plural of a singular bacterium and needs to use the plural verb.
	B) was	C), D) The other sentences surrounding the question use the past tense.
	C) are	Therefore, this sentence must use the past tense as well.
	D) is	

Q40. Absolute Pattern 15: Prepositional Idiom

vent-site bacteria were found to be [40]capable with chemosynthesis;

	A) NO CHANGE	Capable of ~ is the correct form of the idiom.
√	**B) capable of**	C), D) change the original meaning by dropping the word 'capable'.
	C) able to	
	D) available to	

Q41. Absolute Pattern 10: Logical Expression

vent-site bacteria were found to be capable of chemosynthesis; and extremely large concentrations of them were found in samples of [41] vent water thought to be pure.

	A) vent water seemingly without organism
	B) vent water, which was originally considered to be pure
√	**C) pure vent water**
	D) water believed to be devoid of matters in vent

1> The original sentence (thought to be pure) implies that the water that was once believed to be pure is in fact full of bacteria.

2> Only C changed the original meaning of the sentence.

A), B), D) all correspond to the original meaning of the sentence.

Q42. Absolute Pattern 21: Subject-Verb, Pronoun, Noun Agreement

If such an astonishing concentration of organisms [42] were typical of vent outflow, then food within the vent **would** dwarf any contribution from advection.

√	A) NO CHANGE	1> "If-clause' uses 'were,' not 'was', regardless whether the subject is singular or plural.
	B) was	2> The main clause—in the present situation—uses the past tense "would" for the main verb
	C) had been	
	D) would be	3> (D) "would" can't be used in If-clause.

Q43. Absolute Pattern 18: Punctuation Error

Hence, the widely quoted conclusion was reached that bacterial chemosynthesis provides the foundation for hydrothermal-vent food [43] chains—an exciting prospect because no other communities on earth are independent of photosynthesis.

	A) chains—an exciting	1> The question focuses on the punctuation usage for the modifying phrase.
	B) chains, an exciting	2> Either a simple phrase or a clause with a verb can be placed after (A) Dash or (D) Colon as long as it supports the context in the main clause.
√	**C) chains; an exciting**	(B) Comma carries the following phrase "an exciting prospect…" and that's what a comma should do.
	D) chains: an exciting	(C) 1> Semicolon requires a complete clause on both sides. 2> The original sentence after the dash is a phrase, not a clause. 3> Therefore, the semicolon in (C) can't be used.

Q44. PATTERN 1: Adding, Revising, Deleting, Retaining Information

The first reports describing vent faunas proposed **two possible sources of nutrition**: bacterial chemosynthesis, production of food by bacteria using energy derived from chemical changes, and **advection, the drifting of food materials** is from surrounding regions.

Hence, the widely quoted conclusion was reached that bacterial chemosynthesis provides the foundation for hydrothermal-vent food chains—an exciting prospect because no other communities on earth are independent of photosynthesis. [44] **This suggests that bacterial chemosynthesis is not a sufficient source of nutrition for these creatures.**

√	**A) Yes, because it reminds the reader another source of nutrition: advection**
	B) Yes, because it explains that bacterial chemosynthesis is not sufficient source of nutrition
	C) No, because it contradicts to the description in the previous paragraph
	D) No, because it should now focus on why no other communities on earth are independent.

1> As shown above, the author introduced "two possible sources of nutrition."

2> Upon completion of bacterial chemosynthesis, now it's time to discuss the second food-source: advection.

3> The added information will function as a transitional sentence to discuss the second food source.

4> (B) is incorrect because it merely repeats the question.

5> (C) is opposite perception

6> (D) is unrelated issue

24 ABSOLUTE PATTERNS

SAT
Writing and Language
Test 3

ALL THE LOGIC AND RULES

BEHIND THE EVERY SINGLE

SAT QUESTION

Writing and Language Test 3
35 MINUTES, 44 QUEST IONS

Each passage below is accompanied by a number of questions. For some questions, you will consider how the passage might be revised to improve the expression of ideas. For other questions, you will consider how the passage might be edited to correct errors in sentence structure, usage, or punctuation. A passage or a question may be accompanied by one or more graphics (such as a table or graph) that you will consider as you make revising and editing decisions.

Questions 1-11 are based on the following passage.

Sustainable architecture

A modern green design concept is to facilitate sustainable use of the resources – energy, water and other materials – [1] that please both employees and customers.

Glass is a wonder material that combines more than a few advantages, such as transparency, natural day-lighting, blending of exteriors with interiors and [2] sound-proof advantage.

1

Which choice offers the most appropriate introduction to the passage?

A) NO CHANGE
B) all through the complete life cycle of the building including its construction.
C) allowing people to find an alternative amid increasing rental cost
D) that dates back to late 19th century.

2

A) NO CHANGE
B) acoustic control
C) sound dampening function can also be expected
D) the application of effective noise canceling system

CONTINUE

2   2

Glass, a wholly recyclable material, supplies unrestricted occasions for architects as well as designers for the innovative applications in buildings. [3]

The intent of a green building design [4] <u>curtails</u> the demand on non-renewable resources, amplify utilization efficiency of these resources when in use, and [5] <u>augmentation</u> the reuse, recycling, and consumption of renewable resources.

Sustainable architecture that uses glass as a main building material seeks to [6] <u>optimize</u> the negative environmental impact of buildings by efficiency and moderation in the use of materials and energy.

3

At this point, the author considers to add the following sentence.

Glass accomplishes indoor environmental quality and energy efficiency.

Should the author add this sentence?

A) Yes, because it provides how glass plays a noteworthy role as a building material.

B) Yes, because it allows the reader to anticipate how the modern building codes and regulations are maintained

C) No, because other criteria for green buildings should also be presented

D) No, because the passage should focus on sustainable architecture and its main construction materials

4

A) NO CHANGE

B) curtail

C) is being curtailed

D) Is to curtail

5

A) NO CHANGE

B) augments

C) augmenting

D) augment

6

A) NO CHANGE

B) standardize

C) maximize

D) minimize

CONTINUE →

2   2

Sustainable architecture uses [7] awesome approach to energy and ecological conservation in the design of the built environment.

The idea of sustainability, or ecological design, is to ensure that our actions and decisions today do not [8] inhabit the opportunities of future generations.

The industrial glass standards combine [9] a great deal of techniques and technologies to achieve ultra-low energy use. Following its destruction by a tornado in 2007, the town of Greensburg, Kansas (USA) elected to rebuild to highly stringent LEED Platinum environmental standards. Shown is the town's new art center, which integrates its own solar panels and wind generators for energy self-sufficiency.

[10] Effective energy use over the entire life cycle of a building is the most important goal of sustainable architecture.

Numerous passive architectural strategies have been developed over time, [11] examples of those strategies include the arrangement of rooms or the sizing and orientation of windows in a building. The orientation of facades and streets or the ratio between building heights and street widths for urban planning has also been considered.

7

A) NO CHANGE
B) limited
C) open
D) conscious

8

Which choice best combines the underlined sentence?

A) NO CHANGE
B) inhibit
C) include
D) allow

9

A) NO CHANGE
B) a bunch of
C) a lot of
D) much

10

A) NO CHANGE
B) Energy efficiency
C) The application of effective and utilizable energy
D) Energy as an effective source

11

A) NO CHANGE
B) the strategic examples include
C) examples of which include
D) and some strategic examples including

CONTINUE ➤

2
2

Questions 12-22 are based on the following passage.

Pony Express

The Pony Express was a mail service delivering messages, newspapers, mail, and small packages by horseback, using a series of relay stations. This firm was founded by William H. Russell, Alexander Majors, and William B. Waddell, [12] all of them were notable in the freighting business.

During its 19 months of operation, [13] he reduced the time for messages to travel between the Atlantic and Pacific coasts to about 10 days. From April 3, 1860 to October 1861, it became the West's most direct [14] means of east–west communication [15] before the telegraph was established.

12

A) NO CHANGE
B) ,all of whom were notable
C) ,and they were notable
D) ,all of those who were notable

13

A) NO CHANGE
B) they
C) this firm founders
D) The Pony Express mail service delivery firm

14

A) NO CHANGE
B) mean
C) meaning
D) meaningful

15

The author considers to delete the underlined portion, should the author delete it?
A) Yes, because the new issue "telegraph" undermines the integrity of the passage.
B) Yes, because the new invention telegraph undermines the historical importance of the Pony Express, the main theme of the passage.
C) No, because it establishes the reason for the short operation of the service.
D) No, because it provides no specific function for how the new state of California was wired to the rest of the United States.

CONTINUE ➡

2   **2**

[16] This concept of idea of a fast mail route to the Pacific coast was prompted largely by California's newfound prominence and its rapidly growing population. After gold was discovered there in 1848, thousands of prospectors, investors and businessmen made their way to California, at that time

[17] the region was a new territory of the U.S. By 1850, California entered the Union as a free

[18] state. California's population had grown to 380,000.

[19] As a result of the demand for a faster way to get mail to and from this westernmost state became even greater, at the peak of the operations the company expanded employing 6,000 men, thousands of wagons and warehouses. a meatpacking plant, a bank and an insurance company.

16

A) NO CHANGE
B) This conceptual idea
C) Such a concept of idea
D) The idea

17

A) NO CHANGE
B) the state of California was a new territory of the U.S.
C) a new territory of the U.S.
D) it just became the official territory of the U.S.

18

A) NO CHANGE
B) state, whose
C) state with
D) state, which

19

A) NO CHANGE
B) because of
C) because
D) resulting

CONTINUE ▶

2   2

[20] Instead of utilizing a short route and using mounted riders rather than traditional stagecoaches, they proposed to establish a fast mail service between St. Joseph, Missouri, and Sacramento, California, with letters delivered in 10 days, a duration many said was impossible. The initial price was set at $5 per $\frac{1}{2}$ ounce (14 g), then $2.50, and by July 1861 to $1. The founders of the Pony Express hoped to win an exclusive government mail contract, [21] despite that did not come about.

The employers stressed the importance of the pouch. They often said that, if it came to be, the horse and rider should perish before the mochila did.

The mochila was thrown over the saddle and held in place by the weight of the rider sitting on it.

Each corner had a *cantina,* or pocket. Bundles of mail were placed in these cantinas, which were padlocked for safety. [22]

20

A) NO CHANGE
B) By
C) Consequently,
D) On the other hand,

21

A) NO CHANGE
B) however,
C) but
D) and

22

Which choice most logically follows the previous sentence?

A) The mochila could hold 20 pounds of mail along with the 20 pounds of material carried on the horse.
B) Pony Express would end up bankruptcy immediately after the arrival of the telegraph.
C) The greatest beneficiary of Pony Express was not, however, the employers, but the horse retailers.
D) 40 pounds were considered to be lightweight for such a traveling distance.

CONTINUE

2   2

Questions 23-33 are based on the following passage.

But aren't e-cigarettes safer than regular cigarettes?

The FDA admits that some tobacco products have the potential to be [23] less harmful than others. But more evidence is needed.
The agency is exploring this issue with respect to tobacco regulation.

The FDA believes that potential benefit as well as risks [24] are in this new technology.
If certain products, such as e-cigarettes, have reduced toxicity compared to conventional cigarettes; encourage current smokers to switch completely; and/or are not widely used by youth, they may have the potential to reduce disease and death.
But if any product prompts young people to become addicted to nicotine, reduces a person's interest in quitting cigarettes, and/or [25] leading to long-term usage with other tobacco products, the public health impact could be negative.
The FDA encourages manufacturers to explore product innovations that would [26] add potential benefits and minimize risks.

23
A) NO CHANGE
B) more
C) greatly
D) little

24
A) NO CHANGE
B) is
C) will be
D) had been

25
A) NO CHANGE
B) lead
C) leads
D) to be led

26
A) NO CHANGE
B) maximize
C) show
D) minimize

CONTINUE

2   **2**

The final rule allows the FDA to further evaluate and [27] <u>excess</u> the impact of these products on the health of both users and non-users. And it lets the FDA [28] <u>regulate</u> the products based on the most current scientific knowledge.

The FDA considered all manufacturers, including small businesses, when finalizing [29] <u>this rule, and that's the reason why</u> the agency is allowing additional time for small-scale tobacco product manufacturers to comply with certain provisions

27

A) NO CHANGE

B) access

C) accede

D) assess

28

A) NO CHANGE

B) regulates

C) to regulate

D) regulating

29

A) NO CHANGE

B) this rule. That's the reason why

C) this rule, so

D) this rule, that's why

CONTINUE

2

2

In 2016, the FDA stated its position that e-cigarettes are " less likely hazardous for an individual user than continued smoking of traditional cigarettes," although that the net population effect is unknown.

Tobacco Use Among Youth
(In The Past 30 Days)

Usage by Middle School Students Growth		Cigarettes		e-Cigarettes	
	Unites	2011	2017	2011	2017
	%	6%	5%	5%	9%
	Bps		-2		6
Usage by High School Students Growth	%	15%	9%	12%	22%
	Bps		-6.5		15

30

For this question, please refer to the table on the left. At this point, the author wants the conclusion that reflects how e-cigarette regulations should be made in the future.

Which choice best accomplish this goal?

A) FDA should implement e-cigarettes regulations, especially to middle school students because they are the highest e-cigarettes consumers.

B) FDA should delay e-cigarettes regulations because cigarette smoking rates for both middle school and high school students are decreasing already.

C) FDA should implement e-cigarettes regulations because taxations on e-cigarettes are lower than those on conventional cigarettes so it can help reduce students' expenses.

D) FDA should implement e-cigarettes regulations because this new technology has both potential benefits as well as risks

CONTINUE

2

[31] For example, in 2015, the American Academy of Pediatrics strongly recommended against using e-cigarettes to quit smoking. The National Institute on Drug Abuse raises concern over the possibility that they could perpetuate nicotine addiction and thus interfere with quitting, [32]

In August 2014, the American Heart Association released a policy statement concluding that while e-cigarette aerosol is much less toxic [33] then cigarette smoke, there is insufficient evidence for clinicians to counsel smokers to use them as a primary cessation aid.

http://www.fda.gov/TobaccoProducts/Labeling/RulesRegulationsGuidance/ucm246129.htm

31

A) NO CHANGE
B) Moreover,
C) That Is,
D) However,

32

Please refer to the table on the previous page. At this point, the author wants to add an additional statement. Which one best reflects the data?

A) ,stating that e-cigarettes are effective in treating tobacco dependence.
B) ,stating that high school students depend more on e-cigarettes than on cigarette .
C) ,stating e-cigarettes are cheaper way to harm students' health.
D) ,stating that e-cigarettes dependence among middle school students reflects the general public's pattern.

33

A) NO CHANGE
B) compared to
C) in comparison with
D) than

CONTINUE

2   2

Questions 34-44 are based on the following passage.

Midnight in Paris

Midnight in Paris is a 2011 American-French romantic comedy film written and directed by Woody Allen. [34] Being set in Paris, the film [35] by following Gil Pender, a screenwriter, who is forced to confront the shortcomings of his relationship with his materialistic fiancée and their divergent goals, which become increasingly exaggerated as he travels back in time each night at midnight [36] , in which the movie explores themes of nostalgia and modernism.

The film opened to critical acclaim and has commonly been [37] cited as one of Allen's best films in recent years. In 2012, the film won both the Academy Award for Best Original Screenplay and the Golden Globe Awards for Best Screenplay; and was nominated for three other Academy Awards: Best Picture, Best Director and Best Art Direction.

34

A) NO CHANGE
B) Setting
C) Having set
D) Being set

35

A) NO CHANGE
B) followed
C) follows
D) following

36

A) NO CHANGE
B) , in which time
C) , in which midnight
D) , and in which

37

A) NO CHANGE
B) sited
C) sighted
D) sought

CONTINUE

2   2

Gil got lost in the back streets of Paris.

At midnight, a 1920s Peugeot Type 176 car draws up

beside him, and [38] the passengers urge him,

dressed in 1920s clothing, to join them.

They go to a party, where he meets a real life Ernest

Hemingway for the first time.

He encounters Zelda and Scott Fitzgerald, who take

him to meet Ernest Hemingway.

[39] He offers to show Gil's novel to Gertrude Stein,

and Gil goes to fetch his manuscript from his hotel.

However, as soon as he leaves, he finds he has

returned to 2010 and that the bar where the

1920s literati were drinking is a closed laundromat.

Gil attempts to bring Inez to the past with him the

following night, but she becomes [40] impatiently

and peevishly returns to the hotel. Just after she

leaves, the clock strikes midnight and the same car

arrives, this time with Hemingway inside.

Gil spends each of the next few nights in the past.

His late-night wanderings annoys Inez, and

[41] arouses the suspicion of her father, who hires a

private detective to follow him.

38

Which choice best connects the previous portion of

the sentence?

A) NO CHANGE

B) dressed in 1920s clothing, the passengers,
   urge him to join them.

C) the passengers urge him to join them,
   dressed in 1920s clothing.

D) the passengers, dressed in 1920s clothing,
   urge him to join them.

39

A) NO CHANGE

B) They

C) Gil

D) Hemingway

40

A) NO CHANGE

B) peevishly, impatient

C) impatient and peevishly

D) impatiently peevish

41

A) NO CHANGE

B) raises

C) rises

D) arisens

CONTINUE

2

2

Gil spends more and more time with [42] Adriana who leaves Picasso for a brief dalliance with Hemingway.

While Inez shops for expensive furniture, Gil meets [43] Gabrielle, an antique dealer, and fellow admirer of the Lost Generation. Gil returns to 2010 and confronts Inez. Gil breaks up with her and decides to move to Paris. Amid Inez's pique, Gil calmly leaves, [44] after which Inez's father tells her and her mother that he had Gil followed, though the detective has mysteriously disappeared.

42

A) NO CHANGE
B) Adriana, which
C) Adriana, who
D) Adriana, and

43

A) NO CHANGE
B) Gabrielle as an antique dealer
C) Gabrielle, who is an antique dealer,
D) Gabrielle is an antique dealer,

44

Which of the following alternative choices is NOT acceptable?
A) during which
B) following which
C) toward which
D) upon which

TEST 3

WRITING ABSOLUTE PATTERNS

TEST 3
WRITING AND LANGUAGE SECTION PATTERN ANALYSIS

Q1. Absolute Pattern 1: Adding, Revising, Deleting, Retaining Information	
A modern green design concept is to facilitate sustainable use of the resources – energy, water and other materials – [1] that please both employees and customers.	
	A) NO CHANGE
√	B) all through the complete life cycle of the building including its construction.
	C) allowing people to find an alternative amid increasing rental cost
	D) that dates back to late 19th century

The main clause describes the 'sustainable use of the resource.

B) best fits in terms of using sustainable resources.

A) "employee" and C) "rental cost" are not related to the sustainable resources.

D) is incorrect because the sentence states "modern"

Q2. Absolute Pattern 13: Parallel Structure		
Glass is a wonder material that combines more than a few advantages, such as **transparency, natural day-lighting, blending** of exteriors with interiors and [2] sound-proof **advantage**.		
	A) NO CHANGE	A) Redundant error "advantage"
√	B) acoustic control	B) presents the concise parallel structure
	C) sound dampening function can also be expected	C) Parallelism error: the clause with the verb can't suddenly be situated in the lists.
	D) the application of effective noise canceling system	D) Wordy: It can be reduced to (B)

Q3. Absolute Pattern 1: Adding, Revising, Deleting, Retaining Information

Glass accomplishes indoor environmental quality and energy efficiency.

√	A) **Yes, because it provides** how glass plays a noteworthy role as a building **material.**
	B) Yes, because it allows the reader to anticipate how the modern **building codes and regulations** are maintained
	C) No, because other **criteria** for green buildings should also be presented
	D) **No,** because the passage should focus on sustainable architecture and its main construction materials

B) "building codes and regulations" is unrelated word usage.
C) The passage mainly focuses on glass.   D) "No" should change to "Yes"

Q4. Absolute Pattern 13: Parallel Structure

The intent of a green building design [4] curtails the demand on non-renewable resources, **amplify** utilization efficiency of these resources when in use, and [5] **augment**ation the reuse, recycling, and consumption of renewable resources

	A) NO CHANGE	The intent of a green building design is **to curtail**, (to) **amplify**, and (to) **augment**. => The paralleling structure is the main concept in this question.
	B) curtail	1> "The subject "intent" is non-human.
	C) is being curtailed	2> That is, "The intent" itself can't curtail anything.
√	D) **is to curtail**	3> Another clue that suggests (D) should be the answer is "amplify" that uses the root verb instead of singular "curtails", which can only be understood as a list of to-infinitive clause.
		(C) please don't choose "being"

Q5. Absolute Pattern 13: Parallel Structure

The intent of a green building design to curtail the demand on non-renewable resources, amplify utilization efficiency of these resources when in use, and [5] augmentation the reuse, recycling, and consumption of renewable resources

	A) NO CHANGE	1> "to curtail", "(to) amplify", and "(to) augment" are paralleling
	B) augments	2> In a series of To-Infinitive clause, "to" can be dropped from the second list, leaving only the root verb as shown in the above sentence.
	C) augmenting	3> The original sentence is a series of 'to-infinitive clause.'
√	D) **augment**	

Q6. Absolute Pattern 10: Logical Expression

Sustainable architecture that uses glass as a main building material seeks to [6] optimize the negative environmental impact of buildings by efficiency and moderation in the use of materials and energy.

	A) NO CHANGE	"minimize the negative impact" is the only logical expression.
	B) standardize	
	C) maximize	
√	D) minimize	

Q7. Absolute Pattern 3: Colloquialism (Nonstandard Language)

Sustainable architecture uses [7] awesome approach to energy and ecological conservation in the design of the built environment.

	A) NO CHANGE	"awesome" is subjective, not academic and also unsuitable in this journal
	B) limited	is negative
	C) open	is not related and vague word usage
√	D) conscious	**conscious to energy and ecological conservation** is the best choice

Q8. Absolute Pattern 6: Confusing Words

The idea of sustainability, or ecological design, is to ensure that our actions and decisions today do not [8] inhabit the opportunities of future generations.

	A) NO CHANGE	A) "inhabit" means to live
√	B) inhibit	C) and D) are opposite perception
	C) include	
	D) allow	

Q9. Absolute Pattern 10: Logical Expression

The industrial glass standards combine [9] a great deal of techniques and technologies to achieve ultra-low energy use.

	A) NO CHANGE	"a great deal of" is (1) informal and (2) used only for the amount.
	B) a bunch of	"a bunch of" is informal language.
√	**C) a lot of**	"a lot of" can be used in both quantity and quality, and it is formal language.
	D) much	"much" is used only for the quality.

Q10. Absolute Pattern 16: Precision, Concision, Style

[10] Effective energy use over the entire life cycle of a building is the most important goal of sustainable architecture.

	A) NO CHANGE	B is most precise and concise.
√	**B) Energy efficiency**	A), C), D) are wordy.
	C) The application of effective and utilizable energy	
	D) Energy as an effective source	

Q11. Absolute Pattern 7: Conjunction Error

Numerous passive architectural strategies have been developed over time, [11] examples of those strategies include the arrangement of rooms or the sizing and orientation of windows in a building.

	A) NO CHANGE	(C) 'which' functions as a conjunction and links the preceding main clause to the following clause
	B) the strategic examples include	
√	**C) examples of which include**	(A) and (B) violate the comma splice error, combining two clauses without a conjunction.
	D) **and** some strategic examples **including**	(D) has a conjunction "and" but uses the participle "including" instead of a verb "include.", which makes having a conjunction "and" useless.

Q12. Absolute Pattern 7: Conjunction Error

This firm was founded by William H. Russell, Alexander Majors, and William B. Waddell, [12] all of them were notable in the freighting business.

	A) NO CHANGE	B) "whom" functions as a conjunction that links between the primary sentence and the following subordinating clause.
√	B) ,all of **whom** were notable	
	C) ,and they were notable	A) created an independent sentence without having a conjunction.
	D) ,all of those who were notable	C) changes the original meaning.
		D) has no verb. Even if it does, it will still make a comma splice

Q13. Absolute Pattern 17: Pronoun Error

During its 19 months of operation, [13] he reduced the time for messages to travel between the Atlantic and Pacific coasts to about 10 days.

	A) NO CHANGE	1> The previous sentence specifies three people established the company.
√	**B) they**	2> Therefore, it should be "they", not "he"
	C) this firm founders	C) and D) are unnecessarily wordy because this information was already given in the sentence right above.
	D) The Pony Express mail service delivery firm	

Q14. Absolute Pattern 10: Logical Expression

From April 3, 1860 to October 1861, it became the West's most direct [14] means of east–west communication

√	**A) NO CHANGE**	"means", meaning mode and method, is a singular noun.
	B) mean	B) and C) change the original meaning
	C) meaning	D) is the adjective and can't be used.
	D) meaningful	

Q15. Absolute Pattern 1: Adding, Revising, Deleting, Retaining Information

From April 3, 1860 to October 1861, it became the West's most direct means of east–west communication [15] <u>before the telegraph was established.</u>

	A) Yes, because the new issue "telegraph" undermines the integrity of the passage.
	B) Yes, because the new invention telegraph undermines the historical importance of the Pony Express, the main theme of the passage.
√	**C) No, because it establishes the reason for the short operation of the service.**
	D) No, because it provides no specific function for how the new state of California was wired to the rest of the United States.

1> The previous sentence indicates a relatively short period of operation "from 1860 to 1861."

2> The reason for the short operation is clarified in the following phrase.

3> Without having such information, the sentence will lose what it indented to emphasize.

A) and B) are opposite perception. It strengthens instead of "undermines"

D) focuses too much on telegraph

Q16. Absolute Pattern 19: Redundant Error

[16] <u>This concept of idea</u> of a fast mail route to the Pacific coast was prompted largely by California's newfound prominence and its rapidly growing population. Concept means Idea. Therefore, all the remaining choices violate the redundant error.

	A) NO CHANGE	"concept" and "idea" are synonyms.
	B) This conceptual idea	
	C) Such a concept of idea	
√	**D) The idea**	

Q17. Absolute Pattern 5: Comma Splice Error

After gold was discovered there in 1848, thousands of prospectors, investors and businessmen made their way to California, at that time [17] <u>the region was a new territory of the U.S.</u>

	A) NO CHANGE	1> "at that time" is not a conjunction
	B) the state of California was a new territory of the U.S.	2> The original sentence (A), (B) and (D) are all Comma Splice by
√	**C) a new territory of the U.S.**	trying to tie two clauses with "at that time."
	D) it just became the official territory of the U.S.	

Q18. Absolute Pattern 16: Precision, Concision, Style

By 1850, California entered the Union as a free [18] state. California's population had grown to 380,000.

	A) NO CHANGE	1> "a free state" and "California's population" can be reduced into "whose (meaning 'of which') population"
√	**B) state, whose**	2> By doing so, the sentence becomes concise and precise while eliminating the redundancy **"state"** and **"California"**
	C) state with	B) "with" is the preposition that can't carry a clause with the verb.
	D) state, which	D) "which" can't link another noun "population." It should be possessive pronoun like B)

Q19. Absolute Pattern 2: Cause-Effect Relations

[19] As a result of **the demand for** a faster way to get mail to and from this westernmost state **became even greater**, at the peak of the operations the company expanded employing 6,000 men, thousands of wagons and warehouses. a meatpacking plant, a bank and an insurance company.

	A) NO CHANGE	"because" is the only conjunction available to carry and connect the following clause.
	B) because of	_Additional errors_
√	**C) because**	"**became** even greater" and "the **demand for**" hints two facts:
	D) resulting	(1) "**became**: the context is the clause with the verb that requires a conjunction
		(2) "**demand for**": the clear cause clause, not effect clause.
		(A) "As a result" is used to the effect-clause, not the cause-clause.
		(B) is preposition that can't connect the clause.
		(D) is also used to express the consequence, not the cause-effect.

Q20. Absolute Pattern 23: Transitions (Supporting Detail, Contrast, and Consequence)

[20] Instead of utilizing a short route and using mounted riders rather than traditional stagecoaches, they proposed to establish a fast mail service between St. Joseph, Missouri, and Sacramento, California, with letters delivered in 10 days, a duration many said was impossible.

	A) NO CHANGE	1> 'utilizing' becomes the clue word.
√	**B) By**	2> The preposition 'By' is used to express means and method (utilizing).
	C) Consequently,	3> The positive tone in the context shows (A) is incorrect
	D) On the other hand,	A), D) are used to contradict the statement
		C) express the result.

Q21. Absolute Pattern 7: Conjunction Error

The founders of the Pony Express hoped to win an exclusive government mail contract, [21] <u>despite</u> that did not come about.

		Two clauses show the contrasting event.
	A) NO CHANGE	
	B) however,	A) 'despite' is a preposition and can't link the following clause.
√	C) but	B) 'however' requires a semicolon (; + however,)
	D) and	

Q22. Absolute Pattern 1: Adding, Revising, Deleting, Retaining Information

The employers stressed the importance of the pouch. They often said that, if it came to be, the horse and rider should perish before **the mochila** did. **The mochila** was thrown over the saddle and held in place by the weight of the rider sitting on it. Each corner had a *cantina,* or pocket. Bundles of mail were placed in these cantinas, which were padlocked for safety. [22]

√	A) **The mochila** could hold 20 pounds of mail along with the 20 pounds of material carried on the horse.
	B) Pony Express would end up bankruptcy immediately after the arrival of the telegraph.
	C) The greatest beneficiary of Pony Express was not, however, the employers, but the horse retailers.
	D) 40 pounds were considered to be lightweight for such a traveling distance.

(D) is incorrect because it should be placed after (A)

Q23. Absolute Pattern 4: Comparison

The FDA admits that some tobacco products have the potential to be [23] <u>less</u> harmful than others. But more evidence is needed. The agency is exploring this issue with respect to tobacco regulation.

√	A) NO CHANGE	1> "But more evidence is needed." implies that e-cigarette is less toxic and there-
	B) more	fore requires moderate regulations.
	C) greatly	2> That concludes B) and C) should be incorrect.
	D) little	is not used in a comparison and can't link "than others."

Q24. Absolute Pattern 21: Subject-Verb, Pronoun, Noun Agreement

The FDA believes that potential benefit as well as risks [24] <u>are</u> in this new technology.

	A) NO CHANGE	1> "as well as" is not a conjunction, so "risks" can't be the subject.
√	**B) is**	2> The subject should be "benefit" alone, the singular noun, which requires the singular verb "is." (e.g., potential benefit *as well as risks* is in this…)
	C) will be	C) The future tense, and D) The past perfect disagree with the present tense
	D) had been	used in this passage.

Q25. Absolute Pattern 13: Parallel Structure

But if any product **prompts** young people to become addicted to nicotine, **reduces** a person's interest in quitting cigarettes, and/or [25] <u>leading</u> to long-term usage with other tobacco products, the public health impact could be negative.

	A) NO CHANGE	-But if any product **prompts** young people to become addicted to nicotine,
	B) lead	-But if any product **reduces** a person's interest in quitting cigarettes,
		-And/or if any product **leads** to long-term usage with other tobacco products.
√	**C) leads**	As shown above, paralleling structure requires (C) the singular verb.
	D) to be led	

Q26. Absolute Pattern 10: Logical Expression

The FDA encourages manufacturers to explore product innovations that would [26] <u>add</u> potential benefits and minimize risks.

	A) NO CHANGE	"maximize …. and…. minimize" is the correct parallel structure.
√	**B) maximize**	A) "add" and C) "show" are too weak implication that misinterpret the author's intention.
	C) show	
	D) minimize	

Q27. Absolute Pattern 6: Confusing Words

The final rule allows the FDA to further evaluate and (27) <u>excess</u> the impact of these products on the health of both users and non-users. And it lets the FDA (28)<u>regulate</u> the products based on the most current scientific knowledge.

	A) NO CHANGE	A) excess means surplus
	B) access	B) access means to approach
	C) accede	C) accede means to agree
√	**D) assess**	**D) assess means to judge or evaluate**

Q28. Absolute Pattern 21: Subject-Verb, Pronoun, Noun Agreement

And it **lets** the FDA (28) <u>regulate</u> the products based on the most current scientific knowledge.

√	**A) NO CHANGE**	The causative verbs "let, help, make, get" use the additional base verb as a complement.
	B) regulates	B) "regulates" is a singular verb, not the base verb
	C) to regulate	C) "to regulate" is to-infinitive.
	D) regulating	D) "regulating" is a participle.

Q29. Absolute Pattern 16: Precision, Concision, Style

The FDA considered all manufacturers, including small businesses, when finalizing [29] <u>this rule, and that's the **reason why**</u> the agency is allowing additional time for small-scale tobacco product manufacturers to comply with certain <u>provisions</u>

	A) NO CHANGE	1> "reason" and "why" are synonyms, which can't be used simultaneously.
	B) this rule. That's the <u>reason why</u>	2> The correct form of expression is "reason (that)~"
√	**C) this rule, so**	3> (D) is also comma splice errors because it has no proper conjunction to tie the following clause.
	D) this rule, that's why	

Q30. Absolute Pattern 9: Informational Graphs

	A) FDA should implement e-cigarettes regulations, especially to middle school students because they are the highest e-cigarettes consumers.
	B) FDA should delay e-cigarettes regulations because cigarette smoking rates for both middle school and high school students are decreasing already.
	C) FDA should implement e-cigarettes regulations because taxations on e-cigarettes are lower than those on conventional cigarettes so it can help their savings.
	D) FDA should implement e-cigarettes regulations because this new technology has both potential benefits as well as risks

1> The author wants the conclusion that reflects the passage.

2> The last sentence states that "The FDA considered...to comply with certain provisions."

3> For this reason, we know that the regulations are going to be implemented, so (B) can't be the answer.

A) The highest increase is among the high School students, not middle school.

B) The cigarette smoking decrease is not the voluntary cause, but due to the increase of e-cigarette consumption.

C) Unrelated word usage.

Q31. Absolute Pattern 23: Transitions (Supporting Detail, Contrast, and Consequence)

In 2016, the FDA stated its position that e-cigarettes are " less likely hazardous for an individual user than continued smoking of traditional cigarettes," although that the net population effect is unknown. [31] For example, in 2015, the American Academy of Pediatrics strongly recommended against using e-cigarettes to quit smoking

	A) NO CHANGE	Two sentences contradict to each other.
	B) Moreover,	A), B), C) are used to emphasize the previous sentence.
	C) That Is,	
√	**D) However,**	

Q32. Absolute Pattern 9: Informational Graphs

	A) ,stating that e-cigarettes are effective in treating tobacco dependence.
√	**B) ,stating that high school students depend more on e-cigarettes than on cigarette .**
	C) ,stating e-cigarettes are cheaper way to harm students' health.
	D) ,stating that e-cigarettes dependence among middle school students reflects the general public's PATTERN.

B) e-cigarettes dependence among high school students is highest: 16.7% compared to 15.8% in cigarette smoking.

A) is opposite perception

C) and D) are not stated in the passage.

Q33. Absolute Pattern 4: Comparison

In August 2014,the American Heart Association released a policy statement concluding that while e-cigarette aerosol is much less toxic [33] <u>then</u> cigarette smoke, there is insufficient evidence for clinicians to counsel smokers to use them as a primary cessation aid.

A) NO CHANGE	The correct comparative idiom is "Less ~ than."
B) compared to	B), C) There's no such an idiom as 'less ~ compared to' or less ~ in comparison with"
C) in comparison with	
√ **D) than**	

Q34. Absolute Pattern 6: Confusing Words

[34] <u>Being set</u> in Paris, the film <u>follows</u> Gil Pender, a screenwriter, who is forced to confront the shortcomings of his relationship with his materialistic fiancée

A) NO CHANGE	(D) (The film which is) Set in Paris.
B) Setting	"Set in Paris" is the adjective phrase modifying the subject "the film."
C) Having set	(A) "Being" is unnecessary.
	(B) the film can't actively perform "setting" like a human can.
√ **D) Set**	(C) "Having set" means After it has been set.

Q35. Absolute Pattern 21: Subject-Verb, Pronoun, Noun Agreement

Set in Paris, the film [35] by following Gil Pender, a screenwriter, who **is forced** to confront the shortcomings of his relationship with his materialistic fiancée

	A) NO CHANGE	1> The sentence requires the proper verb.
	B) followed	2> The following dependent clause (who **is forced**) indicates the verb should be the present tense.
√	**C) follows**	
	D) following	

Q35. Absolute Pattern 7: Conjunction Error

Set in Paris, the film follows Gil Pender, a screenwriter, who is forced to confront the shortcomings of his relationship with his materialistic fiancée and their divergent goals, which become increasingly exaggerated as he travels back in time each night at midnight [36] , in which the movie explores themes nostalgia and modernism.

√	**A) NO CHANGE**	1> "in which" refers to the moment Gill Pender travels back in times each night at midnight.
	B) , in which time	2> Therefore, it is not necessary to write "time" once more as in (B) or "midnight" as in (C).
	C) , in which midnight	
	D) , and in which	(D) "and" is not needed because "which" is already doing the job.

Q37. Absolute Pattern 6: Confusing Words

The film opened to critical acclaim and has commonly been [37] cited as one of Allen's best films in recent years.

√	**A) NO CHANGE**	Cite means to quote or comment.
	B) sited	B) site means an area
	C) sighted	C) sighted means to be seen
	D) sought	D) sought is the past tense of seek

Q38. Absolute Pattern 12: Modifier (Placement) Error

At midnight, a 1920s Peugeot Type 176 car draws up beside him, and [38] the passengers urge him, dressed in 1920s clothing, to join them.

	A) NO CHANGE
	B) dressed in 1920s clothing, the passengers, urge him to join them.
	C) the passengers urge him to join them, dressed in 1920s clothing.
√	**D) the passengers, dressed in 1920s clothing, urge him to join them.**

D) 1> "the passengers" must have been wearing "1920s clothing."
  2> Therefore, "dressed in 1920s clothing" should be placed next to "the passengers"

(A) is incorrect because "dressed in 1920s clothing" modifies "him," who travels back in time.

(B) also places the modifier besides "him" and separates the subject from the verb "urge" by a comma.

(C) "dressed in 1920s clothing" is the adjective phrase modifying the subject, not the object "them"

Q39. Absolute Pattern 17: Pronoun Error

He encounters Zelda and **Scott Fitzgerald**, who take him to meet **Ernest Hemingway**.
[39] He offers to show Gil's novel to Gertrude Stein,

	A) NO CHANGE	1> There are five people in one sentence, among whom Scott Fitzerald, Ernest Hemingway, and Gil are male.
	B) They	2> It is impossible to identify who "He" is then.
	C) Gil	3> Because the verb "offers" is singular, (B) can't be the answer.
√	**D) Hemingway**	4> (A) "He" and (C) Gil refer to Gil himself, creating an impossible situation. 5> Therefore, it should be Hemingway.

Q40. Absolute Pattern 10: Logical Expression

Gil attempts to bring Inez to the past with him the following night, but she becomes [40] impatiently and peevishly returns to the hotel.

	A) NO CHANGE	C) "(becomes) impatient and peevishly (returns)" is the correct formation.
	B) peevishly impatient	A) "impatiently' is the adverb and can't be the complement of "become." (becomes) impatiently.
√	**C) impatient and peevishly**	B) "peevishly impatient" and D) "impatiently peevish" can't link the verb "returns" because they are adjectives.
	D) impatiently peevish	

Q41. Absolute Pattern 6: Confusing Words

His late-night wanderings annoys Inez, and [41] <u>arouses </u>the suspicion of her father,

√	**A) NO CHANGE**	(A) "arouses suspicion" is correct word, meaning evoke or awaken a feeling or emotion
	B) raises	(B) "raise" means to increase the amount
	C) rises	(C) "rises" means to move from a lower position to a higher one
	D) arisens	(D) "arisen" is a participle and can't put 's' like a verb.

Q42. Absolute Pattern 22: Nonrestrictive Modifier (Inessential Information)

Gil spends more and more time with [42] <u>Adriana who </u>leaves Picasso for a brief dalliance with Hemingway.

	A) NO CHANGE	1>"who leaves Picasso for a brief dalliance with Hemingway. " is used as the non-restrictive (inessential) modifier.
	B) Adriana, which	2> If the clause is not essential to understand the primary meaning of the sentence, the modifier is considered as a nonrestrictive modifier and should be separated by a comma.
√	**C) Adriana, who**	3> Therefore, (A) is incorrect because it uses no comma.
	D) Adriana, and	B) "which" is a connector for things, not a human.
		D) changes the meaning as it becomes ."..and Gil leaves Picasso for a brief dalliance with Hemingway." *dalliance = flirtation. Gil (male) is engaged with Adriana (female), not with Hemingway (male)

Q43. Absolute Pattern 22: Nonrestrictive Modifier (Inessential Information)

While Inez shops for expensive furniture, Gil meets [43] Gabrielle, an antique dealer, and fellow admirer of the Lost Generation

√ **A) NO CHANGE**	1> "an antique dealer" is inessential information.
B) Gabrielle as an antique dealer	2> Therefore, It should be offset by a pair of commas.
C) Gabrielle, who is an antique dealer,	(B) "as" changes the original meaning. Gil didn't meet Garbrielle because her job is an antiques dealer.
D) Gabrielle is an antique dealer,	(C) is wordy. (D) is a sentence.

Q44. Absolute Pattern 15: Prepositional Idiom

Amid Inez's pique, Gil calmly leaves, [44] after which Inez's father tells her and her mother that he had Gil followed,

A) during which	The Preposition "toward" is used for a physical direction.
B) following which	A) Gil calmly leaves during which (during this time) Inez's father tells...
√ **C) toward which**	B) Gil calmly leaves, following which (following Gill's leaving) Inez's...
D) upon which	D) Gil calmly leaves, upon which (upon Gill's leaving) Inez's father tells... As shown above, all the other choices are correct.

SAT

Writing and Language

Test 4

ALL THE LOGIC AND RULES

BEHIND THE EVERY SINGLE

SAT QUESTION

Writing and Language Test 4
35 MINUTES, 44 QUEST IONS

Each passage below is accompanied by a number of questions. For some questions, you will consider how the passage might be revised to improve the expression of ideas. For other questions, you will consider how the passage might be edited to correct errors in sentence structure, usage, or punctuation. A passage or a question may be accompanied by one or more graphics (such as a table or graph) that you will consider as you make revising and editing decisions.

Questions 1-11 are based on the following passage.

Greek Yogurt

Strained yogurt called *kamats matzoon* is traditionally produced by long-term preservation by draining matzoon in cloth sacks. Afterwards it [1] stores in leather sacks or clay pots for a month or more depending on the degree of salting. Strained yogurt (often marketed as "Greek yogurt") has become popular in the United States and Canada, where it is often used as a [2] lower calorie substitute for sour cream.

In 2015, food market research firm Packaged Facts reported that Greek yogurt has a 50 percent share of the yogurt market in the United States. [3] The milk may be concentrated by ultrafiltration to remove a portion of the water before addition of yogurt cultures.

1

A) NO CHANGE
B) will be stored
C) had been stored
D) is stored

2

A) NO CHANGE
B) lower-calorie-substitute
C) lower-calorie substitute
D) substitute of lower calorie

3

Which of the following choices provides the best introduction to this paragraph?

A) NO CHANGE
B) The characteristic thick texture and high protein content are achieved through either or both of two processing steps.
C) Greek yogurt, however, has many drawbacks to mass production
D) Celebrity chef Graham Kerr became an early adopter of strained yogurt as an ingredient, frequently featuring it on his eponymous 1990 cooking show.

CONTINUE ➡

2   2

[4] <u>After culturing,</u> the yogurt may be centrifuged or membrane-filtered to remove whey, in a process analogous to the traditional straining step. Generally, brands [5] <u>are typically described</u> as "strained" yogurt,—[6] <u>including Activia Greek, Chobani, Dannon Light & Fit Greek, Dannon Oikos, FAGE, Stonyfield Organic Oikos, Trader Joe's, and Yoplait.</u>

Other brands of Greek-style yogurt [7] <u>, including</u> Yoplait and some store brands, are made by adding milk protein concentrate and thickeners to standard yogurt to boost the [8] <u>protein's content</u> and modify the texture.

4

A) NO CHANGE
B) After it is done with culturing,
C) Once the yogurt is cultured,
D) Once the culturing process is achieved,

5

A) NO CHANGE
B) are described typically
C) are normally described in the more typical sense
D) are described

6

The writer is thinking of removing the underlined portion of the sentence. If the writer were to delete it, the passage would most likely lose:
A) the relevant information for the second process
B) the specific brand names selling strained yogurt
C) the highly guarded trade details
D) the popularity of Greek Yogurt

7

A) NO CHANGE
B) including
C) : including
D) ,including such as

8

A) NO CHANGE
B) protein-content
C) protein content
D) content of protein

CONTINUE ➡

2   2

With ever increasing demand,

[9] a system that utilizes full automation

and production has become the priority to many

companies.

   The liquid [10] resulting from straining yogurt

is called "acid whey" and is composed of water,

yogurt cultures, protein, a slight amount

of lactose, and lactic acid. It is difficult to dispose

of.

Farmers have used the whey to mix with animal

feed and fertilizer. Using anaerobic digesters,

[11] it can be a source of methane that can be

used to produce electricity.

9

A) NO CHANGE

B) utilizing a fully automated production system
       has become the priority to many companies

.C) a production system that utilizes a full automation
       has become the priority of many companies

.D) many companies are utilizing a fully automated
       production system.

10

A) NO CHANGE

B) results

C) resulted by

D) results in

11

A) NO CHANGE

B) they

C) animal feed and fertilizer

D) farmers

CONTINUE ➡

2   2

Questions 12-22 are based on the following passage.

Aurora

[12] An Aurora is sometimes referred to as a polar light, is a natural light display in the sky, predominantly seen in the high latitude (Arctic and Antarctic) regions. Auroras are produced when the magnetosphere is sufficiently disturbed by the solar wind that the trajectory of charged particles in both solar wind and magnetosphere plasma, mainly in the form of electrons and protons, [13] are precipitated them into the upper atmosphere (thermosphere/exosphere), [14] when their energy is lost. The resulting ionization and excitation of atmospheric constituents emits light of varying colour and complexity. The form of the Aurora, [15] that occurs within bands around both polar regions, is also dependent on the amount of acceleration imparted to the precipitating particles. Precipitating protons generally produce optical emissions as incident hydrogen atoms after gaining electrons from the atmosphere.

[16] Proton Auroras are nature's miracle.
The Aurora frequently appears either as a diffuse glow or as "curtains" that extend approximately in

12

A) NO CHANGE
B) An Aurora,
C) The term Aurora is
D) It is Aurora

13

A) NO CHANGE
B) precipitates
C) is precipitated
D) precipitate

14

A) NO CHANGE
B) where there energy is being lost
C) when the energy is lost.
D) where their energy is lost

15

A) NO CHANGE
B) occurring
C) occurred
D) occurs

16

Which one best fit to the eyewitness accounts of Aurora phenomenon?
A) NO CHANGE
B) Proton Auroras are usually observed at lower latitudes.
C) Proton Auroras usually take place in March
D) Proton Auroras are hard to observe

CONTINUE ➡

2   2

the east-west direction.

At some times, they form "quiet arcs"

[17] , at others ("active Aurora"), the panoramic

view evolves and changes constantly.

[18] Each one consists of many parallel rays,

each lined up with the local direction of the

magnetic field, consistent with Auroras being shaped

by Earth's magnetic field. In-situ particle

measurements confirm that Auroral electrons are

guided by the geomagnetic field, and spiral around

them while moving toward Earth.

The similarity of an Auroral display to curtains is

often enhanced by folds within the arcs. Arcs can

fragment or 'break-up' into separate, at times rapidly

changing, often rayed features that may fill the whole

sky. These are the [19] 'discrete' Auroras, which are

at times bright enough to read a newspaper by at

night. and can display rapid sub-second variations in

intensity. The 'diffuse' Aurora, on the other hand, is

a relatively featureless glow sometimes close to the

limit of visibility. It can be distinguished from

moonlit clouds by the fact that stars can be seen

undiminished through the glow.

17

A) NO CHANGE

B) :at others

C) ;at others

D) with at others

18

Which item could be used as the topic sentence of
this paragraph to establish the main idea?

A) The existing sentence should be the topic sentence

B) You'd probably end up unable to see Aurora

C) If your main purpose is to see Aurora, read this
    article before you book your flight

D) The most distinctive and brightest are the
    curtain-like Auroral arcs.

19

A) NO CHANGE

B) discreet

C) descent

D) deceased

CONTINUE ➤

2

Diffuse Auroras are often composed of patches whose brightness exhibits regular or near-regular pulsations. [20]

A typical Auroral display consist of these forms appears in the above order throughout the night. [21]

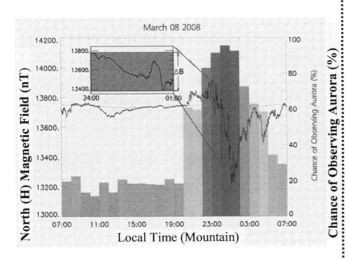

2

Which item would provide the evidence to support the characteristics of the diffuse Auroras?
A) By their nature, the characteristics of diffuse Auroras are elusive to define
B) Diffuse Auroras are often confusing
C) The pulsation period can be typically many seconds, so is not always obvious.
D) The pulsation period provides the most stunning events to the observers

21

The author wants to delete the sentence. If the sentence were deleted, the essay would mainly lose the description concerning
A) the regions diffuse Aurora appear
B) the reason for the reduced luminosity.
C) the sequence and duration of Auroral appearance
D) the important characteristics of Aurora phenomenon

22

All of the following choices accurately support the graph EXCEPT?
A) The magnetic field strength is highest when the chance of observing Aurora is highest
B) The magnetic field strength is lowest when the chance of observing Aurora is highest
C) The chance of observing Aurora is highest after midnight
D) The chance of observing Aurora is lowest in the morning

CONTINUE

2

2

Questions 23-33 are based on the following passage.

My First Solo Flight

Do you have your own dream job? Something that you are willing to spend your lifetime for the future? I dreamt of becoming an architect at first [23] but I realized that it was not for me. One year [24] had passed since I came to Canada, but I still didn't know what I wanted to do in the future. My father and I [25] had a conversation discussing about my future plans. Then he suggested that I take flying lessons to see if I would be interested in flying, so I started learning how to fly at Boundary Bay airport.

This is a story about [26] me, learning how to fly to achieve my goal of becoming an airline pilot.

[27] <1>On September 5th, I went to flying school to practice flying. I have been flying for about a half a year and I just started learning how to land. <2>I needed to do lots of circuits, where I have to circle around the airport in order of crosswind, downwind, base, and final to land the plane smoothly.

<3>I practiced with my instructor every time I came in to fly. <4>My landing skills were showing little progress, so I wasn't sure if I could land the plane by myself.

23

A) NO CHANGE

B) but realized

C) however, I realized

D) but realizing

24

A) NO CHANGE

B) has passed since

C) has passed after

D) was passed after

25

A) NO CHANGE

B) had a conversation about

C) had a consultation about

D) discussed

26

A) NO CHANGE

B) my learning how to fly

C) me, learning and flying

D) me learning how to fly

27

Which of the following sentences in this paragraph is LEAST relevant to the main focus of the essay and therefore should be deleted?

A) Sentence <1>

B) Sentence <2>

C) Sentence <3>

D) Sentence <4>

CONTINUE →

2

2

On September 19th, I went to the flying school to do some circuits. I went outside and checked the plane if there were any problems with it. The plane was fine, so I went out flying with my instructor.

I performed some good smooth landings while we were doing circuits. Suddenly I heard my instructor calling the tower, saying, "I'll send my student out alone." I couldn't believe what I was hearing. I even asked him to repeat what he just said. [28]

My instructor told me exactly what to do after he was gone. I listened very carefully to his instructions. Now, he was gone. My only life insurance was gone. I was all alone in the plane. It felt like I was sitting on a ticking bomb, just waiting to go off if I made a mistake up in the sky.

After he left, I simulated what he [29] told me by saying it out loud to myself. When I was ready, I called the tower and said, "Bay ground, this is Cessna 172 GWZB (Golf Whiskey Zulu Bravo) request for circuit with information Golf." The tower called back and told me to go to the runway. I took a deep breath and started driving the plane to the runway. I never realized until that day how long the runway was.

[30] I was thrilled, excited, nervous, and scared all at the same time.

28

At this point, the author is considering adding the following sentence:

"After hearing the words one more time, I became very nervous because I was going for my first solo flight all by myself. "

Should the author make this addition?

A) Yes, because the essay focuses on his unsettled emotional state

B) Yes, because the essay forebodes the author as the rising national figure

C) No, because the essay focuses on the flight skills, not on the author's personal emotion.

D) No, because it deviates the paragraph's focus on flying practice.

29

A) NO CHANGE

B) had told

C) tells

D) used to tell

30

Which of the following alternatives would NOT be appropriate?

A) I was filled with joy.

B) I was free like a bird.

C) I faced the most complex flying skills

D) I heard the normal apprenticeship requires at least 200 hours of solo flight

CONTINUE ➡

2

2

[31] <u>So nervous</u> that I forgot to switch my radio frequency. I had to switch the frequency to talk to the guy who is responsible for the planes up in the sky and the runway. "Holding short." "Holding short." I replied.

I switched my radio frequency, and tried again. " WZB ready for 25." This time, they gave me clearance for take-off.

I drove on to the runway [32] <u>and taking off</u> with full-power.

When I was up in the sky, I felt a little excited because I was up in the air, alone in the plane, and I was in control of every bit of the plane.

Accidents by Phase of Flight among Apprentice Pilots

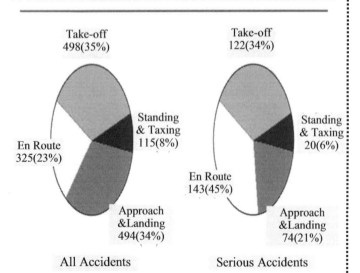

All Accidents   **Serious Accidents**

31

A) NO CHANGE
B) My emotion was very sensitive
C) I was nervous and anxious at the same time
D) Very nervous have I been

32

A) NO CHANGE
B) , taking off.
C) taking off.
D) ,and I took off.

33

Please refer to the information in the pie chart for the following question.

A) Standing & taxing can considerably reduce all accidents
B) En Route can reduce almost half of the serious accidents
C) Approach & landing in all accidents is smaller than that in serious accidents
D) Take-off in serious accidents is insignificantly compared to that in all accidents.

CONTINUE

2

2

Question 34-44 are based on the following passage.

Eastern Philosophy

Some Western thinkers claim that philosophy as such is only characteristic of Western cultures. Martin Heidegger is even reported [34] saying that only Greek and German languages are suitable for philosophizing.

It is still commonplace in Western universities to teach only Western philosophy [35] but ignore Asian philosophy altogether, or consider only newer Western-influenced Asian thought properly "philosophy."

Carine Defoort, herself a specialist in Chinese thought, has offered support for such a "family" view of philosophy, while Rein Raud has presented an argument against it and [36] will offer a more flexible definition of philosophy that would include both Western and Asian thought on equal terms.

In response, OuYang Min argues that philosophy properly is a Western cultural practice and essentially different from *zhexue*, which is what the Chinese have, even though *zhexue* (originally *tetsugaku*) is actually [37] a neologism of newly invented words coined in 1873 by Nishi Amane for describing Western philosophy as opposed to traditional Asian thought.

34

A) NO CHANGE
B) to have said
C) to be said
D) to say

35

A) NO CHANGE
B) but ignores
C) and ignore
D) with ignorance of

36

A) NO CHANGE
B) offered
C) offer
D) had offered

37

A) NO CHANGE
B) the neologism or the newly invented words made
C) the neologism made
D) the neologism of the created words coined

CONTINUE

2   2

Supreme God and the demigods

Some Eastern philosophies have formulated questions on the nature of God and its relationship to the universe based on Monotheistic framework within which it emerged. This has created a dichotomy among some Western philosophies, between secular philosophies and religious philosophies developed within the context of a particular monotheistic [38] religion dogma—especially some creeds of Protestant Christianity, regarding the nature of God and the universe.

Eastern religions have been as concerned by questions relating to the nature of a single God [39] than to the universe's sole creator and ruler. The distinction between the religion and the secular tends to be much less noticeable in Eastern philosophy, and the same philosophical school often contains both religious [40] along with philosophical elements. Thus, some people accept the so-called metaphysical tenets of Buddhism without going to a temple and worshipping. Some have worshipped the Taoist deities [41] divinely and religiously without bothering to delve into the theological underpinnings, while others have embraced the Taoist religion while ignoring the mythological aspects.

38
A) NO CHANGE
B) dogma of religion;
C) religion's dogma:
D) religious dogma,

39
A) NO CHANGE
B) of
C) with
D) as

40
A) NO CHANGE
B) together with
C) as well as
D) and

41
A) NO CHANGE
B) religion
C) religiously
D) with religious mindsets

CONTINUE

2   **2**

Such an arrangement stands in marked contrast to [42] that of some recent philosophy in the West, which has traditionally enforced either a completely unified philosophic/religious belief system, or a sharp and total repudiation of some forms of religion by philosophy.

A common thread that often differentiates Eastern philosophy from Western is the relationship [43] that commonly relates the gods with the universe.

Some Western schools of thought were animistic or pantheistic, such as the classical Greek tradition, while later religious beliefs, [44] influencing the monotheism of the Abrahamic religions, portrayed divinity as more transcendent.

42

A) NO CHANGE

B) those of

C) an arrangement of

D) delete it

43

A) NO CHANGE

B) between the gods and the universe

C) between the gods with the universe

D) between the gods and the universe that find correlations within the common thread

44

A) NO CHANGE

B) had influenced

C) have influenced

D) influenced by

TEST 4

WRITING ABSOLUTE PATTERNS

TEST 4

WRITING AND LANGUAGE SECTION PATTERN ANALYSIS

Q1. Absolute Pattern 24: Verb Tense / Voice Error		
Afterwards it [1] <u>stores</u> in leather sacks or clay pots for a month or more depending on the degree of salting.		
	A) NO CHANGE	Yogurt can't store by itself. It should be a passive voice like (D).
	B) will be stored	The demonstrative context should use the present tense, not the future.
	C) had been stored	It is the past perfect tense.
√	**D) is stored**	

Q2. Absolute Pattern 18: Punctuation Error		
Strained yogurt (often marketed as "Greek Yogurt") has become popular in the United States and Canada, where it is often used with a [2] <u>lower calorie substitute</u> for sour cream.		
	A) NO CHANGE	1> The hyphen is used to make a compound adjective "lower-calorie" that modifies the following noun "substitute."
	B) lower-calorie-substitute	
√	**C) lower-calorie substitute**	2> The hyphen must connect two words that act as one adjective.
	D) substitute of lower calorie	A) needs the hyphen between "lower" and "calorie"
		B) The hyphen should not be used before the noun "substitute."
		D) The possessive preposition "of" and hyphen aren't the same thing.

Q3. Absolute Pattern 1: Adding, Revising, Deleting, Retaining Information

[3] In 2015, food market research firm Packaged Facts reported that Greek yogurt has a 50 percent share of the yogurt market in the United States. **The milk may be concentrated by ultrafiltration** to remove a portion of the water before addition of yogurt cultures.

	A) NO CHANGE
√	B) The characteristic thick texture and high protein content are achieved through either or both of **two processing steps**.
	C) Greek yogurt, however, has many drawbacks to mass production
	D) Celebrity chef Graham Kerr became an early adopter of strained yogurt as an ingredient, frequently featuring it on his eponymous 1990 cooking show.

1> The following sentences describe the Greek yogurt production process.

2> (B) contains "two processing steps" that connects well with the following sentences.

3> (A) is about market share

4> (C) is negative, which is unfit for the context that introduces the advantages of yogurt.

5> (D) is too specific that fits for the example sentence in other body paragraph.

Q4. Absolute Pattern 16: Precision, Concision, Style

[4] After culturing, the yogurt may be centrifuged or membrane-filtered to remove whey, in a process analogous to the traditional straining step.

√ **A) NO CHANGE**	(A) "After culturing" is the modifier for the following main subject "the yogurt" and is precise and concise.
B) After **it is done with** culturing,	(B) "it is done with" is wordy and unnecessary. (C) "the yogurt" repeats the following main subject.
C) Once **the yogurt** is cultured,	(D) is unnecessarily wordy without adding any information. Also, (C) and (D) are comma splice errors: "Once" is an adverb, not a conjunction that connects the following
D) Once the culturing process is achieved,	clause.

Q5. Absolute Pattern 19: Redundant Error

Generally, brands [5] <u>are typically described</u> as "strained" yogurt,

	A) NO CHANGE	(A), (B): "Generally" and "typically" are synonyms.
	B) are described **typically**	(C) "normally", "Generally" and "typically" are all synonyms.
	C) are **normally** described in the more **typical sense**	
√	**D) are described**	

Q6. Absolute Pattern 1: Adding, Revising, Deleting, Retaining Information

Generally, brands are described as "strained" yogurt,—[6] <u>including Activia Greek, Chobani, Dannon Light & Fit Greek, Dannon Oikos, FAGE, Stonyfield Organic Oikos, Trader Joe's, and Yoplait.</u>

	A) the relevant information for the second process	The underlined portion is just the lists of brand names, selling strained yogurt, not (A) "the second process", not (C) high guarded trade details, not (D) the popularity of Greek Yogurt.
√	**B) the specific brand names selling strained yogurt**	
	C) the highly guarded trade details	
	D) the popularity of Greek Yogurt	

Q7. Absolute Pattern 18: Punctuation Error

Other brands of Greek-style yogurt [7] <u>, including</u> Yoplait and some store brands, are made by adding milk protein concentrate and thickeners to standard yogurt to boost the protein content

√	**A) NO CHANGE**	
	B) including	The modifier must be offset by a pair of commas.
	C) : including	The colon contains the meaning "including" and can't be used simultaneously.
	D) ,including such as	"including" and "such as" are synonyms and can't be used simultaneously.

Q8. Absolute Pattern 14: Possessive Determiners and Possessive Noun Error

Yoplait and some store brands are made by adding milk protein concentrate and thickeners to standard yogurt to boost the [8] protein's content and modify the texture.

	A) NO CHANGE	"Protein content" is the compound noun that conveys the single meaning. The other choices try to link two words by using the punctuations that change the original meaning.
	B) protein-content	
√	**C) protein content**	
	D) content of protein	

Q9. Absolute Pattern 16: Precision, Concision, Style

With ever increasing demand, [9] a system that utilizes full automation and production has become the priority to many companies.

	A) NO CHANGE
	B) utilizing a fully automated production system has become the priority to many companies
	C) a production system that utilizes a full automation has become the priority of many companies
√	**D) many companies are utilizing a fully automated production system.**

1> (D) "a fully automated production system" vs. (A) a system that utilizes full automation and production

vs. (C) a production system that utilizes a full automation

As shown above, (A) and (C) are unnecessarily wordy compared to (D).

2> "With ever increasing demand," is the modifier that seeks out the subject. Putting "many companies" as the subject most directly and precisely expresses the modifier.

3> Compared to (D), all the remaining choices are indirect, passive, and wordy.

Q10. Absolute Pattern 12: Modifier (Placement) Error

The liquid [10] resulting from straining yogurt is called "acid whey" and is composed of water

	A) NO CHANGE	1> "straining yogurt" makes "the liquid"
	B) results	2> Therefore, it should be "resulted by straining yogurt as in (C), not "resulting from" as in (A).
√	**C) resulted by**	(B) and (D) are verbs
	D) results in	

Q11. Absolute Pattern 17: Pronoun Error

The liquid resulted by straining yogurt is called "acid whey" and is composed of water, yogurt cultures, protein, a slight amount of lactose, and lactic acid. **It (acid whey)** is difficult to dispose of. Farmers have used the whey to mix with animal feed and fertilizer. Using anaerobic digesters, [11] it can be a source of methane that can be used to produce electricity.

√	**A) NO CHANGE**	(A) "It" refers to acid whey.
	B) they can be	(B) is plural. Whey is singular
	C) animal feed and fertilizer can be	(C) "animal feed and fertilizer" are the ingredients mixed with whey.
	D) farmers can be	D) farmers can't be a source of methane

Q12. Absolute Pattern 21: Subject-Verb, Pronoun, Noun Agreement

[12] An Aurora is *sometimes referred to as a polar light, is a natural light* display in the sky, predominantly seen in the high latitude (Arctic and Antarctic) regions.

	A) NO CHANGE	1> The main verb "**is** a natural light.." is easily identifiable.
√	**B) An Aurora,**	2> Given the verb, the best way to find the answer is to get one without a verb because another verb will cause a comma splice error automatically.
	C) The term Aurora is	3> Therefore, the answer should be (B)
	D) It is Aurora	4> With "An Aurora" as the subject, "sometimes referred to as a polar light," should be considered as the modifier interjected in the middle of the sentence offset by a pair of commas.

Q13. Absolute Pattern 21: Subject-Verb, Pronoun, Noun Agreement

Auroras are produced when the magnetosphere is sufficiently disturbed by the solar wind **that the trajectory** of charged particles in both solar wind and magnetosphere plasma, *mainly in the form of electrons and protons,* [13] are precipitated them into the upper atmosphere

	A) NO CHANGE	When you confront a confusing compound complex sentence:
√	**B) precipitates**	Rule 1: Find a subject and a verb Rule 2: Eliminate any inessential information
	C) is precipitated	
	D) precipitate	1> When the question sentence is such a long compound complex sentence that causes confusion, the actual question will highly likely to start from that-clause. 2> Underpinning this concept, the first step is to find the subject and the verb, regardless of the type of question. 3> Identifying the subject and the verb is crucial in all question types because it solidifies the basic meaning instead of guessing the meaning. 4> In the meantime, any phrase or clause offset by a pair of commas amid the sentence can be ignored for a while. (e.g., *"mainly in the...and protons"*) 5> This removal process will significantly reduce both the complexity of the sentence and your mental energy consumption. 6> Having identified the subject after "that-clause" is "the trajectory," 7> choices (A) and (D) become apparently incorrect because their verbs are plural. 8> (C) is incorrect because "is precipitated" can't link the object "them"

Q14. Absolute Pattern 23: Transitions (Supporting Detail, Contrast, and Consequence)

...mainly in the form of electrons and protons, precipitates them into the upper atmosphere (thermosphere/exosphere), [14] when their energy is lost.

	A) NO CHANGE	(A), (C)
	B) where there energy is being lost	1> "When" connects the time phrase 2>The precedents "into the upper atmosphere" is definitely not the time phrase, but the location (the place adverbial).
	C) when the energy is lost.	3> Therefore, (A) and (C) are incorrect
√	**D) where their energy is lost**	(B) 1> "there" is the indicative pronoun pointing out somewhere. 2> It should be the possessive "their" to link the "energy" 3> Please do not choose "being"

Q15. Absolute Pattern 12: Modifier (Placement) Error

The form of the Aurora, [15] that occurs within bands around both polar regions, is also dependent on the amount of acceleration imparted to the precipitating particles.

	A) NO CHANGE	1> **is** also dependent on" explicitly shows the main verb is already presented and warns us not to use another verb.
√	**B) occurring**	2> Therefore, only (B) should be the correct one.
	C) occurred	3> All remaining options have the verbs.
	D) occurs	(A) "that" can't be placed after the comma because "that" is always used as a restrictive modifier that should be free from a comma.

Q16. Absolute Pattern 1: Adding, Revising, Deleting, Retaining Information

[15] Proton Auroras are nature's miracle.
The Aurora frequently appears either as a diffuse glow or as "curtains" that extend approximately in the east-west direction. At some times, they form [16] "quiet arcs"; at others ("active Aurora"), **the panoramic view evolves and changes constantly**.

	A) NO CHANGE
√	**B) Proton Auroras are usually observed at lower latitudes.**
	C) Proton Auroras usually take place in March
	D) Proton Auroras are hard to observe

1> The keyword in the question is "the eyewitness"

2> Our goal is to find the words related with visual such as "frequently appears" or "the panoramic view evolves and changes constantly."

3> Therefore, the answer is (B)

4> (C) discusses the time of the appearance .

5> (D) is visual but opposite to the passage and is negative.

Q17. Absolute Pattern 16: Precision, Concision, Style

At some times, **they form "quiet arcs"** [16] <u>, at others</u> ("active Aurora"), **the panoramic view evolves** and changes constantly.

	A) NO CHANGE	1> "they form quiet arcs" is the independent clause.
	B) : at others	2> "the panoramic view evolves" is another clause with the verb.
√	C) ; at others	3> A sort of conjunction that can tie these two clauses is needed.
	D) with at others	

1> "they form quiet arcs" is the independent clause.
2> "the panoramic view evolves" is another clause with the verb.
3> A sort of conjunction that can tie these two clauses is needed.
4> Therefore, (A) is incorrect because the comma can't connect two clauses.
5> (D) is incorrect because "with" is preposition that can't link the following clause.
6> The semicolon in (C) functions as a conjunction to show the contrasting view
7> "At some times" and "at others" clearly show the contrasting view. Hence the answer.
8> The colon as shown in (B) may link two clauses. However, the purpose of the colon is to introduce information, not to contrast two clauses.

Q18. Absolute Pattern 1: Adding, Revising, Deleting, Retaining Information

[17] **Each one** consists of many parallel rays, each lined up with the local direction of the magnetic field, consistent with Auroras being shaped by Earth's magnetic field.

	A) The existing sentence should be the topic sentence
	B) You'd probably end up unable to see Aurora
	C) If your main purpose is to see Aurora, read this article before you book your flight
√	D) The most distinctive and brightest are the curtain-like Auroral arcs.

1> The new paragraph cannot start with a pronoun such as "one," "that," "this," "it." "they, each"
2> The precedent that refers to "Each one" must be identified.
3> Therefore, (A) can't be the answer.

B) and C) are not related with the following paragraph.

Q19. Absolute Pattern 10: Logical Expression

These are the [19] 'discrete' Auroras, which are at times bright enough to read a newspaper by at night. and can display rapid sub-second variations in intensity.

√	**A) NO CHANGE**	Discrete = distinctive or unique
	B) discreet	B) discreet = careful. It is often used to the person's characteristic.
	C) descent	C) descent = falling
	D) deceased	D) deceased = dead

Q20. Absolute Pattern 1: Adding, Revising, Deleting, Retaining Information

Diffuse Auroras are often composed of patches whose brightness exhibits regular or near-regular pulsations. [20]

	Question: Which item would provide the <u>evidence to support the characteristics</u> of the diffuse Auroras?
	A) By their nature, the characteristics of diffuse Auroras are elusive to define
	B) The diffuse Auroras are often confusing
√	**C) The pulsation period can be typically many seconds, so is not always obvious.**
	D) The pulsation period provides the most stunning events to the observers

1> The quintessential point in this question is the keywords in the question itself.

2> The keywords are "the evidence and the characteristics"

3> Therefore, any options with the subjective perception can't be the answer such as "elusive to define" as in (A); "confusing " as in (B); "stunning events" as in (D). because all of these options are subjective perspectives.

Q21. Absolute Pattern 1: Adding, Revising, Deleting, Retaining Information

A typical Auroral display consist of these forms appears in the above **order throughout the night.** [21]

	A) the regions diffuse Aurora appear
	B) the reason for the reduced luminosity.
√	C) the **sequence of and duration** of Auroral appearance
	D) the important characteristics of Aurora phenomenon

1> The question is seeking the matching synonyms with the last sentence.

2> The keys in the last sentence are: "order" and "throughout the night"

3> "A typical Auroral display" is the main subject of the sentence, which is not new information; therefore, can't be the significant keyword.

4> "sequence" = "order", and "duration" = "throughout the night.

Q22. Absolute Pattern 9: Informational Graphs

The magnetic field strength is around **13,300 (the lowest)** when the chance of observing aurora is **highest at around 24:00hours**.

√	A) The magnetic field strength is **highest when the chance of observing Aurora is highest**
	B) The magnetic field strength is lowest when the chance of observing Aurora is highest
	C) The chance of observing Aurora is highest after midnight
	D) The chance of observing Aurora is lowest in the morning

Q23. Absolute Pattern 19: Redundant Error

I dreamt of becoming an architect at first [23] but I realized that it was not for me.

	A) NO CHANGE	1> The primary sentence contains 'I' as the main subject.
√	**B) but realized**	2> When the subject in the subordinating clause refers to the same person and there's no other person in the sentence, the subject in the subordinating clause should be removed to avoid the redundancy.
	C) however, I realized	C) The conjunctive adverb 'however' also requires a semicolon before "however"
	D) but realizing	D) "but" is the conjunction that requires the verb. "realizing" is an adjective participle, not a verb.

Q24. Absolute Pattern 24: Verb Tense / Voice Error

One year [24] <u>had passed since</u> **I came to Canada, but** I still didn't know what I wanted to do in the future.

	A) NO CHANGE	1>"I came to Canada" is definitely correct in using the past tense.
√	**B) has passed since**	2> Because the one year period has progressed from one moment in the past until now, this clause should use the present perfect.
	C) has passed after	3> When the present perfect tense is used, "since" must be attached.
	D) was passed after	Can I...? No, using "after" instead of "since" is not okay.

Q25. Absolute Pattern 16: Precision, Concision, Style

My father and I [25] <u>had a conversation discussing about</u> my future plans.

	A) NO CHANGE	(A) "conversation" and "discussing" are synonyms
	B) had a conversation about	(C) "consultation" is too formal language, unfit for the anecdote.
	C) had a consultation about	(D) expresses the precise meaning concisely by employing the verb instead of noun.
√	**D) discussed**	*If a noun and a verb with the same meaning are competing, the verb is always concise and precise. Hence the answer.

Q26. Absolute Pattern 22: Nonrestrictive Modifier (Inessential Information)

This is a story about [26] <u>me, learning how to fly</u> to achieve my goal of becoming an airline pilot.

√	**A) NO CHANGE**	1> "learning how to fly ..." is a nonrestrictive modifier.
	B) my learning how to fly	2> In other words, It is an inessential information, which should be separated by a comma.
	C) me, learning and flying	3> Therefore, D) is incorrect.
	D) me learning how to fly	(B) uses the possessive pronoun "my", trying to connect the nonrestrictive modifier, which becomes difficult to understand and only force the reader to read without holding a breath.
		(C) separates "learning" and "flying…"that changes the original meaning.

Q27. Absolute Pattern 1: Adding, Revising, Deleting, Retaining Information

[27] <1>On September 5th, I went to flying school to practice flying. I have been flying for about a half a year, and I just started learning **how to land**. <2>I needed to do lots of circuits, where I have to circle around the airport in order of crosswind, downwind, base, and **final to land** the plane smoothly. <3>*I practiced with my instructor every time I came in to fly.* <4>**My landing skills** were showing little progress, so I wasn't sure if I could land the plane by myself. practice simulation in detail,

Compared to sentences 1,2, and 4 that illustrate the practicing landing skills, <3> is monotonous and general description. Therefore, it should be deleted.

Q28. Absolute Pattern 1: Adding, Revising, Deleting, Retaining Information

After hearing the words one more time, I became very nervous because I was going for my first solo flight all by myself. "

√	A) **Yes, because the essay focuses on his unsettled emotional state**
	B) Yes, because the essay forebodes the author as the rising national figure
	C) No, because the essay focuses on the flight skills, not on the author's personal emotion.
	D) No, because it deviates the paragraph's focus on flying practice.

This sentence is about the author's first flight that vividly describes his inner mindset.

B) The narrator is an apprentice, far from the rising national figure.

C) The passage focuses on the author's emotion.

D) The sentence does not deviate but adds more ingredients.

Q29. Absolute Pattern 24: Verb Tense / Voice Error

After he left, I simulated what he [29] told me by saying it out loud to myself.

	A) NO CHANGE	1> "what he had told" should have occurred before "he left"
√	**B) had told**	2> Because "he left" is the past tense, "what he had told" should be the past perfect.
	C) tells	
	D) used to tell	

Q30. Absolute Pattern 1: Adding, Revising, Deleting, Retaining Information

Which of the following alternatives would NOT be appropriate?

	A) I was filled with joy.	(D) is irrelevant information .
	B) I was free like a bird.	The passage is based on the personal anecdote, not apprenticeship in general.
	C) I faced the most complex flying skills	A personal anecdote is supposed to be subjective, presenting vivid emotion like (A), (B), (C). (D) is showing numbers however.
√	D) I heard the normal apprenticeship requires at least 200 hours of solo flight	

Q31. Absolute Pattern 2: Cause-Effect Relations

[31] So nervous that I forgot to switch my radio frequency.

√	A) NO CHANGE	1> "so ~ that" clause
	B) My emotion was very sensitive	B) "sensitive" is improper word usage.
		(C) "nervous" and "anxious" are synonyms, a redundant error
	C) I was nervous and anxious at the same time	(D) The following "that I forgot..." indicates the main clause should be the past tense. (D) is present perfect
	D) Very nervous have I been	(A) clearly and precisely uses the So-that clause

Q32. Absolute Pattern 22: Nonrestrictive Modifier (Inessential Information)

I drove on to the runway [32]and taking off with full-power.

	A) NO CHANGE	1> "I drove on to the runway" is the primary clause.
√	B) , taking off with full-power.	2> The best way to consume the remaining underlined portion is to make it as a modifying phrase without adding "and."
	C) taking off with full-power.	(A) "and" is a conjunction that carries a clause with a verb. "taking off" is a participle, not a verb. Therefore, "and" can't be used.
	D) ,and I took off with full-power	(C) requires a comma like (B) because the modifying phrase is nonrestrictive that needs to be separated from the main clause.
		(D) is incorrect for two reasons (1) "I" in the dependent clause is redundant with the "I" in the primary sentence. (2) the meaning becomes wordy, creating a time sequence instead of showing a simultaneous action.

Q33. Absolute Pattern 9: Informational Graphs

	A) Standing & taxing can considerably reduce all accidents
√	**B) En Route can reduce almost half of the serious accidents**
	C) Approach & landing in all accidents is smaller than that in serious accidents
	D) Take-off in serious accidents is insignificant compared to that in all accidents.

A) Standing & taxing can't considerably reduce all accidents because it takes up only 3%.

B) En Route can reduce almost the half of serious accidents because it takes up 45%

C) No, it's greater. Approach & landing in all accidents is 34% while serious accidents is 21%

D) They are about the same: 34 % vs. 35%

Q34. Absolute Pattern 24: Verb Tense / Voice Error

Some Western thinkers claim that philosophy as such is only characteristic of Western cultures. Martin Heidegger is even reported [34] saying that only Greek and German languages are suitable for philosophizing.

	A) NO CHANGE	1> What Martin Heidegger said must come before it is reported.
√	**B) to have said**	2> Therefore, it can not be the future tense like (C) and (D). (A) "saying" indicates the simultaneous happening.
	C) to be said	(B) "to have said" is the past tense for to-infinitive clause.
	D) to say	

Q35. Absolute Pattern 7: Conjunction Error

It is still commonplace in Western universities to teach only Western philosophy [35] but ignore Asian philosophy altogether, or consider only newer Western-influenced Asian thought properly "philosophy."

	A) NO CHANGE	"but" is the conjunction that cancels out the previous clause so that it can emphasize the following sentence.
	B) but ignores	The question clauses, however, are competently paralleling.
√	**C) and ignore**	Therefore, (A) and (B) are incorrect. (D) changes the original meaning, saying that Western universities are ignorant. In a series of To-Infinitive clause, "to" can be dropped from the second list to use only the root verb as shown in (C)
	D) with ignorance of	

Q36. Absolute Pattern 24: Verb Tense / Voice Error

Carine Defoort, herself a specialist in Chinese thought, **has offered** support for such a "family" view of philosophy, while Rein Raud **has presented** an argument against it and [36] will offer a more flexible definition of philosophy

	A) NO CHANGE	1> The primary verb tense in this sentence is the present perfect
√	**B) offered**	(e.g., "has offered", "has presented.")
	C) offer	2> Therefore, the following verb after the conjunction "and" should also be the present perfect.
	D) had offered	(A) is future and (C) is plural, simple present tense
		(D) is the past perfect
		(B) is the present perfect tense: the identical subject (Rein Raud) and the helping verb **(has)**" are simply omitted to make (Rein Raud **has**) offered.

Q37. Absolute Pattern 19: Redundant Error

In response, OuYang Min argues that philosophy properly is a Western cultural practice and essentially different from *zhexue*, which is what the Chinese have, even though *zhexue* (originally *tetsugaku*) is actually [37] the neologism of the newly invented words coined in 1873 by Nishi Amane for describing Western philosophy as opposed to traditional Asian thought.

	A) NO CHANGE	1> the meaning "neologism" is a newly invented word.
	B) the neologism with the newly invented words coined	2> Therefore, (A), (B), and (D) all of them need to be reduced to (C).
√	**C) the neologism made**	
	D) the neologism for the created words coined	

Q38. Absolute Pattern 10: Logical Expression

This has created a dichotomy among some Western philosophies, between secular philosophies and religious philosophies developed within the context of a particular monotheistic
[38] religion dogma—especially some creeds of Protestant Christianity, regarding the nature of God and the universe.

	A) NO CHANGE	(A) "religion" and "dogma" are both nouns and can't be tied together.

	B) dogma of religion;	(B) has three errors:
		  (1) It changes the original meaning.
		  (2) "some creeds" refers to "dogma", not "religion," therefore, the order should be flipped over.
		  (3) The semicolon can't link the following phrase.

	C) religion's dogma:	
√	**D) religious dogma,**	(C) "religion" is an intangible noun that can't be used as the possessive determiner "apostrophe s (D) The adjective "religious" modifies the noun "dogma" correctly.

Q39. Absolute Pattern 15: Prepositional Idiom

Eastern religions have been **as concerned** by questions relating to the nature of a single God [39] than to the universe's sole creator and ruler.

	A) NO CHANGE	Eastern religions have been **as concerned** (by questions relating *to the nature of a single God*) **as** *to the universe's sole creator and ruler*.
	B) of	
	C) with	As seen in the above boldfaced portion of the sentence, "as-as" idiom should be used.
√	**D) as**	

Q40. Absolute Pattern 15: Prepositional Idiom

...the same philosophical school often contains **both** religious [40] along with philosophical elements.

	A) NO CHANGE	"Both~ and" is a correlative conjunction and can't be replaced with other elements.
	B) together with	
	C) as well as	
√	**D) and**	

Q41. Absolute Pattern 19: Redundant Error

Some have worshipped the Taoist deities [41] divinely and religiously without bothering to delve into the theological underpinnings,

	A) NO CHANGE	1> "deities" and "divinely" are synonyms
	B) religion	2> "divinely" also distracts the focus by blocking the keyword "religiously"
√	C) religiously	(B) 1> "Some have worshipped the Taoist deities" is a complete independent sentence.
	D) with religious mindsets	2> Therefore the underlined portion should be an adverb "religiously" to describes the verb "worshipped"
		(D) is wordy

Q42. Absolute Pattern 4: Comparison

Such an arrangement stands in marked contrast to [42] that of some recent philosophy in the West,

	A) NO CHANGE	1> "that of" is used for a comparison, which is not evident in this sentence.
	B) those of	2> The sentence emphasizes "the arrangement", which is not found in recent philosophy in the West.
	C) an arrangement of	3> Therefore, this sentence does not intend to compared anything, but to reveal the fact that some arrangements are not found in some recent philosophy in the West.
√	D) delete it	

Q43. Absolute Pattern 16: Precision, Concision, Style

A **common thread** that **often differentiates** Eastern philosophy from Western is the **relationship** [43] that commonly relates the gods with the universe.

	A) NO CHANGE	The question sentence provides three keywords: (1) differentiate—which ideally embraces the idiom "between ~ and,"
√	**B) between the gods and the universe**	(2) "common thread,"
	C) between the gods with the universe	(3) "relationship"
	D) between the gods and the universe that find correlations within the common thread	(A) "common thread" and "relationship" repeats with "commonly relates"
		(C) "between—with" is unidiomatic
		(D) is wordy and redundant as in (A)

Q44. Absolute Pattern 12: Modifier (Placement) Error

Some Western schools of thought were animistic or pantheistic, such as the classical Greek tradition, while **later religious beliefs**, [44] *influencing the monotheism of the Abrahamic religions*, **portrayed** divinity

Subject — Modifier — Verb

as more transcendent.

	A) NO CHANGE	1> As seen in the above boldfaced portion of the text, "later religious beliefs" is the subject and "portrayed" is the verb.
	B) had influenced	2> Therefore, (B) and (C) can't be the answers because they are verbs.
	C) have influenced	3> The adjective modifier in the middle should be 'influenced by', not "influencing" because the overall past tense can't suddenly shift to on-going situation.
√	D) influenced by	

SAT
Writing and Language
Test 5

ALL THE LOGIC AND RULES

BEHIND THE EVERY SINGLE

SAT QUESTION

Writing and Language Test 5
35 MINUTES, 44 QUEST IONS

Each passage below is accompanied by a number of questions. For some questions, you will consider how the passage might be revised to improve the expression of ideas. For other questions, you will consider how the passage might be edited to correct errors in sentence structure, usage, or punctuation. A passage or a question may be accompanied by one or more graphics (such as a table or graph) that you will consider as you make revising and editing decisions.

Questions 1-12 are based on the following passage

Global Warning

Harvard University The Crimson
 Reproduced with permission

Just when I was starting to get used to the passionate debates [1] characterize meals in Annenberg, a recent dinner conversation threw me a curveball. Last week, I had the unique—and

frustrating—privilege of dining with the last individual on earth who does not believe in global warming.

Or so I thought. Further research indicates that my acquaintance was far from alone; according to a 2008 Gallup poll, about 11 percent of Americans still think that global warming "will never happen." [2]

1

A) that characterize
B) ,which characterizes
C) characterizes
D) characterized

2

At this point, the author is considering adding the sentence below.

  Within the scientific community, this statistic is only three percent.

Should the author add this sentence here?

A) Yes, because it contrasts the views between the public and scientists
B) Yes, because it shows lack of interest in global warming among scientists
C) No, because scientists' view deviates from the main focus of the paragraph
D) No, because 3 percent is too insignificant to emphasize the author's view.

CONTINUE ➤

2

Perhaps most disturbingly, the study reports that 13 percent of Americans believe that no further climate control measures are [3] necessary—in other words, that we as a society should take no action to further reduce carbon emissions or attempt to combat global warming in any way.

Whether these "unbelievers" remain unconvinced [4] and differing interpretations of the data or mere apathy, [5] our stance is highly untenable, but also dangerous. Though it's easy to brush off such wrongheaded beliefs in our relativistic culture, those who think global warming is a hoax are not simply another case of mere "difference of opinion."

These people are gambling [6] the welfare of the entire planet on the off-chance that the majority is incorrect.

Evidence that the average temperature on Earth is rising is abundant and convincing, but I suspect I would be preaching to the converted if I were to summarize it here.

3

Which of the following choices would be LEAST likely be used?
A) necessary—in other words,
B) necessary. In other words,
C) necessary; in other words,
D) necessary, in other words,

4

A) NO CHANGE
B) because
C) due to
D) despite of

5

A) NO CHANGE
B) its
C) their
D) those unbelievers who have their

6

A) NO CHANGE
B) the entire planet's welfare
C) with the entire planet
D) with the entire planet where our welfare is

CONTINUE

2   2

The bottom line is that the scientific community has come to a clear consensus that the evidence of a warming trend is "unequivocal" and [7] It is thus troubling that one in five Americans remain unconvinced by the vast majority of the scientific community that we have an immediate obligation to change our behavior and to protect our planet. Beyond the scientific evidence,[8] a plan of action that reduces carbon emissions based on our moral considerations alone can be achieved.

In an article entitled "Perspectives on Environmental Change: A Basis for Action," Professor Michael B. McElroy of Harvard's Center for Earth and Planetary Physics cites Pope John Paul II's opinion on global warming as he expressed it nearly 20 years ago: "Theology, philosophy and science all speak of a harmonious universe, of a cosmos endowed with its own integrity, its own internal, dynamic nature. This order must be respected. The human race is called to explore this order, [9] examine it with due care, and making use of it. while [10] safeguarding its integrity."

7

Which item best supports the partial statement in this sentence?
A) that human activity has "very likely" been the main cause for that change over the last 50 years.
B) that there's no doubt about it.
C) whether the trend is a transient phenomenon or long-lived feature remains elusive.
D) that there is not enough scientific evidence

8

Which choice best combines the sentence underlined?
A) NO CHANGE
B) one can support a plan of action to reduce carbon emissions based on our moral considerations alone.
C) based on moral considerations alone, we can reduce carbon emissions
D) carbon emissions can be reduced based on our moral considerations alone.

9

A) NO CHANGE
B) to examine it with due care, and to make use of them
C) examine it with due care, and make use of it
D) examine it with due care, and making use of them

10

A) NO CHANGE
B) they should safeguard
C) safeguard
D) safely guarding

CONTINUE

2

McElroy himself reflects that humans do not "have the right to place the balance of the global life support system at risk when there are [11] sensitive actions that can be taken to at least slow the pace of human-induced change." Put another way, the ethical imperative of preserving our planet outweighs the groundless opinions stubbornly maintained by a global warming skeptic.

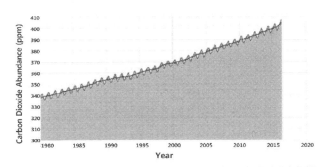

The atmospheric concentration of carbon dioxide

11

A) NO CHANGE
B) sensible
C) serendipitous
D) sense

12

Which person in the passage would most likely consent with the graph?

A) 11 percent of Americans in 2008 Gallup poll
B) 13 percent of Americans in paragraph 2
C) Professor Michael B. McElroy
D) The last individual in paragraph 1

CONTINUE

2

2

Questions 13-22 are based on the following passage.

The Man in Gray –project Gutenberg

The four-faced clock over the information booth on the Upper Level of the Grand Central Station in New York City showed exactly twenty-five minutes after three. Dave Dawson paused in his restless pacing up and down to look at it for the hundredth time in the last half hour. [13] He glared at it, sighed heavily, and made noises deeply in his throat, "Where is that Freddy Farmer guy, anyway?" he grated to himself. "For half an hour I've been pounding shoe leather here waiting for him. Darned if he isn't worse than a woman, not being at a place on time. But [14] he's probably lost. He can stay lost for all I care."

With a sharp nod for emphasis, [15] walking over to the newsstand, he bought a bar of candy.

Dave ignored the look, however, and turned away. He didn't want to talk about the war.

[16] Accordingly, he didn't even want to think about it. Freddy and he were enjoying a much-deserved leave, and they still had four days to go. And until those four days had come and [17] went,

13

A) NO CHANGE
B) Glared at it, sighed heavily, and made noises deeply
C) Glaring at it, sighed heavily, and made noises deep
D) Glared at it, sighed heavily, and made noises deep

14

A) he is
B) he was
C) he has
D) his

15

A) NO CHANGE
B) as he walked over to the newsstand, bought a bar of candy.
C) he walked over to the newsstand and bought a bar of candy.
D) he walked over to the newsstand, and he bought a bar of candy.

16

A) NO CHANGE
B) Firstly,
C) Thus,
D) In fact,

17

A) NO CHANGE
B) was going
C) had gone
D) gone

CONTINUE

2   2

the war could be on another world as far as he was concerned [18] as if the war was occurring in totally different parts on earth.

He let the rest trail off as he saw Freddy Farmer hurrying toward him from the direction of the IRT shuttle train to Times Square. He fixed the English-born air ace with a [19] disgusted eye and watched him approach.

Freddy came up to him all smiles and slightly flushed.

"No!" Dawson snapped. "And my mother taught me never to speak to strangers. So scram, before I call a cop." "Speaking of your New York cops,"

Freddy Farmer chuckled, [20] "I won't be here now, if it hadn't been for a Bobby in the Bronx."

[21] "Bronx?" Dawson exploded. "What the heck were ya doing up there? This morning you said you were going to hear Benny Goodman's band over at the Paramount Theatre."

"And so [22] was I ," Freddy replied with a nod.

18

Which choice best support the previous portion of the sentence ?

A) NO CHANGE

B) from his point of view

C) but he stopped thinking about the war

D) Delete, and ends the sentence by replacing the comma with period

---

19

A) NO CHANGE

B) disgusting

C) disgust

D) disgustingly

20

A) NO CHANGE

B) "I wouldn't have been here now,

C) "I hadn't been here now,

D) "I wouldn't be here now,

21

The literary device used in this sentence is ?

A) Jargon

B) Oxymoron

C) Juxtaposition

D) slang

22

A) NO CHANGE

B) do

C) have

D) did

CONTINUE ➡

2   2

Questions 23-33 are based on the following passage

 Human gene algorithm

[23] When thinking of discovery about the intricate organization of the nervous system, the more it seems remarkable that genes can successfully specify the development of that system. Of all the organs in human body, human brain, especially study of neurons and their connections with one another is considered to be the greatest challenge to scientists. It is a pretty daunting task when thinking of human genes contain [24] so little information to specify which hemisphere of the brain, in each of which occupy a human's 1011 neurons, connects which neurons.

[25] For such reasons, we can assume that there must be an important random factor in neural development.

23

A) NO CHANGE
B) Without a doubt, we discovered
C) The more that is discovered about
D) As we discover

24

A) NO CHANGE
B) too
C) very
D) as

25

At this point, the writer is considering to revise the underlined sentence as below.

> For instance, genes in human body contain so little information that specifying each neuron's role is extremely challenging.

Should this addition be allowed ?

A) Yes, because it supplies additional information about gene connections.
B) Yes, because it further elaborates the intricate, even cryptic, nature of the genes
C) No, because it has already been mentioned
D) No, because specifying neuron's role should have been discussed earlier.

CONTINUE ➤

In particular, that errors [26] <u>must have occurred and do occur</u> in the development of all normal brains. The most vivid expression of such errors [27] <u>occur in</u> genetically identical (isogenic) organisms.

Even when reared under the same conditions, isogenic organisms are [28] <u>rarely</u> exact copies of one another, and their differences have revealed much about the random variations that result from an organism's limited supply of genetic information.

[29] ①In isogenic Daphniae, for example, even though the position, size, and branching pattern of each optic neuron are remarkably constraint, there is some variability in connectivity and the number of synapses varies greatly. ②This variability is probably the result of random scatter beyond the resolution of genetic control and is best termed "imprecision, " since its converse, the degree of clustering about a mean, is conventionally called " precisions."

③ That is why genetic engineering is hard to study as it should deal with more on isogenic Daphniae.

④ Imprecision should be distinguished from developmental mistakes: wrongly migrated neurons, incorrect connections, and the like.

26

Which choice is unacceptable alternative to the underlined sentence ?
A) must and actually occur
B) have and actually occur
C) have occurred and actually did occur
D) must and will occur

27

A) NO CHANGE
B) occurs in
C) occur with
D) occurring with

28

Which choice is LEAST acceptable to the sentence ?
A) a little
B) hardly
C) barely
D) scarcely

29

Which of the following sentences of this paragraph is LEAST relevant to the main focus of the essay and therefore should be deleted?
A) Sentence ①
B) Sentence ②
C) Sentence ③
D) Sentence ④

CONTINUE

2   2

[30] Let us use a computer analogy, minor rounding-off errors occur universally and are analogous to imprecisions, but occasionally binary digit is incorrectly transmitted, perhaps ruining a calculation, and this incorrect transmission is analogous.

Thus, imprecision is a form of inaccuracy, [31] inherently within the limits of design, but mistakes are forms of gross fallibility.

[32]Either imprecision and gross fallibility can plausibly be blamed on the insufficiency of genetic information, since either could be reduced by adding more information. It is universally accepted among information theorists that codes and languages can be made mistake-resistant by incorporating redundancy.

30

A) NO CHANGE
B) To use a computer analogy,
C) Neuroscientists, for further clarification, use a computer analogy,
D) Using a computer analogy can be a way to clarify this issue.

31

Which of the following choices would be appropriate to use?
A) which is both Inherent and congenital
B) thereby inherently congenital
C) inherent
D) that is inherent from the cognitive-developmental stage

32

A) NO CHANGE
B) Both
C) Neither
D) Together with

CONTINUE

2

2

Question 33-44 is based on the following passage.

Virtual Reality (VR)   by San

{ 1 }

Virtual reality or virtual realities (VR), also known as immersive multimedia or computer-simulated reality, is a computer technology that replicates an environment, real or imagined, and simulates a user's physical presence and environment to allow for user interaction.

{ 2 }

Most up-to-date virtual realities are displayed [33] either a computer screen or on a special virtual reality headset, and some simulations include additional sensory information.

Furthermore, virtual reality covers remote communication environments, [34] although unavailable at this time, either through the use of standard input devices such as a wired glove or a keyboard and mouse, or through multimodal devices

{ 3 }

Strides are being made in the realm of education, although much needs to be done. [35] By far, few contents are created that may be used for educational purposes, [36] with most advances are being made in the entertainment industry, but many

---

33

A) NO CHANGE

B) both on a computer screen or with

C) either on a computer screen or with

D) neither on a computer screen nor with

34

Which choice most effectively supports the previous sentence

A) NO CHANGE

B) which allow people to communicate remotely

C) which are still an at embryonic stage

D) which provide the virtual presence of users

35

Which choice would be LEAST acceptable to use?

A) By far,

B) So far,

C) Currently,

D) At present,

36

A) NO CHANGE

B) with the most advances being made

C) with the most advancement is

D) and the most advances being made

CONTINUE

2   **2**

understand and realize the importance of education in VR. The usage of VR in a training perspective is to allow professionals to conduct training in a virtual environment where they can improve their skills without the consequence of failing the operation.[37]

{ 4 }

VR plays an important role in combat training for the military. It allows the recruits to train under a controlled environment. A fully immersive virtual reality and integrated system [38] that uses head-mounted display (HMD), data suits, data glove, and VR weapon are used to train for combat.

[39] ① The simulator would sit on top of the system that reacts to the user inputs and events. ②When the pilot steers the aircraft, the module would turn and tilt accordingly to the provided haptic feedback. ③The flight simulator can range from a fully enclosed module to a series of computer monitors providing the pilot's point of view. ④VR is also used in flight simulation for the Air Force where people are trained to be pilots.

37

What could be the topic of paragraph {3}
A) The application of VR in entertainment
B) The application of VR in training
C) The future of VR
D) The costs and other factors in VR

38

At this point, the author wishes to delete the underlined phrase. Should the author proceeds to delete it or not?
A) Kept, because it helps visualize the sophisticated VR applications in many industries
B) Kept, because it suggests the types of VR tools and accruements currently available
C) Deleted, because listing the tools is unnecessary and could distract the main point
D) Deleted, because the tools are prototype currently unavailable

39

Which choice most effectively arranged the sentence sequence of this paragraph?
A) NO CHANGE
B) ③-②-①-④
C) ④-③-②-①
D) ④-①-②-③

CONTINUE ▶

2

2

The most important reasons for using simulators over learning with a real aircraft are the reduction of transference time between land training and real flight, the safety, economy and [40] control of pollution. By the same token, virtual driving simulations are used to train tank drivers on the bases before allowing them to operate the real vehicle. As these drivers often have [41] better experience than [42] that of any other truck drivers, virtual reality training allows them to compensate this. [43] In the near future, similar projects are expected for all drivers to train prior to drive real vehicles.

40

Which choice would be unacceptable to the sentence?

A) absence

B) reduction

C) generation

D) elimination

41

A) NO CHANGE

B) fewer

C) more

D) less

42

A) NO CHANGE

B) other

C) others

D) any other

43

The author is considering to delete the underlined sentence, should the sentence be deleted?

A) No, because the paragraph loses the structural integrity

B) No, because the passage loses how VR will evolve in the future

C) Yes, because the passage mainly focuses on present development and application

D) Yes, because it does not provide a transition from the previous paragraph.

CONTINUE

2
2

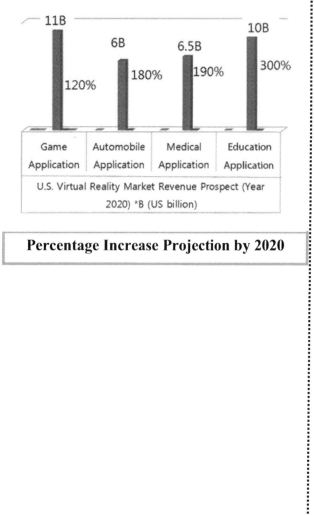

11B
6B
6.5B
10B
120%
180%
190%
300%

| Game Application | Automobile Application | Medical Application | Education Application |

U.S. Virtual Reality Market Revenue Prospect (Year 2020) *B (US billion)

Percentage Increase Projection by 2020

Which choice would LEAST correspond to the statistics shown on the graph?

A) The educational application will experience the highest growth in 2020 among all applications.

B) The highest market revenue in 2020 is game application

C) The growth in medical application is about the same as Automobile application

D) VR applications in the game industry will gradually erode the existing online game industry.

TEST 5

WRITING ABSOLUTE PATTERNS

TEST 5

WRITING AND LANGUAGE SECTION PATTERN ANALYSIS

Q1. Absolute Pattern 12: Modifier (Placement) Error

Just when I was starting to get used to the passionate **debates [1]** _characterize_ _meals in Annenberg_, a recent dinner conversation threw me a curveball. Last week,

√	**A) that characterize**	A) 1>"that characterize meals in Annenberg" describes "debates" as the adjective modifier.
	B) , which characterizes	2> Because "debates" is plural, the plural verb "characterize" should be used.
	C) characterizes	
	D) characterized	B) modifies the "debates" but uses the singular verb "characterizes"
		C), D) are regular verbs, not a modifier.

Q2. Absolute Pattern 1: Adding, Revising, Deleting, Retaining Information

about 11 percent of Americans still think that global warming "will never happen." [2] Within the scientific community, this statistic is only three percent.

√	**A) Yes, because it contrasts the views between the public and scientists**
	B) Yes, because it shows lack of interest in global warming among scientists
	C) No, because scientists' view deviates from the main focus of the paragraph
	D) No, because 3 percent is too insignificant to emphasize the author's view.

A) The author brings up the scientists' view to show 97% of them believe the global warming.

B) The sentence "~among scientists" should change to "~among the public"

C) The author wants to elaborate her thought about global warming based on the scientific justification and therefore "scientists" does not deviates, but emphasizes her belief.

D) is opposite, 3% is very significant because it means 97% believes the global warming.

Q3. Absolute Pattern 18: Punctuation Error

Americans believe that no further climate control measures are [3]necessary—in other words, that we as a society should take no action to further reduce carbon emissions or attempt to combat global warming in any way.

	A) necessary—in other words,	D) is comma splice error
	B) necessary. In other words,	1> After the independent clause, the modifying clause with the verb must carry a connector like the dash in (A), or the semicolon in (C).
	C) necessary; in other words,	
√	**D) necessary, in other words,**	2> Starting a new sentence with the transitional word like in (B) is another method to emphasize the transitional word.

Q4. Absolute Pattern 15: Prepositional Idiom

Whether these "unbelievers" remain unconvinced <u>and</u> differing interpretations **or**

	A) and	"and" is a paralleling conjunction that that connects a clause with a verb.
	B) because	"because" is a cause-effect conjunction that connects a clause with a verb.
√	**C) due to**	means 'caused by' or 'because of' that connects a phrase like the above phrase.
	D) despite of	means without being influenced by, which is opposite of 'due to'

Q5. Absolute Pattern 17: Pronoun Error

Whether **these "unbelievers"** remain unconvinced due to differing interpretations of the data or mere apathy, [5] <u>our stance</u> is highly untenable, but also dangerous.

	A) our stance	A pronoun must have its own precedent.
	B) its stance	C) The precedent "these unbelievers" and "their" are both the 3rd person plural.
√	**C) their** stance	A) "our," the 1st person plural can't receive "these unbelievers"
	D) those unbelievers who have their stance	B) "its" is singular and has no precedent to modify.
		D) (1) "those unbelievers" disagrees with the verb "is" (2) is wordy and redundant.

Q6. Absolute Pattern 14: Possessive Determiners and Possessive Noun Error

These people are gambling [6] the welfare of the entire planet on the off-chance that the majority is incorrect.

√	A) NO CHANGE	B) 1> Apostrophe 's is used exclusively for human, animal, country, organization, etc. 2> For the intangible noun like "welfare," "of" should be used to describe the possessive determiner.
	B) the entire planet's welfare	
	C) with the entire planet	C) changes the meaning
	D) with the entire planet where our welfare is	D) is wordy

Q7. Absolute Pattern 1: Adding, Revising, Deleting, Retaining Information

The bottom line is that the scientific community has come to a clear consensus that the evidence of a warming trend is "unequivocal" and [7]

√	**A) that human activity has "very likely" been the main cause for that change over the last 50 years**
	B) that there's no doubt about it.
	C) whether the trend is a transient phenomenon or long-lived feature remains elusive.
	D) that there is not enough scientific evidence

A) Negative and specific detail best links the previous and the following sentences.

B) is only redundant with "unequivocal" without adding any meaningful information.

C) is directly opposite to the already stated word "unequivocal" and deviates from the negative tone.

D) is directly opposite to the following sentence stating "Beyond the scientific evidence..."

Q8. Absolute Pattern 1: Adding, Revising, Deleting, Retaining Information

Beyond the **scientific evidence**, [8] a plan of action that reduces carbon emissions based on our
moral considerations alone can be achieved.

	A) NO CHANGE
	B) one can support a plan of action to reduces carbon emissions based on our moral considerations alone.
	C) based on moral considerations alone, we can reduce carbon emissions
√	D) carbon emissions can be reduced based on our moral considerations alone.

(A) (1) wordy: "a plan of action" and "can be achieved."

(2) indirect compared to answer (D)

(3) made the misplaced modifier error: "Beyond the scientific evidence" must be connected to "carbon emissions", not "a plan" and putting "based on our moral considerations alone" next to "carbon emissions" is also misplaced.

(B) is wordy and inconsistently shifts the pronoun "our" to "one"

(C) The modifying phrase "Beyond the scientific evidence" should be carried out by the main clause, not by another modifier "based on moral considerations alone." because it will be confusing eventually which phrases modifies which phrases/clause.

(D) First, "carbon emissions" correctly pulls the modifier "Beyond the scientific evidence"

Second, it places the modifier **"based on our moral considerations alone"** as a reason for **"reduction"**

Q9. Absolute Pattern 13: Parallel Structure

The human race is called **to explore** this order, [9]**examine** it with due care, **and making** use of it

	A) The human race is called to explore this order, examine it with due care, and making use of it
	B) to examine it with due care, and to make use of them
√	C) examine it with due care, **and make** use of it
	D) examine it with due care, and making use of them

When to-infinitive clause is presented as a series of information, the preposition "to" can be dropped from the second clause (e.g., " to **explore**, (to) **examine** it, and (to) **make** use of it.)

Choice A, B, and D are all parallelism error.

B) doesn't need to write "to" each time it lists to-infinitive clause.

B), D) also change the pronoun "it" to "them"

Q10. Absolute Pattern 16: Precision, Concision, Style

The human race is called to explore this order, examine it with due care, and make use of it **while** [10] safeguarding its integrity."

√	**A) NO CHANGE**	A) concisely utilizes the subordinating clause without redundancy.
	B) they should safeguard	1> "while" uses "~ing" form to express an on-going situation.
		2> The subject in the subordinating clause, to avoid the repetition, is reduced to the participle (safeguarding)
	C) safeguard	(e. g., "while (*human race is*) safeguarding its integrity.")
	D) safely guarding	B) includes the ambiguous pronoun "they"
		C) uses the plural verb "safeguard"
		D) is wordy

Q11. Absolute Pattern 6: Confusing Words

there are [11] sensitive actions that can be taken

	A) NO CHANGE	sensitive means delicate.
√	**B) sensible**	sensible = moral. The adjective has to be related to morality.
	C) serendipitous	means beneficial.
	D) sense	sense is a noun and can't link to another noun "actions."

Q12. Absolute Pattern 9: Informational Graphs

Which person in the passage would most likely consent with the graph?

	A) 11 percent of Americans in 2008 Gallup poll	As an advocate of global warming trends, the author uses Professor Michael B. McElroy.
	B) 13 percent of Americans in paragraph 2	
√	**C) Professor Michael B. McElroy**	Choice A, B, and D are the group of people who do not believe global warming.
	D) The last individual in paragraph 1	

Q13. Absolute Pattern 13: Parallel Structure

[13] He glared at it, sighed heavily, and made noises deeply in his throat, "Where is that Freddy Farmer guy, anyway?" he grated to himself.

	A) NO CHANGE
	B) Glared at it, sighed heavily, and made noises <u>deeply</u>
	C) Glaring at it, sighed heavily, and made noises deep
√	**D) glared at it, sighed heavily, and made noises deep**

D) (1) meets the parallel structure and (2) uses "deep" correctly as a complement for the causative verb "made."

*The causative verbs 'let', 'get', 'make' 'have' must use an adjective for its complement, not an adverb

A) has two errors: (1) comma splice. The subject "He" shouldn't be used because it changes the adjective modifier to the main sentence, which is already presented in the following clause "Where is that…" (2) the adverb "**deeply**" can't be the complement for the verb "made."

B) The causative verb 'made' uses an adjective 'deep' as a complement, not an adverb 'deeply'

C) "Glaring", "sighed", "made" sequences do not parallel.

Q14. Absolute Pattern 24: Verb Tense / Voice Error

But [14] <u>he's</u> probably lost.

√	**A) he is**	1> The contraction "he's" can be either he is or he was.
	B) he was	2> The surrounding sentences are all present tense. 3> Therefore, the answer also has to be the present tense
	C) he has	
	D) his	B) and C) do not agree with the surrounding tense. D) 'his' is a possessive pronoun.

Q15. Absolute Pattern 12: Modifier (Placement) Error

With a sharp nod for emphasis, [15] <u>walking over to the newsstand, he bought a bar of candy.</u>

	A) NO CHANGE
	B) as he walked over to the newsstand, bought a bar of candy.
√	**C) he walked over to the newsstand and bought a bar of candy.**
	D) he walked over to the newsstand, <u>and he</u> bought a bar of candy.

C) 1> The sentence starts with a prepositional phrase "With a sharp nod for emphasis", which requires its main subject be placed immediately after.

   2> "With a sharp nod~" requires a human subject "he" .

A) 1> Misplaced modifier error: the modifier "With a sharp nod…." can't modify another modifier "walking over….."

   2> It should be carried out by the subjective clause immediately after.

B) 1> "as he walked over" contains the conjunction "as", creating a subordinating clause.

   2> "After all, choice B is not a complete sentence at all but composed of one prepositional phrase and two subordinating clauses.

D) is a redundant error by writing "he" unnecessarily two times for the same person in one sentence.

Q16. Absolute Pattern 23: Transitions (Supporting Detail, Contrast, and Consequence)

He didn't want to talk about the war. [16] <u>Accordingly,</u> he didn't even want to think about it.

	A) NO CHANGE	"In fact" emphasizes the previous sentence as an amplifier.
	B) Firstly,	B) should have a series of examples that extend beyond "Firstly,"
	C) Thus,	A) and C) indicate that there was a reason in the previous sentence.
√	**D) In fact,**	

Q17. Absolute Pattern 24: Verb Tense / Voice Error

And until those four days had come and [17] went,

	A) NO CHANGE	A) 'had come' is the past perfect while 'went' is the simple past.
	B) was going	B) 'was going' is the past progressive tense.
	C) had gone	C) helping verb "had" need not be written again. Leaving only the participle 'gone' sounds much better.
√	**D) gone**	e.g., And until those four days had come and (had) gone.

Q18. Absolute Pattern 19: Redundant Error

And until **those four days** had come and gone, **the war could be on another world** as far as he was concerned [18] as if it was occurring in totally different parts of the earth.

	A) NO CHANGE	D) Deleting the 'as if clause' is the best way to avoid the redundancy.
	B) from his point of view	A) The underlined portion of the sentence is similar to the boldfaced clause.
	C) but he stopped thinking about the war	B) is same as "as far as he was concerned.
√	D) **Delete**	C) The usage of 'but' is not suitable as it cancels out the previous sentence while delivering a similar information.

Q19. Absolute Pattern 10: Logical Expression

He fixed the English-born air ace with a [19] <u>disgusted</u> eye and watched him approach.

√	**A) NO CHANGE**	Adjectives that end 'with -ed' (e.g., 'disgusted') and end with '-ing' (e.g., 'disgusting') are often confusing.
	B) disgusting	
	C) disgust	<u>-ed Adjectives</u> Adjectives that end with '-ed' describe emotions, which tell us how people feel about something.
	D) disgustingly	<u>-ing Adjectives</u> Adjectives that end with '-ing' describe the thing that causes the emotion – a disgusting person makes you feel bad. C), D) can't connect with the noun "eye"

Q20. Absolute Pattern 24: Verb Tense / Voice Error

[20] <u>"I won't be here now,</u> **if it hadn't been** for a Bobby in the Bronx."

	A) NO CHANGE	I WOULDN'T HAVE BEEN here now
√	**B) I wouldn't have been here now,**	IF it HADN'T BEEN for Bobby.
	C) "I hadn't been here now,	
	D) "I wouldn't be here now,	

In the past perfect conditional clause

1> If-clause must use the past perfect tense (had + pp).

2> The main clause must use (would have/could have/should have/must have/might have + p.p)

A) The main clause "I won't be here now." is future tense.

C) "hadn't been" should be used in the if-clause.

D) "wouldn't be" is simple past. It needs to be the past perfect, 'wouldn't have been'

Q21. Absolute Pattern 3: Colloquialism (Nonstandard Language)

[21] "Bronx?" Dawson exploded. "What the heck were ya doing up there?

	A) Jargon	is the specialized language for professionals area such as a legal language
	B) Oxymoron	is contradictory word arrangement to dramatize or ponder the situation
	C) Juxtaposition	is a sort of irony or paradox with a clear, good and evil perception
√	**D) Slang**	The quotation uses conversational, non-standard language.

Q22. Absolute Pattern 21: Subject-Verb, Pronoun, Noun Agreement

you said you were going to hear Benny Goodman's band over at the Paramount Theatre."
"And so [22] was I ,"

	A) NO CHANGE	A) Be-verb (was) can't be replaced with a regular verb (went).
	B) do	B) and C) both are the present tense. It should be the past.
	C) have	
√	**D) did**	So I did (went)

Q23. Absolute Pattern 4: Comparison

[23] When thinking of discovery about the intricate organization of the nervous system, **the more it seems** remarkable that genes can successfully specify the development of that system.

	A) NO CHANGE	"The more,~ the more" is a correlative conjunctional idiom that can't be replaced with other form.
	B) Without a doubt, we discovered	
√	C) **The more** that is discovered about	
	D) As we discover	

Q24. Absolute Pattern 23: Transitions (Supporting Detail, Contrast, and Consequence)

It is a pretty daunting task when thinking of human genes contain [24] so little information to specify which hemisphere of the brain, in each of which occupy a human's 1011neurons, connects which neurons.

	A) NO CHANGE	Too...to affirmative clause
√	**B) too**	Too (+ adjective) … to-infinitive clause automatically builds up a negative tone.
	C) very	(e.g., I am too tired to study. = I can't study)
	D) as	Other adverbs (A), (C), (D) do not have such a function.

Q25. Absolute Pattern 1: Adding, Revising, Deleting, Retaining Information

It is a pretty **daunting task** when thinking of **human genes contain too little information to specify which hemisphere of the brain,** in each of which occupy a human's 1011neurons, connects which neurons. (Premise)

For instance, **genes in human body contain so little information that specifying** each neuron's role is extremely **challenging.**

For such reasons, we can assume that there must be an important random factor in neural development. (Conclusion)

	A) Yes, because it supplies additional information about human body
	B) Yes, because it further elaborates the intricate, even cryptic, nature of the genes
√	**C) No, because it has already been mentioned**
	D) No, because specifying neuron's role should have been discussed earlier.

C) 1> The new sentence is almost identical with the previous sentence. Therefore, it shouldn't be added as it only creates a redundant error.

  2> The previous sentence is the premise for the following conclusion sentence, which should remain.

A) is opposite perception

B) For the very reason that it elaborates in an almost identical way, it should not be rewritten.

Q26. Absolute Pattern 24: Verb Tense / Voice Error

In particular, that errors [26] <u>must have occurred and do occur</u> in the development of all normal brains.

	A) must (occur) and actually occur	1> "have (OCCURRED) and actually occur" is the correct form.
√	**B) have and actually occur**	2> Choice B, however, intentionally dropped "occurred" to avoid redundancy.
	C) have occurred and actually did occur	3> Although avoiding a possible redundancy is a good gesture, it should have been understood that occurred" and "occur" are different from each other.
	D) must (occur) and will occur	4> That is, "occurred" is a participle, while "occur" is a verb, which can't be shared one another or removed.
		All remaining choices are grammatically correct.

Q27. PATTERN 21: Subject-Verb, Noun, Pronoun Agreement

[27] <u>The most vivid **expression** of such errors **occur** in genetically identical (isogenic) organisms.</u>

Subject — Verb

	A) NO CHANGE	1> Whatever comes after the preposition is not a subject (e.g., "**of** *such errors" is not a subject*)
√	**B) occurs in**	
	C) occur with	2> Therefore, the verb has to be the singular verb "occurs"
	D) occurring with	

Q28. Absolute Pattern 6: Confusing Words

Even when reared under the same conditions, isogenic organisms are [28] <u>rarely</u> exact copies of one another

√	**A) a little**	"A little" is used as a positive determiner (e.g., I have a little money.)
	B) hardly	The sentence is looking for a negative adverb that contains the meaning "almost never."
	C) barely	B), C), D) are all negative adverbs, synonym to "rarely"
	D) scarcely	

Q29. Absolute Pattern 1: Adding, Revising, Deleting, Retaining Information

(A) In isogenic Daphniae, for example, ...connectivity and the number of synapses varies greatly.
(B) This variability is probably the result of random scatter...conventionally called " precisions."
(C) *That is why genetic engineering is hard to study* as it should deal with more on isogenic Daphniae.
(D) Imprecision should be distinguished from developmental mistakes: wrongly migrated neurons,...

(C) While all the remaining sentences are describing the characteristic of Isogenic Daphne, and the causes of imprecision, choice C focuses on genetic engineering major in university described nowhere in the passage.

Q30. Absolute Pattern 5: Comma Splice Error

[30] <u>Let us use a computer analogy</u>, **minor rounding-off errors occur** universally and are analogous to imprecisions,   No conjunction   subject   verb

	A) NO CHANGE	1> The preceding portion of the sentence should not be an independent clause with a verb because
√	**B) To use a computer analogy,**	2> the main clause with the subject "minor rounding-off errors" and the verb "occur" has no conjunction to link the additional clause.
	C) Neuroscientists, for further clarification, use a computer analogy.	3> Therefore, the preceding portion of the sentence should remain as a phrase.
	D) Using a computer analogy can be a way to clarify this issue.	4> Except B, everything else is an independent sentence and will be the comma splice error if used.

Q31. Absolute Pattern 19: Redundant Error

Thus, imprecision is a form of inaccuracy, [31] <u>inherently</u> within the limits of design, but mistakes are forms of gross fallibility.

	A) which is both <u>Inherent and congenital</u>	"Inherent", "congenital" and "cognitive-development-al stage" are all synonyms.
	B) thereby <u>inherently congenital</u>	
√	**C) inherent**	
	D) that is <u>inherent from the</u> <u>cognitive</u>-developmental stage	

Q32. Absolute Pattern 15: Prepositional Idiom

[32]Either imprecision **and** gross fallibility can plausibly be blamed on the insufficiency of genetic information,

	A) NO CHANGE	"Both ~ and" is the idiom and can't be replaced with other forms.
√	**B) Both**	
	C) Neither	
	D) Together with	

Q33. Absolute Pattern 13: Parallel Structure

Most up-to-date virtual realities are displayed [33] *either a computer screen or on* a special virtual reality headset

	A) NO CHANGE	1> The correct idiom is "either ~ or"
	B) both on a computer screen or with	2> The structure within the idiom must be exactly the same.
√	**C) either on a computer screen or with**	3> In this case, maintaining the prepositional phrase between "either" and "or" is crucial.
	D) neither on a computer screen nor with	

A) 1> A preposition should be inserted between "either" and "a computer screen" like (C).

2> because "or" phrase carries "on", "either" phrase should also carry a preposition, such as "on."

B) The correct form of idiom is "both ~ and", not "both~ or"

D) is nonsensical.

Q34. Absolute Pattern 1: Adding, Revising, Deleting, Retaining Information

Furthermore, virtual reality **covers remote communication** environments, [34] <u>although unavailable at</u> <u>this</u> <u>time,</u> **either through the use of standard input devices such as** a wired glove or a keyboard and mouse, or through multimodal devices

	A) NO CHANGE	D) provides the directly related and grammatically intact information with the following phrase "either through the use of..."
	B) which allow people to communicate remotely	
	C) which are still at an embryonic stage	B) is redundant with the previous non-underlined portion "covers remote communication"
√	**D) which provide virtual presence of users**	A), C): are negative tone in the positive informative passage.

Q35. PATTERN 23: Transition Words / Phrase for Supporting Detail, Contrast, and Consequence

[35] <u>By far,</u> few contents are created that may be used for educational purposes,

	A) By far,	By far = a great amount of (e.g., Mammoth was by far the largest mammal.)
	B) So far,	B), C), and D) are all synonym.
√	**C) Currently,**	
	D) At present,	

Q36. Absolute Pattern 12: Modifier (Placement) Error

So far, few contents are created that may be used for educational purposes, [36] <u>with most advances</u> **are** <u>being</u> <u>made</u> in the entertainment industry,

	A) NO CHANGE	1> A), C) "with' is preposition that can't carry a clause with a verb.
√	**B) with the most advances being made**	2> Both "are" in (A) and "is" in (C) are verbs.
	C) with the most advancement <u>is</u>	
	D) <u>and</u> the most advances being made	D) starts with the conjunction "and" that requires a verb, which is not found in (D).

Q37. Absolute Pattern 1: Adding, Revising, Deleting, Retaining Information

So far, few contents are created that may be used for educational purposes, with most advances being made in the entertainment industry, but many understand and realize the importance of education and VR.

	A) The application of VR in entertainment	is minor information as is only slighted mentioned
√	**B) The application of VR in training**	is the primary theme of the paragraph
	C) The future of VR	C), D) are minor information as they are only part of the projection in broad theme of VR in education.
	D) The costs and other factors in VR	

Q38. Absolute Pattern 1: Adding, Revising, Deleting, Retaining Information

A fully immersive virtual reality and integrated system [38] that uses head-mounted display (HMD), data suits, data glove, and VR weapon are used to train for combat.

	A) Kept, because it helps visualize the sophisticated VR applications in many industries
√	**B) Kept, because it suggests the types of VR tools and accruements currently available**
	C) Deleted, because listing the tools is unnecessary and could distract the main point
	D) Deleted, because the tools are prototype currently unavailable

B) The underlined portion is about equipment that can be used along with VR system.

A) The paragraph focuses on the military usage, not on many other industries.

C) Listing the tools is necessary and does not distract the main point.

D) Tools are currently used, not the prototype.

Q39. Absolute Pattern 11: Logical Sequence

[39] (4)**VR is also used in flight simulation** for the Air Force where people are trained to be pilots. (3)**The flight simulator can range from** a fully enclosed module to a series of computer monitors providing the pilot's point of view. (1) **The simulator would sit** on top of a hydraulic lift system that reacts to the user inputs and events. (2)**When the pilot steers the aircraft**, the module would turn and tilt accordingly to the provided <u>haptic feedback</u>.

	A) NO CHANGE	In a sentence sequence question, always review your chosen option by reading from the backward order like 4>3>2>1. The reasoning behind this trick is that the conclusion is easier to understand than the introduction.
	B) (3)-(2)-(1)-(4)	
√	C) (4)-(3)-(1)-(2)	
	D) (4)-(1)-(2)-(3)	

Q40. Absolute Pattern 10: Logical Expression

The most important reasons for using simulators over learning with a real aircraft are the reduction of transference time between land training and real flight, the safety, economy and [40] <u>control</u> of pollution.

	A) absence	Generation of pollution is not logical and even nonsensical.
	B) reduction	
√	C) generation	
	D) elimination	

Q41. Absolute Pattern 4: Comparison

As these drivers often have [41] <u>better</u> experience than [42] <u>that of any other</u> truck drivers, virtual reality training allows them to compensate this.

	A) NO CHANGE	Experience is a non-countable noun. Therefore, "less" is correct. A) and C) are opposite from the sentence meaning. B) is used as a countable noun, such as drivers.
	B) fewer	
	C) more	
√	D) less	

Q42. Absolute Pattern 4: Comparison

As these drivers often have less experience than [42] <u>that of any other</u> truck drivers, virtual reality training allows them to compensate this.

	A) NO CHANGE	B) The sentence is comparing the experience between "these drivers" and "other truck drivers"
√	**B) other**	A) "that of" is unnecessary
	C) others	C) 'others' cannot link the following noun, 'drivers'.
	D) any other	D) "than any other" is used for the superlatives. That is, the sentence should contain both the best driver along with "these drivers."

Q43. Absolute Pattern 1: Adding, Revising, Deleting, Retaining Information

[43] <u>In the near future, similar projects are expected for all drivers to train prior to drive real vehicles.</u> The main theme of the passage is about VR, a state-of-the-art technology.

	A) No, because the paragraph loses the structural integrity
√	**B) No, because the passage loses how VR will evolve in the future**
	C) Yes, because the passage mainly focuses on present development and application
	D) Yes, because it does not provide a transition from the previous paragraph.

1> The last sentence predicts the future trends of VR.

2> As the passage moves towards the end, it focuses more on how the application will evolve.

3> Also, the primary role of the last paragraph—regardless of genre—is to help the readers to anticipate the outcome. This is generally acknowledged practice in writing. Therefore, there shouldn't be a problem in this question as well.

A) "structural integrity" and D) "transition" are basically referring to grammar issues, which are ambiguous for exactly what grammar is an issue.

Q44. Absolute Pattern 9: Informational Graphs

D) Increase in VR game does not necessarily mean decrease in existing online game industry.
A) The education application will experience 300% growth, the highest growth in its categories.
B) 11 Billion is the highest among other applications.
C) The automobile (6B) and medical (6.5B) are about the same category based on the sales volume.

SAT
Writing and Language
Test 6

ALL THE LOGIC AND RULES

BEHIND THE EVERY SINGLE

SAT QUESTION

Writing and Language Test 6
35 MINUTES, 44 QUESTIONS

Each passage below is accompanied by a number of questions. For some questions, you will consider how the passage might be revised to improve the expression of ideas. For other questions, you will consider how the passage might be edited to correct errors in sentence structure, usage, or punctuation. A passage or a question may be accompanied by one or more graphics (such as a table or graph) that you will consider as you make revising and editing decisions.

Questions 1-11 are based on the following passage.

On leaving home

I am well acquainted with my suitcase. After all, we've spent a lot of time together: [1] Its moved me back and forth between Canada and America, between my little hometown and a city where no one knows my name, between my parents' house and a college dorm and (most recently) a seedy summer apartment. I know that its wheels squeak at an uncomfortably high pitch. I know that its weight will bang into my calves at every other step [2] so that I skip and hobble in a particular way. canvas suitcase. I know that it exists to displace me—and for that I resent every durable green inch of [3] it for that reason. How tightly am I bound to my location?

1
A) NO CHANGE
B) It's
C) The suitcase
D) It was

2
A) NO CHANGE
B) unless
C) while
D) because

3
A) NO CHANGE
B) the suitcase.
C) it or that.
D) it.

CONTINUE

2

2

My life looks small [4] wraps in cardboard and canvas. Eventually, I can't look anymore.

I need to get out of this [5] used home. I grab my wallet and a map and, with pleasing randomness, decide to visit the Boston Harbor Islands. They seem far and inconvenient, and I am fed up with staying in one place.[6]

Two hours, two buses, and one subway ride later, I am standing inside the Boston Harbor Islands Ferry office. An older woman is in the process of closing the ticket kiosk, and seems annoyed by my presence. "The last ferry to the Islands left at one," she says curtly. Then, registering the look on my face, [7] we soften the atmosphere: "You could just catch the last ferry to Boston, though. There's a lot to do there."

First, I am bewildered. This isn't Boston? Where am I? When did I leave my city? The woman informs me that we are in Hingham, but I've never heard of the town.

4

A) NO CHANGE
B) and wraps
C) wrapping
D) wrapped

5

A) NO CHANGE
B) used to be home.
C) use to-be home.
D) used-to-be home.

6

The author is considering deleting the preceding underlined sentence. Should he make this deletion?

A) Yes, because the sentence contradicts to the narrator's longing for homesickness.
B) Yes, because the sentence contains the word "inconvenient" that the narrator wishes to avoid.
C) No, because the sentence is informative and contributes the narrator's longing for new experience.
D) No, because the sentence sets up the new place other than the narrator's current apartment

7

A) NO CHANGE
B) soften voice whispers:
C) I was softened by the atmosphere:
D) she softens the atmosphere:

CONTINUE

2

2

In desperation, I pull out my map and look for [8] something—anything—that looks interesting. The only destination [9] marked Nantasket Beach that even remotely fits the bill is a little spot on the coast.

I trudge back to the heat-baked highway and wait for the next bus. It takes me another two hours and the advice of a series of strangers, but I eventually make it to my destination.

[10] The sand stretches down from a raised sidewalk in pale sun-bleached yellow dotted with pink and blue umbrellas. The waves froth high enough to sweep even adults off their feet. Shouting kids and screaming gulls and crashing surf produce a beach sound [11] so perfect ,and it feels slightly surreal.

8

A) NO CHANGE
B) something, anything that looks
C) something anything that looks
D) something or anything that looks

9

The best placement for the underlined portion would be:

A) NO CHANGE
B) after the words the bill is
C) after the word that
D) after the word coast

10

At this point, the author wishes to add the following statement:

I grew up in a small beach village.

Would this be a relevant addition here?

A) Yes, because it functions as a topic sentence that link to the following descriptions.
B) Yes, because it informs Nantasket Beach is idyllic.
C) No, because the sentence does not properly link to the following descriptions.
D) No, because it implies that the author's visit is premeditated.

11

A) NO CHANGE
B) as to feel
C) with it feels
D) that it feels

CONTINUE ➡

2

2

Questions 12-22 are based on the following passage.

The new wave of British Heavy Metal

The new wave of British heavy metal (NWOBHM) was a nationwide musical movement that started in the United Kingdom in the late 1970s and [12] have achieved international attention by the early 1980s. Journalist Geoff Barton in a May 1979 [13] coined the term issue of the British music newspaper

Sounds to describe the emergence of new heavy metal bands in the late 1970s, during the period of punk rock's decline and the dominance of new wave music.

Although encompassing [14] variously diversified mainstream and underground styles, the music of the NWOBHM is best remembered for drawing on the heavy metal of the 1970s and infusing [15] it with the intensity of punk rock to produce fast and aggressive songs.

The DIY attitude of the new metal bands led to the spread of raw-sounding, self-produced recordings and [16] a proliferation of independent record labels. Song lyrics were usually about escapist themes such as mythology, fantasy, horror and the rock lifestyle.

12
A) NO CHANGE
B) achieved
C) has achieved
D) has been achieving

13
The best placement for the underlined portion would be:
A) NO CHANGE
B) after the word Geoff Barton
C) after the word newspaper
D) after the word 1970s,

14
A) NO CHANGE
B) diversified in various
C) diverse
D) DELET IT

15
A) NO CHANGE
B) them
C) NWOBHM
D) OMIT the underlined portion

16
A) NO CHANGE
B) independent record labels were proliferated.
C) a proliferation of independent record labels was followed.
D) record labels were proliferated independently.

2

The NWOBHM began as an underground phenomenon growing in parallel to punk but largely ignored by the media. [17] The movement involved mostly young, white, male and working-class musicians and fans, who suffered the hardships brought on by rising unemployment for years after the 1973–75 recession. As a reaction to [18] their bleak reality, they created a community separate from mainstream society to enjoy each other's company and their favourite loud music.

The NWOBHM was heavily criticized for the excessive hype generated by local media in favour of mostly talentless musicians. [19] Consequently, it generated a renewal in the genre of heavy metal music and furthered the progress of the heavy metal subculture, whose updated behavioural and visual codes were quickly adopted by metal fans worldwide after the spread of the music to continental Europe, North America and Asia.

17

At this point, the author wants to add the following sentence:

> It was only through the promotion of rock DJ Neal Kay and *Sounds'* campaigning that it reached the public consciousness and gained radio airplay, recognition and success in the UK.

Would the author make this addition here?

A) Yes, because it provides an important link to the rest of the paragraph.

B) Yes, because it connects well with the previous sentence telling the reason for its unpopularity in the music industry.

C) No, because it strays from the main focus of the essay.

(D) No, because it is directly contradicted to the previous sentence.

18

(A) NO CHANGE

B) NWOBHM's

C) its

D) public's

19

A) NO CHANGE

(B) Nonetheless,

C) For example,

D) Soon,

2

2

The movement spawned perhaps a thousand metal bands [20] ; subsequently, only a few survived the advent of MTV and the rise of the more commercial glam metal in the second half of the 1980s. Among them, Iron Maiden and Def Leppard became international stars. Other groups, such as Diamond Head, Venom and Raven, remained underground, but were a major influence on the successful extreme metal subgenres of the late 1980s and 1990s.[21]

U.K. Album Sales by Genre (in millions)			
	2014	2015	2016
Heavy Metal	29.79	27.82	24.23
Country	47.66	46.13	43.72
Electronic	-	-	8.74
Latin	25.13	16.5	12.35
R&B	77.01	69.89	57.87
Rock	139.6	124.16	103.71
Pop	233	266	299
Alternative	80.92	68.2	53.73
Classical	13.32	12.14	8.96
Jazz	11.79	11.78	8.78

20

A) NO CHANGE
B) ,however,
C) ,and
D) ,but

21

Which choice, if added here, would most effectively conclude the essay?

A) Many bands from the NWOBHM reunited in the 2000s and remained active through live performances and new studio albums.
B) Some critics in 1970s viewed NWOBHM as the significant exponent of the movement
C) Foreign hard rock acts, such as Kiss from the US, Rush from Scorpions from Germany, and especially AC/DC from Australia, climbed the British charts in the same period
D) Each of these bands was in crisis in the mid-to-late 1970s.

22

Given that all of the followings are true, which interpretation would most clearly reflect the passage and the table?

A) Heavy Metal, albeit active in the 2010s, is not getting attention from music industry.
B) Heavy Metal, albeit insignificant in sales, proved to be continuing to increase in sales
C) Heavy Metal, albeit not a major genre, was not the only one experienced decline in sales.
D) Critics, seeking the greatest benefit ,paid more attention on Pop than Heavy Metal

CONTINUE

2

2

Questions 23-33 are based on the following passage.

The Tower of Pisa

The Leaning Tower of Pisa *or simply the Tower of Pisa* is freestanding bell tower of the cathedral of the Italian city of Pisa [23] , and it is known worldwide for its unintended tilt.   [24] Situated behind Pisa's cathedral and is the third oldest structure in the city's Cathedral Square. The tower's tilt began during construction, caused by an inadequate foundation on ground too soft on one side to properly support the structure's weight. [25] Galileo Galilei is said to have dropped two cannonballs of different masses from the tower to demonstrate that [26] its speed of descent was independent of their mass. However, the only primary source for this is the biography *Racconto istorico della vita di Galileo*, written by Galileo's secretary Vincenzo Viviani and published in 1717, long after Viviani's death.

23

A) NO CHANGE
B) which is known
C) , known
D) as known

24

A) NO CHANGE
B) It is situated
C) Being situated
D) The Tower of Pisa, situated

25

If the author wish to delete the underlined portion of the sentence, the paragraph would probably lose:

A) the fascinating feature that attracts tourists from around the world
B) a distinctive look that people talk about the tower
C) the main reason for its look
D) a specific detail that adds serious structural defects behind the construction

26

A) NO CHANGE
B) their
C) it has
D) they have

CONTINUE

2

2

During World War II, the Allies discovered that the Germans were using the tower as an observation post. A U.S. Army sergeant sent to confirm the presence of German troops in the tower [27] which was impressed by the beauty of the cathedral, and thus refrained [28] to order an artillery strike, sparing it from destruction. Numerous efforts have been made to restore the tower to a vertical orientation or at least keep it from falling over. Most of these efforts [29] failed; some worsened the tilt. On February 27, 1964, the government of Italy requested aid in preventing the tower from toppling. [30] Consequently, [31] these people considered important to retain the current tilt, due to the role that this element played in promoting the tourism industry of Pisa.

27

A) NO CHANGE

B) who was impressed

C) was impressed

D) impressed

28

A) NO CHANGE

B) that by ordering

C) from ordering

D) and ordered

29

A) NO CHANGE

B) failed: some worsened the tilt.

C) failed, some worsened the tilt.

D) failed with some worsened the tilt.

30

A) After all

B) However,

C) Nonetheless,

D) Moreover,

31

A) NO CHANGE

B) They were considered

C) It was considered

D) The Italian government considered

CONTINUE

2

A multinational task force of engineers, mathematicians, and historians gathered on the Azores islands to discuss the stabilization methods. <1> It was found that the tilt was increasing in combination with the softer foundations on the lower side. <2> Many methods were proposed to stabilize the tower, including the addition of 800 tonces of lead counterweights to the raised end of the base. <3> The tower and the neighboring cathedral baptistery, and cemetery have been included in the Piazza del DuomoUNESCO World Heritage Site, which was declared in 1987. <4> The tower was closed to the public on January 7, 1990, after more than two decades of stabilization studies and spurred by the abrupt collapse of the Civic Tower of Pavia in 1989. The bells were removed to relieve some weight, and cables were cinched around the third level and anchored several hundred meters away. Apartments and houses in the path of the tower were vacated for safety. The solution chosen to prevent the collapse of the tower was to slightly straighten it to a safer angle by removing 38 cubic metres (1,342 cubic feet) of soil from underneath the raised end.

32

Which of the following sentences is diverting from the main issue in this paragraph?

A) <1>
B) <2>
C) <3>
D) <4>

33

Suppose the author's goal was to write a brief summary describing the timeline of stabilizing the Tower of Pisa.

Would this summary accomplish his goal?

A) Yes, because it details the unique and effortful undertaking made by many scientists including Galilei Galileo

B) Yes, because it chronicles the important events of the project including some debates to stabilize the Tower.

C) No, because it focuses on the historical overview of the leaning Tower with an initial effort to stabilize it.

D) No, because the historical figure like Galileo Galilei's experiment was the main concern.

CONTINUE

2   2

Questions 34-44 are based on the following passage.

Can Dark Knight Rise Again?

Entrepreneur Major Malcolm Wheeler founded National Allied Publications in autumn 1934. The company debuted with the tabloid-sized *New Fun: The Big Comic Magazine* #1 with a cover date of February 1935. The company's second [34] title, *New Comics* #1, appeared in a size close to what would become [35] comic books standard during the period fans and historians [36] call the Golden Age of Comic [37] Books with slightly larger dimensions than today's. That title evolved into *Adventure Comics*, which continued through issue #503 in 1983, becoming one of the longest-running comic-book series. In 2009 DC revived *Adventure Comics* with its original numbering.

34

A) NO CHANGE
B) title, *New Comics* #1
C) title *New Comics* #1,
D) title *New Comics* #1

35

A) NO CHANGE
B) comic's books standard
C) comic's books' standard
D) comic books' standard

36

A) NO CHANGE
B) calls
C) were calling
D) had called

37

A) NO CHANGE
B) Books: with slightly larger
C) Books, with slightly larger
D) Books; slightly larger

CONTINUE ▶

In 1935, Joe Shuster, the future creators of Superman, created Doctor Occult, [38] who was the earliest DC Comics character to still be in the DC Universe. The themed anthology series would become a sensation with the introduction of Batman (May 1939). [39] By then, however, Wheeler-Nicholson had gone. In 1937, in debt to printing-plant owner [40] , Harry Donenfeld—who also published pulp magazines and operated as a principal in the magazine distributorship Independent News—Wheeler-Nicholson had to take Donenfeld on as a partner in order to publish *Detective Comics* #1.

Two DC limited series, *Batman: The Dark Knight Returns* by Frank Miller and *Watchmen* by Moore and artist Dave Gibbons, drew attention in the mainstream press for their [41] dark psychological complexity and promotion of the antihero. These titles helped pave the way for comics to be more widely accepted in literary-criticism circles and to make inroads into the book industry, with collected editions of these series as commercially success-ful trade paperbacks

38
A) NO CHANGE
B) whom was
C) which was
D) who is

39
A) NO CHANGE
B) Since then,
C) After then,
D) Later then,

40
A) NO CHANGE
B) Harry Donenfeld—who
C) , Harry Donenfeld, who
D) Harry Donenfeld who

41
A) NO CHANGE
B) dark psychology, complexity, and promotional
C) dark psychology, complex, and promotion
D) dark psychologically and complexly promotional

CONTINUE ➜

2   2

The comics industry experienced a brief boom in the early 1990s, thanks to a combination of speculative purchasing [42] and several storylines which gained attention from the mainstream media.

DC's extended storylines in which Superman was killed, Batman was crippled, and superhero *Green Lantern* turned into the supervillain Parallax resulted in dramatically increased sales, but the increases were as temporary as the hero's replacements. Sales dropped off as the industry went into a major slump [43] , while manufactured "collectibles" numbering in the millions replaced [44] imagination and reality until fans and speculators alike deserted the medium in droves.

42

At this point, the author wishes to add the following true sentence:

(mass purchase of the books as collectible items, with intent to resell at a higher value as the rising value of older issues was thought to imply that *all* comics would rise dramatically in price)

Should he make this addition here?

A) Yes, because it clarifies what the speculative purchasing is.

B) Yes, because it describes one of consequences that the comics industry benefited from a brief boom in the early 1990s.

C) No, because it would distract readers from the main focus of the paragraph.

D) No, because it creates confusion with the following phrase "and several storylines media.

43

Which of the following alternatives is NOT an acceptable alternative?

A) , and

B) ; in the meantime

C) , but

D) , and simultaneously

44

A) NO CHANGE

B) imagination in reality

C) real imagination

D) imagination with reality

TEST 6

WRITING ABSOLUTE PATTERNS

Test 6 Writing & Language Section Patterns

Q1. Absolute Pattern 17: Pronoun Error

I am well acquainted with my suitcase. After all, **we've spent** a lot of time together: [1] <u>Its</u> moved me back and forth between Canada and America, between my little hometown and a city where **no one knows** my name, between my parents' house and a college dorm and (most recently) a seedy summer apartment.

	A) NO CHANGE	B) 1> It's = It has.
√	**B) It's**	2> Because the overall tense (I am, we've spent, no one knows) surrounding the sentence is present tense, the answer should also be the present tense.
	C) The suitcase	A) "Its" is the singular possessive pronoun. Ex) My house is expensive. Its (my house) wall is made of gold.
	D) It was	C) is repeating, redundant error. D) "It was" is past tense.

Q2. Absolute Pattern 23: Transition Words for Supporting Detail, Contrast, and Consequence

Passage: **I know that** its weight will bang into my calves at every other step [2] <u>so that</u> I skip and hobble in a particular way. canvas suitcase.

	A) NO CHANGE	B) 1> A conditional clause 'unless' shows an action will occur if the other action doesn't follow.
√	**B) unless**	2> Synonyms to unless that carry conditional clause are: *But *Except *Saving *If not *Lest *Without *Unless
	C) while	
	D) because	A) [so that] is used to express the consequence in a cause-and-effect situation. C) [while] is used either in a concessional clause like "in the meantime" or synonym to 'during.' (e.g.,) The poor see their income shrink while the rich see it rises. D) [because] is used to the cause-and-effect

Q3. Absolute Pattern 19: Redundant Error

Passage: I know that it exists to displace me—and **for that** I resent every durable green inch of [3] it for that reason.

→ redundancy ←

	A) NO CHANGE	D) The pronoun "it" refers to narrator's suitcase
	B) the suitcase.	A) "for that reason." is repeating.
	C) it or that.	B) "the suitcase" repeating.
√	**D) it.**	C) "that" is used as a demonstrative pronoun, making "that" unclear.

Q4. Absolute Pattern 10: Logical Expression

Passage: My life looks small [4] wraps in cardboard and canvas.

	A) NO CHANGE	D) My life looks small [4] (*as if My life is being*) **wrapped** in cardboard and canvas.
	B) and wraps	
	C) wrapping	A) "wraps" is a verb. The main verb 'looks' is already stated.
√	**D) wrapped**	B) "and wraps" becomes a verb after the conjunction 'and,.
		C) "wrapping" is used for an on-going situation as if my life is wrapping...

Q 5. Absolute Pattern 18: Punctuation Error

Passage: I need to get out of this [5] used home.

	A) NO CHANGE	D) 1> Hyphenation links two or more words when they come as a single idea before a noun.
	B) used to be home.	2> This is called a **compound adjective**.
	C) used to-be home.	A) [used home.] changes the original meaning.
√	**D) used-to-be home.**	B) [used to be home.] by having no hyphens, all these words are acting independently.
		C) [used to-be home.] is missing one hyphen, so it changes the meaning.

Q6. Absolute Pattern 1: Adding, Revising, Deleting, Retaining Information

	Passage: They seem far and inconvenient, and I am fed up with staying in one place.[6]
	A) Yes, because the sentence contradicts to the narrator's longing for homesickness.
	B) Yes, because the sentence contains the "inconvenient" that the narrator wishes to avoid.
√	C) No, because the sentence contributes the **narrator's longing for new experience**.
	D) No, because the sentence sets up the new place other than the narrator's current apartment

C) "I need to get out of this used-to-be home. I grab my wallet and a map and, **with pleasing randomness,** decide to visit the Boston Harbor Islands. **They seem far and inconvenient, and I am fed up** with staying in one place."

The preceding sentence reveals the narrator's decision and his longing for a new experience.

A) "homesickness" is opposite word usage based on the author's emotion.

B) is opposite emotion. The author wishes to escape from his convenient used-to-be home.

D) The author isn't moving out. He just wants to travel.

Q7. Absolute Pattern 12: Modifier Placement Error

Then, registering the look on my face, [7] we soften the atmosphere: "

	A) NO CHANGE	D) 1> Two people are conversing: the ticket counter clerk and the author.
	B) soften voice whispers:	2> The preceding modifier and the following quote indicate that the clerk is looking at the author's face.
	C) I was softened by the atmosphere:	A) The subject shouldn't be 'we' because one person is supposed to look on the other person's face.
√	**D) she softens the atmosphere:**	B) 1> The subject needs to be human.
		2> 'a soften voice' isn't human that can register.
		C) The subject, "I" can't be the same person in the modifier who is registering the look on his own face.

Q8. Absolute Pattern 18: Punctuation Error

In desperation, I pull out my map and look for [8] something—anything—that looks interesting.

√	**A) NO CHANGE**	A) 1> The main function of a dash is very simple and straightforward: It separates and signifies the word (s), phrase, or clause being interjected in the middle of the sentence.
	B) something, anything that looks	2> In this manner, the function of a pair of dashes is similar to that of a pair of commas.
	C) something anything that looks	3> However, a dash is easy-to-identify so that it impresses the readers.
	D) something or any thing that looks	4> By putting the dashes between 'anything,' the narrator impresses the reader for how desperate he is.

B) It should be a double-commas. The latter part of commas is missing.

C) 'anything' should be separated from the main sentence

D) changes the meaning

Q9. Absolute Pattern 12: Modifier Placement Error

The only destination [9] marked Nantasket Beach that even remotely fits the bill is a little spot on the coast.

	A) NO CHANGE	D) Placing the name right next to the coast can be the best way to modify and describe the coast.
	B) after the words the bill is	A) "marked" becomes the verb
	C) after the word that	B) "bill" and "marked Nantasket Beach" become a phrase that are associated with each other.
√	**D) after the word coast**	C) changes the original meaning.

Q10. Absolute Pattern 1: Adding, Revising, Deleting, Retaining Information

Question: I grew up in a small beach village.

	A) Yes, because it functions as the topic that link to the following descriptions.	C) The following sentences are all about Nantasket Beach and don't link to the narrator's small beach.
	B) Yes, because it informs Nantasket Beach is idyllic.	
√	**C) No, because the sentence does not link to the following descriptions.**	A) It can't function as the topic.
		B) is inconsistent with the question
	D) No, because it implies that the author's visit is premeditated.	D) The author came to the beach by accident.

Q11. Absolute Pattern 23: Transition Words for Supporting Detail, Contrast, and Consequence

Shouting kids and screaming gulls and crashing surf produce a beach sound [11] **so** perfect ,and it feels slightly surreal.

	A) NO CHANGE	D) so ~ that clause
	B) as to feel	A) 1> so ~ that clause is cause-and-effect clause 2> "and" can't replace "that"
	C) with it feels	B) "so ~as" is used to connect a phrase, not a clause. 'to' is preposition for phrase.
√	**D) that it feels**	C) 'with' is preposition. The following clause can't be linked with a preposition.

Q12. Absolute Pattern 24: Verb Tense / Voice Error

The new wave of British heavy metal (NWOBHM) was a nationwide musical movement that started in the United Kingdom in the late **1970s** and [12] have achieved international attention **by** the early **1980s.**

	A) NO CHANGE	C) 1> "by..." is used for time adverbial phrase that requires either the past perfect or the present perfect tense.
	B) achieved	2> In this sentence, using the present perfect is correct because "by the early 1980s" is being compared with "1970s," which uses the simple past tense.
√	**C) has achieved**	3> The subject "the new wave" is singular.
	D) has been achieving	4> So, It needs a singular verb, "has achieved"
		B) 1970 and 1980 can't use the same tense. D) 'achieving' is a progressive tense.

Q13. Absolute Pattern 11: Logical Sequence

Journalist Geoff Barton in **a** May 1979 [13]coined the term **issue of the British music newspaper** *Sounds* to describe the emergence of new heavy metal bands in the late 1970s, during the period of punk rock's decline and the dominance of new wave music.

	A) NO CHANGE	B) The correct sentence is:
√	**B) after the word Geoff Barton**	Journalist Geoff **Barton** *coined* the term in **a** May 1979 **issue of the British music newspaper** *Sounds* to describe the emergence of new heavy metal bands in the late 1970s,
	C) after the word newspaper	A) 1> The original sentence "the term issue" are a noun + a noun, which can't be correct.
	D) after the word 1970s,	2> "**a**" in "in **a** May 1979" indicates the phrase is linked to **"issue of the British music newspaper *Sounds*"**
		C), D) "~1979" phrase and "issue of ~" phrase do not link together.

Q14. Absolute Pattern 19: Redundant Error

Although encompassing [14] variously diversified mainstream and underground styles, the music of the NWOBHM is best remembered for drawing on the heavy metal of the 1970s and infusing [15] it with the intensity of punk rock to produce fast and aggressive songs.

	A) NO CHANGE	C) "diverse," the adjective describes the noun "mainstream".
	B) diversified in various	A), B) "Variously" and "diversified" are synonyms, creating a redundant error.
√	**C) diverse**	D) changes the meaning.
	D) DELETE IT	

Q15. Absolute Pattern 21: Subject-Verb, Pronoun, Noun Agreement

Although encompassing various mainstream and underground styles, the music of the NWOBHM is best remembered for drawing on the heavy metal of the 1970s and infusing [15] it with the intensity of punk rock to produce fast and aggressive songs

√	A) NO CHANGE	A) The pronoun 'it' refers to the music of the NWOBHM.
	B) them	B) The music of the NWOBHM is singular. 'them' is plural
	C) NWOBHM	C) "NWOBHM" already took its position in the main clause and can't be written again in the subordinating clause that can cause a redundant error.
	D) OMIT the underlined portion	D) 'Infusing' requires an object.

Q16. Absolute Pattern 13: Parallel Structure

The DIY attitude of the new metal bands led to **the spread of** raw-sounding, **self-produced recordings** and [16] **a proliferation of** independent record labels. Song lyrics were usually about escapist themes such as mythology, fantasy, horror and the rock lifestyle.

√	A) NO CHANGE	A) The sentence maintains the parallel structure. The original sentence is a series of phrases.
	B) independent record labels were proliferated.	B), C), D are clauses.
	C) a proliferation of independent record labels was followed.	
	D) record labels were proliferated independently.	

Q17. Absolute Pattern 1: Adding, Revising, Deleting, Retaining Information

It was only through the promotion of rock DJ Neal Kay and *Sounds'* campaigning that it reached the public consciousness and gained radio airplay, recognition and success in the UK.

√	**A) Yes, because it provides an important link to the rest of the paragraph.**
	B) Yes, because it connects well with the previous sentence telling the reason for its unpopularity in the music industry.
	C) No, because it strays from the main focus of the essay.
	D) No, because it directly contradicts from the previous sentence.

A) The sentence begins with a negative tone, and then a concession follows, "it was only through"...

Finally, it further introduces how it affected a groups of people in the society positively.

B) 1> The previous sentence is negative tone.

2> the added information is positive tone.

3> Therefore, the added information functions as a concessional clause to connect to the rest of the paragraph.

C), D) The tone and information of this sentence help moving from the previous negative tone to the following positive tone.

Q18. Absolute Pattern 21: Subject-Verb, Pronoun, Noun Agreement

As a reaction to [18] their bleak reality, they created a community separate from mainstream society to enjoy each other's company and their favorite loud music.

√	**A) NO CHANGE**	B) calling its own name is illogical and unnatural.
	B) NWOBHM's	C) is singular pronoun
	C) its	D) The sentence changes its meaning to "public's bleak reality"
	D) public's	

Q19. Absolute Pattern 23: Transition Words for Supporting Detail, Contrast, and Consequence

[19] <u>Consequently,</u> it generated a renewal in the genre of heavy metal music and furthered the progress of the heavy metal subculture, whose updated behavioral and visual codes were quickly adopted by metal fans world-wide after the spread of the music to continental Europe, North America and Asia.

	A) NO CHANGE	B) 1> The previous sentence is negative: The NWOBHM was **heavily criticized** for the excessive hype...
√	**B) Nonetheless,**	2> The following sentence is positive: <u>Nonetheless</u> it generated a renewal...
	C) For example,	3> "nonetheless" is concessional adverb that links (-/+) clauses.
	D) Soon,	A) is used for cause-and-effect.

A) is used for cause-and-effect.

C) is used to support the previous sentence in parallel tone.

D) adverb 'soon' works in a time sequence.

The list of concessional adverbs					
Nevertheless	However	Despite of	Though	Even so	Still

Q20. Absolute Pattern 23: Transition Words for Supporting Detail, Contrast, and Consequence

The movement spawned perhaps **a thousand metal bands** [20] <u>; subsequently,</u> **only a few survived** the advent of MTV and the rise of the more commercial glam metal in the second half of the 1980s.

	A) NO CHANGE	A) and C) are ruled out because two clauses show a clear contradiction. 'subsequently' is used for a cause-and-effect situation.
	B) ,however,	
	C) ,and	B) The correct form of 'however' is ;however,
√	**D) ,but**	C) 'and' is used in parallel situation.

Q21. Absolute Pattern 1: Adding, Revising, Deleting, Retaining Information

Question: Which choice, if added here, would most effectively conclude the essay?

√	**A) Many bands from the NWOBHM reunited in the 2000s and remained active through live performances and new studio albums.**
	B) Some critics in 1970s viewed NWOBHM as the significant exponent of the movement
	C) Foreign hard rock acts, such as Kiss from the US, Rush from Canada, Scorpions from Germany, and especially AC/DC from Australia, climbed the British charts in the same period
	D) Each of these bands was in crisis in the mid-to-late 1970s.

A) follows the chronological sequence.

B) is too extreme for the underground.

C) 1> Foreign groups are out-of-scope.

    2> The central theme of the passage is NWOBHM, the British underground musical bands.

D) The overall tone of the passage is positive. Therefore, the final sentence can't be negative.

Q22. Absolute Pattern 9: Informational Graphs

Given that all of the followings are true, which interpretation would most clearly reflect the passage and the table?

	A) Heavy Metal, albeit active in the 2010s, is <u>not getting attention </u>from music industry.
	B) Heavy Metal, albeit insignificant in sales, proved to be <u>continuing to increase </u>in sales
√	C) Heavy Metal, albeit not a major genre, was **not the only one** experienced decline in sales.
	D) Critics, seeking the greatest benefit ,paid more attention on Pop than Heavy Metal

C) All the rest musical genre except Pop experienced decrease in sales.

A) The sales record proves it gets a decent attention.

B) It continued to decrease three years in a row.

D) Not stated in the table.

Q23. Absolute Pattern 16: Precision, Concision, Style

The Leaning Tower of Pisa *or simply the Tower of Pisa* is freestanding bell tower of the cathedral of the Italian city of Pisa [23] , and it is known worldwide for its unintended tilt.

	A) NO CHANGE	A) "and it is" is unnecessary, causing a wordiness error.
	B) which is known	B) 1> "which is" is unnecessary. 2> It is non-restrictive and requires comma before "which"
√	C) , known	D) "as" is unnecessary and ambiguous.
	D) as known	

Q24. Absolute Pattern 21: Subject-Verb, Pronoun, Noun Agreement

[24] Situated behind Pisa's cathedral and is the third oldest structure in the city's Cathedral Square.

	A) NO CHANGE	A) and C) have no subject and verb.
√	B) It is situated	D) Subject "The Tower of Pisa" is separated from its verb "situated" by a comma, making an incomplete sentence.
	C) Being situated	
	D) The Tower of Pisa, situated	

Q25. Absolute Pattern 1: Adding, Revising, Deleting, Retaining Information

If the author wishes to delete the underlined portion of the sentence, the paragraph would probably lose:

	A) the fascinating feature that attracts tourists from around the world
	B) a distinctive look that people talk about the tower
√	C) the main reason for its look
	D) a specific detail that adds serious structural defects behind the construction

C) The underlined portion of the sentence briefly tells the reason for its tilt.

A) and B) are not mentioned, and inconsistent with the question

D) The sentence doesn't provide specific details.

Q26. Absolute Pattern 17: Pronoun Error

Galileo Galilei is said to have dropped two cannonballs of different masses from the tower to demonstrate that [26] its speed of descent was independent of their mass.

	A) NO CHANGE	B) 'their' speed refers to the two cannonballs.
√	**B) their**	A) and C), "it", the singular pronoun, can't represent two cannonballs.
	C) it has	D) The verb, 'was' is already active in the sentence.
	D) they have	

Q27. Absolute Pattern 21: Subject-Verb, Pronoun, Noun Agreement

Passage: **U.S. Army sergeant** (who was) sent to confirm the presence of German troops in the tower [27] which **was impressed** by the beauty of the cathedral, and thus refrained [28] to order an artillery strike, sparing it from destruction.

	A) NO CHANGE	C) 1> When two verbs are shown in one sentence, the latter one is almost always the real verb.
	B) who was impressed	2> In this sentence, "was impressed", not "sent" is the main verb.
√	**C) was impressed**	A) 'which' needs to be omitted.
	D) impressed	B) 'who' needs to be omitted.
		D) "by the beauty of the cathedral" indicates the verb should be passive

Q28. Absolute Pattern 15: Prepositional Idiom

Passage: A U.S. Army sergeant sent to confirm the presence of German troops in the tower was impressed by the beauty of the cathedral, and thus refrained [28] to order an artillery strike, sparing it from destruction.

	A) NO CHANGE	C) 'refrain ~ from' is the correct version.
	B) that by ordering	A) is the prepositional idiom error.
√	**C) from ordering**	B) 'that' carries a clause, not a phrase.
	D) and ordered	D) changes the meaning of the sentence

Q29. Absolute Pattern 18: Punctuation Error

Most of these efforts [29] failed; some worsened the tilt.

√	**A) NO CHANGE**	A) The semicolon shows two contrasting views.
	B) failed: some worsened the tilt.	B) 1> The colon is used to introduce things.
	C) failed, some worsened the tilt.	2> This sentence, however, simply divides two clauses into two groups: some effort failed while some got worsen.
	D) failed with some worsened the tilt	C) is comma splice error. D) "with" is preposition that can't carry another clause.

Q 30. Absolute Pattern 23: Transition Words for Supporting Detail, Contrast, and Consequence

Passage: [30] Consequently, [31] these people considered important to retain the current tilt, due to the role that this element played in promoting the tourism industry of Pisa.

	A) After all	B) The sentence reveals people's conflicting view concerning the Tower.
√	**B) However,**	A) 'consequently' and 'after all' are used for the cause-and-effect.
	C) Nonetheless,	C) 'Nonetheless' is used to a seemingly contradictory situation and then eventually emphasizes it.
	D) Moreover,	D) 'Moreover' is used to emphasize the previous statement.

Q31. Absolute Pattern 16: Precision, Concision, Style

However, [31] these people considered important to retain the current tilt, due to the role that this element played in promoting the tourism industry of Pisa.

	A) NO CHANGE	A) 1> "these people" are used for the first time in this sentence. 2> It is ambiguous who "these people" are.
	B) They were considered	
	C) It was considered	B) For the same reasoning as A) "They" can't be used.
√	**D) The Italian government considered**	C) 1> The verb "considered" needs to have an object. 2> Therefore, it is ambiguous.

Q 32. Absolute Pattern 11: Logical Sequence

A multinational task force of engineers gathered on the Azores islands to discuss the **stabilization methods**. <1> It was found that **the tilt** was increasing. <2> Many methods were proposed to **stabilize the tower**. <3> The tower has been included in the Piazza del DuomoUNESCO **World Heritage Site**. <4> The tower was closed after more than two decades of **stabilization** studies.

	A) <1>	C) 1> The keywords in surrounding sentences are directly related with the stabilization of the Tower.
	B) <2>	2> UNESCO **World Heritage** Site is not at all related issue.
√	**C) <3>**	
	D) <4>	

Q33. Absolute Pattern 1: Adding, Revising, Deleting, Retaining Information

Suppose the author's goal was to write a brief summary describing the timeline of stabilizing the Tower of Pisa.

	A) Yes, because it details the unique and effortful undertaking made by many scientists <u>including</u> <u>Galilei Galileo</u>
√	B) Yes, because it chronicles the important events of the project including **some debates to stabilize the Tower.**
	C) No, because it focuses on the historical overview of the leaning Tower <u>with</u> an initial effort to stabilize it.
	D) No, because historical figure like <u>Galileo Galilei</u>'s experiment was the main concern

B) The primary concern in this passage is about stabilizing the Tower of Pisa.

A), D) both statements are untrue.

C) An effort to stabilize the Tower takes up more than half of the passage. It is not a minor issue.

Q34. Absolute Pattern 22 : Non-Restrictive Modifier (Inessential Information)

The company's second [34] title, *New Comics #1,* appeared in a size close to what would become
[35] comic books standard

√	**A) NO CHANGE**	A) 1> "*New Comics #1*" doesn't make the sentence incomplete.
	B) title, *New Comics #1*	2> Therefore, it's inessential information.
		3> It needs to be offset by a pair of commas.
	C) title *New Comics #1,*	B) and C) are using only a single comma.
		D) has no comma.
	D) title *New Comics #1*	

Q 35. Absolute Pattern 14: Possessive Determiners and Possessive Noun Error

The company's second title, *New Comics #1,* appeared in a size close to what would become
[35] comic books standard during the period

	A) NO CHANGE	D) Comic books' standard is the correct possessive form
	B) comic's books standard	A) "comic books" and "standard" are nouns that require a connector
	C) comic's books' standard	
√	**D) comic books' standard**	B) and C) apply the wrong possessive forms

Q 36. Absolute Pattern 24: Verb Tense / Voice Error

The company's second title, *New Comics #1,* appeared in a size close to what would become comic books'
standard during the period fans and historians [36] call the Golden Age

√	**A) NO CHANGE**	A) "call" can represent either "(would) call", showing the frequency of the people's reaction in the past or "call" as the demonstrative simple tense.
	B) calls	
	C) were calling	B) is singular
		C) is progressive tense, which is wrong because it can only be used for a short continuous action.
	D) had called	
		D) is past perfect tense

Q 37. Absolute Pattern 18: Punctuation Error

The company's second title, *New Comics* #1, appeared in a size close to what would become comic books' standard during the period fans and historians call the Golden Age of Comic [37] Books with slightly large dimensions **than** today's.

	A) NO CHANGE	C) ",with slightly larger" uses the correct punctuation.
	B) Books: with slightly larger	A) doesn't use a comparison, but it should for the sake of "than".
√	C) Books, with slightly larger	B), D) Colon or semicolon can't be used along with the preposition 'with', unless "with" introduces a series of words.
	D) Books; slightly larger	

Q38. Absolute Pattern 7: Conjunction Error

In 1935, Joe Shuster, the future creators of Superman, created Doctor Occult, [38] who was the earliest DC Comics character to still be in the DC Universe.

	A) NO CHANGE	C) "Doctor Occult" is a character created by Joe Shuster. Therefore, it is non–human, and should be linked to "which."
	B) whom was	
√	C) which was	A) B) and D) who is used for a human precedent.
	D) who is	

Q39. Absolute Pattern 12: Modifier Placement Error

Passage: [39] By then, however, Wheeler-Nicholson **had gone.**

√	A) NO CHANGE	A) 'by,' in time adverbial phrase carries either the present perfect or the past perfect tense.
	B) Since then,	B) 'Since then' is normally used with the present perfect tense, unless two time adverbial phrases are compared in a sentence.
	C) After then,	C) and D) 'After than' and 'later then' are normally used with the simple past tense.
	D) Later then,	

Q40. Absolute Pattern 18: Punctuation Error

Passage: In 1937, in debt to printing-plant owner [40] **, Harry Donenfeld—who also published pulp magazines and operated as a principal in the magazine distributorship Independent News**—Wheeler-Nicholson had to take Donenfeld on as a partner in order to publish *Detective Comics* #1.

	A) NO CHANGE	B) 1> The primary clause with the subject "Wheeler-Nicholson" comes after the modifier.
√	**B) Harry Donenfeld—who**	2> The sentence states that "the printing-plant owner" and "Harry Donenfeld" is the same person.
	C) , Harry Donenfeld, who	3> Therefore, a comma shouldn't separate these two words; otherwise, "Harry Donenfeld" will be the subject.
	D) Harry Donenfeld	A) and C) are incorrect for this reason too.
		4> In this sentence, the modifier "who...News" is offset by a pair of dashes.
		D) is run-on sentence, conflicting with the following main clause and the subject Wheeler.

Q41. Absolute Pattern 10: Logical Expression

Two DC limited series, *Batman: The Dark Knight Returns* by Frank Miller and *Watchmen* by Moore and artist Dave Gibbons, drew attention in the mainstream press for their [41] <u>dark psychological complexity and promotion of the</u> antihero.

√	**A) NO CHANGE** complexity (noun), promotion (noun)	B) 1> "promotional" is adjective. It should be noun like the preceding noun
	B) dark psychology, complexity, and **promotional**	
	C) dark psychology, complex, and promotion of the	C) Noun (psychology), Adjective (complex), Noun (promotion) sequence is parallelism error.
	D) dark psychologically and complexly promotional of the	D) It changes the meaning by changing adjectives into adverbs.

Q42. Absolute Pattern 1: Adding, Revising, Deleting, Retaining Information

(mass purchase of the books as collectible items, with intent to resell at a higher value as the rising value of older issues was thought to imply that *all* comics would rise dramatically in price)

√	A) Yes, because it **clarifies what the speculative purchasing** is.
	B) Yes, because it describes one of <u>the consequences that the comics industry benefited</u> from the brief boom in the early 1990s.
	C) No, because it would <u>distract readers </u>from the main focus of the paragraph.
	D) No, because it <u>creates confusion </u>with the following phrase "and several storylines…media."

A) This information describes what the speculative purchasing is.

B) It might be true statement but is inconsistent with this sentence description.

C) and D) both are negative while the passage is positive.

Q43. Absolute Pattern 23: Transition Words for Supporting Detail, Contrast, and Consequence

Sales dropped off as the industry went into a major slump[43] <u>, while </u>manufactured "collectibles" **numbering in the millions replaced** [44] <u>imagination with reality </u>until fans and speculators alike deserted the medium in droves.

	A) , and	C) 1> 'but' cancels out the previous sentence.
	B) ; in the meantime,	2> Both clauses are negative, so they can't cancel out each other.
√	**C) , but**	A), B), D): All of them are used for the parallel structure
	D) , and simultaneously	

Q44. Absolute Pattern 15: Prepositional Idiom

Sales dropped off as the industry went into a major slump, and manufactured "collectibles" numbering in the millions **replaced** [44] <u>imagination and reality </u>until fans and speculators alike deserted the medium in droves.

	A) NO CHANGE	D) "replaced with" is the correct idiom.
	B) imagination **in** reality	A), B), and C) change the original meaning awkwardly by using the incorrect prepositions.
	C) <u>real imagination</u>	
√	D) imagination **with** reality	

SAT
Writing and Language
Test 7

ALL THE LOGIC AND RULES

BEHIND THE EVERY SINGLE

SAT QUESTION

Writing and Language Test 7
35 MINUTES, 44 QUESTIONS

Each passage below is accompanied by a number of questions. For some questions, you will consider how the passage might be revised to improve the expression of ideas. For other questions, you will consider how the passage might be edited to correct errors in sentence structure, usage, or punctuation. A passage or a question may be accompanied by one or more graphics (such as a table or graph) that you will consider as you make revising and editing decisions.

Questions 1-11 are based on the following passage.

John Glenn and the Limits of Possibility

John Glenn, the first American to orbit the Earth [1] by circling the planet, a World War II veteran, and United States Senator for a tenure of 24 years, died on Thursday. He was 95.
[2] A native Ohioan who grew up in Ohio, I admired John Glenn. Glenn achieved an almost mythically larger-than-life status in American culture when he returned from space in 1962. From his journey in orbit on, Glenn continued to make Ohio and the United States proud. Both [3] because he achieved incredible feat and the way he handled himself with humility and plain-spoken grace, Glenn was an ideal role model.

1
A) NO CHANGE
B) circling the planet,
C) where he circled the planet
D) OMIT the underlined portion

2
A) NO CHANGE
B) Admiring a native Ohioan John Glenn, I grew up.
C) Admiring John Glenn as a native Ohioan, I grew up.
D) As a native Ohioan, I grew up admiring John Glenn.

3
A) NO CHANGE
B) because his incredible achievements as well as
C) because of his incredible achievements and
D) because of his incredible achievements and also because of

CONTINUE

2

2

He embodied so many characteristics teachers and parents want young people to learn about—and he was a homegrown legend. Having studied history for the last four years, [4] my perspective on why John Glenn is a hero has changed. My conviction that Glenn's legacy is important and my belief in the inspirational power of his life story [5] ; however, is unaltered. Glenn was a lionhearted warrior, an undaunted explorer, [6] and he was a judicious statesman. <1>Glenn announced he would run for the Senate the day he retired from NASA in 1964, though he wasn't elected until 1974. <2>He was a fighter pilot in two wars, then a Navy and Marine test pilot, before being selected as one of the original "Mercury Seven" astronauts. <3>His famous orbit of earth was the culmination of twenty years of extraordinary feats of daring.

<4>In 1998, while still a sitting Senator, he returned to space at age 77, the oldest person ever to do so.

4

A) NO CHANGE
B) I changed my perspective on why John Glenn is a hero.
C) change of my perspective on why John Glenn is a hero has come upon me.
D) why John Glenn is a hero has changed.

5

A) NO CHANGE
B) however,
C) , however,
D) OMIT the underlined portion

6

A) NO CHANGE
B) who was a judicious statesman
C) and statesman who was judicious
D) and judicious statesman

7

For logic and sequence of this paragraph, sentence <1> should be placed:
A) NO CHANGE
B) after sentence <2>
C) after sentence <3>
D) after sentence <4>

CONTINUE

After officially retiring from the Senate, he helped found the John Glenn Institute for Public Service and Public Policy at The Ohio State University where he taught. <u>He continued to give lectures and visit schools until the end of his life</u>. [8]

John Glenn had one of the most impressive resumes in history. But accomplishments and accolades aside, [9] <u>sheer immensity that Glenn provided by devoting</u> to others—whether measured in time, energy, or personal risk—was itself heroic.

Glenn's passing is a reminder that an optimistic vision of America is possible. Without turning Glenn into a marble demigod or valorizing the cultural milieu from which he came, for that we be dishonest and a disservice to the man, I admire his human courage and his unwavering commitment to causes greater than himself. I respect the way he used his celebrity to create a platform from which he could unselfishly multiply his ability to do good.

8

The author is considering deleting the preceding sentence (He continued…).Should the author delete it?

A) Yes, because the sentence disrupts the paragraph's attention to John Glenn's career as a heroic astronaut.

B) Yes, because the sentence inappropriately shifts the focus of the paragraph from John Glenn, a hero to a philanthropist.

C) No, because the sentence is consistent with the paragraph's focus on the aspects of John Glenn's philanthropic activities after the retirement

D) No, because the sentence logically links the author's preference of Glenn as a philanthropist to astronaut.

9

A) NO CHANGE
B) the sheer immensity of Glenn's devotion
C) Glenn devoted with sheer immensity
D) Glenn devoted sheerly and immensely

CONTINUE

2   2

And I try to remember, without having lived through his most historic accomplishments myself, what it [10] was like to be inspired by a humble individual who dared to test the limits of possibility that transcends our limitations.[11]

A) NO CHANGE

B) will like to be

C) is like to be

D) DELTE IT

The author is considering deleting the underlined portion of the sentence. Should the author delete it?

A) Yes, because the portion shifts its focus from John Glenn as a heroic human being to just a human being.

B) Yes, because the portion does not deliver any meaningful information.

C) No, because the portion is emphasizing undaunted character John Glenn presented

D) No, because the portion logically concludes the essay.

CONTINUE

2

2

Questions 12-22 are based on the following passage.

Sarah Margaret Fuller Ossoli (1810 – 1850) [12] , is commonly known as Margaret Fuller, was an American journalist, critic, and women's rights advocate associated with the American transcendentalism movement. She was the first full-time American female book reviewer in journalism. Her book *Woman in the Nineteenth Century* is considered the first major feminist work in the United States. [13] Born in Cambridge, Massachusetts, [14] she was given a substantially early education by her father, Timothy Fuller.

She became the first editor of the transcendentalist
 (1)
Journal *The Dial* in 1840, before joining the New
 (2)   (3)
York Tribune under Horace Greeley in 1844. [15]
 (4)

12

A) NO CHANGE
B) ,commonly known as
C) ,was commonly known as
D) ,who is commonly known as,

13

If the author were to delete the preceding sentence, the paragraph would primarily lose information that
A) reveals social and racial bias Sarah Fuller encountered at that time it was published.
B) indicates the time and place the book was written
C) establishes the historic value of the book
D) describes the type of occupation Sarah Fuller worked

14

A) NO CHANGE
B) Sarah
C) it was Sarah Margarete Fuller who
D) this first major feminist in the United States

15

Which of the following information is not essential to understand the work and job of Sarah Fuller?
A) the first editor (1)
B) The Dial (2)
C) in 1840 (3)
D) under Horace Greeley (4)

CONTINUE ➤

2

2

By the time she was in her 30s, Fuller [16] had earned a reputation as the best-read person in New England and became the first woman allowed to use the library at Harvard College. Her seminal work, *Woman in the Nineteenth Century*, was published in 1845. A year later, she was sent to Europe for the *Tribune* as its first female correspondent. She and her confidant Jane Kimberly soon became involved in the revolutions in Italy and she allied [17] her with Giuseppe Mazzini. She had a relationship with Giovanni Ossoli, [18] with whom she had a child. All three members of the family died in a shipwreck off Fire Island, New York, as they were traveling to the United States in 1850. Fuller's body was never recovered.

16

A) NO CHANGE
B) earned
C) has earned
D) had been earning

17

A) NO CHANGE
B) herself with Giuseppe Mazzini
C) with Giuseppe Mazzini
D) her being with Giuseppe Mazzini

18

A) NO CHANGE
B) with who
C) who
D) whose

CONTINUE

Many other advocates for women's rights and feminism, including [19] that of Susan B. Anthony, [20] cite Fuller as a source of inspiration. Many of her contemporaries ,however, were supportive, including her former friend Harriet Martineau. She said that Fuller was a talker [21] more than an activist. Shortly after Fuller's death, her importance faded; the editors who prepared her letters to be published, believing her fame would be short-lived, censored or altered much of her work before publication.

19

A) NO CHANGE
B) people such as Susan B. Anthony,
C) those of Susan B. Anthony,
D) Susan B. Anthony,

20

A) NO CHANGE
B) sighted
C) cited
D) site

21

A) NO CHANGE
B) less than
C) rather than
D) less then

22

Suppose the author's goal was to write a brief essay about the life of an early feminist. Would this summary successfully fulfill the author's goal?

A) Yes, because the summary offers Susan Anthony's major events as a feminist
B) Yes, because the summary reveals social injustice Sarah Fuller encountered.
C) No, because the summary focuses more on the impact of Susan Anthony as her mentor
D) No, because the summary represents an early feminist' unfolded personal life rather than civil work.

CONTINUE

2   2

Questions 23-33 are based on the following passage.

A shape-memory ally

A shape-memory alloy (SMA) is an alloy that "remembers" its original shape and that when deformed returns to its pre-deformed shape [23] that heated. This material is a lightweight, solid-state [24] alternative to conventional actuators such as hydraulic, pneumatic, and motor-based systems. Shape-memory alloys have applications in robotics and automotive, aerospace and biomedical industries. The two main types of shape-memory alloys are copper-aluminum-nickel, and nickel-titanium (NiTi) alloys but SMAs can also be created [25] by alloy of zinc, and copper, and gold, and iron. Although iron-based and copper-based SMAs, such as Fe-Mn-Si, Cu-Zn-Al and Cu-Al-Ni, are [26] commercially available in the market and cheaper than NiTi, NiTi which bases SMAs are preferable for most applications [27] due to their stability, practicability and superior thermo-mechanic performance.

23

A) NO CHANGE
B) when
C) by
D) OMIT the underlined portion

24

Which of the following alternatives to the portion would NOT be acceptable?
A) replacement for
B) substitute for
C) enhancement to
D) equivalent to

25

A) NO CHANGE
B) with alloying zinc, copper, gold and iron.
C) with alloy of zinc, copper, gold and iron.
D) by alloying zinc, copper, gold and iron.

26

A) NO CHANGE
B) commercially available as a marketable product
C) commercial.
D) commercially available

27

Which of the following alternatives to the underlined portion would NOT be acceptable?
A) because their stability
B) because of their stability
C) owing to their stability
D) thanks to their stability

CONTINUE

2 **2**

NiTi alloys change from austenite to martensite upon cooling; M_f is the temperature at which the transition to martensite completes upon cooling. [28] Repeated use of the shape-memory effect may lead to a shift of the characteristic transformation temperatures (this effect is known as functional [29] fatigue, as it is closely related with a change of microstructural and functional properties of the material). The maximum temperature at which SMAs can no longer be stress induced is called M_d, where the SMAs are [30] permanently deformed.

28

Which one establishes a visual contrast to the image in the precedent sentence?

A) The first consumer commercial application was a shape-memory coupling for piping.

B) Intelligent Reinforced Concrete (IRC), which incorporates SMA wires embedded within the concrete can sense cracks and contract to heal macro-sized crack.

C) There have been, however, limited studies on using these materials in auto body.

D) During heating A_s and A_f are the temperature at which the transformation from martensite to austenite starts and finishes.

29

Which of the following alternatives to the underlined portion would NOT be acceptable?

A) exhaustion

B) weakness

C) stress

D) depression

30

Which of the following alternatives to the underlined portion would NOT be acceptable?

A) irrevocably

B) irreversibly

C) irreparably

D) forever

CONTINUE ➡

2   **2**

The transition from the martensite phase to the austenite phase is only dependent on temperature and stress, not time, as most phase changes are, as there is no diffusion involved. Similarly, the austenite structure receives its name from steel alloys of [31] <u>a similar and comparable</u> structure. It is the reversible diffusion less transition between these two phases that results in special properties. [32] <u>Martensite</u> can be formed from austenite by rapidly cooling carbon-steel, this process is not reversible, so steel does not have shape-memory properties.

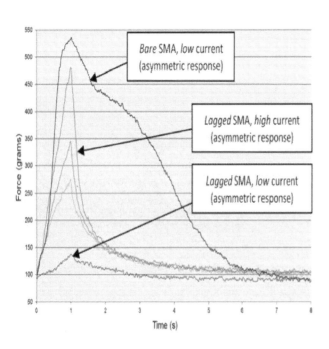

Time (s)

31

A) NO CHANGE
B) a comparable configuration and similar
C) a similar structure which is comparable.
D) similar

32

A) NO CHANGE
B) While martensite
C) With martensite
D) By martensite

33

The graph demonstrates the feasibility of SMA actuators that use conductive "lagging" method on which thermal paste is rapidly transferred from the SMA. Using this method, manufacturers can expect:
A) A significant reduction time in both Bare SMA low current and Lagged SMA, low current
B) A significant reduction time both Bare SMA low current and Lagged SMA, high current
C) A significant reduction time in Lagged SMA high current only.
D) A significant reduction time in Lagged SMA low current only.

CONTINUE

2   2

Questions 34-44 are based on the following passage.

Thomas Carmichael Hindman, Jr.

Thomas Carmichael Hindman, Jr. (January 28, 1828 – September 27, 1868) was a lawyer, United States Representative from the 1st Congressional District of Arkansas, [34] and he was a major general in the Confederate States Army during the American Civil War. After receiving his primary education in Ripley, he [35] had attended the Lawrenceville Classical Institute and graduated with honors in 1843. <1> Afterwards, he raised a company in Tippah County for the 2nd Mississippi regiment in the Mexican–American War. <2> Hindman served during the war as a lieutenant and later as a captain of his company. <3> He studied law, and was admitted to the state bar in 1851. <4>After the war, he returned to Ripley. He was elected as the Democratic Representative from Arkansas's 1st congressional district in the Thirty-sixth Congress from March 4, 1859, to March 4, 1861, but [36] had been declined to serve after the onset of the Civil War and Arkansas's secession from the Union. [37] Instead, Hindman waited wisely until war was over.

34

A) NO CHANGE
B) who was a major general
C) and was a major general
D) and *major general*

35

Which of the following is most logical sequences in this paragraph?
A) NO CHANGE
B) <1>,<4>,<2>,<3>
C) <1>,<2>,<4>,<3>
D) <4>,<1>,<2>,<3>

36

A) NO CHANGE
B) had declined
C) was declined
D) declined

37

At this point, the author wishes to provide a specific example on the efforts being made by Hindman to further his desire, which one would best accomplish this purpose?
A) NO CHANGE
B) Instead, Hindman joined the armed forces of the Confederacy.
C) Instead, Hindman sought peaceful resolution to end the Civil war.
D) Instead, Hindman moved to Mexican town of Carlota, where he engaged in coffee planting and attempted to practice law.

CONTINUE →

2   **2**

He commanded the Trans-Mississippi Department, and later raised and commanded "Hindman's Legion" for the Confederate States Army. After the war, Hindman avoided surrender to the federal government [38] by fleeing to Mexico City. After the execution of Maximilian I of Mexico, Hindman submitted a petition [39] to request for a pardon to President Andrew Johnson, but it was denied. Hindman, nonetheless, returned to his former life in Helena. He became the leader of the "Young Democracy" [40] , there he rebuilt a new political organization that was willing to accept the Reconstruction for the restoration of the Union. He was assassinated on September 27, 1868, at his Helena home. As the American Civil War approached, Hindman was a passionate voice for secession and was primarily Arkansas's most prominent Fire-Eater.

With war approaching, Hindman resigned from Congress and recruited a regiment at Helena, which was mustered into Confederate service. He requested the state government for muskets, clothing and ten days of rations [41] so that his men could "fight for our country".

38

A) NO CHANGE
B) into
C) towards
D) via

39

A) NO CHANGE
B) by officially requesting
C) and appealed to authority with respect
D) OMIT the underlined portion

40

A) NO CHANGE
B) , a new political organization
C) , it became a new political organization
D) ; a new political organization

41

A) NO CHANGE
B) so as
C) so as to
D) in order for

CONTINUE ➤

2

He and his regiment were soon active participants in the disastrous Kentucky Campaign, followed soon after that by fierce fighting at the Battle of Shiloh in April 1862, [42] when he was slightly wounded. After his recovery, Hindman was promoted [43] to the rank of major general and was appointed commander of the Trans-Mississippi Department to prevent an invasion by the Union troops led by Samuel Curtis.

Events in Arkansas had taken a terrible turn for the worse. Most units had been stripped from the state for service east of the Mississippi River. When Hindman arrived in Little Rock, Arkansas, he found that his command was bare of soldiers, penniless, defenseless, [44] although no immediate threat was visible, Meantime, the Federal Army was approaching dangerously from the northwest.

42

Which of the following choices would NOT be acceptable?
A) NO CHANGE
B) where
C) but
D) a time that

43

Which one clearly adds objective and specific information that illustrates Hindman's army career?
A) NO CHANGE
B) to the envious rank
C) to rank that everyone aspires
D) to the rank that became critical in his army career

44

Which choice would most effectively maintain logical consistency?
A) NO CHANGE
B) consequently, Hindman attempted inevitable surrender .
C) and dreadfully exposed to its enemy.
D) but had a hope in politics that still called for him.

TEST 7

WRITING ABSOLUTE PATTERNS

Test 7 Writing & Language Section Patterns

Q1. Absolute Pattern 19: Redundant Error

John Glenn, the first American to orbit the Earth [1] by circling the planet,

	A) NO CHANGE	redundant error
	B) **circling the planet,**	redundant error
	C) where he **circled the planet**	redundant error
√	**D) OMIT the underlined portion**	

Q2. Absolute Pattern 12: Modifier Placement Error

[2] A native Ohioan who grew up in Ohio, I admired John Glenn.

	A) NO CHANGE	A) is redundant error.
	B) Admiring a native Ohioan John Glenn, I grew up.	"A native Ohioan" and "grew up in Ohio" are basically the same meaning.
	C) Admiring John Glenn as a native Ohioan, I grew up.	B), C) "Admiring…" should be placed next to "I grew up."
√	**D) As a native Ohioan, I grew up admiring John Glenn.**	

Key point: Choices A, B, C are all misplaced modifiers. Modifier should be placed right next to the one that it modifies. only D satisfies this arrangement.

Q3. Absolute Pattern 7: Conjunction Error

Both [3] because he achieved incredible feat and **the way** he handled himself with humility and plain-spoken grace, Glenn was an ideal role model.

	A) NO CHANGE	C) 1> The non-underlined portion " **the way...grace**" is a phrase, not a clause.
	B) because his incredible achievements as well as	2> The underlined portion is a clause. 3> Therefore, the underlined portion should also be a phrase, which can't use a conjunction.
√	**C) because of his incredible achievements and**	A), B) 1> "because" is a conjunction that links to clause. 2> It is a parallelism error that conflicts with the following phrase.
	D) because of his incredible ar-hievements and also because of	B) "as well as" D) "also because of" can be and should be replaced with "and"

Q4. Absolute Pattern 12: Modifier Placement Error

Having studied history for the last four years, [4] <u>my perspective on why John Glenn is a hero has changed.</u>

	A) NO CHANGE	B) 1> "Having studied ~" implies the subject has to be human.
√	**B) I changed my perspective on why John Glenn is a hero.**	2> The subject is human 'I'
	C) <u>change</u> of my perspective on why John Glenn is a hero has come upon me	A) The subject 'my perspective' is non-human.
		C), D) Both 'change' and 'why' are used as a subject and can't carry the modifier "having studied".
	D) <u>why</u> John Glenn is a hero has changed.	

Q5. Absolute Pattern 7: Conjunction Error

My conviction that Glenn's legacy is important and my belief in the inspirational power of his life story [5] <u>; however,</u> is unaltered.

	A) NO CHANGE	C) a pair of commas should offset "however" when used in the middle of the sentence.
	B) however,	
√	**C) , however,**	A) semicolon + "however" is used when "however" carries a subordinating clause.
	D) OMIT the underlined portion	B) 'however' needs a pair of commas, not one.
		D) changes the original meaning

Q6. Absolute Pattern 13: Parallel Structure

Glenn was a lionhearted **warrior,** an undaunted **explorer,** [6] <u>and he was a **judicious statesman**</u>.

	A) NO CHANGE	D) warrior, explorer, and judicious statesman are correct parallel structure.
	B) **who was** a judicious statesman	
	C) **and statesman who was** judicious	A), B), C) are all parallelism error
√	**D) and judicious statesman**	

Q7. Absolute Pattern 11: Logical Sequence

Question: **For logic and sequence of this paragraph**, sentence <1> should be placed:

	A) NO CHANGE	Sentence sequence question can often be solved easily by reading the sentence from backward in 4,3,2,1 order, instead of 1,2,3,4 because finding the conclusion is often easier than finding the introduction sentence.
	B) after sentence <2>	
√	**C) after sentence <3>**	
	D) after sentence <4>	

<2>He was a fighter pilot in two wars, then a Navy and Marine test pilot, before being selected as one of the **original "Mercury Seven" astronauts**. (Topic)

<3>His **famous orbit** of earth was the **culmination of** twenty years of extraordinary feats of daring. (The supporting detail)

<1>Glenn announced he **would run for the Senate** the day **he retired from NASA in** 1964, though he wasn't elected until 1974. (Example)

<4>In 1998, **while still a sitting Senator**, he returned to space at age 77, the oldest person ever to do so.

Q8. Absolute Pattern 1: Adding, Revising, Deleting, Retaining Information

He **continued to give lectures** and visit schools until the end of his life. [8]

Question: The author is **considering deleting** the preceding sentence (He continued…).Should the author delete it?

	A) Yes, because the sentence <u>disrupts the paragraph's</u> attention to John Glenn's career as a heroic astronaut.
	B) Yes, because the sentence <u>inappropriately shifts</u> the focus of the paragraph from John Glenn, a hero to a philanthropist.
√	**C) No, because the sentence is consistent with the paragraph's focus on the aspects of John Glenn's philanthropic activities after the retirement**
	D) No, because the sentence logically links the <u>author's preference</u> of Glenn as a philanthropist to as an astronaut.

C) 1> The previous sentence describes his later life after the retirement.

2> Therefore, sentence 8 should not be deleted.

3> For this reason, options A and B are incorrect.

D) The author respects Glenn as a philanthropist as well as an astronaut

Q9. Absolute Pattern 10: Logical Expression

But accomplishments and accolades aside, [9] sheer immensity that Glenn provided by devoting to others—whether measured in time, energy, or personal risk—**was** itself heroic.

	A) NO CHANGE	B) "**sheer immensity**" is the subject that counteract and highlights the modifier "accomplishment accolades"
√	**B) sheer immensity of Glenn's devotion**	A) is wordy. "provided by devoting" can be reduced to 'devotion'
	C) **Glenn devoted** with sheer immensity	C), D) Run-on: "devoted" becomes a verb, while having the main verb "was" already.
	D) Glenn **devoted** sheerly and immensely	D) "sheerly and immensely" sound awkward.

Q10 Absolute Pattern 24: Verb Tense / Voice Error

And I try to remember, without **having lived** through his most historic accomplishments myself, what it [10] **was** like to be inspired by a humble individual who dared to test the limits of possibility that transcends our limits.[11]

√	A) NO CHANGE	'having lived,' meaning after he had lived (the past perfect situation) corresponds to the simple past "was" in the main verb.
	B) **will** like to be	'will' is used for the future tense
	C) **is** like to be	'is' is used for the present tense
	D) DELTE IT	Change of meaning. "like to be" implies the author's imagination

Q11. Absolute Pattern 19: Redundant Error

...who dared to **test the limits of possibility** that transcends our limitations.[11]

Question: The author is considering **deleting the underlined portion** of the sentence. Should the author delete it?

	A) Yes, because the portion shifts its focus from John Glenn as a heroic human being to just a human being.
√	B) Yes, because the portion **does not deliver any meaningful information**.
	C) No, because the portion is emphasizing undaunted character John Glenn presented
	D) No, because the portion logically concludes the essay.

"**test the limits of possibility**" and "that transcends our limitations" are essentially identical phrases.

Q12. Absolute Pattern 12: Modifier Error

Sarah Margaret Fuller Ossoli (1810 – 1850) [12] *, is commonly known as Margaret Fuller,* **was** an American journalist, critic, and women's rights advocate associated with the American transcendentalism movement.

	A) NO CHANGE	B) A pair of commas offsetting the modifier properly separates it from the main clause.
√	**B) ,commonly known as**	A) "is" should be removed because "was", the main verb, already exists.
	C) ,**was** commonly known as	C) "was" is not necessary
	D) ,**who is** commonly known as	D) "who is" is not necessary because it simply functions as a complementizer.

Q13. Absolute Pattern 1: Adding, Revising, Deleting, Retaining Information

Her book *Woman in the Nineteenth Century* is considered the **first major feminist work** in the United States. [13]

	A) reveals **social and racial bias** Sarah Fuller encountered at that time it was published.	C) It is the first major feminist work
	B) indicates the **time and place the book was written**	A) racial bias is not mentioned in the sentence
√	**C) establishes the historic value of the book**	B) can't be primarily information
	D) describes the **type of occupation** Sarah Fuller worked	D) her occupation is inconsistent with the sentence.

Q14. Absolute Pattern 17: Pronoun Error

Born in Cambridge, Massachusetts, [14] **she** was given a substantially early education by her father, Timothy Fuller.

	A) NO CHANGE	B)
√	**B) Sarah**	1> The first sentence of each paragraph can't start with a pronoun.
	C) it was Sarah Margarete Fuller who	2> The person's name must be given first before using the corresponding pronoun.
	D) this first major feminist in the United States	A) Ambiguous pronoun
		C) Wordy D) Wordy + ambiguous

Q15. Absolute Pattern 1: Adding, Revising, Deleting, Retaining Information

She became <u>the first editor </u>of the transcendentalist Journal *The Dial* <u>in 1840,</u> before joining the New *York*
          (1)   (2)   (3)

Tribune <u>under Horace Greeley</u> in 1844. [15]
          (4)

Question: Which of the following information is **not essential** to understand the work and job of Sarah Fuller?	
A) the first editor (1)	D) "under Horace Greeley" is not necessary to understand the other essential information.
B) The Dial (2)	
C) in 1840 (3)	Choice (A),(B),(C) are necessary information because they are directly related with Fuller.
√ **D) under Horace Greeley (4)**	

Q16. Absolute Pattern 24: Verb Tense / Voice Error

By the time she was in her 30s, Fuller [16] <u>had earned </u>a reputation as the best-read person

√	**A) NO CHANGE**	past perfect	A) 'By' in time adverbial phrase refers to the completion of action; therefore, the tense has to be perfect tense such as past perfect, present perfect, or future perfect.
	B) earned	simple past	
	C) has earned	present perfect	C) The present perfect tense is incorrect because "she was~"
	D) had been earning	progressive	indicates the past occurrence.

Q17. Absolute Pattern 17: Pronoun Error

She and her confidant Jane Kimberly soon became involved in the revolutions in Italy and she allied [17] <u>her with Giuseppe Mazzini.</u>

	A) NO CHANGE	B) The reflective pronoun 'herself' must be used with the corresponding subject. Therefore, herself clearly refers to Fuller.
√	**B) herself with Giuseppe Mazzini**	
	C) with Giuseppe Mazzini	A) "she" and "her" are unclear. It could be Fuller or Jane. C) "she" is unclear. It could be Fuller or Jane.
	D) her being with Giuseppe Mazzini	D) 'being' cannot be used

ABSOLUTE PATTERN | Test 7

Q18. Absolute Pattern 17: Pronoun Error

She had a relationship with Giovanni Ossoli, [18] **with whom** she had a child.

√	**A) NO CHANGE**	A) Preposition 'with' requires the <u>objective</u> relative pronoun Preposition + Whom.
	B) with who	B) 'with' is a preposition that must carry an objective "whom".
	C) who	C) 'who' alone can't connect to the following subject 'she.'
	D) whose	D) 'whose' is possessive that requires a noun.

Q19. Absolute Pattern 4: Comparison

Many other advocates for women's rights and feminism, including [19] <u>that of **Susan B. Anthony**</u>, cite Fuller as a source of inspiration

	A) NO CHANGE	'that of' is ambiguous and should be deleted.
	B) people <u>such as</u> Susan B. Anthony,	'such as' is redundant with 'including'
	C) <u>those of</u> Susan B. Anthony,	'those of' is ambiguous and should be deleted.
√	**D) Susan B. Anthony,**	"including Susan"' is the best reference.

Q20 Absolute Pattern 10: Logical Expression

Many other advocates for women's rights and feminism, including Susan B. Anthony, [20] <u>cite</u> Fuller as a source of inspiration.

	A) NO CHANGE	'cite' is present tense while other surrounding sentences are past tense.
	B) sighted	'sighted' means saw
√	**C) cited**	"cited" properly maintains the same tense with other surrounding sentences
	D) sited	site means a construction area

Q21. Absolute Pattern 4: Comparison

She said that Fuller was a talker [21] more than an activist

	A) NO CHANGE	The sentence is about the criticism Fuller received from other activists. Therefore, it has to be 'less than', instead of 'more than.'
√	B) less than	
	C) rather then	C) and D) both are using 'then', instead of 'than.' 'then' means by that time.
	D) less then	

Q22. Absolute Pattern 1: Adding, Revising, Deleting, Retaining Information

Many other advocates for women's rights and feminism, including Susan B. Anthony cited Fuller as a source of inspiration.

Question: Suppose the author's goal was to write a brief essay about the life of an early feminist.
Would this **summary** successfully fulfill the author's goal?

	A) Yes, because the summary offers Susan Anthony's major events as a feminist
√	B) Yes, because the summary reveals social injustice Sarah Fuller encountered.
	C) No, because the summary focuses more on the impact of feminism in general.
	D) No, because the summary represents an early feminist' unfolded personal life rather than civil work.

The keyword in the question is 'summary' that encourages us to read the concluding paragraph.

A), C) are incorrect because the main character is Sarah Fuller, not Susan or feminism in general.

D) The personal life story of Sarah Fuller is only briefly mentioned.

Q23 Absolute Pattern 7: Conjunction Error

A shape-memory alloy (SMA) is an alloy that "remembers" its original shape and that **when deformed** returns to its pre-deformed shape [23] that heated.

	A) NO CHANGE	B) 1> The original sentence was "when (its deformed shape is) heated. "
√	B) when	2> The preceding parallel structure also gives a clue "**when** (its original shape is) deformed returns to…." **when** (its deformed shape is) heated.
	C) by	A) 'that' is used as an indicative pronoun as if it sounds "that heated shape"
	D) OMIT	C) "by" is preposition. Preposition can't link to the subordinating clause.
		D) omitting is not an option to link the 'shape' to 'heated.'

Q24. Absolute Pattern 10: Logical Expression

This material is a lightweight, solid-state [24] alternative to conventional actuators

Question: Which of the following alternatives to the portion would **NOT** be acceptable?

	A) replacement for	C) alternative does not necessarily mean better or enhancement
	B) substitute for	The other options are all synonyms
√	**C) enhancement to**	
	D) equivalent to	

Q25 Absolute Pattern 15: Prepositional Idiom

The two main types of shape-memory alloys are copper-aluminum-nickel, and nickel-titanium (NiTi) alloys but SMAs can also be created [25] by **alloy of** zinc, copper, gold, and iron.

	A) NO CHANGE	D) "by +~ing" is used to describe means and method
	B) with alloying zinc, copper, gold and iron.	(A) "by alloy" should change to "by alloying"
	C) with alloy of zinc, copper, gold and iron.	(B) "with" should be replaced to "by"
		(C) Changes the meaning.
√	**D) by alloying zinc, copper, gold and iron.**	

Q26. Absolute Pattern 19: Redundant Error

Although iron-based and copper-based SMAs, such as Fe-Mn-Si, Cu-Zn-Al and Cu-Al-Ni, are [26] commercially available **in the market** and cheaper than NiTi, NiTi which bases SMAs are preferable

	A) NO CHANGE	D) is succinct and precise.
	B) commercially available as a marketable product	Commercially available means marketable, causing a redundant error.
	C) commercial	A), B) are redundant error
√	**D) commercially available**	C) changes the meaning

Q27. Absolute Pattern 23: Transition Words for Supporting Detail, Contrast, and Consequence

Although iron-based and copper-based SMAs, such as Fe-Mn-Si, Cu-Zn-Al and Cu-Al-Ni, are commercially available and cheaper than NiTi, NiTi which bases SMAs are preferable for most applications [27] <u>due to their stability,</u> practicability and superior thermo-mechanic performance.

Question: Which of the following alternatives to the underlined portion would **NOT** be acceptable?

√	**A) because their stability**	A) 1> Although look alike, 'because' and 'because of' are different.
	B) because <u>of</u> their stability	2> The former is conjunction that links to another clause, while the latter is preposition that links to a phrase, not a clause.
	C) owing <u>to</u> their stability	3> The underlined portion of the original sentence is phrase, not a clause.
	D) thanks <u>to</u> their stability	B), C), and D) are all fine with linking the following phrase.

Q28. Absolute Pattern 1: Adding, Revising, Deleting, Retaining Information

<u>NiTi alloys change from</u> austenite <u>to</u> martensite upon **cooling;** M_f is the **temperature** at which the **transition** to martensite **completes upon cooling.** [28]

Question: Which one establishes **a visual contrast** to the image in the precedent sentence?

	A) The <u>first consumer commercial application</u> was a shape-memory coupling for piping.
	B) Intelligent Reinforced Concrete (IRC), which incorporates SMA wires embedded within the <u>concrete can sense cracks and contract</u> to heal macro-sized crack.
	C) There have been, however, <u>limited studies</u> on using these materials in auto body.
√	**D) During heating** A_s **and** A_f **are the temperatures at which the transformation from martensite to austenite starts and finishes.**

The question asks <u>visual contrast.</u>
The preceding sentence has keywords such as **cooling, temperature, transition, complete upon cooling.**

D) has similar keywords that illustrate visual contrast such as **heating, temperatures, starts and finishes.**

To sum up, while the preceding clause shows the cooling process, the added information presents the heating process, which visualizes its contrasting process.

Q29 Absolute Pattern 10: Logical Expression

Repeated use of the shape-memory effect may lead to a shift of the characteristic transformation temperatures (this effect is known as **functional** [29] fatigue,

Question: Which of the following alternatives to the underlined portion would **NOT** be acceptable?

	A) exhaustion	D) depression is most likely used to human psychology, not to material in this category.
	B) weakness	A), B), C) are all synonyms that can be alternately used with fatigue.
	C) stress	The keyword is "functional" right before fatigue.
√	**D) depression**	

Q30. Absolute Pattern 10: Logical Expression

The maximum temperature at which SMAs can no longer be stress induced is called M_d, where the SMAs are [30] permanently **deformed**.

Question: Which of the following alternatives to the underlined portion would **NOT** be acceptable?

	A) irrevocably	A), B), C): All refer to the condition that is unable to recover.
	B) irreversibly	Choice (D) "forever", however, does not have such a meaning.
	C) irreparably	It is simply a synonym to the word permanent.
√	**D) forever**	The keyword is 'deformed'.

Q31 Absolute Pattern 19: Redundant Error

Similarly, the austenite structure receives its name from steel alloys of [31] a similar and comparable structure.

	A) NO CHANGE	D) is concise and direct.
	B) a comparable configuration and similar	A) "similar" and "comparable" are synonyms
	C) a similar structure which is comparable	A), B), and C) are all redundant error
√	**D) similar**	

Q32. Absolute Pattern 5: Comma Splice Error

[32] <u>Martensite **can be formed**</u> from austenite by rapidly cooling carbon-steel, **this process is not reversible**, so steel does not have shape-memory properties.

	A) NO CHANGE	B) 1> Because there is no conjunction in the second clause starting with "this process is…"),
√	**B) While martensite**	
	C) <u>With</u> martensite	2> we should make one in the underlined portion by changing the independent sentence into a subordinating clause,
	D) <u>By</u> martensite	3> We can do this by putting "While" . A) The original sentence is a comma splice error, requiring a conjunction. C), D) Preposition cannot link to a clause.

Q33 Absolute Pattern 9: Informational Graphs

Following chart demonstrates the feasibility of SMA actuators that use conductive "lagging" method on which thermal paste is rapidly transferred from the SMA. Using this method, manufacturers can expect:

	A) a significant reduction time in both Bare SMA low current and <u>Lagged SMA, low current</u>
√	**B) a significant reduction time in both Bare SMA low current and Lagged SMA, high current**
	C) a significant reduction time in <u>Lagged SMA high current only</u>.
	D) a significant reduction time in <u>Lagged SMA low current only</u>

Setting aside Force, the graph shows a significant reduction time in **both Bare SMA low current and Lagged SMA, high current**

Q34. Absolute Pattern 13: Parallel Structure

Thomas Carmichael Hindman, Jr. (January 28, 1828 – September 27, 1868) was a **lawyer, United States Representative** from the 1st Congressional District of Arkansas, [34] **and** he was **a major general** in the Confederate States Army during the American Civil War.

	A) NO CHANGE	D) The original sentence lacks the parallelism by placing a clause "and he was a major general" in the middle of the parallel structure.
	B) **who was** a major general	B) 'who' is complementizer and unnecessary.
	C) **and was** a major general	C) 'was' is unnecessary.
√	D) **and** *major general*	

Q35. Absolute Pattern 11: Logical Sequence

Passage: <1> Afterwards, he raised a company in Tippah County for the 2nd Mississippi regiment in the Mexican–American War. <2> Hindman served during the war as a lieutenant and later as a captain of his company. <3> He studied law, and was admitted to the state bar in 1851. <4>After the war, he returned to Ripley.

Question: Which of the following is most **logical sequences in** this paragraph?

Answer Keywords: <1> Afterwards, he **raised a company** in Tippah County for the 2nd Mississippi regiment in the Mexican–American War. <2> Hindman served during the war as a lieutenant and later as **a captain of his company**. <4>**After the war, he returned** to Ripley. <3> **He studied law,** and was admitted to the state bar in 1851.

√	B) <1>,<4>,<2>,<3>	Once your selection is completed, try to read them backward: <3><2><4><1>. It will confirm your choice.

Q36. Absolute Pattern 24: Verb Tense / Voice Error

He **was elected** as the Democratic Representative from Arkansas's 1st congressional district in the Thirty-sixth Congress from March 4, 1859, to March 4, 1861, but [36] <u>had been declined</u> to serve after the onset of the Civil War and Arkansas's secession from the Union.

	A) NO CHANGE	D) 1> The past tense is employed throughout the passage.
	B) had declined	2> Therefore, this sentence should also use the simple past.
	C) was declined	A) is past perfect, passive.
		B) is past perfect.
√	**D) declined**	C) is passive.

Q37 Absolute Pattern 1: Adding, Revising, Deleting, Retaining Information

He was elected as the Democratic Representative from Arkansas's 1st congressional district in the Thirty-sixth Congress from March 4, 1859, to March 4, 1861, but declined to serve after the onset of the Civil War and Arkansas's secession from the Union. [37]

Question: At this point, the author wishes to provide **a specific example** of the efforts being made by Hindman to further his desire, which one would best accomplish this purpose?

	A) Instead, Hindman waited wisely until war was over.
√	**B) Instead, Hindman joined the armed forces of the Confederacy**
	C) Instead, Hindman sought a peaceful resolution to end the Civil war.
	D) Instead, Hindman moved to Mexican town of Carlota, where he engaged in coffee planting and attempted to practice law.

B) The previous and the following paragraphs describe his decision to serve in the army, which naturally links to choice B.

A), C), D) are all negative contrary to the rest of the paragraphs.

Q38. Absolute Pattern 15: Prepositional Idiom

He commanded the Trans-Mississippi Department, and later raised and commanded "Hindman's Legion" for the Confederate States Army. After the war, Hindman avoided surrender to the federal government [38]by fleeing to Mexico City.

√	**A) NO CHANGE**	Preposition 'by' is used to describe a means or a method
	B) into	'into' means getting inside.
	C) towards	"towards" is used for a direction.
	D) via	"via" is used for a direction.

Q39. Absolute Pattern 19: Redundant Error

After the execution of Maximilian I of Mexico, Hindman submitted a petition [39] to request for a pardon to President Andrew Johnson, but it was denied. Hindman, nonetheless, returned to his former life in Helena.

	A) NO CHANGE	The meaning "Petition" and options A), B), C) are synonyms; therefore, they should be deleted.
	B) by officially requesting	
	C) and appealed to authority with respect	
√	**D) OMIT the underlined portion**	D) is clear and concise

Q40. Absolute Pattern 16: Precision, Concision, Style

He became the leader of the "Young Democracy" [40] , there **he rebuilt** a new political organization that was willing to accept the Reconstruction for the restoration of the Union.

	A) NO CHANGE	B) 1> It is clear and concise
√	**B) , a new political organization**	2> The simplification rule is the concept that makes sentence concise without losing the original meaning.
	C) , **it became** a new political organization	A), C) 1> Comma splice error. 2>"there he rebuilt" is a new clause.
	D) ; a new political organization	C) "it became" is a new clause D) Semi-colon is used to link a clause, not for a phrase.

Q41. Absolute Pattern 7: Conjunction Error

Passage: He requested the state government for muskets, clothing and ten days of rations [41]so that **his men could fight** for our country

√	**A) NO CHANGE**	A) Only 'so- that' carries a subordinating clause
	B) so as	B), C), D) are all prepositions and carries a phrase, not a clause.
	C) so as to	
	D) in order for	

Q42. Absolute Pattern 7: Conjunction Error

He and his regiment were soon active participants in the disastrous Kentucky Campaign, **followed soon after that by fierce fighting at the Battle of Shiloh in April 1862,** [42]when he was slightly wounded.

	A) NO CHANGE	C) 1> Conjunction 'but' cancels out the previous clause.
	B) where	2> The main clause and the following dependent clause are not in the conflicting relation.
√	**C) but**	
	D) a time that	B) 'where' links to the 'Kentucky Campaign.' A), D) try to connect ' in April 1862.'

Q43. Absolute Pattern 1: Adding, Revising, Deleting, Retaining Information

After his recovery, Hindman was promoted [43] to the rank of major general and was appointed commander of the Trans-Mississippi Department to prevent an invasion by the Union troops led by Samuel Curtis.

√	**A) NO CHANGE**	A) Informing his rank illustrates Hindman's specific army career
	B) to the envious rank	B), C) are subjective information.
	C) to rank that everyone aspires	
	D) to the rank that became critical in his army career	D) only repeats the question.

Q44. Absolute Pattern 1: Adding, Revising, Deleting, Retaining Information

positive   Negative

When Hindman arrived in Little Rock, Arkansas, he found that his command **was bare of soldiers**, **penniless, defenseless,** [44] **although no immediate threat** was visible, and dreadfully exposed to its enemy. Meantime, the Federal Army was approaching **dangerously** from the northwest.

Question: Which choice would most effectively maintain logical consistency?

	A) NO CHANGE	C) is consistent with the previous description.
	B) consequently, Hindman attempted inevitable surrender.	
√	C) **and dreadfully exposed to its enemy.**	A) and B) are opposite description. A) There was immediate threat
	D) but had a hope in politics that still called for him.	B) Hindman didn't surrender.
		D) is inconsistent with other sentence

SAT
Writing and Language
Test 8

ALL THE LOGIC AND RULES

BEHIND THE EVERY SINGLE

SAT QUESTION

Writing and Language Test 8
35 MINUTES, 44 QUESTIONS

Each passage below is accompanied by a number of questions. For some questions, you will consider how the passage might be revised to improve the expression of ideas. For other questions, you will consider how the passage might be edited to correct errors in sentence structure, usage, or punctuation. A passage or a question may be accompanied by one or more graphics (such as a table or graph) that you will consider as you make revising and editing decisions.

Questions 1-11 are based on the following passage.

Let's Engage the Silent Majority

I didn't expect Donald Trump to be President of the United States. I hoped and prayed he would lose. Throughout the election cycle, I tried to remain detached from the endless fear and bigotry that seemed to spew out of the Trump political machine. For me, my parents, and my community, this election was too personal, <u>even though I tried to be detached from this fear</u>. [1]

I am an undocumented [2] <u>immigrant, one</u> of the many directly under threat in Donald Trump's plan to deport all 11.5 million undocumented immigrants in the United States.

1

The author is thinking of deleting the underlined clause "even though...this fear" from the preceding sentence. Should he make this decision?

A) Yes, because this clause is unnecessary.
B) Yes, because the sentence is more focused without this clause.
C) No, because this clause describes the author's subconscious anxiety.
D) No, because this clause provides unidentified new information without evidence.

2

A) NO CHANGE
B) immigrant. One
C) immigrant, who is one
D) immigrant; one

CONTINUE

2   2

In addition, I am a visa-overstayer—one of about 4.6 million that he would prioritize [3] Trump has said in his deportation campaign. I'm terrified of my place in this country and am crippled by the seeming inevitability of the sweeping actions on immigration Trump has promised to the American people. He says he will cancel DACA, cancel funding to sanctuary cities, [4] and deport me, my parents, and members of my community. But in the face of uncertainty and overwhelming despondency, I refuse to be silenced.

President Trump directly threatens the physical and emotional wellbeing of me and all other undocumented people living in the US. [5] His presidency is built on a fundamental misunderstanding of the immigration system, on the notion that the nation's supposed vulnerability is the fault of undocumented immigrants, Muslims, and Latinos.

I don't write to concede defeat in the face of bigotry— our community will not be silent as our families are separated and our livelihoods dismantled. [6] You may write to ask for Donald Trump's pity or compassion when it comes to immigration.

3

The best placement for the underlined portion would be:

A) NO CHANGE

B) after the word In addition

C) after the word that

D) after the word campaign.

4

The author is thinking of removing the underlined portion. If he removes it, the paragraph would lose:

A) A shift in the mood from concern to reality

B) Overall summary of the paragraph

C) A shift in the mood from general to personal

D) A signal of hope

5

Which choice most efficiently introduces the description that follows in this sentence?

A) NO CHANGE

B) Members of my community support Trump,

C) Latinos attribute this consequence to Muslims,

D) His new immigration policy will not make immediate impact on the immigration system,

6

A) NO CHANGE

B) If I have time and courage, I will

C) I will not proclaim to

D) Neither do I

CONTINUE

2   2

I speak to my fellow undocumented Americans [7] directly and unswervingly, but my message is for everyone: Let us begin a dialogue with those who seek to suppress and deport us. For many who celebrate Trump, this election is a reassertion of their belief that undocumented immigrants do not deserve a place in this country. It is counterproductive (and impossible) to insulate ourselves from these voices, especially now that their views have been legitimized by the President himself. [8] We will be deported soon anyway. As undocumented immigrants, [9] I cannot crave to be part of U.S. citizens right away. Our immigration status is [10] fortunately tied up in our identity, so that we cannot exist without drawing attention to the systems that define us, the systems [11] by which this world—our world, the world we share with all those around us—is built. Just by living and breathing in America, we create pressure, we force reexamination, and therefore we are seen as a threat. Perhaps the hardest part of being undocumented is understanding that our futures depend on the worldviews and political leanings of other people.

7

A) NO CHANGE
B) directly,
C) directly based upon unswervingness
D) in direct motion

8

Which one best illustrates the author's emotional state?
A) NO CHANGE
B) We must engage.
C) We must accept the reality and respect Trump's decision.
D) The only way that we can legitimate ourselves is to leave the country.

9

A) NO CHANGE
B) exploiting politics is beyond our reach.
C) to raise political voice is next to impossible
D) we don't choose to be political

10

A) NO CHANGE
B) unexpectedly
C) undoubtedly
D) inextricably

11

A) NO CHANGE
B) on which
C) through which
D) from which

CONTINUE

2   2

Questions 12-22 are based on the following passage.

Oil Spill

An oil spill is the release of a liquid petroleum hydro-carbon into the environment, especially marine areas, [12] due to human activity, and is a form of pollution. The term is usually applied to marine oil spills, where oil is released into the ocean or coastal waters, but spills may also occur on land.

[13] Crude oil spill release from tankers offshore platforms, drilling rigs and wells, and spills of refined petroleum products (such as gasoline, diesel) and their by-products—[14] many such oil spills damage our environment to the irreversible point.

Oil spills penetrate into the structure of the plumage of birds and the fur of mammals, reducing its insulating ability, and making them more vulnerable to temperature fluctuations [15] but much less buoyant in the water.

12

Which of the following alternatives is NOT acceptable?
A) because of
B) because
C) result of
D) caused by

13

A) NO CHANGE
B) Crude oil spill release from tankers;
C) Crude oil spill release from tankers,
D) Crude oil spill release from tankers—

14

Which choice most effectively establishes threats to the environment?
A) NO CHANGE
B) oil spill removal process involves enormous work as expansive as the ocean, but it's by far the most effective solution.
C) it is irony that major oil refinery companies have cleanup companies, which generate revenue by the oil spills made by their parent company.
D) government policy has become strict enough to control the damage to the environment.

15

A) NO CHANGE
B) and
C) yet
D) resulting

CONTINUE

2

2

Cleanup and recovery from an oil spill are difficult [16] and depends upon many factors, including the type of oil spilled, the temperature of the water (affecting evaporation and biodegradation), and the types of shorelines and beaches involved.

[17] Technology that controls the ocean temperature to prevent evaporation and biodegradation is considered as state-of-the-art technology. Oil spills can have disastrous consequences for society [18] ; economically, environmentally, and socially.

16

A) NO CHANGE

B) and depend

C) , which depends

D) that depends

17

Which one provides details that best help the reader understand enormous tasks for oil clean up

A) NO CHANGE

B) Generally, over 70% of accidents occur in the ocean

C) Spills may take weeks, months or even years to clean up.

D) Over the last few decades, oil spill clean up technology has experienced dramatic advancement

18

A) NO CHANGE

B) : economically, environmentally, and socially.

C) ,environmentally economical and social.

D) economically, environmentally, socially.

CONTINUE

2   **2**

[19] As a result, oil spill accidents have initiated intense media attention and political uproar, bringing many together in a political struggle concerning government response to oil spills and [20] air pollution control in major cities in coastal area. Crude oil and refined fuel spills from tanker ship accidents have damaged vulnerable ecosystems in Alaska, the Gulf of Mexico, the Galapagos Islands, France, the Sundarbans, Ogoniland, and many other places.

19

A) NO CHANGE
B) In the meantime,
C) Then,
D) For example,

20

Which choice is most consistent with the previous portion of the sentence?

A) NO CHANGE
B) increase in budget to develop renewable energy source
C) what actions can best prevent them from happening.
D) energy conserving education to the public

21

Suppose the author's goal was to write a brief summary illustrating the hazardous impact of oil spills.
Would this summary fulfill the author's goal?

A) Yes, because the summary offers some of the consequences that oil spill creates
B) Yes, because the summary encourages establishing more strict government policy against oil spill prevention
C) No, because the summary focuses more on economic impact than on environmental impact
D) No, because the summary also represents struggles oil refinery companies experience to meet the government environment standards

CONTINUE ➤

2   **2**

*Oil spill control guidelines for the surface area of shorelines

Film thickness			Quantity spread	
Appearance	inches	mm	nm	gal/ sq. m i
Barely visible	0.0000015	0.0000380	38	25
Silvery sheen	0.0000030	0.0000760	76	50
First trace of color	0.0000060	0.0001500	150	100
Bright bands of color	0.0000120	0.0003000	300	200
Colors begin to dull	0.00004	0.0010000	1000	666
Colors are much darker	0.0000800	0.0020000	2000	1332

22

Please refer to the table and the passage.

In order to estimate quantity of oil spilled, all of following the variables must be available EXCEPT

A) Oil film thickness

B) Quantity spread

C) Total surface area

D) Direction of wind and current

CONTINUE ➡

2

Questions 23-33 are based on the following passage.

An Advanced Practice Registered Nurse

An advanced practice registered nurse (APRN) [23] ,which is a nurse with post-graduate education in nursing. APRNs are prepared with advanced didactic and clinical education, knowledge, skills, and scope of practice in nursing.

<1>In 2004, It recommended that advanced practice registered nurses move the entry level degree to the doctorate level by 2015. <2>APRN defines a level of nursing practice [24] that utilizes extended and expanded skills in assessment, planning, diagnosis and evaluation of the care required. <3>Nurses practicing at this level are educationally prepared at the post-graduate level [25] upon completion of post-graduate programs. <4> It also defines the basis of advanced practice is the high degree of knowledge, skill, and experience that [27] apply to the nurse-patient/client relationship.

23
A) NO CHANGE
B) was
C) is
D) OMIT the underlined portion

24
Which of the following alternatives would NOT be acceptable?
A) ,which utilizes
B) utilizing
C) utilized
D) —utilizing

25
A) NO CHANGE
B) , once they are professionally ready.
C) if they are well-prepared in the post-graduate level programs.
D) OMIT the underlined portion.

26
Which of the following is most logical sequences of this paragraph?
A) NO CHANGE
B) <1>,<4>,<2>,<3>
C) <2>,<3>,<1>,<4>
D) <2>,<3>,<4>,<1>

27
A) NO CHANGE
B) are utilizable and applicable
C) is applied
D) are applied

CONTINUE

2 2

APRNs [28],who demonstrate effective integration of theory, practice and experiences [29] along with increasing degrees of autonomy in judgments and interventions. Intensive post-graduate education is designed to teach an APRN to use multiple approaches to decision-making, manage the care of individuals and groups, [30] to engage in collaborative practices with the patient or client to achieve best outcomes. Each nurse specialty, especially NPs, can have sub-specialties or concentrations in a specific field or patient population in healthcare, [31] each of them has a unique history and context, but shares the commonality of being an APRN.

28

A) NO CHANGE
B) ,which demonstrate
C) demonstrate
D) demonstrates

29

Which of the following alternatives to the underlined portion would NOT be acceptable?

A) together with
B) plus
C) as well as
D) in company with

30

A) NO CHANGE
B) engaging
C) engage
D) by engaging

31

A) NO CHANGE
B) each of which
C) each and every single NP
D) and each of which

CONTINUE

2   2

[32] <u>Because </u>education, accreditation, and certification are necessary components of an overall approach to preparing an APRN for practice, these roles are regulated by legislation and specific professional regulation. While APRNs are educated differently depending on their specific specialty, all APRNs are now trained at the graduate level and are required to attain at least a master's degree.

[33] <u>International Council of Nurses established such regulations only in 1977.</u>

32

Which alternative word is NOT acceptable?

A) For
B) As
C) Since
D) Although

33

Which choice provides an accurate and effective summary of this paragraph?

A) NO CHANGE
B) A registered nurse who has acquired the expert knowledge must maintain high work ethics.
C) An advanced practice registered nurse (APRN) is generally considered high paying job.
D) Generally, a Master of Science in Nursing is their field of concentration.

CONTINUE

Questions 34-44 are based on the following passage.

Black Cat By Edgar Allan Poe

From my infancy I was noted for the docility and humanity of my disposition. I was especially fond of animals, and was indulged by my parents with a great variety of pets. With these I spent most of my time, and never was so happy [34] when feeding and caressing them. To those [35],whom have cherished an affection for a faithful and sagacious dog, I [36] need hardly be at the trouble of explaining the nature or the intensity of the gratification thus derivable. There is something in the unselfish and self-sacrificing love of a brute, which goes directly to the heart of him who has had frequent occasion to test the paltry friendship and gossamer fidelity of mere Man. I married early, and [37] in my wife was happy to find a disposition not uncongenial with my own.

34

A) NO CHANGE
B) as when
C) that when
D) than when

35

A) NO CHANGE
B) ; whom
C) , who
D) who

36

Which of the following alternatives would NOT be acceptable?
A) need scarcely
B) need not
C) hardly don't need to
D) don't need to

37

The best placement for the underlined portion would be:
A) NO CHANGE
B) after the word find
C) after the word disposition
D) after the word own

CONTINUE

UNAUTHORIZED COPYING OR REUSE OF ANY PART OF THIS PAGE IS ILLEGAL   **259**

2   2

[38] <u>With my partiality for domestic pets being observed,</u> she lost no opportunity of procuring those of the most agreeable kind. We had birds, gold fish, a fine dog, rabbits, a small monkey, and a cat.

This latter was a remarkably large and beautiful animal, entirely black, and sagacious to an astonishing degree. In speaking of his intelligence, my wife, who at heart was not a little tinctured with superstition, made frequent allusion to the ancient popular notion [39] <u>that domestic pets owners reduce their mental depression up to 20%.</u>

Pluto — this was the cat's name — was my favorite pet and playmate. I alone fed him, and he attended me wherever I went about the house. It was even with difficulty that I could prevent him [40] <u>to</u> following me through the streets.

Our friendship lasted, in this manner, for several years, [41]<u>during which period</u> my general temperament and character — through the instrumentality of the Fiend Intemperance — had (I blush to confess it) experienced a radical alteration for the worse.

38

A) NO CHANGE
B) Observing my partiality for domestic pets,
C) I gave partiality for domestic pets,
D) I gave partiality for domestic pets, which

39

Which one further illustrates the narrator's comments about ancient popular notion?

A) NO CHANGE
B) ,which regarded all black cats as witches in disguise.
C) that my parents used to tell me when I was young.
D) ,which lingered in my mind always.

40

A) NO CHANGE
B) from
C) with
D) DELETE IT

41

A) NO CHANGE
B) during
C) and
D) however

CONTINUE →

2   2

I suffered myself to use intemperate language to my

at length, I even offered her personal violence. My

pets, [42] of course, were made to feel the change in

my disposition. I not only neglected, but ill-used

them. For Pluto[43] ,however, I still retained

sufficient regard to restrain me from maltreating him,

as I made no scruple of maltreating the rabbits, the

monkey, or even the dog, when by accident, or

through affection, they came in my way. But my

disease grew upon me — for what disease is like

Alcohol! — and at length even Pluto, who was now

becoming old, [44] additionally somewhat

peevish — even Pluto began to experience the effects

of my ill temper.

42

Which of the following alternatives would NOT be acceptable?

A) gradually,
B) naturally,
C) sadly,
D) affectionately,

43

A) NO CHANGE
B) ; however,
C) however,
D) however

44

A) NO CHANGE
B) consequently
C) basically
D) necessarily

TEST 8

WRITING ABSOLUTE PATTERNS

Test 8 Writing & Language Section Patterns

Q1. Absolute Pattern 19: Redundant Error

Throughout the election cycle, **I tried to remain detached from the endless fear** and bigotry that seemed to spew out of the Trump political machine. For me, my parents, and my community, this election was too personal, **even though I tried to be detached from this fear.** [1]

Question: The author is thinking of deleting the clause "even though...this fear" from the preceding sentence. Should he make this decision?

√	**A) Yes, because this clause is unnecessary.**
	B) Yes, because the sentence is more <u>focused without this clause</u>.
	C) No, because this clause <u>emphasizes the author's subconscious anxiety.</u>
	D) No, because this clause provides <u>unidentified new information without evidence.</u>

A) It should be removed due to redundancy.

B) It is not the matter of focus, but the matter of redundancy.

C) 1> The author's subconscious anxiety was explained in the preceding clause as well.

   2> Therefore, redundancy.

D) This clause is not new. It's redundant

Q2. Absolute Pattern 16: Precision, Concision, Style

I am an undocumented [2] <u>immigrant, one </u>of the many directly under threat in Donald Trump's plan to deport all 11.5 million undocumented immigrants in the United States.

√	**A) NO CHANGE**	Precise and concise modifier
	B) immigrant. **One**	It can't be separated into two sentence because "One..." is a phrase, not a sentence.
	C) immigrant, **who** is one	Unnecessary conjunction
	D) immigrant**; one**	Semicolon requires a clause. The following modifier is a phrase.

As long as it is placed properly, a modifier that sits right next to the word it describes does not require a conjunction like (C) or semicolon like (D).

Q3. Absolute Pattern 12: Modifier Placement Error

In addition, I am a visa-overstayer—one of about 4.6 million **that he** would prioritize [3]Trump has said in his deportation campaign.

Question: The best placement for the underlined portion would be:

	A) NO CHANGE	C) 'that Trump had said he would...' is the correct placement.
	B) after the word In addition	A) is pronoun Error. The first sentence in a new paragraph can't start with a pronoun.
√	**C) after the word that**	

	D) after the word campaign.	B) 1> Changes the original meaning.
		  2> The sentence becomes "Trump had said I am…"
		
		D) 1> Change of original meaning.
		  2> The sentence becomes "the campaign Trump had said"

Q4. Absolute Pattern 1: Adding, Revising, Deleting, Retaining Information

He says he will cancel DACA, cancel funding to sanctuary cities, [4]and deport me, my parents, and members of my community.

Question: The author is thinking of removing the underlined clause. If he removes it, the paragraph would lose:

	A) a shift in the mood from concern to reality	C) Retaining this information adds tension and drives the situation to more personal
	B) overall summary of the paragraph	A) Adding "parents" doesn't shift the concern to the reality.
√	C) a **shift in the mood** from general to **personal**	
	D) a signal of hope	B) 1> The essay is not about his parents 2> Therefore, it loses no summary. D) is opposite

Q5. Absolute Pattern 1: Adding, Revising, Deleting, Retaining Information

[5]His presidency is built on a fundamental misunderstanding of the immigration system, on the notion that the **nation's supposed vulnerability is the fault of undocumented immigrants**,

Question: Which choice most efficiently introduces the description that follows in this sentence?

√	**A) NO CHANGE**	A) Retaining this information adds clear cause-effect relations
	B) Members of my community support Trump,	B), D) are opposite perception.
	C) Latinos attribute this consequence to Muslims,	
	D) His new immigration policy will not make immediate impact on the immigration system,	C) is not stated in the passage and inconsistent with the question

Q6. Absolute Pattern 10: Logical Expression

I don't write to concede defeat in the face of bigotry—our community will not be silent as our families are separated and our livelihoods dismantled. [6] You may write to ask for Donald **Trump's pity or compassion** when it comes to immigration.

	A) NO CHANGE	D) is consistent with the preceding sentence
	B) If I have time and courage, I will	A), B) are positive that interrupts the negative tone of the passage
	C) I will not proclaim to	C) "proclaim" is extreme and not suitable word.
√	**D) Neither do I**	

Q7. Absolute Pattern 19: Redundant Error

I speak to my fellow undocumented Americans [7] directly and unswervingly,

	A) NO CHANGE	B) is direct and concise.
√	**B) directly,**	A), C) 1> "directly" and "unswervingly" are synonyms 2> By removing synonym, information becomes concise
	C) directly based upon unswervingness	
	D) in direct motion	D) is wordy

Q8. Absolute Pattern 1: Adding, Revising, Deleting, Retaining Information

It is **counterproductive (and impossible) to insulate ourselves** from these voices, especially now that their views have been legitimized by the President himself. [8]We will be deported soon anyway.

Question: Which one best illustrates the author's emotional state?

A) NO CHANGE	B) 1> The author wants to fight against Trump's decision.
√ **B) We must engage.**	2> Therefore, the answer should maintain the same active tone.
C) We must accept the reality and respect Trump's decision.	
D) The only way that we can legitimate ourselves is to leave the country.	3> The rest of the choices are ruled out simply because of their passive tone.

Q9. Absolute Pattern 17: Pronoun Error

As undocumented immigrants, [9]I cannot crave to be part of U.S. citizens right away.

	A) NO CHANGE	D) immigrants (plural) = we (plural)
	B) exploiting politics is beyond our reach.	Modifier 'immigrants' is plural. Therefore, the subject in the main clause must be human in plural form.
	C) to raise political voice is next to impossible	A) 1> Pronoun error. 2> "immigrants" (plural) "I" (singular)
√	D) **we** don't choose to be political	B), C) "exploiting politics, "to raise political voice" cannot modify "undocumented immigrants" because they are non-human objects

Q10. Absolute Pattern 10: Logical Expression

Our immigration status is [10]fortunately **tied up** in our identity,

	A) NO CHANGE	'tied up' is negative word. "fortunately" is positive
	B) unexpectedly	"unexpectedly" dilutes the strong word "tied up"
	C) undoubtedly	"undoubtedly" dilutes the strong word "tied up"
√	D) **inextricably**	'inextricably' means complexly tied up.

Q11. Absolute Pattern 15: Prepositional Idiom

Passage: we cannot exist without drawing attention to the systems that define us, the systems [11]<u>by which</u> this world—our world, the world we share with all those around us—is **built.**

	A) NO CHANGE	
√	**B) on which**	'built on' is the correct prepositional idiom
	C) through which	
	D) from which	

Q12 Absolute Pattern 15: Prepositional Idiom

Passage: An oil spill is the release of a liquid petroleum hydrocarbon into the environment, especially marine areas, [12]<u>due to </u>human activity,

	A) because of	B) 1> 'because of' and 'because ' are not the same thing.
√	**B) because**	2> 'because' is conjunction that connects subordinating clause.
	C) result of	3> "because of" is preposition that can take on only a word or a short phrase like "human activity."
	D) caused by	C), D) are prepositions as well.

Q13. Absolute Pattern 13: Parallel Structure

[13] <u>Crude oil spill release from **tankers**</u> offshore **platforms,** drilling rigs and **wells,** and spills of refined petroleum products (such as gasoline, diesel) and their **by-products**—[14]**many such oil spills damage our environment** to the irreversible point.

	A) NO CHANGE	C) **"tankers, platforms, wells, by-products"** set the correct parallel structure.
	B) Crude oil from <u>tankers;</u>	A) 'tankers' and 'offshore' should be separated using a comma because "tankers" and "offshore platforms" are nouns and can't be tied together.
√	C) Crude oil spill release from **tankers,**	B) Semicolon connects a clause. 'offshore platforms' is not a clause
	D) Crude oil spill release from <u>tankers—</u>	D) A pair of dashes makes it subject of the sentence.

1> The above boldface font (takers, platform, wells, by-products) shows the parallel structure.

2>The main sentence hides all the way back, next to the "dash," "many such oil spills...."

3> The preceding phrases are modifiers that need to maintain parallelism.

Q14. Absolute Pattern 1: Adding, Revising, Deleting, Retaining Information

—[14]many such **oil spills damage our environment** to the irreversible point.

Question:_ Which choice most effectively establishes **threats to the environment**?

√	**A) NO CHANGE** (The question keywords "threats to the environment' suggest the answer should be negative.)	B), C), D) are all positive.
	B) oil spill removal process involves enormous work as expansive as ocean, <u>but it's by far the most effective solution.</u>	
	C) it is irony that major <u>oil refinery companies </u>have cleanup companies, which <u>generate revenue </u>by the oil spills made by their parent company.	
	D) <u>government policy has become strict enough </u>to control the damage to the environment.	

Q15. Absolute Pattern 7: Conjunction Error

and making them more vulnerable to temperature fluctuations [15] <u>but </u>much less buoyant in the water.

	A) NO CHANGE	B) The preceding phrase is paralleling with the following phrase, requiring 'and'
√	**B) and**	A), C) Contradictory conjunction 'but' or "yet" cancels out the preceding phrase.
	C) yet	D) "resulting" is used for cause-effect relation.
	D) resulting	

Q16. Absolute Pattern 21: Subject-Verb, Pronoun, Noun Agreement

Cleanup and recovery from an oil spill are difficult [16] **and** <u>depends </u>upon many factors,

	A) NO CHANGE	B) The subject 'cleanup and recovery' is plural, so is the verb 'depend'
√	**B) and depend**	A) 1> a punctuation error: when clauses share the same subject, comma shouldn't be placed. 2> the subject-verb agreement error: "depends" is singular.
	C) , which <u>depends</u>	
	D) that <u>depends</u>	C), D) 1> the subject-verb agreement error 2> "which" or "that" are ambiguous as they don't specify which is being modified

Q17. Absolute Pattern 1: Adding, Revising, Deleting, Retaining Information

[17] <u>**Technology**</u> that controls the ocean temperature to prevent evaporation and biodegradation is considered as <u>**state-of-the-art technology**</u>.

Question: Which one provides details that best help the reader understand enormous tasks for oil clean up	
A) NO CHANGE	C) The question keywords 'enormous tasks' implies quantity. Choices A, B, D are all related to the quality.
B) Generally, over 70% of accidents occur <u>in the ocean</u>	
√ **C) Spills may take weeks, months or even years to clean up.**	A), D) are quality, illustrating advanced skills
D) Over the last few decades, oil <u>spill clean up technology</u> has experienced dramatic advancement	B) is unrelated issue (location)

Q18. Absolute Pattern 18: Punctuation Error

Oil spills can have disastrous consequences for society [18] <u>**; e**conomically, environmentally, and socially.</u>

A) NO CHANGE	Semicolon error
√	**B) : economically, environmentally, and socially.**	Colon is used properly to introduce a list
	C) ,environmentally economical and social.	It changes the meaning
	D) economically, environmentally, socially.	Punctuation error

The purpose of 'colon' is very straightforward: it introduces things. The sentence structure wouldn't be a matter: a word, series of words, sentences, phrase, etc, are all acceptable after the colon.

For option A, semicolon functions as conjunction and requires a clause to link.

Option D requires a comma before "economically" because the following three adverbs are non-restrictive (inessential elements) and therefore need to be separated from the main clause.

Q19. Absolute Pattern 23: Transition Words for Supporting Detail, Contrast, and Consequence

[19] <u>As a result,</u> **oil spill accidents have initiated intense media attention** and political uproar,

√	**A) NO CHANGE**	The preceding text explicitly suggests that the following sentence requires an adverb with consequence.
	B) In the meantime,	'In the meantime' is used to contrast the information like 'while' or 'on the contrary'.
	C) Then,	'Then' is used to indicate the time sequence or concession.
	D) For example,	'For example' is used to support the preceding information.

The following adverbs are also used for consequence.

Correspondingly	Thus	In respect to	In that event
Subsequently	Hence	In consequence	Therefore

Q20. Absolute Pattern 1: Adding, Revising, Deleting, Retaining Information

bringing many together in a political **struggle concerning government response to oil spills** and [20] <u>air pollution control in major cities in coastal area.</u>

	A) NO CHANGE	A), B), D) are all unrelated issues with oil spills.
	B) increase in budget to develop <u>renewable energy source</u>	
√	**C) what actions can best prevent them from happening.**	
	D) <u>energy conserving education</u> to the public	

Q21. Absolute Pattern 1: Adding, Revising, Deleting, Retaining Information

Question: Suppose the author's goal was to write a **brief summary illustrating the hazardous impact** of oil spills. Would this summary successfully fulfill the author's goal?

√	**A) Yes, because the summary offers some of the consequences that oil spill creates**
	B) Yes, because the summary encourages establishing more strict <u>government policy</u> against oil spill prevention
	C) No, because the summary focuses more on <u>economic impact than on environmental impact</u>
	D) No, because the summary also represents struggles <u>oil refinery companies</u> experience to meet the government environment standards

B), D) are not stated in the passage.   C) is a minor issue.

Q22. Absolute Pattern 9: Informational Graphs

Question:_In order to estimate quantity of oil spilled, all of the following variables must be available **EXCEPT**

	A) Oil film thickness	film thickness is mentioned in the table
	B) Quantity spread	quantity spread is mentioned in the table
	C) Total surface area	total surface area can be calculated using the table
√	**D) Direction of wind and current**	Although an integral factor, wind direction is not mentioned in the passage.

Q23. Absolute Pattern 21: Subject-Verb, Pronoun, Noun Agreement

An advanced practice registered nurse (APRN) [23] ,which is a nurse with post-graduate education in nursing.

	A) NO CHANGE	",which" should be removed.
	B) was	The surrounding sentences use the present tense and must follow the same tense.
√	**C) is**	The subject 'APRN' requires the main verb 'is'
	D) OMIT	This option should be omitted from your selection.

Q24. Absolute Pattern 10: Logical Expression

APRN **defines** a level of nursing practice [24] that **utilizes** extended and expanded skills,

Question:_Which of the following alternatives would **NOT** be acceptable?

	A) ,which utilizes	C) "utilized" becomes the verb in past tense.
	B) utilizing	A),B),D): all of them use the proper form of punctuations and conjunctions to function as a modifier.
√	**C) utilized**	
	D) —utilizing	

Q25. Absolute Pattern 19: Redundant Error

Nurses practicing at this level are **educationally prepared at the post-graduate level** and may work in either a specialist or generalist capacity, [25] upon completion of post-graduate programs.

	A) NO CHANGE	A), C) are redundant error, repeating the preceding clause.
	B) once they are professionally ready.	
	C) if they are well-prepared in the post-graduate level programs.	B) is comma splice error
√	D) OMIT the underlined portion.	

Q26. Absolute Pattern 11: Logical Sequence

Question: Which of the following is most **logical sequences** of this paragraph?

	A) NO CHANGE	<2> **APRN defines a level of nursing practice** that utilizes extended and expanded skills, diagnosis and evaluation of the care required.
	B) <1>,<4>,<2>,<3>	<3> **Nurses practicing at this level** are educationally **prepared at the post-graduate level.**
	C) <2>,<3>,<1>,<4>	
√	D) <2>,<3>,<4>,<1>	<4> **It also** defines **the basis of advanced practice** is the high degree of knowledge, skill and experience that apply to the nurse-patient/client relationship.
		<1> In 2004, It **recommended that advanced practice** registered nurses move the entry level degree to the doctorate level by 2015.

APRN defines a level -> at this level->It also defines->In 2004, It

Q27. Absolute Pattern 21: Subject-Verb, Pronoun, Noun Agreement

It also defines the basis of advanced practice is **the high degree** of knowledge, skill, and experience that [27] apply to the nurse-patient/client relationship.

	A) NO CHANGE	C) The verb "is applied" agrees with the subject 'the high degree"
	B) are utilizable and applicable	A) The verb needs to be passive voice because "the high degree " can't "apply by itself.
√	C) is applied	
	D) are applied	B) "utilizable" and "applicable" are synonyms, redundant error. The verb is plural.

Q28. Absolute Pattern 21: Subject-Verb, Pronoun, Noun Agreement

APRNs [28],who **demonstrate** effective integration of theory, practice and experiences [29]along with increasing degrees of autonomy in judgments and interventions.

	A) NO CHANGE	C) The sentence does not have a verb. By simply removing 'who', we can make a verb.
	B) ,which demonstrate	
√	**C) demonstrate**	A) ', who' should be removed.
		B) ',which' should be removed.
	D) demonstrate**s**	D) The subject 'APRNs' is plural. "demonstrates" is singular.

Q29. Absolute Pattern 3. Colloquialism (Nonstandard Language)

APRNs demonstrate effective integration of theory, practice and experiences [29]along with increasing degrees of autonomy in judgments and interventions.

Question: Which of the following alternatives to the underlined portion would **NOT** be acceptable?

	A) together with	B) PLUS' is colloquial language and can't be used in writing.
√	**B) plus**	A), C), D) are all synonyms and can be used in written form.
	C) as well as	
	D) in company with	

Q30. Absolute Pattern 13. Parallel Structure

Intensive post-graduate education is designed to teach an APRN **to use** multiple approaches to decision-making, **manage** the care of individuals and groups, [30] to engage in collaborative practices with the patient or client to achieve best outcomes;

	A) NO CHANGE	The above parallel structure should be: "to use~, (to) manage~, (to) engage~."
	B) engaging	C) 'To-infinitive' clause in parallel structure can drop 'to' from the second to-infinitive clause and use the base verb only.
√	**C) engage**	
	D) by engaging	A) 'to' should be removed
		B), D) "engaging" is gerund.

Q31. Absolute Pattern 7.Conjunction Error

Each nurse specialty, especially NPs, can have sub-specialties or concentrations in a specific field or patient population in healthcare, [31]<u>each of them </u>has a unique history and context, but shares the commonality of being an APRN.

	A) NO CHANGE	B) In order to link these two clauses, we need to have a proper subordinating conjunction. "which" is used as a conjunction
√	**B) each of which**	A) Comma splice error. "each of them~" does not have a conjunction to link the previous sentence.
	C) each and every single NP	C) Comma splice error. "each" and "every" are redundant.
	D) **and** each of **which**	D) It has two conjunctions. "and" and "which".

Q32. Absolute Pattern 7.Conjunction Error

[32] <u>Because </u>education, accreditation, and certification are necessary components of an overall approach to preparing an APRN for practice, these roles are regulated by legislation and specific professional regulation

	A) For	'For', 'As', 'Since' are all synonyms to 'Because'
	B) As	
	C) Since	
√	**D) Although**	'Although' is used for concessional clause.

Q33. Absolute Pattern 1: Adding, Revising, Deleting, Retaining Information

While APRNs **are educated** differently depending on their specific **specialty,** all APRNs are now **trained at the graduate level** and are required to attain at least a **master's degree.**
[33] **<u>International Council of Nurses</u>** <u>established such regulations only in 1977.</u>

	A) NO CHANGE
	B) A registered nurse who has acquired the expert knowledge must maintain high <u>work ethics</u>.
	C) An advanced practice registered nurse (APRN) is generally considered <u>high paying job</u>.
√	**D) Generally, a Master of Science in Nursing is their field of concentration.**

D) is the only education-related sentence.

A) No new information should be introduced suddenly.

B), "work ethics" and C) "high paying job" are not directly related to APRN education.

Q34. Absolute Pattern 4: Comparison

With these I spent most of my time, and never was **so happy** [34] <u>when </u>feeding and caressing them.

	A) NO CHANGE	B) "so…as" is correlative conjunction that always works as a pair, and other alternatives cannot replace this form.
√	**B) as when**	
	C) that when	
	D) than when	

Q35. Absolute Pattern 17: Pronoun Error

To those [35],<u>whom</u> **have cherished** an affection for a faithful and sagacious dog, I [36] <u>need hardly </u>be at the trouble of explaining the nature or the intensity of the gratification thus derivable.

	A) NO CHANGE	D) "who" is the correct subjective pronoun.
	B) ;whom	A) and B) 'whom' is objective and should not be placed before verb.
	C) ,who	
√	**D) who**	C) comma should not be used in restrictive (essential) modifier. "who have cherished… dog" is an essential modifier in the sentence. (example) -I love wonder woman **WHO is** my heroin. -Wonder woman **WHOM I** loved married to Batman.

Q36. Absolute Pattern 8: Double Negative Error

To those who have cherished an affection for a faithful and sagacious dog, I [36] <u>need hardly </u>be at the trouble of explaining the nature

Question:_ Which of the following alternatives would NOT be acceptable?

	A) need scarcely	C) Double negative error: both 'hardly' and 'don't' are negative. It should remove either one of them.
	B) need not	
√	**C) hardly don't need to**	
	D) don't need to	

Q37. Absolute Pattern 1: Adding, Revising, Deleting, Retaining Information

I married early, and [37] in my wife was happy to find **a disposition** not uncongenial with my own.

	A) NO CHANGE	B) "...and was happy to find in **my wife a disposition** not uncongenial' is an ideal arrangement.
√	**B) after the word find**	
	C) after the word disposition	A) Change of meaning: It appears to be ' my wife was happy'
	D) after the word own	C) Change of meaning: in my **wife not uncongenial with my own** D)"...with my own in my wife" doesn't make sense.

Key point: choice C: 'not uncongenial' has to be compared with disposition , not wife.

Q38. Absolute Pattern 12: Modifier Error

[38] With my partiality for domestic pets **being** observed, **she** lost no opportunity of procuring those of the most agreeable kind.

	A) NO CHANGE	Wordiness error and passive. *do not choose 'being'
√	**B) Observing my partiality for domestic pets,**	"she" was "observing my partiality"
	C) **I** gave partiality for domestic pets,	is comma splice
	D) **I** gave partiality for domestic pets, which	"which" is ambiguous and not needed

Q39. Absolute Pattern 1: Adding, Revising, Deleting, Retaining Information

In speaking of his intelligence, my wife, who at heart was not a little tinctured with **superstition,** made frequent allusion to the **ancient popular notion**[39] that **domestic pets owners can reduce their mental depression up to 20%.**

Question: Which one further illustrates the narrator's comments about ancient popular notion?

	A) NO CHANGE (The statement is more like modern one)	Inconsistent with the question
√	**B) , *which regarded* all black cats as witches in disguise.**	Most compatible with ancient notion
	C) that my parents used to tell me when I was young.	Inconsistent with the question
	D) , which lingered in my mind always.	Too vague expression

Q40. Absolute Pattern 15: Prepositional Idiom

It was even with difficulty that I could **prevent** him [40] <u>to</u> following me through the streets.

	A) NO CHANGE	
√	**B) from**	**"prevent** something or someone **from…"** is the correct idiom
	C) with	
	D) DELETE IT	

Q41. Absolute Pattern 7: Conjunction Error

Our friendship lasted, in this manner, for several years, [41], <u>during which </u>my general temperament and character — through the instrumentality of the Fiend Intemperance — had (I blush to confess it) experienced a **radical alteration** for the worse.

√	**A) NO CHANGE**	"for several years, during which (period)" is the correct conjunction for time.
	B) during	"during" is preposition and can't carry a clause.
	C) and	'and' is used for parallel structure. The primary sentence and the dependent clause are not based on the parallel (equal) concept.
	D) however	'however' is adverb and requires a semicolon to use it.

Q42. Absolute Pattern 23: Transition Words for Supporting Detail, Contrast, and Consequence

I suffered myself to use intemperate language to my at length, I even offered her personal **violence**. **My pets**, [42]<u>of course,</u> **were made to feel** the change in my disposition.

Question: Which of the following alternatives would **NOT be acceptable**?

	A) gradually,	Negative (connotation)
	B) naturally,	Negative (connotation)
	C) sadly,	Negative
√	**D) affectionately,**	Positive

Q43. Absolute Pattern 18: Punctuation Error

I not only neglected but ill-used them. For Pluto [43], **however,** I still retained sufficient regard to restrain me from maltreating him,

√	A) NO CHANGE	When 'however' is used in the middle of the sentence, it should have a pair of commas that offset 'however'.
	B) ; however,	Semicolon + however is used to connect the main and subordinating clause.
	C) however,	'however' cannot be used with a single comma in the middle of the sentence.
	D) however	'however' cannot be used without a punctuation

Q44. Absolute Pattern 23: Transition Words for Supporting Detail, Contrast, and Consequence

But my disease grew upon me — for what disease is like Alcohol! — and at length even **Pluto, who was now becoming old,** [44] additionally **somewhat peevish** — even Pluto began to experience the effects of my ill temper.

	A) NO CHANGE	
√	B) consequently	Aging causes Pluto becomes peevish as a consequence
	C) basically	
	D) necessarily	

SAT
Writing and Language
Test 9

ALL THE LOGIC AND RULES

BEHIND THE EVERY SINGLE

SAT QUESTION

Writing and Language Test 9
35 MINUTES, 44 QUESTIONS

Each passage below is accompanied by a number of questions. For some questions, you will consider how the passage might be revised to improve the expression of ideas. For other questions, you will consider how the passage might be edited to correct errors in sentence structure, usage, or punctuation. A passage or a question may be accompanied by one or more graphics (such as a table or graph) that you will consider as you make revising and editing decisions.

Questions 1-11 are based on the following passage.

WikiLeaks

WikiLeaks is an international [1] non-profitable journalistic organization that publishes secret information, news leaks, and classified media from anonymous sources, [2] mainly from organizations or individuals who do not disclose their names. Its website, initiated in 2006 in Iceland by the organization Sunshine Press, claimed a database of more than 1.2 million documents within a year of its launch. Julian Assange, an Australian Internet activist, is generally described as its founder, editor-in-chief, and director. Hrafnsson is also a member of Sunshine Press Productions, [3] along with Assange, Hrafnsson and Gavin MacFadyen are the only known members outside.

1
A) NO CHANGE
B) non-profit journal organization
C) non-profitable journalism organization
D) non-profit journalistic organization

2
A) NO CHANGE
B) however, the origin of information is normally not disclosed.
C) —although the information is not readily verifiable.
D) DELETE IT.

3
A) NO CHANGE
B) in conjunction with,
C) together with Assange,
D) and with Assange

CONTINUE

2

2

The group has released a number of [4] significantly pivotal documents that have become front-page news items. Early releases included documentation of equipment expenditures and holdings in the Afghanistan war and a report informing a corruption investigation inKenya. In April 2010, WikiLeaks published gunsight footage from the 12 July 2007 Baghdad airstrike in which Iraqi journalists were among those killed by an AH-64 Apache helicopter, known [5] to be the *Collateral Murder* video. In July of the same year, WikiLeaks released

[6] ,a compilation of more than 76,900 documents about the War in

Afghanistan, Afghan Diary to the world.

WikiLeaks [7] relies on some degree on volunteers and previously described its founders as a mixture of Asian dissidents, journalists, mathematicians, and start-up company technologists from the United States.

4

A) NO CHANGE
B) significant and pivotal documents
C) significant documents, which is pivotal
D) significant documents

5

Which of the following alternatives to the underlined portion would NOT be acceptable?

A) to be
B) as
C) for
D) to

6

The best placement for the underlined portion would be:

A) NO CHANGE
B) After the word "year,"
C) After the word "Diary"
D) After the word "world"

7

A) NO CHANGE
B) reliance on some degree to
C) reliance to some degree on
D) relies to some degree on

CONTINUE

2   **2**

WikiLeaks progressively [8] adopt a more traditional publication model and no longer accepts either user comments or edits.

As of June 2009, the website had more than 1,200 registered volunteers and listed an advisory board comprising Assange, his deputy Jash Vora and seven other people, [9] some of them denied any association with the organization.

According to the WikiLeaks website, its goal is "to bring important news and information to the public. One of our most important activities is to publish original source material alongside our news stories, [10] for example, readers and historians alike can see evidence of the truth."

Another of the organization's goals is to ensure that journalists and whistleblowers are not prosecuted for emailing sensitive or classified documents. The online "drop box" is described by the WikiLeaks website as "[11] an innovative, security and anonymous way for sources to leak information to WikiLeaks journalists."

8

A) NO CHANGE
B) had adopted
C) is under the influence of drastic adoption with
D) adopts

9

A) NO CHANGE
B) some people
C) some of who
D) some of whom

10

A) NO CHANGE
B) so
C) because
D) moreover,

11

A) NO CHANGE
B) an innovative, secure, and anonymous
C) an innovatively secure and anonymous
D) an innovatively and securely anonymous

CONTINUE ➡

Questions 12-22 are based on the following passage.

ISIS

The Islamic State of Iraq and Syria (ISIS) is a Salafi jihadist militant group that follows a fundamentalist, Wahhabi doctrine of Sunni Islam.

The [12] group adopted the name Islamic State and its idea of a caliphate have been widely criticized from the United Nations, [13] various governments refuted, and mainstream Muslim groups rejecting its statehood or caliphhood.

The group first began referring to itself as Islamic State or IS in June 2014, [14] which it proclaimed itself a worldwide caliphate and named Abu Bakr al-Baghdadi as its caliph. The group has been designated a terrorist organization by the United Nations. Over 60 countries are directly or indirectly waging war against ISIL. [15] Adopted at social media, ISIL is widely known for its videos of beheadings.

12
A) NO CHANGE
B) groups' adoption of
C) adoption of group
D) group's adoption of

13
A) NO CHANGE
B) along with various governments,
C) various governments,
D) both various governments

14
A) NO CHANGE
B) whom
C) that
D) when

15
A) NO CHANGE
B) Adept
C) Addicted
D) Annexed

CONTINUE

2   **2**

[16] The United Nations holds ISIL responsible for human rights abuses and war crimes, and Amnesty International has charged the group with ethnic cleansing on a "historic scale" in northern Iraq. Around the world, Islamic religious leadershave overwhelmingly condemned ISIL's ideology.

The United Nations [17] holds ISIS responsible for human rights abuses and war crimes, and Amnesty International has charged the group with ethnic cleansing on a "historic scale" in northern Iraq. Around the world, [18] ISIS gained prominence when it drove Iraqi government forces out of key cities in its Western Iraq and capturing Mosul.

16

In the preceding sentence, the writer is considering replacing " beheadings." with " beheadings: soldiers, civilians, journalists and aid workers
Should the writer make this revision?

A) Yes, because it fixes the incomplete sentence.

B) Yes, because it gives added information about the atrocity of the group.

C) No, because it unnecessarily lists examples that should be placed elsewhere.

D) No, because it is not proper to mention the occupations in this sentence.

17

A) NO CHANGE

B) hold

C) is held

D) are held

18

Which choice maintains the essay's negative tone and most strongly supports the writer at this point?

A) NO CHANGE

B) Islamic religious leaders have overwhelmingly condemned ISIS's ideology and actions.

C) ISIS has long argued that the group has the true path of true Islam and that its actions reflect the religion's real teachings or virtues.

D) Some extremists in countries like U.S. Russia, Israel, Turkey, Saudi Arabia hold the same opinion with the leaders in ISIS

CONTINUE ➤

2   2

In June 2014, Saudi Arabia moved troops to [19] their borders with Iraq, after Iraq lost control [20] of, or withdrew from, strategic crossing points that then came under the control of ISIL, or tribes that supported ISIL.

In late January 2015, it was reported that ISIS members infiltrated the European Union and disguised themselves as civilian refugees who were emigrating from the war zones of Iraq. An ISIS representative claimed that ISIS [21] had successfully smuggled 4,000 fighters, and that the smuggled fighters were planning attacks in Europe in retaliation for the airstrikes carried out against ISIS targets in Iraq and Syria.

[22] In the meantime, experts believe that this claim was exaggerated to boost their stature and spread fear, and acknowledged that some Western countries were aware of the smuggling.

19

A) NO CHANGE
B) there borders
C) it's border
D) its border

20

Which of the following alternatives to the underlined portion would NOT be acceptable?
A) of, or withdrew from, strategic
B) of (or withdrew from) strategic
C) of —or withdrew from—strategic
D) of, or withdrew from strategic

21

A) NO CHANGE
B) successfully smuggled
C) smuggled with success
D) had been successfully smuggled

22

A) NO CHANGE
B) Granted,
C) However,
D) Since

CONTINUE

2

2

Questions 23-33 are based on the following passage.

Quantum Physics

Quantum mechanics is a fundamental branch of physics concerned with processes [23] involving: for example, atoms and photons. <A> System such as these which [24] obey quantum mechanics can be in a quantum superposition of different states, [25] unlike classical physics. <B> Early quantum theory was profoundly reconceived in the mid-1920s. <C> The [26] reconceived theory is formulated in various specially developed mathematical formalisms. <D> Important applications of quantum theory include superconducting magnets, light-emitting diodes, and the laser transistor and semiconductors such as the microprocessor, medical and research imaging such as magnetic resonance imaging and electron microscopy, and explanations for many biological and physical phenomena.

23

A) NO CHANGE
B) involving; for example,
C) involving for example
D) involving, for example,

24

A) NO CHANGE
B) obeys quantum mechanics
C) abeyance of
D) have obeyed

25

A) NO CHANGE
B) unlike classical physics superposition
C) unlike that of classical physics
D) unlike in classical physics

26

Which of the following alternatives to the underlined portion would NOT be acceptable?
A) conceptualized
B) rehabilitated
C) redesigned
D) recalibrated

27

At this point, the writer wishes to introduce the practicality of Quantum mechanics.
Which sentence can be the best topic sentence for the new paragraph?
A) <A> System such as ...
B) <B> Early quantum theory...
C) <C> The reconceived...
D) <D> Important applications of...

CONTINUE →

2   **2**

When quantum mechanics was originally formulated, it was applied to models [28] whose correspondence limit was non-relativistic classical mechanics. For instance, the well-known model of the quantum harmonic oscillator uses an explicitly non-relativistic expression for the kinetic energy of the oscillator, and is thus a quantum version of the classical harmonic oscillator. Early attempts to merge quantum mechanics [29] for special relativity has involved the replacement of the Schrödinger equation with a covariant equation. [30] For example, these theories were successful in explaining many experimental results, they had certain unsatisfactory qualities stemming from their neglect of the relativistic creation and annihilation of particles. A fully relativistic quantum theory required the development of quantum field theory, which applies quantization to a field [31]—less than a fixed set of particles.

The first complete quantum field theory, quantum electrodynamics, provides a fully quantum description of the electromagnetic interaction.

28

A) NO CHANGE
B) whom
C) which
D) that

29

A) NO CHANGE
B) with special relativity involved
C) to special relativity had involved
D) into special relativity involves

30

A) NO CHANGE
B) While,
C) Due to
D) Moreover,

31

A) NO CHANGE
B) similar to
C) the same as
D) rather than

CONTINUE ⮕

2   2

The full [32] apparatus's of quantum field theory is often unnecessary for describing electrodynamic systems. A simpler approach, one that has been employed since the inception of quantum mechanics, is to treat charged particles as quantum mechanical objects being acted on by a classical electromagnetic field.

32

A) quantum field of apparatus

B) apparatus' quantum field

C) apparatus of quantum field

D) quantum field's apparatus

33

Suppose the writer's primary purpose had been to describe the difference between Quantum physics and classical physics.

Would this essay accomplish that purpose?

A) Yes, because it discusses both theories

B) Yes, because it focuses primarily on the early stage of Quantum theory that heavily depended on Classical Physics

C) No, because it focuses more on Classical Physics and its influence upon Quantum Physics

D) No, because it focuses more on Quantum Physics and its conceptual understanding.

CONTINUE ➡

2   2

Questions 34-44 are based on the following passage.

Frankenstein, or the Modern Prometheus
By Mary Wollstonecraft Shelley

You will rejoice to hear that no disaster [34] accompany the commencement of an enterprise which you have regarded with such evil forebodings. Do you understand this feeling? This breeze, which has travelled from the regions [35] for which I am advancing, gives me a foretaste of those icy climes. Inspirited by this wind of promise, [36] what a fervent and vivid moment.

I try in vain to be persuaded that the pole is the seat of frost and [37] desolation, it ever presents itself to my imagination as the region of beauty and delight. There, Margaret, the sun is forever visible, [38] its broad disk just skirting the horizon and diffusing a perpetual splendor. There--for with your leave, my sister, I will put some trust in preceding navigators-- there snow and frost are banished; and, sailing over a calm sea, we may be wafted to a land surpassing in wonders and in beauty every region hitherto discovered on the habitable globe.

34

A) NO CHANGE
B) had accompanied
C) is to be accompanied
D) has accompanied

35

A) NO CHANGE
B) to
C) towards
D) in

36

A) NO CHANGE
B) more fervent and vivid had my daydream become.
C) I have become more fervent and vivid
D) there has become more fervent and vivid in my daydream.

37

A) NO CHANGE
B) desolation; it ever
C) desolation that ever
D) desolation: it ever

38

A) NO CHANGE
B) it's
C) there is
D) there are

CONTINUE

2   **2**

I write a few lines in haste to say that I am safe--and well advanced on my voyage. This letter will reach England by a merchantman now on its homeward voyage from Archangel; more fortunate than [39] me, who may not see my native land, perhaps, for many years. I [40] am, however, in good spirits, my men are bold and apparently firm of purpose, nor do the floating sheets of ice that continually pass us, indicating the dangers of the region towards which we are advancing, [41] appearing dismay them. We have already reached a very high latitude; but it is the height of summer, and although not so warm as in England, the southern gales, which blow us speedily towards those shores which I so ardently desire to attain, breathe a degree of renovating warmth which I had not expected.

No incidents [42] has hitherto befallen us that would make a figure in a letter. One or two stiff gales and the springing of a leak are accidents which [43] experiencing navigators scarcely remember to record, and I shall be well content if nothing worse happen to us during our voyage.

39

A) NO CHANGE

B) myself

C) mine

D) I

40

A) NO CHANGE

B) am however in good spirits:

C) am, however, in good spirits:

D) am, however, in good spirits,

41

A) NO CHANGE

B) appear to

C) appears to

D) that appear to

42

A) NO CHANGE

B) has hitherto befall

C) have hitherto befallen

D) have already befall

43

A) NO CHANGE

B) experienced

C) is experienced

D) experience

CONTINUE ➡

2

2

So strange an accident [44] has happened to us and I cannot forbear recording it, although it is very probable that you will see me before these papers can come into your possession.

44

A) NO CHANGE

B) has happened to us that I

C) had happened to us and me

D) happened to us and I

TEST 9

WRITING ABSOLUTE PATTERNS

Test 9 Writing & Language Section Patterns

Q1. Absolute Pattern 10: Logical Expression

WikiLeaks is an international [1]non-profitable journalistic organization

A) NO CHANGE	D) Either "non-profit" or "not-for-profit" journalistic (adjective) organization (noun) is the correct usage.
B) non-profit **journal** organization	
C) non-**profitable** journalism organization	B) Both 'journal' and 'organization' are noun and can't be combined.
√ D) **non-profit journalistic** organization	A), C) "non-profitable" is not standard usage.

Q2. Absolute Pattern 19: Redundant Error

WikiLeaks is an international non-profit journalistic organization that publishes secret information, news leaks, and classified media from **anonymous sources**, [2] mainly from organizations or individuals who do not disclose their names.

A) NO CHANGE	D) The underlined portion is redundant with the word anonymous source"
B) however, the origin of information is normally not disclosed.	A), B), and C) are repeating the already written information.
C) —although the information is not readily verifiable.	
√ D) DELETE IT.	

Q3. Absolute Pattern 5: Comma Splice Error

Hrafnsson is also a member of Sunshine Press Productions, [3] along with Assange, Hrafnsson and Gavin MacFadyen are the only known members outside.

A) NO CHANGE	D) 1> "and" is a conjunction
B) in conjunction with Assange,	2> "and" links the previous clause with the following clause.
C) together with Assange,	A), B), and C)
√ D) **and with Assange**	"along with", "in conjunction with" and "together with" are not conjunctions, and can't connect the clause.

Q4. Absolute Pattern 19: Redundant Error

The group has released a number of [4] <u>significantly pivotal documents</u> that have become front-page news items.

	A) NO CHANGE	D) is most concise.
	B) significant and pivotal documents	A), B), C) Redundant Error.
	C) significant documents, which is pivotal	
√	**D) significant documents**	"significantly" and "pivotal" are synonyms, causing a redundancy.

Q5. Absolute Pattern 24: Verb Tense / Voice Error

In April 2010, WikiLeaks published gunsight footage from the 12 July 2007 Baghdad airstrike in which Iraqi journalists were among those killed by an AH-64 Apache helicopter, known [5] <u>to be</u> the *Collateral Murder* video.

√	**A) to be**	A) 1> "to be" is used for the future tense. 2> "In April 2010." indicates the past.
	B) as	All the remaining options work well with the past tense.
	C) for	
	D) to	

Q6. Absolute Pattern 12: Modifier Placement Error

In July of the same year, WikiLeaks released [6] <u>, a compilation of more than 76,900 documents about the War in Afghanistan,</u> Afghan Diary to the world.

	A) NO CHANGE	C) The correct sentence:
	B) After the word "year,"	In July of the same year, WikiLeaks released Afghan War Diary, <u>a compilation of more than 76,900 documents about the War in Afghanistan,</u> to the world.
√	**C) After the word "Diary"**	
	D) After the word "world"	1> The modifier "a compilation… Afghanistan" is so long that
		2> it separates the verb "released" from the object "Afghan Diary", blurring the original meaning.

Q7. Absolute Pattern 15: Prepositional Idiom

WikiLeaks [7] relies on some degree to volunteers and previously described its founders as a mixture of Asian dissidents, journalists, mathematicians, and start-up company technologists from the United States.

	A) NO CHANGE	D) "to some degree" + "relies on" => **relies _to some degree_ on**
	B) reliance on some degree to	B), C) 'Reliance' is noun. The sentence requires a verb, 'reles'
	C) reliance to some degree on	
√	D) relies to some degree on	

Q8. Absolute Pattern 24: Verb Tense / Voice Error

WikiLeaks progressively [8] adopt a more traditional publication model and no longer **accepts** either user comments or edits.

	A) NO CHANGE	D) 1> The simple past tense (adopted) should be ideal in this sentence.
	B) had adopted	2> However, having none in the options, the best alternative is to maintain the same present tense as used in the same sentence.
	C) is under the influence of drastic adoption with	A) 1> Subject-verb agreement error. 2> "WikiLeaks" the title of the organization, is singular noun and therefore should use the singular verb.
√	D) adopts	B) 1> "had adopted" is past perfect tense. 2> the adjacent verb "accepts" is the present. 3> Tense can't jump from present to past perfect.
		C) is wordy

Q9. Absolute Pattern 7: Conjunction Error

As of June 2009, the website had more than 1,200 registered volunteers and listed an advisory board comprising Assange, his deputy Jash Vora and seven other people, [9] some of them denied any association with the organization.

	A) NO CHANGE	D) "whom" is used as a conjunction that links the previous clause.
	B) some people	A) and B) 1> Comma splice error. 2> No conjunction is used to link the subordinating clause "some of them..." or "some people"
	C) some of who	
√	D) some of whom	C) 1> "who" is subjective. 2> "of" is preposition. 3> Therefore, "whom", the objective pronoun must be used after the preposition.

Q10. Absolute Pattern 23: Transition Words for Supporting Detail, Contrast, and Consequence

According to the WikiLeaks website, its goal is "to bring important news and information to the public. One of our most important activities is to publish **original source material** alongside our news stories, [10] for example, readers and historians alike **can see evidence** of the truth."

	A) NO CHANGE	B) "so" means "for this reason."
√	**B) so**	C) 1> The cause appeared already in the previous sentence.
	C) because	2> It should use 'so', or 'therefore', or 'thus.' to show the consequence.
	D) moreover,	D) is used to backup the consequence.

Q11. Absolute Pattern 13: Parallel Structure

The online "drop box" is described by the WikiLeaks website as "[11] an **innovative, security** and **anonymous** way for sources to leak information to WikiLeaks journalists."

	A) NO CHANGE	B) innovative (Adjective), secure (Adjective), and anonymous (Adjective) = The parallel structure.
√	**B) an innovative, secure, and anonymous**	
	C) an innovatively secure and anonymous	A) innovative (Adjective), security (Noun), and anonymous (Adjective) parallelism error.
	D) an innovatively and securely anonymous	C), D) change the meaning

Q12. Absolute Pattern 14: Possessive Determiners and Possessive Noun Error

The [12] group adopted the name Islamic State and its idea of a caliphate *have been widely criticized* from the United Nations, various governments refuted, and mainstream Muslim groups rejecting its statehood ...

	A) NO CHANGE	D)
	B) groups' adoption of	1> "adopted" is not the main verb.
		2> *have been widely criticized* " is the main verb.
	C) adoption of group	3> "The group's adoption...State" parallels with the following phrase "and its
√	**D) group's adoption of**	idea of a caliphate".
		A) uses "adopted" as the main verb.
		B) "groups" is plural. It is a singular.
		C) group" and the following word "the name doesn't link

Q13. Absolute Pattern 13: Parallel Structure

The group's adoption of the name Islamic State and its idea of a caliphate have been widely criticized from **the United Nations**, [13] <u>various governments</u> refuted, **and mainstream Muslim groups** rejecting its statehood or caliphhood.

	A) NO CHANGE	C) "the United Nations, (Noun) <u>various governments (Noun),</u> and mainstream Muslim groups (Noun).
	B) along with various governments,	A) The verb 'refuted" should be deleted to make it as the parallel structure.
√	C) **various governments,**	
	D) both various governments	B), D) "along with" or "both" are unnecessary

Q14. Absolute Pattern 7: Conjunction Error

The group first began referring to itself as Islamic State or IS in June 2014, [14] <u>which</u> it proclaimed itself a worldwide caliphate and named Abu Bakral-Baghdadi as its caliph

	A) NO CHANGE	D) "when" links to "June 2014"
	B) whom	A) "which" is ambiguous.
	C) that	B) is for a human precedent
√	D) **when**	C) might work only were there no comma after '2014'

Q15. Absolute Pattern 10: Logical Expression

Passage: [15] <u>Adopted</u> at social media, ISIL is widely known for its videos of beheadings.

	A) NO CHANGE	B) Adept means skillful.
√	B) **Adept**	A) Adopted = taking over someone's child
	C) Addicted	C) addicted = obsessed
	D) Annexed	D) annexed = to be combined

Q16. Absolute Pattern 1: Adding, Revising, Deleting, Retaining Information

Adept at social media, ISIL is widely known for its videos of beheadings.

	A)	Yes, because it fixes the incomplete sentence.
√	**B)**	**Yes, because it gives added information about the atrocity of the group.**
	C)	No, because it unnecessarily lists examples that should be placed elsewhere.
	D)	No, because it is not proper to mention the occupations in this sentence.

B) By providing information of those actual victims, the revised sentence emphasizes the organization's atrocity.

A) There's no grammar error.

C) It's not mentioned nowhere else.

D) It is necessary to list explicitly who the victims were.

Q17. Absolute Pattern 21: Subject-Verb, Pronoun, Noun Agreement

The United Nations [17] holds ISIS responsible for human rights abuses and war crimes, and Amnesty International has charged the group with ethnic cleansing on a "historic scale" in northern Iraq.

√	**A) NO CHANGE**	A) "The United Nations" is one entity, one organization, and singular.
	B) hold	B) is plural
	C) is held	C), D) are passive
	D) are held	

Q18. Absolute Pattern 1: Adding, Revising, Deleting, Retaining Information

Around the world, [18] ISIS gained prominence when it drove Iraqi government forces out of key cities in its Western Iraq and capturing Mosul.

Question: Which choice maintains the essay's <u>negative tone and most strongly support the writer at this point</u>?

	A) NO CHANGE	B) is negative towards the ISIS.
√	**B) Islamic religious leaders have overwhelmingly condemned ISIS's ideology and actions.**	A) is neutral narrative tone
	C) ISIS has long argued that the group has the true path of true Islam and that its actions reflect the religion's real teachings or virtues.	C) is positive towards the ISIS.
		D) is inconsistent with the question as it deviates from the main issue
	D) Some extremists in countries like U.S. Russia, Israel, Turkey, Saudi Arabia hold the same opinion with the leaders in ISIS	

Q19. Absolute Pattern 14: Possessive Determiners and Possessive Noun Error

In June 2014, Saudi Arabia moved troops to [19] <u>their borders</u> with Iraq,

	A) NO CHANGE	D) 1> The subject "Saudi Arabia" is singular.
	B) there borders	2> "its" is singular possessive pronoun.
	C) it's border	A) is possessive plural pronoun
√	**D) its border**	B) "there" is place adverb
		C) "It's" is the contraction for either it has or it is

Q20. Absolute Pattern 18: Punctuation Error

In June 2014, Saudi Arabia moved troops to its borders with Iraq, after Iraq lost control [20] <u>of, or withdrew from, strategic</u> crossing points that then came under the control of ISIL, or tribes that supported ISIL.

	A) of, or withdrew from, strategic	D) 1> uses only one comma.
	B) of (or withdrew from) strategic	2> If a phrase or a word within a sentence simply adds extra information, it must be separated from the main clause using a necessary punctuation.
	C) of —or withdrew from—strategic	
√	**D) of, or withdrew from strategic**	A) a pair of commas, B) parenthesis, C) double dashes separate the interjected modifier from the main clause.

Q21. Absolute Pattern 24: Verb Tense / Voice Error

An ISIS representative **claimed** that ISIS [21] <u>had successfully smuggled</u> 4,000 fighters, and that the smuggled fighters were planning attacks in Europe in retaliation for the airstrikes carried out against ISIS targets in Iraq and Syria.

√	**A) NO CHANGE**	A) 1> "claimed" is past tense.
	B) successfully <u>smuggled</u>	2> smuggle should have occurred before the claim.
	C) <u>smuggled</u> with success	3> "**had** successfully **smuggled**" is the past perfect.
	D) <u>had been</u> successfully smuggled	B) and C) are simple past, pointing that "claimed" and "smuggled" were occurring at the same time, an illogical situation.
		D) is passive voice. It sounds as if ISIS were victims.

Q22. Absolute Pattern 7: Conjunction Error

[22] <u>In the meantime,</u> experts believe that this claim was exaggerated to boost their stature and spread fear, and acknowledged that some Western countries were aware of the smuggling.

	A) NO CHANGE	C) 1> 'however' cancels out the preceding sentence.
	B) Granted,	2> The two sentences between the adverb "however" present the contrasting views.
√	C) However,	
	D) Since	A) 'In the meantime' means meanwhile
		B) 'Granted' means acknowledged
		D) 'since' means because

Q23. Absolute Pattern 18: Punctuation Error

Quantum mechanics is a fundamental branch of physics concerned with processes [23] <u>involving: for example,</u> atoms and photons.

	A) NO CHANGE	D) "for example" should be separated from the main sentence by off setting with a pair of commas.
	B) involving; for example,	
	C) involving for example	A) a colon functions as "for example"
√	D) involving, for example,	B) a semi-colon carries a clause.
		C) lacks punctuation

Q24. Absolute Pattern 24: Verb Tense / Voice Error

System such as these which [24]<u>obey</u> quantum mechanics can be in a quantum superposition of different states,...

√	A) NO CHANGE	A) 1> "obey" is plural because 2> "these" is plural.
	B) obeys	B) "obeys" is plural.
	C) abeyance of	C) is noun
	D) have obeyed	D) 1> "have obeyed" is present perfect. 2> Demonstrative statement like this passage should use the simple present tense as used in the surrounding sentences.

Q25. Absolute Pattern 4: Comparison

System such as these which obeys quantum mechanics can be in a quantum superposition of different states, [25] <u>unlike classical physics.</u>

	A) NO CHANGE	Please read the following revised sentence.
	B) unlike classical physics superposition	<u>Unlike classical physics, system such as these</u> obeys quantum mechanics. As seen above, "classical physics" is being compared with "system"
√	C) **unlike that of classical physics**	Therefore, it requires "that" (system)
	D) unlike in classical physics.	B) "physics" and "superposition" are both nouns, so one of which should be a possessive form. D) "that" is missing as in (A).

Q26. Absolute Pattern 10: Logical Expression

The [26]<u>reconceived </u>theory is formulated in various specially developed mathematical formalisms.

	A) conceptualized	Reconceived means an idea taken into mind.
√	**B) rehabilitated**	B) means to restore to healthy condition after imprisonment
	C) redesigned	D) means recalculated
	D) recalibrated	A), C), D) are all synonyms to reconceived.

Q27. Absolute Pattern 11: Logical Sequence

Quantum mechanics is a fundamental branch of physics concerned with processes involving: atoms and photons. <A> **System such as these** which obey quantum mechanics can be in a quantum superposition of different states, unlike classical physics. <B> **Early quantum theory** was profoundly reconceived in the mid-1920s. <C> **The reconceived theory** is formulated in various specially developed mathematical formalisms. <D> **Important applications of quantum theory** include ..

	A) <A> System such as …	D) Application means practicality.
	B) <B> Early quantum theory…	
	C) <C> The reconceived...	
√	D) **<D> Important applications of...**	

Q28. Absolute Pattern 14: Possessive Determiners and Possessive Noun Error

When quantum mechanics was originally formulated, it was applied to models [28] <u>whose</u> correspondence limit was non-relativistic classical mechanics.

√	A) NO CHANGE	A) 1> "whose" means 'of which' (of the models')
		2> "whose" inks "models" to "correspondence limit (noun).
	B) whom	
	C) which	B) "whom" is used only for the human
	D) that	C), D) 1> 'which' and 'that' are not possessive 2> Therefore, they can't link another noun "correspondence"

Q29. Absolute Pattern 24: Verb Tense / Voice Error

Early attempts to merge quantum mechanics [29] <u>for special relativity has involved</u> the replacement of the Schrödinger equation with a covariant equation.

	A) NO CHANGE	B) "involved," the past tense is required because the subject "Early attempts" implies the past activity.
√	**B) with special relativity involved**	
	C) to special relativity <u>had involved</u>	A) 1> "Early attempts" is the subject, plural, and indicates the past occurrence.
		2> "has involved" is present and singular.
	D) into special relativity <u>involves</u>	
		C) 1> "had involved" is past perfect tense.
		2> The past perfect tense can't be used independently.
		3> It normally carries the simple past tense.
		D) "involves" is present tense.

Q30. Absolute Pattern 23: Transition Words for Supporting Detail, Contrast, and Consequence

[30] <u>For example,</u> these theories **were successful** in explaining many experimental results, they had certain **unsatisfactory qualities** stemming from their neglect of the relativistic creation and annihilation of particles.

	A) NO CHANGE	B) 1> The sentence discusses the contradicting positions—"successful" and
√	**B) While,**	"unsatisfactory."
	C) Due to	2> "While", should be used in this contradictory circumstance.
	D) Moreover,	A), D) are used to emphasize the previous statement.

A), D) are used to emphasize the previous statement.

C) is used for the cause-and-effect.

Q31. Absolute Pattern 4: Comparison

While these theories were **successful** in explaining many experimental results, they had **certain unsatisfactory** qualities stemming from their neglect of the relativistic creation and annihilation of particles. **A fully relativistic quantum theory required the development of quantum field theory, which applies quantization to a field** [31]—**less than** a fixed set of particles.

	A) NO CHANGE	D) 1> The previous sentence discusses a sort of disappointment.
	B) similar to	2> The following sentence diagnoses the problems and provides the solution.
	C) the same as	3> That is, the scientists needed "the quantization to a field, where neither
√	**D) rather than**	the relativistic creation can be neglected nor annihilation of particles be created.

4> Therefore, "rather than" is the correct answer.

Q32. Absolute Pattern 14: Possessive Determiners and Possessive Noun Error

The full [32] apparatus's of quantum field theory is often unnecessary for describing electrodynamic systems.

	A) quantum field of apparatus	C) "quantum field" links to the following word "theory," creating the correct "quantum field theory"
	B) apparatus' quantum field	
√	**C) apparatus of quantum field**	A), D) 1> There's no "apparatus theory"
	D) quantum field's apparatus	2> Apparatus means tool or system.

B), D) 1> "apparatus" or "field" is non-human object

2> Therefore, they can't be "apparatus'" or "field's"
It should use "of" for possessive determiner.

Q33. Absolute Pattern 1: Adding, Revising, Deleting, Retaining Information

Question: Suppose the writer's primary purpose had been to describe the difference between Quantum physics and classical physics. Would this essay accomplish that purpose?

	A) Yes, because it discusses both theories
	B) Yes, because it focuses primarily on the early stage of Quantum theory that heavily depended on Classical Physics
	C) No, because it focuses more on Classical Physics and its influence upon Quantum Physics
√	**D) No, because it focuses more on Quantum Physics and its conceptual understanding.**

D) The main theme is Quantum Physics, not Classical Physics as the title stated.

Q34. Absolute Pattern 24: Verb Tense / Voice Error

You will rejoice to hear that no disaster [34] accompany the commencement of an enterprise which **you have regarded** with such evil forebodings.

	A) NO CHANGE	D) 1> The narration and the subordinating clause (have regarded) indicate the past experience.
	B) had accompanied	2> The closest tense should then be the present perfect.
	C) is to be accompanied	
√	**D) has accompanied**	A) is plural. It should be singular because the subject is singular. B) 1> "had accompanied" is past perfect, which should be supported by the simple past tense in the same sentence. 2> It can't jump from present to past perfect. C) is for the future.

Q35. Absolute Pattern 15: Prepositional Idiom

This breeze, which has traveled from the regions [35] for which I am **advancing,** gives me a foretaste of those icy climes.

	A) NO CHANGE	D) "towards" is used to describe the movement to a certain destination (e.g., advancing towards San Francisco.)
	B) to	
√	**C) towards**	
	D) in	

Q36. Absolute Pattern 12: Modifier Placement Error

Inspired by this wind of promise, [36] what a fervent and vivid moment .

	A) NO CHANGE	C) 1> The sentence begins with the modifier "inspired by"
	B) more fervent and vivid had my daydream become.	
√	C) **I** have become more fervent and vivid	2> Only human subject can be inspired.
	D) there has become more fervent and vivid in my daydream.	

Q37. Absolute Pattern 18: Punctuation Error

I try in vain to be persuaded that the pole is the seat of frost and [37] desolation, it ever presents itself to my imagination as the region of beauty and delight.

	A) NO CHANGE	Semicolon can link the contradictory clause
√	**B) desolation; it ever**	B) Only semicolon can link another clause with a contradiction.
	C) desolation that ever	A) is comma splice error.
	D) desolation: it ever	When two sentences are combined, there must be a connector, either conjunction or semicolon.
		C) 1> Given that two clauses are contradicting,
		2> "that" can't represent the contradictory clause.
		D) It uses a colon. The colon is used to introduce things, not to contradict.

Q38. Absolute Pattern 5: Comma Splice Error

There, Margaret, the sun is forever visible, [38] its broad disk just skirting the horizon and diffusing a perpetual splendor.

√	**A) NO CHANGE**	A) 1> The primary clause "the sun...visible," ends with the comma.
	B) it's	2> which means the following statement should be a phrase.
	C) there is	3> Were it a clause, it will be a comma splice error.
	D) there are	4> only (A) is phrase.
		B), C), D) are all clauses with verbs, causing a comma splice error.

Q39. Absolute Pattern 17: Pronoun Error

This letter will reach England **by a merchantman** now on its homeward voyage from Archangel; more fortunate than [39] <u>me</u>, who may not see my native land, perhaps, for many years.

	A) NO CHANGE	D) 1> "I" is subjective pronoun that compares with a merchantman.
	B) myself	To illustrate, the original sentence can be divided into two parts: "**A merchantman is** more fortunate." and "**I am** less fortunate."
	C) mine	2> that can be combined into "A merchantman is more fortunate than I (am)."
√	**D) I**	A) is objective: "**A merchantman is** more fortunate." and "**me am.**" is incorrect sentence.
		B) "myself" can't be used alone; it should come along with I. C) is a possessive

Q40. Absolute Pattern 18: Punctuation Error

I [40] <u>am, **however,** in good **spirits; my men**</u> are bold and apparently firm of purpose, nor do the floating sheets of ice that continually pass us, indicating the dangers of the region towards which we are advancing,

√	**A) NO CHANGE**	A) 1> "however" should be offset by a pair of commas when inserted in the middle of the clause like (A) or (D).
	B) am however in good spirits:	2> "my men are bold…" is another clause that requires either conjunction or semicolon.
	C) am, however; in good spirits:	
	D) am, however, in good spirits,	B), C), and D) don't follow the standard punctuation described above. (D) is comma splice.

Q41. Absolute Pattern 21: Subject-Verb, Pronoun, Noun Agreement

I am, however, in good spirits; my men are bold and apparently firm of purpose, **nor do the floating sheets of ice** *that continually pass us, indicating the dangers of the region towards which we are advancing,* [41] <u>appearing</u> dismay them.

	A) NO CHANGE	B) 1> The conjunction "nor" signals the subordinating clause will follow.
√	**B) appear to**	2> "the floating sheets" is the subject in the subordinating clause.
	C) appears to	3> *"that continually….advancing,"* is a quick interjection modifying the ice.
	D) that appear to	4> The quick interjection above is offset by a pair of commas, indicating that the subordinating clause is not completed yet and still waits for the verb.
		5> "appear" (plural) corresponds to the subject "the floating sheets." (plural)
		A) is adjective
		C) 1> The subject "the floating sheets" is plural. 2> "appears to" is singular.
		D) should drop 'that'

Q42. Pattern 21: Subject-Verb, Pronoun, Noun Agreement

No incidents [42] has hitherto befallen us that would make a figure in a letter.

	A) NO CHANGE	C) The subject "incidents" (plural) requires the plural verb have + befallen. Hitherto= so far.
	B) has hitherto befall	
√	**C) have hitherto befallen**	A) and B) "has" is singular; therefore incorrect.
	D) have already befall	B) and D) "befall" has to be 'befallen' (the participle of befall)
		D) The adverb 'already' should be deleted.

Q43. Absolute Pattern 10: Logical Expression

One or two stiff gales and the springing of a leak are accidents **which** [43] underline{experiencing} **navigators scarcely remember** to record, and I shall be well content if nothing worse happen to us during our voyage.

	A) NO CHANGE	It should be "experienced" as the navigator who is experienced, not experiencing.
√	**B) experienced**	
	C) is experienced	C) is verb. The verb "remember" is already given.
	D) experience	D) is noun and can't link to the following noun "navigator."

Q44. Absolute Pattern 7: Conjunction Error

So strange an accident[44] has happened to us and I cannot forbear recording it, although it is very probable that you will see me before these papers can come into your possession.

	A) NO CHANGE	B) "So-that" clause (a cause-effect) is evident in this sentence.
√	**B) has happened to us that I**	A) "and" can't replace "that" in "so-that" clause.
	C) had happened to us and me	C) is past perfect and using the incorrect pronoun "and me"
	D) happened to us and I	D) is simple past. The surrounding sentence shows the present tense should be used.

SAT
Writing and Language
Test 10

ALL THE LOGIC AND RULES

BEHIND THE EVERY SINGLE

SAT QUESTION

Writing and Language Test 10
35 MINUTES, 44 QUESTIONS

Each passage below is accompanied by a number of questions. For some questions, you will consider how the passage might be revised to improve the expression of ideas. For other questions, you will consider how the passage might be edited to correct errors in sentence structure, usage, or punctuation. A passage or a question may be accompanied by one or more graphics (such as a table or graph) that you will consider as you make revising and editing decisions.

Questions 1-11 are based on the following passage.

AIRBNB

Airbnb is an online marketplace that enables people to list, [1] browsing a place to stay temporarily, then rent vacation homes for a processing fee.

It has over 1,500,000 listings in 34,000 cities and 191 countries. Founded in August 2008 and [2] headquartered in San Francisco, California, the company is privately owned and operated. Shortly after moving to San Francisco in October 2007, Brian Chesky created the initial concept for AirBed & Breakfast. The original site offered short-term living quarters, breakfast, and a unique business networking opportunity for attendees who were unable to book a hotel in the saturated market.

1

A) NO CHANGE
B) find,
C) look for other people's house
D) searching for,

2

A) NO CHANGE
B) San Francisco as its headquarter
C) headquarter in San Francisco,
D) Airbnb has its headquarter in San Francisco

CONTINUE

2   2

At the time, roommates Chesky and Gebbia could not afford the rent for their loft in San Francisco. They made their living room into a bed and breakfast, accommodating three guests on air mattresses and providing homemade breakfast.

In February 2008, technical architect Nathan Blecharczyk joined as the third co-founder of Air Bed & Breakfast. During the company's initial stages, the founders focused on high-profile events where alternative lodging was [3] plenty.

The site Airbedandbreakfast.com officially launched on August 11, 2008.

To help fund the site, the founders created special edition breakfast cereals, with presidential candidates Barack Obama and John McCain as the inspiration for "Obama O's" and "Cap'n McCains". In two months, 800 boxes of cereal were sold at $40 each, [4] it has generated more than $30,000 for the company's incubation.

[5] With the website already built, they used the fund to fly to New York to meet users and promote the site. They returned to San Francisco with a profitable business model to present to West Coast investors.

3

A) NO CHANGE
B) not very close by
C) scarce
D) easily found

4

A) NO CHANGE
B) generating more than
C) that generated more than
D) thereby generating more than

5

Which choice best connects the sentence with the previous paragraph?
A) NO CHANGE
B) Hotel industries became wary of the company by that time.
C) Although the initial business plan seemed rosy, the reality waiting for them was the opposite.
D) Airbnb soon became the multibillion company

CONTINUE

2 **2**

In March 2009, the name Airbedandbreakfast.com was shortened to Airbnb.com, and [6] the site's content expanded from air beds and shared spaces to a variety of properties including entire homes and apartments.

On May 25, 2011, [7] actor, and partner at A-Grade Investments Ashton Kutcher, announced a significant investment in the company and his role as a strategic brand advisor for the company.

6

A) NO CHANGE

B) the site contents

C) the content's site

D) the site's content

7

A) NO CHANGE

B) an actor and a partner

C) actor and partner

D) actor as a partner

CONTINUE

2

In July 2014, Airbnb revealed design revisions to their site and mobile app and introduced a new logo. Some considered the new icon to be visually similar to genitalia, [8] also a consumer survey by **Survata** showed only a minority of respondents thought this was the case.

[9] In the past, businesses were regulated by zoning laws, but Mayor Steven Fulop stated that the city does not have enough inspectors to deal the number of local units being rented out, approximately 300 of which rented through the service as of that date, and that rapid-evolving technology such as Airbnb made doing so impossible. Under the new legislation, Airbnb pays the city 6 percent hotel tax on the residential properties whose owners rent temporary living space to tourists for under 30 days, which is estimated to bring $1 million in revenue to the city, and expand tourist capacity beyond the city's 13 existing hotels.

8

A) NO CHANGE
B) but
C) nevertheless
D) moreover

9

At this point, the writer is considering adding the following sentence.

> In October 2015, Jersey City, New Jersey became the first city in the New York metropolitan area to legalize Airbnb, and add it to their existing body of hotels and motels that pay taxes.

Should the writer make this addition here?

A) Yes, because it supports the main argument in the passage and one city Mayor's effort to expand business
B) Yes, because it provides a meaningful connection to the following sentences
C) No, because it should set up the argument for the benefit of the business
D) No, because this article focuses on the initial stage of the company

CONTINUE

2   **2**

Airbnb will also provide insurance protection to homeowners in the event damage done to their residence by renters. The new laws will not pre vent condominium associations from voting to prohibit use of Airbnb in [10] them.

[11] Giving the growth of international users, Airbnb opened 6 additional international offices in early 2012. These cities include Paris, Milan, Barcelona, Copenhagen, Moscow, and Sao Paulo.

10

A) NO CHANGE
B) it
C) those buildings.
D) their buildings.

11

A) NO CHANGE
B) Having given
C) After Airbnb was given
D) To give

CONTINUE

2

2

Questions 12-22 are based on the following passage.

NASA Confirms Evidence That Liquid Water Flows on Today

New findings from NASA's Mars Reconnaissance Orbiter (MRO) provides the strongest evidence yet that liquid water flows intermittently on present-day Mars. Using an imaging spectrometer on MRO, [12] it detected signatures of hydrated minerals on slopes where mysterious streaks are seen on the Red Planet. These darkish streaks appear to ebb and flow over time. They darken and appear to flow down steep slopes during warm seasons, and then fade in cooler seasons. They appear in several locations on Mars when temperatures are above minus 10 degrees Fahrenheit (minus 23 Celsius) [13] but disappear at colder times.

[14] When we search for an extraterrestrial life, our quest on Mars has been to 'follow the water,' in our search for life in the universe, and now we have convincing science that validates what we've long suspected, said John Grunsfeld, astronaut and associate administrator of NASA's Science Mission Directorate in Washington.

12

A) NO CHANGE
B) they
C) researchers
D) Mars

13

A) NO CHANGE
B) and disappear
C) however, disappear
D) while disappearing

14

A) NO CHANGE
B) Because searching for an extra-terrestrial life is our goal,
C) As we search for an extraterrestrial life,
D) delete the underlined portion, and starts the sentence with "Our quest…".

CONTINUE

2　　　　　　　　　　　　　　　　　　　　　　　　　　**2**

"This is a significant development, as it appears to confirm that water [15] —albeit briny—is flowing today on the surface of Mars."

These downhill flows, known as recurring slope lineae (RSL), often have been described as possibly related [16] to water.

　The new findings of hydrated salts on the slopes point to what that relationship may be to these dark features. The hydrated salts would lower the freezing point of a liquid brine, [17] just as salt on roads here on Earth causes ice and snow to melt more rapidly. Scientists say it's likely a shallow subsurface flow, with enough water wicking to the surface to explain the darkening.

15

Which of the following alternatives would NOT be appropriate?
A) ,albeit briny,
B) (albeit briny)
C) although briny
D) ,though briny,

16

A) NO CHANGE
B) with potential liquid
C) with conceivable water
D) to obtainable water

17

At this point, the author wishes to delete the underlined phrase. Should the author proceeds to delete it or not?
A) Keep, because it confirms the same molecules of salts on Mars' surface and Earth.
B) Keep, because it helps visualize the process of melting ice
C) Delete, because it undermines the passage's central theory
D) Delete, because the description doesn't fit to the academic journal

CONTINUE

2 **2**

[18] They are hypothesized to be formed by flow of briny liquid water on Mars. The image is produced by draping an orthorectified (RED) image (ESP_031059_1685) on a Digital Terrain Model (DTM) of the same site produced by High Resolution Imaging Science Experiment (University of Arizona). Vertical exaggeration is 1.5."We found the hydrated salts only when the seasonal features were widest, [19] which suggests that either the dark streaks themselves and a process that forms them is the source of the hydration. In either case, the detection of hydrated salts on these slopes means that water plays a vital role in the formation of these streaks," said Lujendra Ojha of the Georgia Institute of Technology (Georgia Tech) [20] in Atlanta, lead author of a report on these findings published Sept. 28 by Nature Geoscience. Ojha first noticed these puzzling features as a University of Arizona undergraduate student in 2010, using images from the MRO's High Resolution Imaging Science Experiment (HiRISE).

18

At this point, the writer is considering adding the following sentence in this new paragraph.

The dark streaks here are up to few hundred meters in length.

Should the writer make this addition here?

A) Yes, because a new paragraph cannot start with a pronoun.
B) Yes, because the exact measurement is an essential factor to determine the quality of briny liquid.
C) No, because the information is not directly related with the paragraph.
D) No, because the hypothesis is not fully confirmed to suggest the measurement.

19

A) NO CHANGE
B) which suggest that either the dark streaks themselves or a process that forms them is
C) suggested that either the dark streaks themselves or a process that forms them is
D) , suggesting that either the dark streaks themselves or a process that forms them are

20

A) NO CHANGE
B) in Atlanta lead
C) in Atlanta, leading
D) in Atlanta leads

CONTINUE

2   **2**

The new site study pairs HiRISE observations with mineral mapping by MRO's Compact Reconnaissance Imaging Spectrometer for Mars (CRISM).[21]

So far, HiRISE actually acquired 9137 images (Table 1), but from 2 to 3 times as much downlink data volume as expected, so the average image sizes are larger than previously expected. Ojha chose to acquire larger images rather than more images because it was operationally easier and because of a lifetime concern related to the number of on–off cycles to the FPS.

Table 1		
Image types acquired in the PSP.		
	Number acquired in PSP	% of total images
Total images	9137	100
Standalone small images	3465	38
Coordinated and ride-along images with other teams	5672	62
Stereo images / enhanced size	2064	23
Off-nadir observations	6839	75
Nadir observations including non-mineral zones	2298	25

Dwayne Brown / Laurie Cantillo
Headquarters, Washington
http://www.nasa.gov/press-release/nasa-confirms-evidence-that-liquid-water-flows-on-today-s-mars

21

At this point, the writer wants to further reinforce Ojhas research. Which choice most effectively accomplish this goal?

A) Using the HiRISE, he documented RSL at dozens of mineral sites on Mars.

B) Using the HiRISE, he was able to solve on-off cycles to the FPS.

C) Using the HiRISE, he acquired the average-size images.

D) Using the HiRISE, he chose to document more images as many as possible.

22

The writer wants the information in the passage to correspond as closely as possible with the information in the table.

Given that goal described in the passage would remain unchanged, on which research should Ojha conduct?

A) Standalone small images

B) Off-nadir observations

C) Stereo images with enhanced size

D) Nadir observations including non-mineral zones

CONTINUE →

2

2

Questions 23-33 are based on the following passage.

Louis Armstrong

Louis Armstrong, nicknamed Satchmo or Pops, was an American trumpeter, composer, singer and occasional [23] actor. Luis Armstrong is considered as the most influential figures in jazz. His career spanned five decades, from the 1920s to the 1960s [24] ,different eras in jazz.

Coming to prominence in the 1920s as an "inventive" trumpet and cornet player, Armstrong [25] was not officially trained in jazz, shifting the focus of the music from collective improvisation to solo performance.

Armstrong was one of the first truly popular African-American entertainers to "cross over", whose skin color was secondary to his music in [26] likeminded fans' passion.

23

A) NO CHANGE
B) actor, and Luis Armstrong
C) actor
D) actor, who

24

Which of the following alternatives would NOT be appropriate?
A) , different eras in Jazz
B) −different eras in Jazz
C) : different eras in Jazz
D) ; different eras in Jazz

25

The writer wants to convey an attitude of genuine interest and respect to the later life of the musician. Which choice best accomplishes this goal?
A) NO CHANGE
B) was born when United States of America was severely experiencing racially the Divided States of America.
C) started his career by taking an unenviable position at the backstage.
D) was a foundational influence

26

Which choice most effectively sets up the contrast in the sentence and is consistent with the information in the rest of the passage?
A) NO CHANGE
B) the racially divided country.
C) the professional music industry
D) the society back in the 1930s.

CONTINUE ➡

2

2

His artistry and personality allowed him socially acceptable to access the upper echelons of American society which [27] <u>were highly open</u> for black men of his era.

[28] ①Armstrong was born into a poor family in New Orleans, Louisiana, and was the grandson of slaves.

②He spent his youth in poverty, in a rough neighborhood known as "the Battlefield", which was part of the Storyville legal prostitution district.

③ His mother Mary "Mayann" Albert (1886–1927) then left Louis and his younger sister, Beatrice Armstrong Collins, in the care of his grandmother, Josephine Armstrong, and at times, his Uncle Isaac.

④At five, he moved back to live with his mother and her relatives. He attended the Fisk School for Boys, where he most likely had early exposure to music. He brought in some money [29] <u>as a paperboy</u> but also by finding discarded food and selling it to restaurants, but it was not enough to keep his mother from prostitution. He [30] <u>often hang</u> out in dance halls close to home, where he observed everything from licentious dancing to the quadrille.

27

A) NO CHANGE
B) appreciated
C) were accessible
D) were unapproachable

28

To improve the cohesion and flow of this paragraph, the writer wants to add the following sentence.

His father, William Armstrong, abandoned the family when Louis was an infant and took up with another woman.

The sentence would most logically be placed after

A) sentence 1
B) sentence 2
C) sentence 3
D) sentence 4

29

A) NO CHANGE
B) working as a paperboy
C) not only as a paperboy
D) selling papers

30

A) NO CHANGE
B) was hang
C) often hung
D) was hanging

CONTINUE ➡

2   2

After dropping out of the Fisk School at age eleven, Armstrong [31] joined a quartet of boys who sang in the streets for money. He also started to get into trouble. Cornet player Bunk Johnson said he taught Armstrong (then 11) to play by ear at Dago Tony's Tonk in New Orleans, [32] however in his later years Armstrong gave the credit to Oliver. Armstrong hardly looked back at his youth as the worst of times but drew inspiration from it instead: "Every time I close my eyes blowing that trumpet of mine—I look right in the heart of good old New Orleans... It has given me something to live for." [33]

31

A) NO CHANGE
B) had joined
C) has joined
D) was joined

32

A) NO CHANGE
B) in spite of
C) because
D) although

33

Which choice most effectively concludes the sentence and paragraph?

A) NO CHANGE
B) "Well...New Orleans indeed was such a beautiful land.
C) I regret things could have been better if I was a well-behaved kid.
D) Who knew I would be the king of music?

CONTINUE

2

2

Questions 34-44 are based on the following passage.

DRONE

An unmanned aerial vehicle (UAV), commonly known as a drone, as an unmanned aircraft system (UAS), or by several other names, is an aircraft without a human pilot aboard. The flight of UAVs may operate with various degrees of autonomy: either under remote control by a human operator, or under fully [34] and exhaustively by onboard computers. [35] Compared to manned aircraft, UAVs are often preferred for missions that are too [36] boring for humans. They originated mostly in military applications, although their use is expanding in commercial, scientific, recreational, agricultural, and other applications [37] such as, policing and surveillance, aerial photography, agriculture and drone racing. The term [38] ,more widely used by the public, "drone was given in reference to the resemblance of male bee that makes loud and regular sounds.

34

A) NO CHANGE
B) and categorically
C) and thoroughly
D) delete it

35

A) NO CHANGE
B) When you compare
C) Comparing
D) After the comparison

36

A) NO CHANGE
B) dangerous and distanced
C) theoretical
D) organized

37

A) NO CHANGE
B) , such as
C) ; such as,
D) such as:

38

The best placement for the underlined portion would be:
A) NO CHANGE
B) after "drone"
C) after "given"
D) after "bee"

CONTINUE

This term emphasizes the importance of elements other than the aircraft [39] ,indicating the significance of several elements of drone.

It includes several elements [40] ,such as ground control stations, data links, and other support equipment. Many similar terms are in use.

A UAV is defined as a powered, aerial vehicle that [41] do not carry a human operator, uses aerodynamic forces to provide vehicle lift, can fly autonomously or be piloted remotely, can be expendable or recoverable, and carry a lethal or nonlethal payload.

39

A) NO CHANGE
B) as it indicates the significance of several elements.
C) an indication of its term's significance.
D) delete the underlined portion.

40

Which of the following alternatives would NOT be appropriate?
A) , including ground control stations,
B) : ground control stations,
C) —ground control stations,
D) like ground control stations,

41

A) NO ERROR
B) does not carry a human operator, uses aero dynamic forces to provide vehicle lift, could fly autonomously or be piloted remotely, can be expendable
C) do not carry a human operator, uses aerodynamic forces to provide vehicle lift, fly autonomously or be piloted remotely, can be expendable
D) does not carry a human operator, uses aerodynamic forces to provide vehicle lift, can fly autonomously or be piloted remotely, expendable

CONTINUE

2   **2**

[42] Therefore, missiles are not considered UAVs because the vehicle itself is a weapon that is not reused, though it is also unmanned and in some cases remotely guided.

The relation of UAVs to remote controlled model aircraft is unclear. [43] Some jurisdictions base their definitions on size or weight; however, the US Federal Aviation Administration defines any unmanned flying craft as a UAV regardless of size.

[44] The UAV's global military market is dominated by United States and Israel. The US held a 60% military-market share in 2006. It operated over 9,000 UAVs in 2014. From 1985 to 2014, exported drones came predominantly from Israel (60.7%) and the United States (23.9%); top importers were the United Kingdom (33.9%) and India (13.2%).

42

A) NO CHANGE
B) Moreover,
C) For example,
D) Although,

43

At this point, the author wishes to delete the underlined phrase. Should the author proceeds to delete it or not?

A) Keep, because it provides a specific example of the previous sentence.
B) Keep, because it provides the reason for the inclusion of remote controlled model aircraft to UAV.
C) Delete, because it interrupts the flow of the paragraph by illustrating an unsettled decision
D) Delete, because it weakens the focus of the passage by shifting to remote controlled model aircraft.

44

Which of the following sentences is LEAST applicable as an alternate sentence?

A) The UAV's global market is dominated by United States and Israel.
B) As the related technology improves, there has been a huge expansion in the UAV's global military market in less than a decade.
C) UAV's global market, however, faces some serious privacy issues as it expands exponentially.
D) The U.S. Department of Defense has released a new statistics that shows Israel as the second largest market controller, next to the U.S.

TEST 10

WRITING ABSOLUTE PATTERNS

Test 10 Writing & Language Section Patterns

Q1. Absolute Pattern 13: Parallel Structure

Airbnb is an online marketplace that enables people **to list**, [1] browsing a place to stay temporarily, then **rent** vacation homes for a processing fee.

	A) NO CHANGE	B) maintains the parallel structure. *"to list, find, then rent."*
√	**B) find,**	A), C), D) are all wordy that can be reduced to "find."
	C) look for other people's house	
	D) searching for,	

Q2. Absolute Pattern 13: Parallel Structure

It has over 1,500,000 listings in 34,000 cities and 191 countries. **Founded in** August 2008 and [2] **headquartered in** San Francisco, California, the company is privately owned and operated.

√	**A) NO CHANGE**	A) 1> It starts with "founded in", 2> it should maintain the same structure "headquartered in."
	B) San Francisco as its headquarter	
	C) headquarter in San Francisco,	B) "California" should be linked to "San Francisco," instead of "its headquarter.
	D) Airbnb has its headquarter in San Francisco	C) "headquarter" is used as a noun, creating a new subject
		D) is a complete sentence, causing many errors, starting with a comma splice.

Q3. Absolute Pattern 10: Logical Expression

During the company's initial stages, the founders focused on high-profile events where alternative lodging was [3] plenty.

	A) NO CHANGE	A), D): customers wouldn't use the new lodging offering company if there are plenty of rooms available.
	B) not very close by	
√	**C) scarce**	B) The sentence is not about lodging distance, but scarcity.
	D) easily found	

Q4. Absolute Pattern 12: Modifier Placement Error

In two months, 800 boxes of cereal were sold at $40 each, [4] it has generated more than $30,000 for the company's incubation.

	A) NO CHANGE	A) is comma splice error.
√	**B) generating more than**	C) "that clause" cannot be followed by comma.
	C) that generated more than	D) "thereby" is unnecessary.
	D) thereby generating more than	

Q5. Absolute Pattern 1: Adding, Revising, Deleting, Retaining Information

[5] With the website already built, they used the fund to fly to New York to meet users and promote the site.

√	A) NO CHANGE	A) The startup company is still in the embryonic stage and it reflects the initial stage of the company.
	B) Hotel industries became wary of the company by that time.	
	C) Although the initial business plan seemed rosy, the reality waiting for them was opposite	B) changes the focus of the passage.
	D) Airbnb soon became the multibillion company	C) Negative tone, while the overall tone in the passage is positive about Airbnb.
		D) doesn't fit to the startup company.

Q6. Absolute Pattern 14: Possessive Determiners and Possessive Noun Error

In March 2009, the name Airbedandbreakfast.com was shortened to Airbnb.com, and
[6] the site content expanded from air beds and shared spaces to a variety of properties including entire homes and apartments.

	A) NO CHANGE	A), B) Both "site" and "content" are nouns, either one of which must be a possessive to the other noun.
	B) the site contents	
	C) the content's site	C) The site should be the possessive, not the content.
√	**D) the site's content**	

Q7. Absolute Pattern 20: Restrictive Modifier (Essential Information)

On May 25, 2011, [7] actor, and partner at A-Grade Investments Ashton Kutcher announced a significant investment in the company and his role as a strategic brand advisor for the company.

	A) NO CHANGE	C) Actor and Ashton Kutcher is one individual and should not be separated by a comma.
	B) an actor and a partner	B) article "an" and "a" make two people as if an actor and a partner are different people.
√	C) actor and partner	D) 1> a comma after "a partner" technically severs the subject from the verb.
	D) actor as a partner,	2> "as a partner changes the original meaning as if the actor limits his role as a partner.

Q8. Absolute Pattern 7: Conjunction Error

Some considered the new icon to be visually similar to genitalia, [8] also a consumer survey by Survata showed **only a minority** of respondents thought this was the case.

	A) NO CHANGE	B) Two sentences show the contrasting view with a single issue.
√	B) but	Therefore, conjunction 'but' should be used.
	C) nevertheless	A), C), D) are all conjunctive adverbs. They are not the conjunction. That is, they cannot connect the following clause without a semicolon.
	D) moreover	Therefore, they are all incorrect regardless of their rhetorical meaning.
		A) and D) are used to add and expand the description.
		C) means despite what has been said and done.

Q9. Absolute Pattern 1: Adding, Revising, Deleting, Retaining Information

Question: Should the writer make this addition here?

	A) Yes, because it supports the main argument in the passage and one city Mayor's effort to expand business
√	B) Yes, because it provides a meaningful connection to the following sentences
	C) No, because it should set up the argument for the benefit of the business
	D) No, because this article focuses on the initial stage of the company

B) The following sentence requires the added information.

A) The Mayor tries to regulate the business, not "expanding it."

C) It's opposite. The following sentence provides the argument for the benefit of the city of New York

D) "No" should change to "Yes"

Q10. Absolute Pattern 14: Possessive Determiners and Possessive Noun Error

The new laws will not prevent condominium associations from voting to prohibit use of Airbnb in [10] them.

	A) NO CHANGE	D) indicates the condominium associations' buildings.
	B) it	A), B) are ambiguous that could indicate many singular or plural nouns in the sentence.
	C) those buildings	
√	**D) their buildings**	C) 'those buildings' implies that the specific buildings have already been mentioned in the previous sentence.

Q11. Absolute Pattern 24: Verb Tense / Voice Error

[11] Giving the growth of international users, Airbnb opened 6 additional international offices in early 2012. These cities include Paris, Milan, Barcelona, Copenhagen, Moscow, and Sao Paulo.

	A) NO CHANGE	B) 1> "Having given" means After it had been given.
√	**B) Having given**	2> " The primary sentence shows that the company opened its new offices after it grew its users.
	C) After Airbnb was given	A) is the present progressive, implying the simultaneous occurrence.
		C) 1> is passive. It should be active.
	D) To give	2> Using "Airbnb" two times in one sentence causes a redundant error.
		D) is the future tense.

Q12. Absolute Pattern 17: Pronoun Error

Using an imaging spectrometer on MRO, [12] it detected signatures of hydrated minerals on slopes where mysterious streaks are seen on the Red Planet.

	A) NO CHANGE	
	B) they	
√	**C) researchers**	Only researchers (human) can use "an imaging spectrometer on MRO"
	D) Mars	

Q13. Absolute Pattern 13: Parallel Structure

They appear in several locations on Mars when temperatures are above minus 10 degrees Fahrenheit (minus 23 Celsius), [13] but disappear at colder times.

	A) NO CHANGE	B) The sentence is in parallel structure that needs the conjunction "and."
√	**B) and disappear**	A) "but," C) "however", D) "while" are used to contradict or cancel out the preceding sentence. This sentence maintains the parallel structure.
	C) however, disappear	
	D) while disappearing	

Q14. Absolute Pattern 19: Redundant Error

[14] When we search for an extraterrestrial life, our quest on Mars has been to 'follow the water,' **in our search for life** in the universe, and now we have convincing science that validates what we've long suspected," said John Grunsfeld, astronaut and associate administrator of NASA's Science Mission Directorate in Washington.

	A) NO CHANGE	A), B), C) are all redundant with the following phrase in the same sentence.
	B) Because searching for an extra-terrestrial life is our goal,	
	C) As we search for an extraterrestrial life,	
√	D) delete the underlined portion, and starts the sentence with "Our quest...."	

Q15. Absolute Pattern 18: Punctuation Error

This is a significant development, as it appears to confirm that water [15] —albeit briny—is flowing today on the surface of Mars."

	A) NO CHANGE	Inessential Information should be separated from the main sentence using a pair of punctuation.
	B) (albeit briny)	
√	**C) although briny**	Choice C didn't use any punctuation.
	D) ,albeit briny,	A) a pair of dashes, B) parenthesis, D) a pair of commas, all of which offset the inessential information from the main clause.

Q16. Absolute Pattern 19: Redundant Error

These downhill flows, known as recurring slope lineae (RSL), often have been described as **possibly** related [16] to water.

√	**A) NO CHANGE**	All the other choices are redundant to the word "possibly"
	B) with <u>potential</u> liquid	
	C) with <u>conceivable</u> water	
	D) to *obtainable* water	

Q17. Absolute Pattern 1: Adding, Revising, Deleting, Retaining Information

The hydrated salts would lower the freezing point of a liquid brine, [17] <u>just as salt on roads here on Earth causes ice and snow to melt more rapidly.</u> Scientists say it's likely a shallow subsurface flow, with enough water wicking to the surface to explain the darkening.

	A) Keep, because it confirms the same molecules of salts on Mars' surface and Earth.	B) "just as" clearly indicates the author's intention to help visualize the previous statement.
√	**B) Keep, because it helps visualize the process of melting ice**	A) The clause doesn't confirm the same molecules.
	C) Delete, because it undermines the passage's central theory	C), D) Visualization neither undermines the theory nor unfits for the academic journal.
	D) Delete, because the description doesn't fit to the academic journal	

Q18. Absolute Pattern 1: Adding, Revising, Deleting, Retaining Information

Question: The dark streaks here are up to few hundred meters in length.

Should the writer make this addition here?

√	**A) Yes, because a new paragraph cannot start with a pronoun.**
	B) Yes, because the exact measurement is an essential factor to determine the quality of briny liquid.
	C) No, because the information is <u>not directly related </u>with the paragraph.
	D) No, because the hypothesis is <u>not fully confirmed </u>to suggest the measurement

A) No paragraph can begin with a pronoun in the first sentence.

B) The description "the quality of briny liquid," isn't supported by or mentioned in the passage.

C) The following sentence describes that there are relations between the sentences.

D) The following sentence fully confirms the measurement.

Q19. Absolute Pattern 21: Subject-Verb, Pronoun, Noun Agreement

We found the hydrated salts only when the seasonal features were widest, [19]<u>which suggests that **either** the dark streaks themselves **and** a process that forms them is</u> the source of the hydration.

	A) NO CHANGE	B) 1> "either...or" is the correct form.
√	B) **which suggest** that either the dark streaks themselves **or a process** that forms them **is**	2> The subject is "a process," a singular; therefore, the verb, "is" is correct.
	C) **suggested** that either the dark streaks themselves **or a process** that forms them **are**	C), D) 1> Tense error: "suggested," is past tense.
	D) **suggesting** that either the dark streaks themselves **or a process** that forms them **are**	2> the verb, "are" is incorrect.

Q20. Absolute Pattern 22 : Non-Restrictive Modifier (Inessential Information)

In either case, the detection of hydrated salts on these slopes means that water plays a vital role in the formation of these streaks," **said Lujendra Ojha of the Georgia Institute of Technology [20] in Atlanta, lead author** of a report on these findings published Sept. 28 by Nature Geoscience.

√	**A) NO CHANGE**	A) The non-restrictive modifier should be separated by comma.
	B) in Atlanta lead	B) Without a comma, the modifier blurs the line between the main clause and the modifier, causing several errors such as the change of meaning.
	C) in Atlanta, leading	
	D) in Atlanta leads	C) 1> changes the original meaning 2> "leading author" sounds as if Lujendra Ojha is leading another author.
		D) uses "leads" as a verb causing 1> the changes of meaning 2> comma splice error.

Q21. Absolute Pattern 1: Adding, Revising, Deleting, Retaining Information

The **new site study** pairs HiRISE observations with **mineral mapping** by MRO's Compact Reconnaissance Imaging Spectrometer for Mars [21] So far, HiRISE actually acquired 9137 images, but from 2 to 3 times as much downlink data volume as expected, so the average **image sizes are larger** than previously expected. Ojha chose to acquire larger images rather than more images **because it was operationally easier** and because of a lifetime concern related to the number of on–off cycles to the FPS.

√	A) Using the HiRISE, he documented RSL at dozens **of mineral sites on Mars.**	A) "The new site study" and "mineral sites" correspond correctly to support each other's description.
	B) Using the HiRISE, he was able to solve on-off cycles to the FPS.	B) The passage didn't say he solved on-off cycles. It only hints that he was able to operate easily.
	C) Using the HiRISE, he acquired average-size images	
	D) Using the HiRISE, he chose to document more images as many as possible.	C), D) are opposite to the passage.

Q22. Absolute Pattern 9: Informational Graphs

So far, HiRISE actually acquired 9137 images, <u>but from 2 to 3 times as much downlink data volume as expected, so the average image sizes are larger than previously expected.</u> Ojha chose to acquire larger images rather than more images because it was operationally easier and because of a lifetime concern related to the number of on–off cycles to the FPS.

	A) Standalone small images	As described above, The on-going research will focus on C)
	B) Off-nadir observations	
√	**C) Stereo images with enhanced size**	
	D) Nadir observations including non-mineral zones	

Q23. Absolute Pattern 16: Precision, Concision, Style

Louis Armstrong, nicknamed Satchmo or Pops, was an American trumpeter, composer, singer and occasional [23] <u>actor. Luis Armstrong</u> is considered as the most influential figures in jazz.

	A) NO CHANGE	D) links the following clause while simplifying the entire sentence.
	B) actor, and Luis Armstrong	A), B) are redundant error. These options repeat Luis Armstrong unnecessarily, which can be avoided by linking with 'who.'
	C) actor	
√	D) actor, who	C) is run-on sentence.

Q24. Absolute Pattern 18: Punctuation Error

Passage: His career spanned five decades, from the 1920s to the 1960s [24]<u>, different eras in jazz.</u>

	A) , different eras in Jazz	D) 1> A semicolon requires a clause on both sides.
	B) –different eras in Jazz	2> "different eras in Jazz" is not a clause. A), B), C): comma, dash, and colon, all of which can carry a phrase.
	C) : different eras in Jazz	
√	**D) ; different eras in Jazz**	

Q25. Absolute Pattern 1: Adding, Revising, Deleting, Retaining Information

Passage: Coming to prominence in the 1920s as an "inventive" trumpet and cornet player, Armstrong [25] was not officially trained in jazz, shifting the focus of the music from collective improvisation to solo performance.

	A) NO CHANGE	D) is positive and expresses the author's respect to the musician's later life success.
	B) was born when United States of America was severely experiencing racially the Divided States of America.	
	C) started his career by taking an unenviable position at the backstage.	A), C) are negative. B) is inconsistent with the question. It rather shows the back ground information.
√	D) was a foundational influence	C) is opposite. The question asks "the later life," not the starting career.

Q26. Absolute Pattern 1: Adding, Revising, Deleting, Retaining Information

Passage: Armstrong was one of the first truly popular African-American entertainers to "cross over," whose skin color was secondary to his music in [26] likeminded fans' passion.

	A) NO CHANGE	B) sets up the direct contrast to racial issues introduced in the sentence. Other options are not necessarily related to racial issue.
√	B) the racially divided country.	
	C) the professional music industry	
	D) the society back in the 1930s.	

Q27. Absolute Pattern 10: Logical Expression

His artistry and personality allowed him socially acceptable to access the upper echelons of American society which [27] were highly open for black men of his era.

	A) NO CHANGE	A), B), C) are all opposite
	B) appreciated	
	C) were accessible	
√	D) were unapproachable	

Q28. Absolute Pattern 11: Logical Sequence

[28] 1.Armstrong was born into a poor family in New Orleans, Louisiana, and was the grandson of slaves. 2. He spent his youth in poverty, in a rough neighborhood known as "the Battlefield," which was part of the Storyville legal prostitution district. 3. **His mother Mary "Mayann" Albert (1886–1927) then left** Louis and his younger sister, Beatrice Armstrong Collins, in the care of his grandmother, Josephine Armstrong, and at times, his Uncle Isaac. 4.At five, he moved back to live with his mother and her relatives. He attended the Fisk School for Boys, where he most likely had early exposure to music.

	A) sentence 1	C) "His mother...then left" shows the chronological sequence.
√	**B) sentence 2**	A) and B) illustrate Armstrong's youth.
	C) sentence 3	D) Sentence 4 describes young Louis tapped into the world of his musical life.
	D) sentence 4	

Q29. Absolute Pattern 7: Conjunction Error

He brought in some money [29] <u>either</u> as a paperboy **but also** by finding discarded food and selling it to restaurants, but it was not enough to keep his mother from prostitution.

	A) NO CHANGE	C) "not only...but also" is a correlative conjunction that can't be replaced with other format.
	B) working as a paperboy	
√	**C) not only as a paperboy**	A) "either...but also" isn't the correct idiom
	D) selling papers	B). D) can't reduce the first half of the "not only...but also" conjunction.

Q30. Absolute Pattern 10: Logical Expression

Passage: He [30] <u>often hang</u> out in dance halls close to home, where he **observed** everything from licentious dancing to the quadrille.

	A) NO CHANGE	C) Hung is the past tense of hang. The following verb "observed" suggests to use the past tense.
	B) was hang	
√	**C) often hung**	A) is present tense
	D) was hanging	D) 1> The progressive tense shows only a short continues and repeated action.
		2> "often" indicates the frequent occurrences in the past.
		3> Therefore, progressive tense can't be applied.

Q31. Absolute Pattern 24: Verb Tense / Voice Error

After dropping out of the Fisk School at age eleven, Armstrong [31] joined a quartet of boys **who sang** in the streets for money

√	**A) NO CHANGE**	A) 1> The entire passage uses the past tense. 2> To maintain the parallel structure, this sentence must use the past tense as well.
	B) had joined	
	C) has joined	B) 1> is past perfect.
	D) was joined	2> The situation is reversed. "Joining a quarter…" should come later, not before.
		C) 1> is present perfect. 2> The overall passage uses the past tense.
		D) is passive voice. "he was joined by someone" doesn't make sense.

Q32. Absolute Pattern 7: Conjunction Error

Cornet player Bunk Johnson said he taught Armstrong (then 11) to play by ear at Dago Tony's Tonk in New Orleans, [32] however in his later years Armstrong gave the credit to Oliver.

	A) NO CHANGE	D) is coordinating conjunction for concessional statement.
	B) in spite of	
	C) because	A) The conjunctive adverb 'however,' requires a semicolon like ":however,"
		B) means even though and can't be used for a clause.
√	**D) although**	C) is used for the cause-and-effect situation.

Q33. Absolute Pattern 1: Adding, Revising, Deleting, Retaining Information

"Every time I close my eyes blowing that trumpet of mine—I look right in the heart of good old New Orleans... It has given me something to live for." [33]

√	**A) NO CHANGE**
	B) "Well...New Orleans indeed was such a beautiful land.
	C) I regret things could have been better if I was a well-behaved kid.
	D) Who knew I would be the king of music?

A) The sentence does not require further conclusion.

B) It shifts its focus to New Orleans.

C) is negative. The entire passage is positive.

D) A self-congratulatory tone doesn't connect well with the previous sentence

Q34. Absolute Pattern 10: Logical Expression

The flight of UAVs may operate with various degrees of autonomy: either under remote control by a human operator, or under fully [34] and exhaustively by onboard computers.

	A) NO CHANGE	A), B), C) are all synonyms to "fully."
	B) categorically	
	C) thoroughly	
√	**D) delete it**	

Q35. Absolute Pattern 10: Logical Expression

[35] Compared to manned aircraft, UAVs are often preferred for missions that are too [36] boring for humans. The subject is 'UAVs', which is supported by its introductory modifier 'Compared to manned aircraft'. The original form of this sentence was "When UAVs are compared to manned aircraft,"

√	**A) NO CHANGE**	A) "Compared" is the contraction of "When UAVs are compared (to manned aircraft)"
	B) When you compare	
	C) Comparing	B) "you" changes the subject.
	D) After the comparison	C) 1> The subject "UAVs" is non-human. 2> Therefore, "UAVs comparing" is illogical. D) is wordy.

Q36. Absolute Pattern 10: Logical Expression

Compared to manned aircraft, UAVs are often preferred for missions that are too [36] boring for humans.

	A) NO CHANGE	B) The storyline emphasizes the out-of-reach to human control.
√	**B) dangerous and distanced**	A), C), D) do not reflect the primary functions of the UAVs
	C) theoretical	
	D) organized	

Q37. Absolute Pattern 18: Punctuation Error

They originated mostly in military applications, although their use is expanding in commercial, scientific, recreational, agricultural, and other applications [37] <u>such as,</u> policing and surveillance, aerial photography, agriculture and drone racing.

	A) NO CHANGE	B) Comma should be placed before "such as"
√	**B) , such as**	A), C) Comma can't be placed after such as.
	C) ; such as,	D) A colon and 'such as' perform the same function. Therefore, they can't be
	D) such as:	placed simultaneously.

Q38. Absolute Pattern 11: Logical Sequence

The **term** [38] <u>,more widely used by the public,</u> "**drone** was given in reference to the resemblance of male bee that makes loud and regular sounds.

	A) NO CHANGE	Correct sentence:
√	**B) after "drone"**	The **term drone**, more widely used by the public, was given ~.
	C) after "given"	B) 1> "The term" and "drone" can't be separated.
	D) after "bee"	2> "more widely used by the public," indicates "drone."
		3> Therefore, it should be placed after "drone."

Q39. Absolute Pattern 19: Redundant Error

This term emphasizes the importance of elements other than the aircraft
[39] <u>,indicating the significance of several elements of drone.</u>

	A) NO CHANGE	The underlined portion is redundant, and has to be removed.
	B) as it indicates the significance of several elements.	
	C) an indication of its term's significance.	
√	**D) delete the underlined portion.**	

Q40. Absolute Pattern 19: Redundant Error

It **includes** several elements [40] ,such as ground control stations, data links, and other support equipment.

√	A) , **including** ground control stations,	A) "including" is repeating.
	B) : ground control stations,	B) "colon" [:]
		C) "dash" [—]
	C) —ground control stations,	D) "like"
	D) like ground control stations,	All the other options are used to introduce thing (s).

Q41. Absolute Pattern 21: Subject-Verb, Pronoun, Noun Agreement

Passage: A UAV is defined as a powered, aerial vehicle that [41] **do** not carry a human operator, uses aerodynamic forces to provide vehicle lift, can fly autonomously or be piloted remotely, can be expendable or recoverable, and carry a lethal or nonlethal payload.

	A) NO ERROR
	B) does not carry a human operator, uses aerodynamic forces to provide vehicle lift, could fly autonomously or be piloted remotely, can be expendable
	C) do not carry a human operator, uses aerodynamic forces to provide vehicle lift, fly autonomously or be piloted remotely, can be expendable
√	D) **does** not carry a human operator, **uses** aerodynamic forces to provide vehicle lift, **can fly** autonomously or **be** piloted remotely, **expendable**

D) "does", "uses", "can fly", "(can) be", "(can be) expendable"

The correct sentence:

A UAV is defined as a powered, aerial **vehicle** that **does not** carry a human operator, **uses** aerodynamic forces to provide vehicle lift, **can fly** autonomously or (can) **be** piloted remotely, (can be) **expendable** or recoverable,...

* "(can)" and "(can be)" are removed to avoid redundancy and prevent the slow progression of expression.

A) 1> "Vehicle," the subject for that-clause, is singular. 2> "does," the singular verb, is required.

B) "could" is past tense, defying the present tense applied in the essay.

C) "fly" is plural. => "flies"

Q42. Absolute Pattern 23: Transition Words for Supporting Detail, Contrast, and Consequence

Passage: [42] <u>Therefore,</u> missiles are not considered UAVs because the vehicle itself is a weapon that is not reused, though it is also unmanned and in some cases remotely guided.

	A) NO CHANGE	C) The following sentence describes the missiles that further specify what cannot be defined as UAV.
	B) Moreover,	
√	C) For example,	A) 'Therefore' is used to illustrate consequence.
	D) Although,	B) 'Moreover' is used to support the preceding information.
		D) 'Although' is used to illustrate the contrasting view

Q43. Absolute Pattern 1: Adding, Revising, Deleting, Retaining Information

Question: At this point, the author wishes to delete the underlined phrase. Should the author proceeds to delete it or not?

√	**A) Keep, because it provides a specific example of the previous sentence.**
	B) Keep, because it provides the reason for the inclusion of remote controlled model aircraft to UAV
	C) Delete, because it interrupts the flow of the paragraph by illustrating an unsettled decision.
	D) Delete, because it weakens the focus of the passage by shifting to remote controlled model aircraft.

A) The sentence must be kept. There should always be a supporting detail that backup the topic sentence.

B) The previous sentence (The topic) illustrates why the definition of UVAs is still unclear.

C), D) both run counter to the central purpose of the previous sentence.

Q44. Absolute Pattern 1: Adding, Revising, Deleting, Retaining Information	
Question: Which of the following sentences is LEAST applicable as an alternate sentence?	
	A) The UAV's global market is dominated by United States and Israel.
	B) As the related technology improves, there has been a huge expansion in the UAV's global military market in less than a decade.
√	C) UAV's global market, however, faces **some serious privacy** issues as it expands exponentially.
	D) The U.S. Department of Defense has released a new statistics that shows Israel as the second largest market controller, next to the U.S.

C)

1> It switches the focus on a privacy issue, which is not discussed in the passage.

2> The negative tone also runs opposite to the overall positive tone of UAVs expansion in the passage.

3> A), B), and D) All of them share the positive aspects of UAV expansion and connect well with the overall flow and tone of the preceding sentence.

SAT
Writing and Language
Test 11

ALL THE LOGIC AND RULES
BEHIND THE EVERY SINGLE
SAT QUESTION

Writing and Language Test 11
35 MINUTES, 44 QUESTIONS

Each passage below is accompanied by a number of questions. For some questions, you will consider how the passage might be revised to improve the expression of ideas. For other questions, you will consider how the passage might be edited to correct errors in sentence structure, usage, or punctuation. A passage or a question may be accompanied by one or more graphics (such as a table or graph) that you will consider as you make revising and editing decisions.

Questions 1-11 are based on the following passage.

The World Digital Library

The World Digital Library (WDL) is an international digital library operated by UNESCO and the United States Library of Congress. The WDL [1] had stated that its mission is to [2] promoting international and intercultural understanding, expand the volume and variety of cultural content on the Internet, [3] provide resources for educators, scholars, and general audiences, and build capacity in partner institutions to narrow the digital divide within and among countries.

1

A) NO CHANGE
B) have stated
C) state
D) has stated

2

A) NO CHANGE
B) promotion of
C) promote and encourage
D) promote

3

A) NO CHANGE
B) by providing
C) to provide
D) which provides

CONTINUE

2

2

[4] Brown University is taking the major role among university participants.

The library intends to make available on the Internet, free of charge and in multilingual format, significant primary materials from cultures around the world, including manuscripts, maps, rare books, musical scores, recordings, films, prints, photographs, architectural drawings, and other significant cultural materials. [5]

4

Which choice best connects the sentence with the previous paragraph?

A) As written on the passage

B) It aims to expand non-English and non-western content on the Internet, and contribute to scholarly research.

C) It is a well-known fact that the Royal Library of Alexandria, Egypt, founded by Ptolemy, is considered to be the greatest ancient library in human civilization.

D) As the mode of modern information is becoming more digitized than paper-printed, the role of librarians is also shifting dramatically.

5

At this point, the author wishes to add the following information.

--encompassing materials obtained from many countries.

Should the author make this addition here?

A) Yes, because it provides added information of the materials.

B) Yes, because it connects well with the previous sentence.

C) No, because dash creates a punctuation error.

D) No, because it violates redundant error.

CONTINUE ⟶

2   **2**

After almost 20 years without participation, the United States [6] , which re-established its permanent delegation to the United Nations Educational, Scientific and Cultural Organization (UNESCO) in 2003. Dr. James H. Billington, Librarian of Congress, was nominated as a commissioner of the U.S. National Commission to UNESCO and [7] has been invited to give a plenary speech at its inaugural conference in June 2005. [8] His speech entitled *A View of the Digital World Library,* which described a vision in which the rich collections that "institutions, libraries, and museums have preserved could be given back to the world free of charge and in a new form far more universally accessible than any forms that have preceded it."

6

A) NO CHANGE
B) that re-established
C) by re-establishing
D) re-established

7

A) NO CHANGE
B) had been
C) was
D) is

8

Which choice combines the underlined portion of the sentence most effectively?

A) NO CHANGE
B) His speech, entitled *A View of the Digital World Library*, described a vision in which the rich collections that "institutions, libraries, and museums have preserved
C) With his speech, entitled *A View of the Digital World Library*, described a vision in which the rich collections that "institutions, libraries, and museums have preserved
D) His speech, entitled *A View of the Digital World Library*, described a vision, the rich collections, institutions, libraries, and museums

CONTINUE ▶

2   **2**

Google Inc. became the first partner of this public–private partnership and donated $3 million to support development of the World Digital Library in 2005.

The WDL opened with 1,236 items. As of late 2015, it lists more than 12,000 items from nearly 200 countries, dating back to 8,000 BCE.

At the National Commission's 2006 annual conference [9] ,which has been held every year since its establishment, Dr. John Van Oudenaren, Senior Advisor for the World Digital Library at the Library of Congress, outlined a project plan for bringing Dr. Billington's vision to fruition.

Foremost was the belief that the World Digital Library should engage partners in planning the four main project areas: technical architecture, selection, governance, and [10] garnering funding. This was achieved in December 2006, [11] that 45 national library directors, library technical directors, and cultural and educational representatives from UNESCO met in Paris to discuss the development of the World Digital Library.

9

A) NO CHANGE
B) ,held every year since its establishment,
C) that has been held yearly since its establishment
D) delete the underlined portion.

10

A) NO CHANGE
B) fund
C) funding
D) collecting working capital

11

A) NO CHANGE
B) in
C) in which
D) when

CONTINUE

2   2

Questions 12-22 are based on the following passage.

From Charles Darwin Autobiography

[12] German Editor, Gunter Schiller

[13] having written to me for an account of the

development of my mind and character with

some sketch of my autobiography, I have thought

that the attempt would amuse me, and might

possibly interest my children or their children.

[14] I had found no difficulty, for life is nearly

over with me. I have taken no pains about my style of

writing.

I was born at Shrewsbury on February 12th,

1809, and my earliest recollection goes back only to

when I was a few months over four years old, when

we went to near Abergele for sea-bathing, and I

recollect some events and places there with some little

distinctness.

My mother died in July 1817, when I was a little over

eight years old, and [15] it is odd that I can remember

hardly anything about her except her death-bed.

12

A) NO CHANGE
B) German Editor, Gunter Schiller,
C) German Editor Gunter Schiller,
D) German Editor Gunter Schiller

13

A) NO CHANGE
B) written
C) wrote
D) has written

14

A) NO CHANGE
B) Nor have I found difficulty,
C) Finding not difficulty,
D) Without finding difficulty,

15

A) NO CHANGE
B) its
C) it was
D) it had been

CONTINUE ▶

2　　　　　　　　　　　　　　　　　**2**

In the spring of this same year I was sent to a day-school in Shrewsbury, where I stayed a year. I have been told that I was much slower in learning than my younger sister Catherine, and I believe that I was in many ways a naughty boy. Mrs. Darwin was a Unitarian and attended Mr. Case's chapel. But [16] both he and his brother were christened and intended to belong to the Church of England. My taste for natural history, and more especially for collecting, was well developed. I tried to make out the names of plants [17] and collected all sorts of things, shells, seals, franks, coins, and minerals. The passion for collecting which leads a man to be a systematic naturalist, a virtuoso, or a miser, was very strong in me, and was clearly innate, [18] as none of my sisters or brother ever had this taste.

16

A) NO CHANGE
B) both him and his brother
C) both his and brother
D) both he as well as his brother

17

At this point, the writer is considering adding the following sentence.

　—Rev. W.A. Leighton brought a flower to school and taught us how by looking at the inside of the blossom the name of the plant could be discovered, which greatly roused my curiosity—

Should the writer make this addition here?

A) Yes, because it is consistent with the previous sentence and provides some added information.
B) Yes, because it enlightens us as well on how to find names of plants.
C) No, because it interrupts the paragraph's description of young Charles Darwin.
D) No, because Rev. W.A. Leighton is inessential character and is unnecessary to introduce.

18

A) NO CHANGE
B) but
C) and
D) moreover,

CONTINUE ➤

2   **2**

I may here also confess that as a little boy I was much given to inventing deliberate [19] falsehoods, and this was always done for the sake of causing excitement. [20] Moreover, I once gathered much valuable fruit from my father's trees and hid it in the shrubbery, and then ran in breathless haste to spread the news that I had discovered a hoard of stolen fruit. I must have been a very simple little fellow when I first went to the school. ① A boy the name of Garnett took me into a cake shop one day, and bought some cakes for which he did not pay, as the shop man trusted him. ②When we came out I asked him why he did not pay for them, and he instantly answered, "Why, do you not know that my uncle left a great sum of money to the town on condition that every tradesman should give whatever was wanted without payment to anyone who wore his old hat and moved it in a particular manner?" and he then showed me how it was moved. ③He then went into another shop where he was trusted, and asked for some small article, moving his hat in the proper manner, [21] but he was such a naïve boy as I recall.

[22] When we came out he said, "Now if you like to go by yourself into that cake-shop (how well I remember its exact position) I will lend you my hat.

19

Which choice most effectively combines the sentences at the underlined portion?
A) NO CHANGE
B) falsehood, whereas
C) falsehood, indeed,
D) falsehood, consequently,

20

A) NO CHANGE
B) Thus,
C) For instance,
D) In the meantime,

21

Which choice most closely matches the stylistic pattern established earlier in the sentence?
A) NO CHANGE
B) , so that the tradesman could remember the remarks from the boy's uncle.
C) , and of course obtained it without payment.
D) , and mentioned about his uncle to the tradesman.

22

To make the passage most logical, the sentence should be placed
A) where it is now.
B) after sentence 1
C) after sentence 2
D) after sentence 3

CONTINUE

2   2

Questions 23-33 are based on the following passage.

The Greenhouse gas effects

Greenhouse gas concentrations in the atmosphere will continue to increase [23] unless the billions of tons of our annual emissions decrease substantially. Increased concentrations are expected to increase Earth's average temperature, influence the patterns and amounts of precipitation, reduce ice and snow cover, as well as permafrost, raise sea level, and increase the acidity of the oceans. [24]

Temperature [25] increases and other climate changes may directly impact our food and water supply, ecosystems, coasts, and human health. The bars in the bottom box indicate what temperatures and impacts are expected under the high and low emissions scenarios, which are determined by our actions.

23

Which choice offers the most logical information to support the entire passage?

A) NO CHANGE

B) although there is nothing we can do about it

C) , but some folks believe that it's an overblown media tactic.

D) ,which accumulate in our atmosphere

24

At this point, the author wishes to add the following phrases.

   The mechanism is named after a faulty analogy with the effect of solar radiation passing through glass and warming a greenhouse. The way a green house retains heat is fundamentally different

Should the author make this addition here?

A) Yes, because it provides the added examples from the previous discussion.

B) Yes, because unlike the previous information, the addition brings more objective and mechanical function of the Greenhouse.

C) No, because some of the additions are redundant and unnecessarily wordy.

D) No, because it blurs the focus of the sentence

25

A) NO CHANGE

B) ,which increases fast

C) has been dramatically increased

D) increase

CONTINUE ➤

2

2

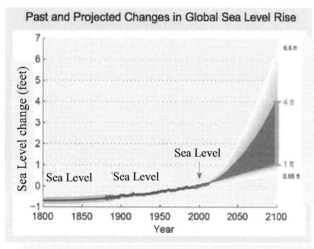

U.S. National Climate Assessment, 2014

The magnitude and rate of future climate change will primarily depend on many uncertain factors.

Among many noted estimates, the IPCC's "SRES" scenarios have been frequently used to make projections of future climate change.

The SRES scenarios are "baseline" (or "reference") scenarios, which means that the current or future measures that limit GHG emissions are not to be rigidly defined.[27]

Emissions projections of the SRES scenarios are [28] comparable in range to the baseline emissions, which are broad in scenarios that have been developed by the scientific community.

26

According to the information in the passage, which choice offers an accurate interpretation of the data in the chart?

A) Sea-level changes present the unclear relationship with the greenhouse

B) Thermal expansion in atmosphere is the direct effects of global warming but not the volume of water

C) The future sea level tells that drastic emission control won't make much difference.

D) The future sea level will be controlled within decades by our effort

27

Which choice supports the previously mentioned sentence?

A) They are, by far, the best, and therefore, should be employed as the most trusted guidelines

B) They forecast only up to 10 years of measurement.

C) They should never be practically applied.

D) They may function as a guideline.

28

A) NO CHANGE

B) comparable and relative to the baseline emissions scenarios broadly

C) broadly comparable to the baseline emissions scenarios

D) comparable to the baseline emissions scenarios, which are broad.

CONTINUE ➤

2   2

Many greenhouse gases stay in the atmosphere for long periods of time. [29] As a result, even if emissions stopped increasing, atmospheric greenhouse gas concentrations would continue to increase and remain elevated for hundreds of years. Even if we stabilized concentrations and the composition of today's atmosphere, (which would require a dramatic reduction in current greenhouse gas emissions), surface air temperatures [30] will continue to warm. This is because [31] the oceans, which store heat, take many decades to fully respond to higher greenhouse gas concentrations. The ocean's response to higher greenhouse gas concentrations and higher temperatures will continue to [32] effect climate over the next several decades to hundreds of years.

Therefore, over the next several millennia, projections suggest that global warming [33] could affect the global economy.

Even if emissions were drastically reduced, global temperatures would remain close to their highest level for at least 1,000 years

29

A) NO CHANGE
B) But,
C) On the other hand,
D) Nonetheless,

30

A) NO CHANGE
B) would continue
C) are going to continue
D) are continuing

31

A) NO CHANGE
B) the oceans which store heat
C) the oceans, that store heat,
D) the oceans store heat

32

A) NO CHANGE
B) affect
C) endanger
D) push negatively

33

A) NO CHANGE
B) could be significantly reduced
C) could be possibly reversed
D) could be irreversible.

CONTINUE

2   **2**

Questions 34-44 are based on the following passage.

Café de Cat

Cat cafés are quite popular in Japan, with Tokyo being home to 58 cat cafés as of 2015. [34] Other forms of pet [35] rental such as rabbit cafés, are also common in Japan. [36] There are various types of cat café in Japan, some feature specific categories of cat such as black cats, fat cats, rare breed cats or ex-stray cats. Every cat café in Japan is required to obtain a license and comply with the strict requirements and regulations of the nation's Animal Treatment and Protection Law.

34

At this point, the author considers to add the following information,

> The popularity of cat cafés in Japan is attributed to many apartments forbidding pets, and to provide cats relaxing companionship in what may otherwise be a stressful and lonely urban life.

Should the author add this information here?

A) Yes, because it establishes the psychological role cat can impart to its owner.

B) Yes, because it gives further explanations behind their popularity.

C) No, because such a detail doesn't fit in the introductory paragraph

D) No, because it mentions positive effects only to the place where side-effects should be presented.

35

A) NO CHANGE

B) rental, such as rabbit cafes,

C) rental, such as rabbit cafes

D) rental such as rabbit cafes

36

Which of the following choices would NOT be an alternate sentence?

A) Japan: some featuring specific categories of cat, such as black cats, fat cats, or ex-stray cats.

B) Japan, such as black cats cafe, fat cats cafe, or ex-stray cats cafe.

C) Japan, to name a few with black cats cafe, or ex-stray cats cafe.

D) Japan; which featuring specific categories of cat such as black cats, fat cats, or ex-stray cats.

CONTINUE

2

2

Japanese cat cafés feature strict rules to ensure cleanliness and animal welfare, in particular seeking to ensure that the cats are not disturbed by [37] excessive and unwanted attention, such as by young children or when sleeping. Many cat cafés also seek to raise awareness of cat's welfare issues, such as abandoned and stray cats.

Cat cafés have been spreading across North America [38] after 2014. The goal in North America generally is to help get cats adopted by partnering with local cat rescuers. ①The cat cafés across this region have come together to create The North American Cat Cafe Embassy. ②Saturday, October 17, 2015 saw the opening of Ontario's first cat café located in Guelph, Ontario. ③ The first cat café to open in North America was Le Café des Chats/Cat Café Montreal in Montreal, Canada, which opened its doors to the public in August 2014 [39] ,with 8 cats adopted from local shelters. ④ Catfe opened in Vancouver, British Columbia on December 14, 2015 and Kitty Cat Café and Pet Me Meow are both planning cafés for Toronto to open in 2015.

37
A) NO CHANGE
B) excessively
C) excess
D) excessed

38
A) NO CHANGE
B) in
C) by
D) since

39
Which of the following choices would NOT be an appropriate alternative phrase?
A) –having 8 cats adopted from local shelters.
B) ,which started with 8 cats adopted from local shelters.
C) , by home-staying 8 cats adopted from local shelters.
D) , 8 cats were adopted from local shelters.

40
To make this paragraph most logical, sentence ②Saturday, should be placed
A) Where it is now
B) Before sentence ①The cat
C) After sentence ③ The first
D) After sentence ④ Catfe

CONTINUE

Cat cafés in the United States differ from those in many other countries by their focus on adoptions. Hundreds of animals have been adopted through [41] their efforts. [42] Also, in United States, compliance with governmental food service regulations is required. The area where the cats are playing or being considered for adoption must be entirely separated from the area where food and drink are served. For example, a newly adopted cat must leave [43] without passing a food serving area through a separate door.

In May 2015, Grand Rapids, Michigan, announced Happy Cat Cafe will open sometime in 2016. They are hoping to partner with The Humane Society of West Michigan. The cafe raised $26,821 on Kickstarter with 549 backers.

In October 2015, the Blue Cat Cafe opened in Austin, Texas, [44] thereby partnering with the Austin Humane Society as a cafe and adoption center. It has live music for cats.

41
A) NO CHANGE
B) Catcafe
C) Its
D) Animal rescuers'

42
A) NO CHANGE
B) Consequently,
C) While,
D) Delete the underlined portion and change ' in the United States...' to "In the United States"

43
A) NO CHANGE
B) through a separate door, without passing a food serving area.
C) a food serving area through a separate door..
D) through a food serving area, without passing a separate door.

44
A) NO CHANGE
B) whereby it partners
C) in which it partners
D) partnering

TEST 11

WRITING ABSOLUTE PATTERNS

Test 11 Writing & Language Section Patterns

Q1. Absolute Pattern 24: Verb Tense / Voice Error

The WDL [1] had stated that its mission is to [2] promoting international and intercultural understanding, expand the volume and variety of cultural content on the Internet,(3) provide resources for educators, scholars, and general audiences, and build capacity in partner institutions to narrow the digital divide within and among countries.

	A) The past perfect tense	D) 1> This is a demonstrative statement that normally uses the simple present tense (e.g., The sun **rises**. William Shakespeare **is** the greatest playwright in history.)
	B) have stated	
	C) state	2> Having no simple present in the options, the second best alternative should be using (D) the present perfect.
√	**D) has stated**	B) and C): 1> Subject-verb agreement error.
		2> The subject WDL is singular. "have" and "state" are plural verbs.

Q2. Absolute Pattern 13: Parallel Structure

The WDL states that its mission is [2] to **promoting** international and intercultural understanding, **expand** the volume and variety of cultural content on the Internet, **provide** resources for educators, scholars, and general audiences, and **build** capacity in partner institutions to narrow the digital divide within and among countries.

	A) NO CHANGE	D) 1> The statement "its mission is" implies the future action.
	B) promotion of	2> To-infinitive clause performs the future action.
		3> The above sentence is using "to-infinitive clause" in a parallel structure.
	C) to promote and encourage	4> "to" can be dropped from the second to-infinitive clause, and use the base verb only: *"to promote, (to) expand, (to) provide, and (to) build."*
√	**D) to promote**	A) "~ing" is used for on-going concern
		B) is noun C) "promote and encourage' is redundant

Q3. Pattern 13: Parallel Structure

The WDL states that its mission is **to promote** international and intercultural understanding, **expand** the volume and variety of cultural content on the Internet,(3) **provide** resources for educators, scholars, and general audiences, and **build** capacity in partner institutions to narrow the digital divide

√	**A) NO CHANGE**	As seen in the previous question, "provide" best meets the parallel structure.
	B) by providing	
	C) to provide	
	D) which provides	

Q4. Absolute Pattern 1: Adding, Revising, Deleting, Retaining Information

[4] Brown University is taking the major role among university participants.

	A) As written on the passage
√	**B) It aims to expand non-English and non-western content on the Internet, and contribute to scholarly research.**
	C) It is a well-known fact that the Royal Library of Alexandria, Egypt, founded by Ptolemy, is considered to be the greatest ancient library in human civilization.
	D) As the mode of modern information is becoming more digitized, the role of librarians is also shifting dramatically.

1> The previous paragraph describes the international and intercultural promotion

2> The following paragraph describes the multilingual format.

3> Therefore, choice B, which states "the non-English content," is the most suitable topic.

Q5. Absolute Pattern 1: Adding, Revising, Deleting, Retaining Information

At this point, the author wishes to add the following information --encompassing materials obtained from many countries. —- Should the author make this addition here?

	A) Yes, because it provides added information of the materials.	A), B) The inclusion will only repeat the same information mentioned just earlier. C) There is no punctuation issue.
	B) Yes, because it connects well with the previous sentence.	
	C) No, because the usage of the dash is a punctuation error.	
√	**D) No, because it violates a redundant error.**	

Q6. Pattern 21: Subject-Verb, Pronoun, Noun Agreement

After almost 20 years without participation, the United States [6] ,which re-established its permanent delegation to the United Nations Educational, Scientific and Cultural Organization (UNESCO) in 2003.

	A) NO CHANGE	D) The sentence requires a verb. A), B) "which" and "that" technically function as a conjunction, creating the sentence without a verb. C) Missing verb
	B) that re-established	
	C) by re-establishing	
√	**D) re-established**	

Q7. Absolute Pattern 24: Verb Tense / Voice Error

Dr. James H. Billington, Librarian of Congress, was nominated as a commissioner of the U.S. National Commission to UNESCO and [7] has been invited to give a plenary speech at its inaugural conference in June 2005.

	A) NO CHANGE	C) 1> The previous clause uses the simple past tense. 2> The following clause contains "2005" that requires simple past tense.
	B) had been	A) is present perfect and passive
√	**C) was**	B) is the past perfect, passive
	D) is	D) is simple present

Q8. Absolute Pattern 16: Precision, Concision, Style

[8] His speech entitled *A View of the Digital World Library,* which described a vision in which the rich collections that "institutions, libraries, and museums have preserved could be given back to the world free of charge and in a new form far more universally accessible than any forms that have preceded it."

	A) NO CHANGE	Missing verb
√	B) **His speech**, entitled *A View of the Digital World Library,* **described** a vision in which the rich collections that "institutions, libraries, and museums have preserved	
	C) <u>With</u> his speech, entitled *A View of the Digital World Library*, described a vision in which the rich collections that "institutions, libraries, and museums have preserved	
	D) His speech, entitled *A View of the Digital World Library,* described a vision, the rich collections, institutions, libraries, and museums	

B) clears the errors in the original sentence by

1>offsetting a pair of commas to the quick interjection modifier "entitled...World library".

2> using the proper subject-verb arrangement (His speech...described)

C) has no subject. 'With' should be deleted.

D) changes the original meaning, creating an awkward sentence " institutions, libraries, and museums could be given back…"

Q9. Absolute Pattern 19: Redundant Error

At the National Commission's 2006 annual conference [9],<u>which has been held every year since its</u> <u>establishment,</u>

	A) NO CHANGE	A), B), C) are redundant.
	B) ,held <u>every year</u> since its establishment,	All of them repeat the word 'annual' in a slightly different manner.
	C) that <u>has been held yearly since</u> its establishment	
√	D) **delete the underlined portion.**	

Q10. Absolute Pattern 16: Precision, Concision, Style

Foremost was the belief that the World Digital Library should engage partners in planning the four main project areas: technical architecture, selection, governance, and [10]garnering funding.

	A) NO CHANGE	A) 'funding' already contains the meaning 'garnering," redundancy.
	B) fund	B) is a verb.
√	C) funding	C) "Funding" maintains the parallel structure.
	D) collecting working capital	D) is wordy

Q11. Absolute Pattern 7: Conjunction Error

This was achieved in December 2006, [11]that 45 national library directors, library technical directors, and cultural and educational representatives from UNESCO met in Paris to discuss the development of the World Digital Library.

	A) NO CHANGE	'that' can't link the time clause, due to the comma after "2006"
	B) in	'in' is preposition, which can't carry a clause
	C) in which	'in which' can be understood as 'where' but not 'when'.
√	D) when	The time phrase should be linked by 'when'

Q12. Absolute Pattern 20: Restrictive Modifier (Essential Information)

[12] German Editor, Gunter Schiller [13] having written to me for an account of the development of my mind and character with some sketch of my autobiography, I have thought that the attempt would amuse me, and might possibly interest my children or their children.

	A) NO CHANGE	D) 1> German Editor and Gunter Schiller is one person.
	B) German Editor, Gunter Schiller,	2> Gunter Schiller should be treated as an essential information.
	C) German Editor Gunter Schiller,	3> In fact, "Gunter Schiller (who)" is more important than "German Editor (what)" to maintain the logical sentence.
√	D) German Editor Gunter Schiller	4> Therefore, The name should not be offset by a pair of commas

Q13. Absolute Pattern 24: Verb Tense / Voice Error

German Editor Gunter Schiller [13] having written to me for an account of the development of my mind and character with some sketch of my autobiography, I **have thought** that the attempt would amuse me, and might possibly interest my children or their children.

		The usage of 'having'
√	A) NO CHANGE	1> The main verb "have thought" is the present perfect.
	B) written	2> German Editor's action indicates that he acted earlier, requiring past tense.
	C) wrote	3> Therefore, the answer should be "having written." (meaning after he wrote)
	D) has written	B) The participle 'written' is expressed in a passive voice 'being written,'
		C) and D) are verbs, creating several critical errors, such as comma splice, run-on, etc.

Q14. Absolute Pattern 23: Transition Words for Supporting Detail, Contrast, and Consequence

[14] I **had found** no difficulty, **for** life is nearly over with me. I have taken no pains about my style of writing.

	A) NO CHANGE	B) The previous portion should be the primary sentence that contains the subject and verb.
√	B) Nor have I found difficulty,	A) "had found" is past perfect. The past perfect tense can't be used along with the present tense "have taken"
	C) Finding not difficulty,	
	D) Without finding difficulty,	C) and D) aren't even sentences

Q15. Absolute Pattern 24: Verb Tense / Voice Error

My mother died in July 1817, when I was a little over eight years old, and [15] it is odd **that I can** remember hardly anything about her except her death-bed.

√	A) NO CHANGE	A) 1> This autobiography passage is a narrative form.
	B) its	2> The present tense is the most ideal tense in narration.
	C) it was	3> The other non-underlined portion also uses the present tense.
	D) it had been	B) 'its' is a possessive pronoun, and has no verb.
		C) is simple past
		D) is past perfect.

Q16. Absolute Pattern 15: Prepositional Idiom

But [16] both he and his brother were christened and intended to belong to the Church of England;

		Correlative conjunction "both ~ and"
√	A) NO CHANGE	A) The subjective pronoun 'he' should be used after the conjunction "But"
	B) both him and his brother	B) 'him' is objective pronoun.
	C) both his and brother	C) 'his' is possessive pronoun.
	D) both he as well as his brother	D) The idiom "both ~ and" can't be replaced with "both ~ as well as."

Q17. Absolute Pattern 1: Adding, Revising, Deleting, Retaining Information

At this point, the writer is considering adding the following sentence.

—Rev. W.A. Leighton brought a flower to school and taught us how by looking at the inside of the blossom the name of the plant could be discovered, which greatly roused my curiosity—
Should the writer make this addition here?

√	A) Yes, because it is **consistent with the previous sentence** and provides some added information.
	B) Yes, because it enlightens us as well on how to find names of plants.
	C) No, because it interrupts the paragraph's description of young Charles Darwin.
	D) No, because Rev. W.A. Leighton is inessential character and is unnecessary to introduce.

The previous sentence introduces young Darwin's innate penchant for nature.

The following sentence further sketches his early curiosity for nature.

B) The reader is not mentioned and therefore unnecessary.

C), D) The added information makes the passage more descriptive.

Q18. Absolute Pattern 23: Transition Words for Supporting Detail, Contrast, and Consequence

The passion for collecting which leads a man to be a systematic naturalist, a virtuoso, or a miser, was very strong in me, and was clearly innate, [18] <u>as</u> none of my sisters or brother ever had this taste.

	A) NO CHANGE	Two clauses are contradicting to each other. Therefore, the conjunction "but" must be used.
√	**B) but**	
	C) and	A) 'as,' equalizes the idea.
		C) 'and' is used for a parallel structure.
	D) moreover,	D) 'moreover' is used to add or emphasize the previous sentence.

Q19. Absolute Pattern 23: Transition Words for Supporting Detail, Contrast, and Consequence

I may here also confess that as a little boy I was much given to inventing deliberate [19] <u>falsehoods, and</u> this was always done for the sake of causing excitement.

√	**A) NO CHANGE**	Conjunction "and." is required because the sentence flows within the parallel structure.
	B) falsehood, whereas	
		B) 'whereas' means 'on the contrary,' and it expresses opposite view.
	C) falsehood, indeed,	C), and (D) are incorrect because they are adverbs, not conjunction, and therefore can't tie the following clause like "and" can.
	D) falsehood, consequently,	C) 'indeed' is used to emphasize the previous statement.
		D) "consequently" is used for the cause-and-effect relation.

Q20. Absolute Pattern 23: Transition Words for Supporting Detail, Contrast, and Consequence

[20]<u>Moreover,</u> I once gathered much valuable fruit from my father's trees and hid it in the shrubbery, and then ran in breathless haste to spread the news that I had discovered a hoard of stolen fruit.

	A) NO CHANGE	C) 1> 'For instance' adds details to the topic sentence.
	B) Thus,	2> The previous sentence sketches young Charles Darwin's childhood naivety.
√	**C) For instance,**	A) 'Moreover' is used to add up another complementary statement
	D) In the meantime,	B) 'Thus' is used to reveal the consequence.
		D) 'In the meantime,' is used to show the different perspective from the previous statement

Q21. Absolute Pattern 1: Adding, Revising, Deleting, Retaining Information

He then went into another shop where he was trusted, and asked for some small article, moving his hat in the proper manner, [21] but he was such a naïve boy as I recall.

	A) NO CHANGE	A) "naïve" doesn't fit in the description about the boy. He steals from the shop.
	B) so that the tradesman could remember the remarks from the boy's uncle.	B) and D) are part of lies the boy intrigued young Charles Darwin, not a true statement.
√	C) and of course obtained it without payment.	
	D) while mentioning about his uncle to the tradesman.	

Q22. Absolute Pattern 1: Adding, Revising, Deleting, Retaining Information

When we came out he said, "Now if you like to go by yourself into that cake-shop (how well I remember its exact position) I will lend you my hat.

	A) where it is now.	The current position is correct. It is young Charles Darwin's turn to steal.
	B) after sentence 1	
	C) after sentence 2	
√	D) after sentence 3	

Q23. Absolute Pattern 1: Adding, Revising, Deleting, Retaining Information

Greenhouse gas concentrations in the atmosphere will continue to increase [23] unless the billions of tons of our annual emissions decrease substantially.

Which choice offers the most logical information to support the entire passage?

√	A) NO CHANGE	A) The topic sentence, the title, and the following passage are all about warning against the greenhouse gas emission. This sentence well presents the negative mood.
	B) although there is nothing we could do about it	B) This statement is too regressive.
	C) , but some folks believe that it's an overblown media tactic.	C) is opposite perception from the author's main view
	D) ,which concentrates in our atmosphere	D) simply rewrites the terminology of Greenhouse.

Q24. Absolute Pattern 1: Adding, Revising, Deleting, Retaining Information

Q. At this point, the author wishes to add the following phrases.
The mechanism is named after a faulty analogy with the effect of solar radiation passing through glass and warming a greenhouse. The way a green house retains heat is fundamentally different
Should the author make this addition here?

	A) Yes, because it provides added examples of the previous discussion.
	B) Yes, because unlike the previous information, the addition brings more objective and mechanical function of the Greenhouse.
	C) No, because some of the additions are redundant and unnecessarily wordy.
√	**D) No, because it blurs the focus of the sentence**

1> (The Previous Sentence) <u>Earth's average temperature, influence the patterns</u> and amounts of precipitation, reduce ice and snow cover, as well as permafrost, raise sea level, and increase the acidity of the oceans. [24]

2> (The Following Sentence) Temperature [25] <u>increases and other climate changes may directly impact</u> our food and water supply, ecosystems, coasts, and human health.

Both previous and following sentences discuss the Earth temperature change caused by the Greenhouse.

3> The question asks whether the new sentence introducing the <u>origin of the term</u> "greenhouse" can be inserted in the middle. The answer is D) No.

Q25. Pattern 21: Subject-Verb, Pronoun, Noun Agreement

Temperature [25] <u>increases</u> and other climate changes **may directly impact** our food and water supply, ecosystems, coasts, and human health.

	A) NO CHANGE	"Temperature increase and other climate changes" should be the subject, not a verb.
	B) ,which increases fast	We know this by looking at the verb "'may directly impact"
	C) has been dramatically increased	
√	**D) increase**	A) uses "increases" as a verb B) is wordy C) changes the meaning of the entire sentence.

Q26. Absolute Pattern 9: Informational Graphs

According to the information in the passage, which choice offers an accurate interpretation of the data in the chart?

	A) Sea-level changes present the unclear relationship with greenhouse effect
	B) Thermal expansion in atmosphere is the direct effects of Atlantic temperature anomaly
√	**C) The future sea level tells that drastic emission control won't make much difference.**
	D) The future sea level will be controlled within decades by our effort

(Topic Sentence): Greenhouse gas concentrations in the atmosphere will continue to increase unless the billions of tons of our annual emissions decrease substantially…. as well as permafrost, raise sea level,

(Concluding Sentence): Even if emissions were drastically reduced, global temperatures would remain close to their highest level for at least 1,000 years

C) is correct according to the graph.

A) is direct opposite to the first and the last sentences of the passage as well as the graph.

B) "Thermal expansion in atmosphere" is not mentioned in the passage.

D) is direct opposite to the concluding sentence.

Q27. Absolute Pattern 1: Adding, Revising, Deleting, Retaining Information

Among many noted estimates, the IPCC's "SRES" scenarios have been frequently used to make projections of future climate change. The SRES scenarios are "baseline" (or "reference") scenarios, which means that the current or future measures that limit GHG emissions are not to be rigidly defined. [27]

	Which choice supports the previously mentioned sentence?
	A) SRES are, by far, the best, and therefore, should be employed as the most rigid guidelines
	B) SRES forecast only up to 10 years of measurement.
	C) SRES should never be practically applied.
√	**D) SRES may function as the guidelines.**

Based on the underlined portion of the sentence, only D) should be the answer.

A), C) are opposite to the statement.

B) is not stated in the passage.

Q28. Absolute Pattern 16: Precision, Concision, Style

Emissions projections of the SRES scenarios are [28] comparable **in range to** the baseline emissions, **which are broad** in scenarios that have been developed by the scientific community.

	A) NO CHANGE	A) "which are broad" is wordy and changes the original meaning.
	B) comparable and relative to the baseline emissions scenarios broadly	
√	C) **broadly comparable to the baseline emissions scenarios**	B) "comparable" and "relative" are synonym.
	D) comparable to the baseline emissions scenarios, which are broad.	D) "scenarios are broad" \changes the meaning.

Q29. Absolute Pattern 2: Cause-Effect Relations

Many greenhouse gases stay in the atmosphere for long periods of time. [29] As a result, even if emissions stopped increasing, atmospheric greenhouse gas concentrations would continue to increase and remain elevated for hundreds of years.

√	A) **NO CHANGE**	A) The cause-and-effect situation requires "because" or similar transitional word.
	B) But,	B) cancels out the previous sentence.
	C) On the other hand,	C) suggests a different view.
	D) Nonetheless,	D) means despite what has been said and done.

Q30. Absolute Pattern 24: Verb Tense / Voice Error

Even **if we stabilized** concentrations and the composition of today's atmosphere, (which would require a dramatic reduction in current greenhouse gas emissions), surface air temperatures [30] will continue to warm.

	A) NO CHANGE	1> If-clause uses the past tense for the present situation
√	B) **would continue**	2> "if we stabilized" indicates that the verb in the main clause also has to be the past tense.
	C) are going to continue	A) is future. C), D) are present tense .
	D) are continuing	

Q31.   Pattern 22 : Non-Restrictive Modifier (Inessential Information)

This is because [31] <u>the oceans, which store heat,</u> take many decades to fully respond to higher green-house gas concentrations.

√	A) NO CHANGE	'which store heat' is non-essential information. Therefore, it should be offset by a pair of commas to separate it from the main clause.
	B) the oceans which store heat	B) hasn't got a pair of commas
	C) the oceans, that store heat,	C) "that" cannot be followed by a comma.
	D) the oceans store heat	D) "store" is a verb. The main verb "take" is already presented.

Q32. Pattern 6: Confusing Words

The ocean's response to higher greenhouse gas concentrations and higher temperatures will continue to [32] <u>effect</u> climate over the next several decades to hundreds of years.

	A) NO CHANGE	B) "affect" is normally used as a verb.
√	B) affect	A) "effect" is more often used as a noun
	C) endanger	C) and D) change the meaning drastically.
	D) push negatively	

Q33. Absolute Pattern 10: Logical Expression

Therefore, over the next several millennia, projections suggest that global warming [33] could affect the global economy.

	A) NO CHANGE	D) Throughout the passage, the author's primary concern is the irreversible dire impact of the greenhouse. The author describes the global warming trends will not change.
	B) could be significantly reduced	
	C) could be possibly reversed	A) is new information, not supported by neither the previous nor the following sentence.
√	D) could be irreversible	B) and C) are opposite perception

Q34. Absolute Pattern 1: Adding, Revising, Deleting, Retaining Information

At this point, the author considers to add the following information,

The popularity of cat cafés in Japan is attributed to many apartments forbidding pets, and to provide cats relaxing companionship in what may otherwise be a stressful and lonely urban life.

Should the author add this information here?

	A) Yes, because it establishes the <u>psychological role cat can impart</u> to its owner.
√	**B) Yes, because it gives further explanations behind their popularity.**
	C) <u>No</u>, because such a detail doesn't fit in the introductory paragraph
	D) <u>No</u>, because it mentions positive effects only to the place where side-effects should be presented.

A) 1> "psychological…" is offbeat in tone and theme. 2> The main theme is Cat Café, not cat.

C) The degree of details in this sentence is necessary to support the topic sentence.

D) The overall essay is written from the positive point.

Q35. Absolute Pattern 18: Punctuation Error

Other forms of pet [35] <u>rental such as rabbit **cafés, are**</u> also common in Japan.

	A) NO CHANGE	C) 1> "such as" phrase should be separated from the main clause by comma.
	B) rental, such as rabbit cafes,	A) and D) Comma should separate "such as" from the main clause.
√	**C) rental, such as rabbit cafes**	B) Comma separates the verb from its main clause.
	D) rental such as rabbit cafes	

Q36. Absolute Pattern 18: Punctuation Error

Question: Which of the following choices would NOT be an alternate sentence?

	A) Japan: some featuring specific categories of cat, such as black cats, fat cats, or ex-stray cats.
	B) Japan, such as black cats cafe, fat cats cafe, or ex-stray cats cafe.
	C) Japan, to name a few with black cats cafe, or ex-stray cats cafe.
√	D) **Japan, which featuring** specific categories of cat such as black cats, fat cats, or ex-stray cats.

D) 1> "which" must carry a clause. 2> starting with "featuring" is a phrase, not a clause.

3> It should either remove 'which' or fix 'which featuring' to "which features."

A) A colon carries any type of statement as long as it introduces things.

B) 'such as' presents a series of example   C) 'to name a few' presents a series of example.

Q37. Absolute Pattern 10: Logical Expression

Japanese cat cafés feature strict rules to ensure cleanliness and animal welfare, in particular seeking to ensure that the cats are not disturbed by [37] excessive and unwanted **attention**, such as by young children or when sleeping.

√	**A) NO CHANGE**	A) "attention" is a noun that requires an adjective "excessive."
	B) excessively	B) is adverb, which is used to describe an adjective or verb, not noun.
	C) excess	C) means surplus
	D) excessed	D) is passive form of adjective "excess".

Q38. Absolute Pattern 15: Prepositional Idiom

Cat cafés have been spreading across North America [38] after 2014.

	A) NO CHANGE	A) 1> 'after' and 'since' are not interchangeable.
	B) in	2> 'since' should be used when the primary clause uses the present perfect or past perfect tense.
	C) by	
√	**D) since**	B) "in" and C) "by" can't replace 'since'

Q39. Pattern 5: Comma Splice Error

The first cat café to open in North America was Le Café des Chats/Cat Café Montreal in Montreal, Canada, which opened its doors to the public in August 2014 [39], with 8 cats adopted from local shelters.

	A) –having 8 cats adopted from local shelters.	D) Comma splice error.
	B) ,which started with 8 cats adopted from local shelters.	A) A single dash emphasizes the following modifier that can carry any form of statement.
	C) ,by home-staying 8 cats adopted from local shelters.	B) 'which' functions as a conjunction that allows the subordinating clause to follow
√	D) , 8 cats **were adopted** from local shelters.	C) The preposition 'by' carries a gerund, 'home-staying, which is an ideal form of this sentence structure.

Q40. Absolute Pattern 11: Logical Sequence

Question: To make this paragraph most logical, sentence 2 should be placed

	A) Where it is now	Based on the chronological sequence, sentence 2 should be located after sentence 3.
	B) Before sentence 1	
√	**C) After sentence 3**	
	D) After sentence after 4	

<1>.The cat cafés across this region have come together to create The North American Cat Cafe Embassy.

<2> Saturday, **October 17, 2015** saw the opening of Ontario's first cat café located in Guelph, Ontario.

<3> The first cat café to open in North America was Le Café des Chats/Cat Café Montreal in Montreal, Canada, which opened its doors to the public in **August 2014 ,** with 8 cats adopted from local shelters.

<4>. Catfe opened in Vancouver, British Columbia on **December 14, 2015** and Kitty Cat Café and Pet Me Meow are both planning cafés for **Toronto to open in 2015.**

Q41. Absolute Pattern 17: Pronoun Error

Cat cafés in the **United States** differ from **those** in many **other countries** by **their** focus on adoptions. Hundreds of **animals** have been adopted through [41] **their** efforts.

	A) NO CHANGE	A) ambiguity error. 1> The pronoun "their" indicates too many antecedents, blurring what it actually refers to. "their" could be "Cat cafes", "those" or other countries" 2> In this case, avoiding pronoun is the best way.
	B) Catcafe	
	C) Its	B) The noun must be the possessive to connect "efforts."
√	**D) Animal rescuers'**	C) The singular pronoun 'Its' can't represent any word in the sentence.

Q42. Absolute Pattern 23: Transition Words for Supporting Detail, Contrast, and Consequence

[42]Also, in United States, compliance with governmental food service regulations is required.

√	**A) NO CHANGE**	A) 1> The previous sentence introduces the different function of Catcafé in U.S, focusing on adoption.
	B) Consequently,	2> The following sentence further explores the regulations using "Also."
	C) While,	B) 'Consequently,' is used for cause-and-effect situation.
	D) Delete	C) 'while' is mainly used for contradiction.

Q43. Pattern 12: Modifier Placement Error

For example, [43] a newly adopted cat must **leave** without passing a food serving area **through a separate door.**

	A) NO CHANGE	B) "leave through a door" is the correct modifier
√	B) **through a separate door**, without passing a food serving area.	A) It sounds as if "food serving area" is in a separate door.
	C) a food serving area through a separate door.	C) changes the meaning, "cat must leave a food serving area." (Are cats already there?)
	D) through a food serving area, without passing a separate door.	D) changes the meaning ("cat.. can't pass a separate door.")

Q44. Absolute Pattern 16: Precision, Concision, Style

In October 2015, the Blue Cat Cafe opened in Austin, Texas, [44] thereby partnering with the Austin Humane Society as a cafe and adoption center. It has live music for cats.

	A) NO CHANGE	'partnering ~ ' is much more clear expression.
	B) whereby it partners	A), B), C) all contain unnecessary conjunctive adverbs that are ambiguous for which they stand for.
	C) in which it partners	
√	D) **partnering**	

SAT

Writing and Language

Test 12

ALL THE LOGIC AND RULES

BEHIND THE EVERY SINGLE

SAT QUESTION

Writing and Language Test 12
35 MINUTES, 44 QUESTIONS

Each passage below is accompanied by a number of questions. For some questions, you will consider how the passage might be revised to improve the expression of ideas. For other questions, you will consider how the passage might be edited to correct errors in sentence structure, usage, or punctuation. A passage or a question may be accompanied by one or more graphics (such as a table or graph) that you will consider as you make revising and editing decisions.

Questions 1-11 are based on the following passage.

BREXIT

The United Kingdom European Union membership referendum, also known as the EU referendum and the Brexit [1] referendum, which a referendum that took place on Thursday 23 June 2016 in the United Kingdom to [2] gauge support for the country's continued membership in the European Union. The referendum result was not legally binding. The result was split [3] with the constituent countries of the United Kingdom, with a majority in England and Wales voting to leave, and a majority in Scotland and Northern Ireland, voting to remain.

To start the process to leave the [4] EU, which is expected to take several years, the British government will have to invoke Article 50 of the Treaty on European Union.

1
A) NO CHANGE
B) referendum, are a referendum
C) referendum, as a referendum
D) referendum, was a referendum

2
Which of the following alternatives would NOT be appropriate?
A) check
B) measure
C) see
D) alter

3
A) NO CHANGE
B) into
C) between
D) in

4
A) NO CHANGE
B) EU expects
C) EU, expecting
D) EU and to expect

CONTINUE →

2   2

The UK government has announced formal process of leaving the EU [5] although revoking the vote might be possible.

Membership of the EU had long been a topic of debate in the United Kingdom. [6] The country joined the European Economic Community (EEC, or "Common Market") in 1973.

Britain Stronger in Europe was the official group campaigning for the UK to remain in the EU and was led by the Prime Minister David Cameron and Chancellor George Osborne. [7] Other campaign groups, political parties, businesses, trade unions, newspapers and prominent individuals were also involved, and each side had supporters from across the political spectrum.

5

Which choice provides a supporting example that emphasizes the main point of the sentence?

A) NO CHANGE

B) ,confirming the due date by March 2019.

C) , confirming Brexit was driven by the official process

D) , using term "hard Brexit" rather than "soft Brexit"

6

If the writer were to delete the underlined portion, the sentence would primarily lose:

A) The meaning of EEC

B) The formal step to leave E.U. after the referendum.

C) The description of historical overview.

D) The importance of EEC to the United Kingdom.

7

At this point, the author wishes to add the following information.

> Vote Leave was the official group campaigning for the UK to leave the EU and was fronted by the Conservative MPs Boris Johnson and Michael Gove.

Should the author make this addition here?

A) Yes, because it provides added information about the history of conflicts.

B) Yes, because it connects with the previous sentence.

C) No, because it is mentioned in the following sentences.'

D) No, because it is not persuasive.

CONTINUE ➡

2   2

Financial markets [8] were reacted negatively in the immediate aftermath of the result. Investors in worldwide stock markets lost more than the [9] equivalent of 2 trillion United States dollars on 24 June 2016, making it the worst single-day loss in history. The market losses amounted to 3 trillion US dollars by 27 June. The value of the pound sterling against the US dollar fell to a 31-year low. The UK's and the EU's sovereign debt credit rating was also lowered by Standard & Poor's. By 29 June, the markets had returned to growth and the value of the pound had begun to rise.

Immediately after the result, the Prime Minister [10] David Cameron had announced he would resign, having campaigned unsuccessfully for a "remain" vote on behalf of Britain Stronger in Europe and HM Government. He was succeeded by Theresa May on 13 July.

8
A) NO CHANGE
B) were in great reaction
C) reacted by
D) reacted

9
Which of the following alternatives would NOT be appropriate?
A) equivocal to
B) equal to
C) tantamount to
D) nearly

10
Which choice combines the underlined sentence most effectively?
A) NO CHANGE
B) David Cameron followed the result, Cameron announced that he would resign, after he campaigned
C) David Cameron announced he would resign, having campaigned
D) David Cameron, by announcing that he would resign, having campaigned

CONTINUE

2

2

United Kingdom European Union membership referendum

Should the United Kingdom remain a member of the European Union or leave the European Union?

Location	United Kingdom
Date	23 June 2016

Results		
	Votes	**%**
Leave	**17,410,742**	**51.89%**
Remain	16,141,241	48.11%
Valid votes	33,551,983	99.92%
Invalid or blank votes	25,359	0.08%
Total votes	**33,577,342**	**100.00%**
Registered voters/ turnout	46,500,001	72.21%

11

In reference to the passage, which choice offers an accurate interpretation of the table on the left ?

A) The table results reflect the cause of the former Prime Minister David Cameron's leaving the office.

B) The referendum result was legally binding.

C) As the referendum confirmed, United Kingdom will start the formal process of leaving the EU immediately.

D) As the referendum confirmed, the Leave group will leave the EU, and the Remain group will remain in the EU.

CONTINUE

2   2

Questions 12-22 are based on the following passage.

Are we alone?

{ Paragraph 1 }

Many scientists believe we are not alone in the universe. It's probable, they say, that life could have [12] rise on at least some of the billions of planets thought to exist in our galaxy alone -- just as it did here on planet Earth. This basic question about our place in the Universe is one that may be answered by scientific investigations. (A)

{ Paragraph 2 }

Experts from NASA and its partner institutions addressed this question on July 14, at a public talk held at NASA Headquarters in Washington. [13] They outlined NASA's roadmap to the search for life in the [14] universe, it was an ongoing journey that involves a number of current and future telescopes. Sometime in the near future, people will be able to point to a star and say, 'that star has a planet like Earth'," says Sara Seager, professor of planetary science and physics at the Massachusetts Institute of Technology in Cambridge, Massachusetts. [15] However, the impression of how common planets are in the Milky way adversely creates backlash among scientists. (B)

12

A) NO CHANGE
B) raise
C) arisen
D) arouse

13

A) NO CHANGE
B) He
C) It
D) Those

14

A) NO CHANGE
B) universe, and an ongoing journey
C) universe because it was an ongoing journey
D) universe, an ongoing journey

15

Which choice emphasizes the anticipation of some scientists believing the existence of a planet like Earth.

A) NO CHANGE
B) There are 100 billion planets in our Milky Way galaxy
C) Astronomers have currently discovered the evidential proof that there is no chance for Venus to sustain life.
D) Astronomers acknowledge that under the current technology, there are many obstacles to materialize our space safari project.

CONTINUE ▶

2

2

{ Paragraph 3 }

NASA's quest to study planetary systems around other stars started with ground-based observatories, then moved to space-based assets like the Hubble Space Telescope, the Spitzer Space Telescope, and the Kepler Space Telescope. Today's telescopes can look at many stars and tell if they have one or more orbiting planets.(C)

[16] However, they can determine if the planets are the right distance away from the star to have liquid water, the key ingredient to life as we know [17] it.

{ Paragraph 4 }

The NASA roadmap will continue with the launch of the Transiting Exoplanet Surveying Satellite TESS) in 2017 and the James Webb Space Telescope. These upcoming telescopes [18] would find and characterize [19] a host of new exoplanets—those planets that orbit other stars—expanding our knowledge of their atmospheres and diversity. The Webb telescope and WFIRST-AFTA will lay the groundwork, and future missions will extend the search for the nearby planets that are similar to Earth in size and mass, a key step in the search for life.
(D)

16
A) NO CHANGE
B) Although at this phase,
C) Even more,
D) Therefore,

17
A) NO CHANGE
B) liquid water is the essential to sustain life.
C) water can be used to form life.
D) that the planets' distance is a way to under stand whether liquid water exists or not.

18
A) NO CHANGE
B) will find
C) have to find
D) that find

19
Which choice most dramatically emphasizes the massive scale of upcoming discovery using the telescope observation projects?
A) NO CHANGE
B) more reliable data of
C) groundbreaking discovery of
D) the actual photographs of

CONTINUE

2   2

"This technology we are using to explore exoplanets is real," said John Grunsfeld, astronaut and associate administrator for NASA's Science Mission Directorate in Washington. "The James Webb Space Telescope and the next advances are happening now. These are not dreams -- this is what we do at NASA."

[20] After its launch in 2009, Kepler has dramatically changed what we know about exoplanets, finding most of the more than 5,000 potential exoplanets, of which more than 1700 have been confirmed. The Kepler observations have led to estimates of billions of planets in our galaxy, and shown that most planets within one astronomical unit are less than three times the diameter of Earth. Kepler also found the first Earth-size planet to orbit in the "habitable zone" of a star, the region where liquid water can pool on the surface.

20

A) NO CHANGE
B) Having followed
C) With
D) Since

21

Suppose the writer's primary purpose is to describe the possibility of searching for life.

Would this essay accomplish that purpose?

A) Yes, because it tells about a variety of challenges the scientists face along with their searching for life in exoplanets.

B) Yes, because it focuses primarily on scientists' application of a various types of telescopes and other methods in quest of searching for life in the universe.

C) No, because it focuses mainly on the projects to be undertaken in the future.

D) No, because it focuses on the limited applications within the scope of modern technology in finding life in the universe.

22

The writer wants to add the following sentence to the essay:

What are the next steps to finding life elsewhere?

The sentence would most logically be placed at point:

A) A in {Paragraph 1}
B) B in {Paragraph 2}
C) C in {Paragraph 3}
D) D in {Paragraph 4}

CONTINUE ⟶

2   2

Questions 23-33 are based on the following passage.

Black ice

Black [23] ice, sometimes called clear ice, refers to a thin coating of glaze ice on a surface, especially on roads. The ice itself is not black, but visually transparent, [24] allowing the often black road below to be seen through it. The typically low level of noticeable ice pellets, snow, or sleet [25] surrounds black ice means that areas of the ice are often practically invisible to drivers or people stepping on it. [26] Their is, thus, a risk of skidding and subsequent accidents due to the unexpected loss of traction. The term *black ice* in the United States is often incorrectly used to describe any type of ice that forms on roadways, even when standing water on roads turns to ice as the temperature falls below freezing. Correctly defined, black ice is formed on relatively dry roads, rendering it invisible to drivers. It occurs when in the textures present in all pavements very slightly below the top of the road surface contain water or moisture, thereby presenting a dry surface to tires until that water or moisture freezes and expands; drivers then find they are riding above the road surface on a honeycombed invisible sheet of ice.

23

Which of the following alternatives to the underlined portion would NOT be acceptable?
A) ice, sometimes called clear ice, refers
B) ice—sometimes called clear ice—refers
C) ice, sometimes called clear ice refers
D) ice (sometimes called clear ice) refers

24

If the writer were to delete the underlined portion of the sentence, it would primarily lose:
A) an idea that emphasizes the reason for an optical illusion
B) a statement that introduces the main focus of the following paragraph.
C) an unnecessary detail that contradicts information presented earlier in the paragraph.
D) a vivid image that most observers want to find out beneath the Black Ice.

25

A) NO CHANGE
B) surrounding black ice meaning
C) surrounding black ice means
D) surrounding black ice mean

26

A) NO CHANGE
B) Their have been
C) There is
D) There are

CONTINUE

2   2

Because it represents only a thin accumulation, black ice is highly transparent and thus difficult to see as compared with snow, frozen slush, or thicker ice layers. [27] In addition, it often is interleaved with wet pavement, which is nearly identical in [28] appearance, this makes driving, cycling or walking on affected surfaces extremely dangerous. Deicing with salt   (sodium chloride) is effective to down temperatures of about −18 °C (0 ° F).

At below −18 °C, black ice can form on roadways when the moisture from automobile exhaust condenses on the road surface. Such conditions caused multiple accidents in Minnesota when the temperatures dipped below −18 °C for a prolonged period of time in December 2008. [29] With salt's ineffectiveness at melting ice at these temperatures compounds the problem. Black ice may form even when the ambient temperature is several degrees above the freezing point of water 0 °C (32 °F), [30] if the air warms suddenly after a prolonged cold spell that has left the surface of the roadway well below the freezing point temperature.

27

A) NO CHANGE
B) On the contrary,
C) Consequently,
D) In spite of such a thin accumulation,

28

Which of the following alternatives to the underlined portion would NOT be acceptable?
A) appearance, which makes
B) appearance, making
C) appearance. This makes
D) appearance, this makes

29

A) NO CHANGE
B) Salt's
C) Salt
D) Sodium Chloride

30

In the preceding sentence, the underlined portion of if-clause primarily serves to indicate:
A) that black ice phenomenon could occur in many southern states with mild temperature
B) the strikingly complex characteristics of Black Ice
C) that technique to prevent black ice is not very well developed at present
D) the atmospheric conditions that lead to Black Ice formation under certain temperature.

CONTINUE ▶

2   2

On December 1, 2013, heavy post-Thanksgiving weekend traffic encountered black ice on the westbound I-290 expressway in Worcester, Massachusetts. A chain reaction series of crashes resulted, involving three tractor-trailers and over 60 other vehicles. The ice [31] had formed suddenly on a long downward slope, [32] surprising drivers coming over the crest of a hill, who could not see crashed vehicles ahead until it was too late to stop on the slick pavement. Bridges and overpasses can be especially dangerous. Black ice forms first on bridges and overpasses because air can circulate both above and below the surface of the elevated roadway, causing the bridge pavement temperature to drop more rapidly.

31

A) NO CHANGE
B) formed suddenly in a matter of seconds
C) has formed suddenly
D) formed suddenly

32

A) NO CHANGE
B) surprised
C) surprisingly alarmed
D) cautioning

33

Suppose the writer's primary purpose has been to write an essay summarizing the road trip safety education in winter. Would this essay accomplish that purpose?

A) Yes, because it discusses the complete road trip safety measures in winter driving
B) Yes, because it demonstrates the National Transportation Safety Board's effort to educate the dangers of Black Ice.
C) No, because it focusses instead on what the Black Ice is, and how it forms.
D) No, because it focuses instead on describing the method of distinguishing Black Ice from White Ice.

CONTINUE

2   2

Questions 34-44 are based on the following passage.

9 TO 5 GROUP

In 2005 Brad Neuberg used "coworking" to describe a physical space which he originally called a "9 to 5 group". Neuberg organized a co-working [34] <u>site called the "Hat Factory"</u> in San Francisco, a live-work loft that was home to three technology workers, and open to others during the day. Brad was also one of the founders of Citizen Space, the first "Work Only" co-working space. Now, co-working places exist worldwide, with over 700 locations in the United States alone. Since 2006 a few studies have shown the number of co-working spaces and available seats have roughly doubled each year, [35] <u>incrementing nearly as much as two times within twelve-month cycle</u>. San Francisco continues to have a large presence in the co-working community [36] <u>and being home to</u> a growing number of co-working places including RocketSpace, Sandbox Suites, and Citizen Space.

34

A) NO CHANGE
B) site called, the "Hat Factory",
C) site called, the "Hat Factory"
D) site called the "Hat Factory",

35

A) NO CHANGE
B) almost reaching 200 percent increase.
C) impressively expanding its numbers every twelve-month.
D) delete the underlined portion.

36

A) NO CHANGE
B) homing to
C) and has home to
D) and is home to

CONTINUE

2

2

The New York co-working community has also been evolving rapidly in places like Regus and Rockefeller Group Business Center. [37] The demand for co-working in Brooklyn neighborhoods is almost never ending. [38] Despite of the rise in the Millennials workforce, nearly one in 10 workers in the Gowanus area work from home that adds the reason for high demand. The industrial area of Gowanus, Brooklyn is seeing a surge in new startups like Co-workers, which are redesigning old buildings into new co-working spaces.

Some co-working places were developed by nomadic Internet entrepreneurs [39] lured by an enormous financial interest.

A 2007 survey showed that many employees worry about feeling isolated and losing human interaction if they were to telecommute. Roughly a third of both private and public-sector workers also reported that they didn't want to stay at home during work.

37

The writer is considering adding the following sentence:
> Several new startups like WeWork have been expanding all over the city.

Should the writer make this addition here?

A) Yes, because it connects the paragraph's point about the rapid expansion of co-working community in the certain region.

B) Yes, because it explains the significant number of startup business in New York

C) No, because it should focus and address only one startup company and shouldn't include information about other startups.

D) No, because it deviates from the paragraph's focus on major building like Rockefeller Group Business Center

---

38

A) NO CHANGE
B) Due to
C) For example,
D) In addition to

39

Which choice maintains the essay's positive tone and most strongly supports the main theme of the essay?

A) NO CHANGE
B) seeking an alternative to working in coffee shops and cafes, or to isolation in index pendent or home offices.
C) wanting to find a place both to live and work
D) who were often dripped away from the mainstream of the industry.

CONTINUE

2

2

As of 2012, the U.K. is among the most responsive European country to the idea of collaborative working, with a special focus on London. The city leads the co-working market not only for the large number of co-working places it offers but also for the [40] variety of places that exist to fit the differing needs among start-ups, entrepreneurs and freelancers, who avoid the existing office structure. Camden Collective is a regeneration project in London [41] that re-purposes previously vacant and underused properties, and opened its first 'wire-less wall-less' co-working space in 2009. In March 2012 Google along with several local partners opened a co-working place in the heart of East London. Campus London is located in Tech City and helps multiple start-ups to grow under the same roof, by mentoring them and giving them the chance to learn more through the events that run everyday, [42] through which Campus London assists many startups. In June 2013, the U.K. Government announced it would be applying co-working principles to a new pilot scheme for its 'One Public Sector Estate' strategy covering 12 local authorities in England which will encourage councils to work with central government departments and other bodies so that staff share buildings.

40

Which of the following alternatives to the underlined portion would NOT be acceptable?
A) mobile
B) unique
C) conventional
D) non-traditional

41

If the writer were to delete the underlined portion of the sentence, the essay would primarily lose details that:
A) illustrate some of the Camden collective Project's features that transformed old buildings
B) hint Google's considerable contribution
C) support the essay's claim that London has become the hub of the co-working community in the world
D) clarify an unfamiliar term "Camden collective Projects"

42

A) NO CHANGE
B) whereby startups receive valuable mentoring
C) through which Campus London provides daily events
D) Delete the underlined portion

CONTINUE

2   2

Co-working is also becoming more common in continental Europe, with the startup metropolis Berlin being a major booster for this development. [43] This kind of working environment is not exclusive to big cities. Also smaller urban areas with many young and creative people and especially university cities may offer coworking places, with *Cowork Greifswald* in Germany being one example. Cooperations between co-working spaces and academic environments are focused.

43

A) NO CHANGE
B) For example, this kind
C) Generally speaking, this kind
D) Commonly, this kind

44

Suppose the writer's primary purpose has been to explain how co-working environment has become new trends throughout North America and Europe. Would this essay accomplish that purpose?

A) Yes, because it describes the architectural design of New York co-working places.
B) Yes, because it enumerates a number of events that successfully transformed old buildings and incubate startup entrepreneurs
C) No, because it focuses more specifically on the major startup supporters like Google or Rockefeller Group Business Center.
D) No, because it focuses on positive prospects only, while there exist plausible negatives.

TEST 12

WRITING ABSOLUTE PATTERNS

Test 12 Writing & Language Section Patterns

Q1. Absolute Pattern 21: Subject-Verb, Pronoun, Noun Agreement

The United Kingdom European Union membership referendum, ***also known as the EU referendum and the Brexit [1] referendum,*** *which* is a referendum that took place on Thursday 23 June 2016 in the United Kingdom to gauge support for the country's continued membership in the European Union.

	A) NO CHANGE	'which' should be removed. "is" should be "was"
	B) referendum, <u>are</u> a referendum	Two errors: using the plural verb and the present tense.
	C) referendum, <u>as</u> a referendum	Verb is missing.
√	**D) referendum, was** a referendum	Uses the singular, past tense verb

1> The subject is singular "the United Kingdom European Union membership **referendum,**"

2> The non-restrictive modifier (quick interjection) "also known as….the Brexit referendum," is offset by a pair of commas because it is inessential information.

3> The above subject <1> must have the main verb right after the second comma.

4> "that took place on Thursday 23 June 2016" indicates the main verb requires the past tense.

Q2. Absolute Pattern 10: Logical Expression

Passage: ... took place on Thursday 23 June 2016 in the United Kingdom to [2]<u>gauge</u> support for the country's continued membership in the European Union.	
Question: Which of the following <u>alternatives would NOT</u> be appropriate?	
A) check B) measure C) see are all synonyms to gauge.	
√ **D) alter**	"alter" means 'to change.'

Q3. Absolute Pattern 15: Prepositional Idiom

Question: The result was split [3] <u>with</u> the constituent countries of the United Kingdom, with a majority in England and Wales ***voting to leave***, **and** a majority in Scotland and Northern Ireland, ***voting to remain***.

	A) NO CHANGE	"Between ~and" is idiomatic phrase
	B) into	Ex) **between** apple **and** tomato.
√	**C) between**	1> Generally, the prepositional idiom pattern—finding a pair of words—is easy.
	D) in	2> <u>However, when the former part of the idiom is capped in, while the latter one is disclosed</u>, the question becomes harder. 3> When multiple choices offer only clueless prepositions, you should <u>find if there's any structural similarity in the sentence.</u> 4> In this question, the parallel structure <u>*'voting to remain.' and 'voting to leave'*</u> can be a clue. 5> You can always ignore pronouns like person's or country names.

Q4. Absolute Pattern 12: Modifier Placement Error

Passage: To start the process to leave the [4] <u>EU</u>*, **which is expected** to take several years,* the British **government will have to** invoke Article 50 of the Treaty on European Union.

√	**A) NO CHANGE**	1> The non-restrictive modifier (inessential information) **"which is...years"** is offset by a pair of commas. 2> It modifies "leaving EU."
	B) EU expects	It sounds as if "EU expects..."
	C) EU, expecting	It should be passive "expected", not active "expecting." Otherwise, "EU" will be the subject.
	D) EU and to expect	It changes the original meaning.

Q5. Absolute Pattern 1: Adding, Revising, Deleting, Retaining Information

Passage: The UK government has announced formal process of leaving the EU [6] although revoking the vote might be possible.

Question: Which choice provides a supporting example that emphasizes the main point of the sentence?

	A) NO CHANGE	Opposite and contradicts to each other
√	**B) ,confirming the due date by March 2019.**	emphasized by exact dates
	C) ,confirming Brexit was driven by the official process	Redundant error
	D) ,using the term "hard Brexit" rather than "soft Brexit".	unrelated example

B) The exact date of leaving emphasizes the previous portion of the sentence.

A), 'although' cancels out the previous portion of the sentence, rather than emphasizes it.

C) repeats the main clause.

Q6. Absolute Pattern 1: Adding, Revising, Deleting, Retaining Information

Passage: Membership of the EU had **long been a topic of debate** in the United Kingdom. [6] The country joined the European Economic Community (EEC, or "Common Market") in **1973**.

Question: If the writer were to delete the underlined portion (adjusting the capitalization as needed), the sentence would primarily lose:

	A) the meaning of EEC	Minor issue
	B) the formal step to leave E.U. after the referendum.	Unrelated word usage
√	**C) the description of historical overview**	**had long been, 1973**
	D) the importance of EEC to the United Kingdom.	Opposite perception

A) "EEC" is mentioned first time in this sentence; therefore, there's nothing to lose.

C) The information adds more historical credibility to support the previous sentence.

D) The BREXIT is the voting process to leave the E.U because UK believes E.U. and EEC is not important.

Q7. Absolute Pattern 1: Adding, Revising, Deleting, Retaining Information

Passage: Britain Stronger in Europe **was the official group campaigning for the UK to remain in the EU and was led by** the Prime Minister David Cameron and Chancellor George Osborne. [7]

Question: At this point, the author wishes to <u>add the following information.</u>
Vote Leave was the official group campaigning for the UK to leave the EU and was fronted by the Conservative MPs Boris Johnson and Michael Gove.
Should the author make this addition here?

	A) Yes, because it provides added information about the <u>history of conflicts.</u>	Unrelated issue
√	**B) Yes, because it connects with the previous sentence.**	
	C) No, because it is <u>mentioned in the following sentences.</u>	Not mentioned
	D) No, because it is <u>not persuasive enough.</u>	Opposite

The previous sentence discusses the group backing the UK to remain in the EU.

The following sentence, representing the opposite group, is an ideal addition.

A) repeats the previous sentence, therefore, is not related with this question.

D) It's persuasive.

Q8. Absolute Pattern 21: Subject-Verb, Pronoun, Noun Agreement

Passage: Financial markets [8] <u>were reacted</u> negatively in the immediate aftermath of the result.
Using a passive voice is illogical in this sentence.

	A) NO CHANGE	D) Active and concise.
	B) were in great reaction	A), B), C) 1> If the sentence intends to use the passive voice, it should have a clear agent for the passive verb.
	C) reacted by	For instance, "The operation was conducted <u>by the chief surgeon</u>." (the chief surgeon is the agent that must have the passive voice).
√	**D) reacted**	2> Without having an agent, it has no point to change the active voice to passive voice.
		A) is passive B) is wordy C) 'reacted by" is used as an adjective phrase, not a verb. They all contain passive tone.

Q9. Absolute Pattern 10: Logical Expression

Passage: Financial markets reacted negatively in the immediate aftermath of the result. Investors in worldwide stock markets lost more than the [9] equivalent of 2 trillion United States dollars on 24 June 2016

Question: Which of the following alternatives would NOT be appropriate?

√	A) equivocal to	equivocal means unclear
	B) equal to	equivalent means the same.
	C) tantamount to	tantamount means equal
	D) nearly	nearly means equivalent

Q10. Absolute Pattern 24: Verb Tense / Voice Error

Passage: [10] **Immediately after the result,** the Prime Minister David Cameron **had announced** he would resign, having campaigned unsuccessfully for a "remain" vote on behalf of Britain Stronger in Europe and HM Government.

	A) NO CHANGE	'had announced' is past perfect. The tense is reversed.
	B) David Cameron followed the result, Cameron announced he would resign, after he campaigned	
√	C) David Cameron **announced he would resign, having campaigned**	
	D) David Cameron, by announcing that he would resign, having campaigned	

C) **"Immediately after the result," (or immediately after the result was given)** points out that both 'the result' and 'the announcement' occurred at the same time.

A) "had announced" is the past perfect, illustrating that the announcement occurred before the result was given, which is opposite and almost impossible situation.

B) Comma splice error + a redundant error ("Cameron" is written two times in one sentence although he is the only person in the sentence.)

D) No verb.

Q11. Absolute Pattern 9: Informational Graphs

Question: In **reference to the passage**, which choice offers an accurate interpretation of the table on the left ?

√	**A)** The **table results** reflect **the cause** of the former Prime Minister David Cameron's **leaving the office**.
	B) The referendum result was <u>legally binding</u>.
	C) As the referendum confirmed, United Kingdom will start the formal process of <u>leaving the EU immediately.</u>
	D) As the referendum confirmed, the Leave group will leave the EU, <u>and the Remain group will remain in EU.</u>

B) The first paragraph indicates it is not legally binding.

C) The second paragraph indicates that leaving the EU will take several years.

D) Remain group cannot remain in EU.

Q12. Absolute Pattern 24: Verb Tense / Voice Error

Passage: Many scientists believe we are not alone in the universe. It's probable, they say, that life **could have** [12] <u>rise</u> on at least some of the billions of planets thought to exist in our galaxy alone -- just as it did here on planet Earth.

	A) NO CHANGE	Rise means emerge. Rise is base verb.
	B) raise	Raise means to move upward
√	**C) arisen**	"could have" requires the past participle. "arisen" (rise=> rose => arisen)
	D) arouse	Arouse means evoke feeling

Q13. Absolute Pattern 17: Pronoun Error

Passage: **Experts** from NASA and its partner institutions addressed this question on July 14, at a public talk held at NASA Headquarters in Washington. [13]They outlined NASA's roadmap to the search for life in the [14]universe.

√	**A) NO CHANGE**	**"Experts" is the subject, which is plural.**
	B) He	The subject 'Experts" is plural. 'He' is singular
	C) It	'It' is singular. NASA itself can't outline NASA's roadmap.
	D) Those	"Those" is used as either the possessive pronoun like 'those cars' or an indicative object like ' I like those too,' none of which works in this sentence.

Q14. Absolute Pattern 16: Precision, Concision, Style

Passage: They outlined NASA's roadmap to the search for life in the [14]universe, it was an ongoing journey that involves a number of current and future telescopes.

	A) NO CHANGE	<u>As a rule of thumb, the shortest option has a higher probability</u>
	B) and an ongoing journey	When all four options carry the exactly same wordings, among which some use a conjunction connecting with a following clause, while others have no conjunction because the wordings are made of a phrase, not a clause, the one without conjunction is almost always the answer because the question is seeking the precise and concise style. That's why the answer is (D)
	C) because it was an ongoing journey	(A) comma splice
√	**D) universe, an ongoing journey**	(B) 'an ongoing journey' is not a clause. Therefore, "and" is unnecessary.
		(C) 'because' is used to a cause-effect relation.

Q15. Absolute Pattern 1: Adding, Revising, Deleting, Retaining Information

Question: Which choice emphasizes the <u>anticipation of some scientists believing the existence of planet like Earth.</u> .**(The question is positive; therefore, it is seeking a positive answer)**

	A) However, the impression of how common planets are in the Milky way <u>adversely creates backlash</u> among scientists.	All the other options are negative
√	**B) There are just too many planets out there in our Milky Way galaxy**	
	C) Astronomers have currently discovered the evidential proof that <u>there is no chance</u> for Venus to sustain life.	
	D) Astronomers acknowledge that under the current technology there <u>are many obstacles</u> to materialize our space safari project.	

Q16. Absolute Pattern 23: Transition Words for Supporting Detail, Contrast, and Consequence

Today's telescopes can look at many stars and tell if they have one or more orbiting planets. [16] <u>However,</u> **they can determine** if the planets are the right distance away from the star to have liquid water, the key ingredient to life as we know [17]it.

	A) NO CHANGE	C) 1> The adverb 'even more' amplifies the preceding sentence.
	B) You bet!	2> The original sentence is positively paralleling with the following sentence, requiring "Even more."
√	**C) Even more,**	A) Conjunctive adverb "however" cancels out the previous sentence.
	D) Therefore,	B) "You bet!" is informal colloquial language that should be avoided.
		D) 'Therefore' is used for consequence.

Q17. Absolute Pattern 16: Precision, Concision, Style

Passage: Even more, **they can determine** if the planets are the right distance away from the star to have liquid water, the key ingredient to life as we know [17]<u>it.</u>

√	**A) NO CHANGE**	The pronoun "it" is correctly used to summarize the information.
	B) <u>liquid water is essential to sustain life</u>	(B), (C), (D) All three options are redundant as they repeat the previous sentence without adding any new information.
	C) <u>water can be used to form life.</u>	
	D) that the planets' <u>distance is a way to understand whether liquid water exists or not.</u>	

Q18. Absolute Pattern 24: Verb Tense / Voice Error

Passage: These **upcoming** telescopes [18]<u>**would** find</u> and characterize [19] a host of new exoplanets—those planets that orbit other stars —expanding our knowledge of their atmospheres and diversity.

	A) NO CHANGE	The word 'upcoming' signals the future tense. 'would' is past tense
√	**B) will find**	"These upcoming" hints that the future tense is required.
	C) have to find	Change of meaning. "have to" is an interrogative that forces someone to do.
	D) that find	No verb.

Q19. Absolute Pattern 10: Logical Expression

Passage: These upcoming telescopes will find and characterize [19] a host of new exoplanets -- those planets that orbit other stars -- expanding our knowledge of their atmospheres and diversity.

Question: Which choice most dramatically emphasizes the **massive scale** of upcoming discovery using the telescope observation projects?

√	**A) NO CHANGE**	Quantity vs. Quality
	B) more <u>reliable</u> data of	A) 1> "host" means a lot or massive. 2> The keyword in the question is "the massive scale," which quantifies the size of the future discovery project.
	C) <u>groundbreaking</u> discovery of	
	D) the <u>actual photographs</u> of	B) and C) are quality value that cannot be quantified. D) is not related issue to the question.

Q20. Absolute Pattern 23: Transition Words for Supporting Detail, Contrast, and Consequence

Passage: [20] <u>After</u> its launch in 2009, Kepler **has dramatically changed** what we know about exoplanets, finding most of the more than 5,000 potential exoplanets, of which more than 1700 have been confirmed.

	A) NO CHANGE	'after' cannot replace 'since.'
	B) Having followed	'Having followed' means "After it (had) followed"
	C) With	change of original meaning.
√	**D) Since**	The present perfect tense (have/has + p.p) requires "since."

Q21. Absolute Pattern 1: Adding, Revising, Deleting, Retaining Information

Suppose the writer's primary purpose has been to describe the possibility of searching for life. Would this essay accomplish that purpose?

	A) Yes, because it tells about a <u>variety of challenges</u> the scientists face along with their searching for life in exoplanets.	A) and D) are negative, while the passage maintains the positive tone.
√	B) Yes, because it focuses primarily on scientists' **application of new types of telescopes and other methods**	A) also forgot to mention about the telescopes, the main apparatus appears in this passage.
	C) <u>No,</u> because it focuses mainly on the projects to be <u>undertaken in the future</u>.	C) The passage introduces both the present and the future project.
	D) <u>No,</u> because it focuses on the <u>limited applications</u> within the scope of modern technology in finding life in the universe	

Q22. Absolute Pattern 1: Adding, Revising, Deleting, Retaining Information

Question: The writer <u>wants to add</u> the following sentence to the essay: What are the next steps to finding life elsewhere? The sentence would most logically be placed at Point:

√	**A) A in Paragraph 1**	<u>**This basic question about**</u> our place in the Universe is one that may be answered by scientific investigations. (A)
	B) B in Paragraph 2	However, the impression of how common planets are in the Milky way adversely creates backlash among scientists. (B)
	C) C in Paragraph 3	Today's telescopes can look at many stars and tell if they have one or more orbiting planets.(C)
	D) D in Paragraph 4	The Webb telescope and WFIRST-AFTA will lay the groundwork, and future missions will extend the search for the nearby planets that are similar to Earth in size and mass, a key step in the search for life. (D)

A) The following sentence starts with "This basic question." implying the response to the question. Therefore, the previous sentence should very likely to be asking this question.

Q23. Absolute Pattern 18: Punctuation Error

Black [23]<u>ice, *sometimes called clear ice,* refs</u> to a thin coating of glaze ice on a surface, especially on roads.

Question: Which of the following alternatives to the underlined portion would **NOT** be acceptable?

	A) ice<u>,</u> sometimes called clear ice<u>,</u> refers	C) 1> "sometimes called clear ice" is a quick-interjection that modifies the subject, 'Black ice.'
	B) ice—sometimes called clear ice—refers	2> This modifier is inessential information.
√	**C) ice, sometimes called clear ice refers**	3> Therefore, it should be offset by a pair of commas on both sides to indicate that it's not a part of the main sentence but describes further the subject "Black ice"
	D) ice <u>(sometimes called clear ice)</u> refers	4> it misses one comma after "ice".

C) 1> "sometimes called clear ice" is a quick-interjection that modifies the subject, 'Black ice.'
2> This modifier is inessential information.
3> Therefore, it should be offset by a pair of commas on both sides to indicate that it's not a part of the main sentence but describes further the subject "Black ice"
4> it misses one comma after "ice".

B) and D) function as the same way as a pair of comma.

Q24. Absolute Pattern 1: Adding, Revising, Deleting, Retaining Information

The ice itself is not black, but visually transparent, [24] allowing the often black road below to be seen through it.

Question: If the writer were to delete the underlined portion of the sentence, it would primarily lose:

√	**A) an idea that emphasizes the reason for an optical illusion**
	B) a statement that introduces main focus of the following paragraph.
	C) an unnecessary detail that contradicts in formation presented earlier in the paragraph.
	D) a clear image that conveys what most observers want to find out behind the black ice.

A) 1> The preceding portion of the sentence is the **cause**, which "allows (allowing)" black road to be seen through it" (**the effect**)   C) It is a necessary detail.

Q25. Absolute Pattern 21: Subject-Verb, Pronoun, Noun Agreement

The typically low **level** of noticeable ice pellets, snow, and sleet [25] surrounds black ice means that areas of the ice are often practically invisible to drivers or people stepping on it.

	A) NO CHANGE	A) uses both "surrounds" and "means" as the verbs.
	B) surrounding black ice meaning	B) has no verb by using both "surrounding" and "meaning" as the adjective phrase.
√	**C) surrounding black ice means**	C) properly use the verb "means" to describe the subject "level" and by using "surrounding" as an adjective phrase.
	D) surrounding black ice mean	D) The subject is "level"; therefore, the verb has to be "means"

Q26. Absolute Pattern 21: Subject-Verb, Pronoun, Noun Agreement

[26] Their is, thus, **a risk of skidding and subsequent accidents** due to the unexpected loss of traction

	A) NO CHANGE	D) Plural subjects "a risk of skidding" and "subsequent accidents" require plural verb "are."
	B) Their have been	A), B) "Their" is possessive pronoun. (e.g., Their house is smaller than his.)
	C) There is	C) "is" should be "are"
√	**D) There are**	

Key point: Some students may think that the subject is "a risk', a singular noun that comprises "**a risk of** (skidding and subsequent accidents). That concept is incorrect because "a" (article) is used only for a singular noun. "accidents" is plural and can't stand together with "a" that proves "a risk of skidding" and "subsequent accidents" are different incidents. Hence, the plural subject.

Q27. Absolute Pattern 23: Transition Words for Supporting Detail, Contrast, and Consequence

Because it represents only a thin accumulation, black ice is highly transparent and thus difficult to see as compared with snow, frozen slush, or thicker ice layers. [27] <u>In addition,</u> it often is interleaved with wet pavement, which is nearly identical in [28] appearance, this makes driving, cycling or walking on affected surfaces extremely dangerous.

√	**A) NO CHANGE**	A) 1> 'In addition' is used to support the previous subordinating clause "Because."
	B) On the contrary,	2> The following sentence adds information by further elaborating its appearance.
	C) Consequently,	B), D) drive the explanation to the opposite direction.
	D) In spite of such a thin accumulation,	C) The consequence has already been mentioned using the 'because clause. ("black ice is highly transparent…")

Q28. Absolute Pattern 12: Modifier Placement Error

In addition, it often is interleaved with wet pavement, which is nearly identical in [28] <u>appearance, this makes driving,</u> cycling or walking on affected surfaces extremely dangerous.

Question: Which of the following alternatives to the underlined portion would **NOT** be acceptable?

	A) appearance, which makes	D) is a comma splice error.
	B) appearance, making	A) "which makes" or B) ",making" efficiently describe the effect of the appearance.
	C) appearance. This makes	
√	**D) appearance, this makes**	C) starting with a new sentence is an alternative

Q29. Absolute Pattern 14: Possessive Determiners and Possessive Noun Error

Passage: [29] <u>With salt's</u> ineffectiveness at melting ice at these temperatures compounds the problem.

	A) NO CHANGE	"With" is a preposition, carrying a prepositional phrase, not a subject
√	**B) Salt's**	It properly links to the subject "ineffectiveness"
	C) Salt	C) and D) both have to be a possessive form to link the following noun 'ineffectiveness.'
	D) Sodium Chloride	

Q30. Absolute Pattern 1: Adding, Revising, Deleting, Retaining Information

[30] if the air warms suddenly after a prolonged cold spell that has left the surface of the roadway well below the freezing point temperature.

Question: In the preceding sentence, the clause " if the air warms... freezing point temperature." primarily serves to indicate:

	A) that black ice phenomenon could occur in many southern states with the mild temperature.
	B) the strikingly complex characteristics of black ice
	C) that technique to prevent black ice has yet to be developed at present
√	**D) the atmospheric conditions that lead to Black Ice formation under the certain temperature.**

1>The relations between the previous and the following clauses are a cause-and-effect.

2> The main clause states that even in the ambient weather, Black Ice forms.

3> The reasons for the phenomenon are then described: "the surface of the roadway keeps below the freezing point temperature for awhile."

B) The statement is true, but the question is not seeking the characteristics. It wants the cause-effect relations.

A) and C): 1> The passage does not mention about southern states or technique.

2> Adding new information is incorrect.

Q31. Absolute Pattern 24: Verb Tense / Voice Error

Passage: The ice [31]had formed suddenly on a long downward slope, [32] surprising drivers coming over the crest of a hill, who could not see crashed vehicles ahead until it was too late to stop on the slick pavement.

	A) NO CHANGE	D) 1> The key point in this question is "suddenly."
	B) formed suddenly in a matter of seconds	2> The word "suddenly" indicates the immediate occurrence; therefore, we should use the simple past tense as used in the surrounding sentences.
	C) has formed suddenly	
√	**D) formed suddenly**	A) The past perfect is incorrect tense. B) Redundant error C) The present perfect is incorrect.

Q32. Absolute Pattern 10: Logical Expression

The ice formed **suddenly** on a long downward slope, [32] **_surprising drivers_** coming over the crest of a hill, who could not see crashed vehicles ahead until it was too late to stop on the slick pavement.

√	**A) NO CHANGE**	"The ice formed suddenly" indicates the situation with a brief moment in time that the drivers' reaction has to be shown instantaneous as well using the "ing" form.
	B) surprised	"surprised" is verb and can't be used as a verb because "crashed" is the main verb.
	C) surprisingly alarmed	'surprising' and 'alarmed' are synonyms, redundant error
	D) cautioning	changes the original meaning. "surprise" and "caution" are antonym

Q33. Absolute Pattern 1: Adding, Revising, Deleting, Retaining Information

Question: Suppose the writer's primary purpose has been to write an essay summarizing the road trip safety education in winter. Would this essay accomplish that purpose?

	A) Yes, because it discusses the complete road trip safety measures in winter driving
	B) Yes, because it demonstrates the National Transportation Safety Board's effort to educate the dangers of black ice.
√	**C) No, because it focusses instead on what the Black Ice is, and how it forms.**
	D) No, because it focuses instead on describing the method of distinguishing Black Ice from White Ice.

The passage isn't related with the road trip safety education at all.

D) White ice is scarcely mentioned.

Q34. Absolute Pattern 20: Restrictive Modifier (Essential Information)

Neuberg organized a co-working [34] site called the "Hat Factory" in San Francisco, a live-work loft that was home to three technology workers, and open to others during the day.

√	A) NO CHANGE	"Hat Factory" should not be offset by a pair of commas.
	B) site called, the "Hat Factory,"	No pair of comma is necessary for essential information.
	C) site called, the "Hat Factory"	A comma in the front of "the"
	D) site called the "Hat Factory,"	A comma after "Factory"

The sentence is restrictive. That is, "Hat Factory" is essential information, and offsetting a pair of comma around "the Hat Factory" can leave the entire sentence incomplete.

Q35. Absolute Pattern 19: Redundant Error

Since 2006 a few studies have shown the number of co-working spaces and available seats have roughly **doubled each year**, [35] incrementing nearly as much **as two times** within **twelve-month** cycle.

	A) NO CHANGE	redundant error (doubled each year)
	B) almost reaching 200 percent.	redundant error (doubled)
	C) impressively expanding its numbers every twelve-month	redundant error (each year)
√	D) delete the underlined portion	

Q36. Absolute Pattern 21: Subject-Verb, Pronoun, Noun Agreement

San Francisco continues to have a large presence in the co-working community, [36] and being home to a growing number of co-working places including RocketSpace, Sandbox Suites, and Citizen Space.

	A) NO CHANGE	It changes to passive voice. *please do not choose 'being.'
	B) homing to	Colloquialism error. It sounds unidiomatic and non-standard.
	C) and has home to	"has home to" should be "is home to"
√	D) and is home to	"and (San Francisco) is home to …." is the correct parallel structure.

Q37. Absolute Pattern 1: Adding, Revising, Deleting, Retaining Information

The New York co-working community has also been evolving rapidly in places like Regus and Rockefeller Group Business Center. [37]

Question: The writer is considering adding the following sentence: Several new startups like WeWork have been expanding all over the city. Should the writer make this addition here?

√	A) Yes, because it connects the paragraph's point about the rapid expansion of co-working community in the certain region.	B) The main theme is not startup companies, but the proliferation of co-working facilities.
	B) Yes, because it explains the significant number of startup business in New York	C) is only one of the startups mentioned in the first paragraph.
	C) No, because it should focus on one main coworking company "the Hat Factory"	D) is not stated in the passage.
	D) No, because it deviates from the paragraph's focus on major building like Rockefeller Group Business Center	

Q38. Absolute Pattern 23: Transition Words for Supporting Detail, Contrast, and Consequence

Cause   Effect

[38] Despite of the rise in the Millennials workforce, nearly one in 10 workers in the Gowanus area work from home that adds the reason for high demand.

	A) NO CHANGE	despite of = not affected by
√	B) Due to	due to = because of
	C) For example,	'for example' and 'in addition to' are used to add up information to the previous sentence.
	D) In addition to	

The sentence is the cause-effect structure. Therefore, it needs 'due to.'

Q39. Absolute Pattern 1: Adding, Revising, Deleting, Retaining Information

Some co-working places were developed by **nomadic** Internet entrepreneurs [39] lured by an enormous financial interest.

Question: Which choice maintains the essay's positive tone and most strongly support the main theme of the essay?

	A) NO CHANGE	B) 1> 'nomadic' means wondering from place to place. 2> The modifier supports the needs of nomadic internet entrepreneurs.
√	**B) seeking an alternative to working in coffee shops and cafes, or to isolation in independent or home offices.**	
	C) wanting to find a place to both live and work	A) ":lured by" is negative word, not positive.
	D) who were often dripped away from the main stream of the industry.	C) Co-working place is not a residence D) is negative term

Q40. Absolute Pattern 10: Logical Expression

The city leads the co-working market not only for the large number of co-working places it offers but also for the [40] variety of places that exist **to fit the differing needs among start-ups, entrepreneurs and freelancers, who avoid the existing office structure.**

Question: Which of the following alternatives to the underlined portion would NOT be acceptable?

	A) mobile	A), B), D) 1> All fit into the requirements for the co-working space described in the passage.
	B) unique	2> The main theme of the co-working facilities excludes conventional place.
√	**C) conventional**	3> (C) is antonym to the Bold faced fonts of the sentence as well as "non-traditional" as in (D).
	D) non-traditional	

Q41. Absolute Pattern 1: Adding, Revising, Deleting, Retaining Information

Camden Collective is a regeneration project in London [41] that re-purposes previously vacant and underused properties, and opened its first 'wire-less wall-less' co-working space in 2009.

Question: If the writer were to delete the underlined portion of the sentence, the essay would primarily lose details that:

√	A) illustrate some of the Camden collective Project's features that transformed old buildings
	B) hint Google's considerable contribution
	C) support the essay's claim that London has become the hub of the co-working community in the world
	D) clarify the unfamiliar term "Camden collective Projects"

A) "re-purpose" = transformed; "previously vacant" = old, features, buildings
The underlined portion shows how the project transformed the old building into the co-working facilities.

B) This passage is hardly related with Google.

C) Co-working community in the world is not discussed.

D) Understanding the term 'Camden Collective Projects' does not provide any significance.

Q42. Absolute Pattern 19: Redundant Error

Passage: **Campus London** is located in Tech City and **helps multiple start-ups** to grow under the same roof, by **mentoring them and giving them the chance to learn more through the events that run everyday**, [42] through which **Campus London assists many startups**

	A) NO CHANGE	The underlined portion is redundant	A), B), C) contain very similar information to
	B) whereby startups receive valuable mentoring		the previous portion of the sentence without
	C) through which Campus London provides daily events		adding extra information.
√	D) Delete the underlined portion		

Q43. Absolute Pattern 23: Transition Words for Supporting Detail, Contrast, and Consequence

Co-working is also becoming more common in continental Europe, with the startup metropolis Berlin being a major booster for this development. [43] This kind of working environment is not exclusive to big cities.

√	A) NO CHANGE	A) The sentence develops its issue by itself, and no additional transitional word is needed.
	B) For example, this kind	
	C) Generally speaking, this kind	
	D) Commonly, this kind	

Q44. Absolute Pattern 1: Adding, Revising, Deleting, Retaining Information

Suppose the writer's primary purpose has been to explain how co-working environment has become new trends throughout North America and Europe. Would this essay accomplish that purpose?

	A) Yes, because it describes the architectural design of New York co-working places.
√	**B) Yes, because it enumerates a number of events that successfully transformed old buildings and incubate startup entrepreneurs**
	C) No, because it focuses more on the major startup supporters like Google or Rockefeller Group Business Center.
	D) No, because it focuses on positive prospects only, while there are plausible negatives.

Key point: The main theme of the essay is the proliferation of co-working environment and facilities that help incubate startups. In that sense, it fulfills its purpose.

A) The Architectural design of New York is not mentioned.

C) The startup supporters like Google was only remotely mentioned.

D) Negative points are not mentioned.

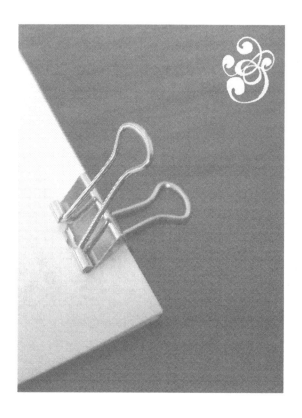

Chapter 3

A. COLLEGE BOARD PSAT WRITING PATTERN ANALYSIS

B. COLLEGE BOARD SAT WRITING PATTERN ANALYSIS

C. 70 SAT HACKERS ABSOLUTE PATTERNS FOR THE SENTENCE ERROR QUESTIONS

PSAT COLLEGE BOARD OFFICIAL TEST
PATTERN ANALYSIS

To download the test, please visit:
https://collegereadiness.collegeboard.org/pdf/psat-nmsqt-practice-test-1.pdf

The PSAT Official Test is the property of the College Board.
Due to the copyright protection, the original text is extensively condensed.
To understand the full concept of this analysis, it is critical to study the previous chapters including the seven practice tests before you proceed.

PSAT COLLEGE BOARD OFFICIAL GUIDE
WRITING AND LANGUAGE SECTION PATTERS

Q1. Absolute Pattern 19: Redundant Error

Passage keywords: yearly, annually

	A) yearly, annually	Redundancy
	B) annually, each year	Redundancy
√	**C) annually**	
	D) yearly, annually	Redundancy

Q2. Absolute Pattern 4: Comparison

	A) big	(D) The meaning "primary" itself contains the superlative.
	B) things	1> The phrase 'one of the' suggests the superlative is coming. 2> Therefore, (A) 'big' is incorrect
	C) things	(B), (C) 'things' is colloquial (nonstandard language) and also ambiguous.
√	**D) primary**	

Q3. Absolute Pattern 21: Subject-Verb, Noun, Pronoun Agreement

Passage keywords: American (singular)

	A) spend	C) The singular verb in the adjective clause
	B) have spent	1> "the average American spend" modifies (or supports) the subject "The hours", serving as an adjective clause.
√	**C) spends**	2> Even though it is in the middle of the sentence working as an adjective for the main subject,
	D) are spent	3> it still needs to follow the subject-verb agreement. 4> "the average American" is singular (the singular subject in the adjective clause). 5> Therefore, the verb "spend" should be "spends." (the singular verb in the adjective clause) A) Plural B) The present perfect D) Passive

Q4. Absolute Pattern 7: Conjunction Error

Passage keywords: As long as, and

	A) As long as, and	D) **'as long as' is subordinating conjunction. (e.g., as long as you stay)**
	B) workers;	1> The sentence starts with "as long as"
		2> Because it is subordinating conjunction, it should carry a clause. "companies continue…".
	C) ,managers, should	3> After this subordinating clause, the main clause should be following, starting with the main subject and verb, <u>not another conjunction "and"</u>.
√	**D) workers,**	4> To sum up, the original sentence has two conjunctions, instead of one.
		*As introduced in Chapter 2, finding an error that has no conjunction is easy, but an error having two conjunctions is paradoxically harder.
		(A) has two conjunctions: "as long as" and "and"
		(B) Semicolon functions as a conjunction, creating a double-conjunction error like (A)
		(C) 1> The subject "manager" is separated from the verb "should" by a comma. 2> The subject and the verb can't be separated by a comma.

Q5. Absolute Pattern 11: Logical Sequence

Passage keywords: [1] workers, lack of sleep [3] average American, 1970s [2] combat, problem [4] work efficiency

Sentence sequence: [1] Topic (Main concern) => [3] Supporting details (Historical overview & Data) => [2] Analysis => [4] Solution

	A) AS IT IS	[1] Topic (Main concern) => [2] Analysis => [3] Supporting details (Historical overview & Data)=> [4] Solution
	B) before 1	[3] Supporting details (Historical overview & Data) => [1] Topic (Main concern) => [2] Analysis => [4] Solution
√	**C) after 1**	As introduced in Ch.2, reviewing the sequence in backward is easier because identifying the conclusion is easier than identifying the introduction.
	D) after 4	[1] Topic (Main concern) => [2] Analysis => [4] Solution => [3] Supporting details (Historical overview & Data)

*So easier is finding the conclusion than finding the introduction that it is critical concept to read backward in order (e.g., 4>3>2>1)

Q6. Absolute Pattern 1: Adding, Revising, Deleting, Retaining Information

Passage keywords: adding (Positive)

√	A) benefit	Positive
	B) methodology	Not stated in the passage (New info.)
	C) No, not important	Negative
	D) contradicts	Negative

Q7. Absolute Pattern 1: Adding, Revising, Deleting, Retaining Information

Passage keywords: long-term health

	A) weekly attendance	Inconsistent with the question
√	B) lower risk, heart attack	Synonym or similar perception
	C) health, costs	Not stated in the passage (New info.)
	D) employees, efficient	Inconsistent with the question

Q8. Absolute Pattern 13: Parallel Structure

Passage keywords: block, play, waking

	A) waking	verb, verb, gerund
√	B) wake	verb, verb, verb
	C) to wake	verb, verb, to-infinitive
	D) waking of	verb, verb, preposition

Q9. Absolute Pattern 15: Prepositional Idiom

Passage keywords: "their workers" suggests more than three people

	A) throughout	Extreme word usage. 'throughout means in every single part or person
√	**B) among**	**For more than three people/objects**
	C) between	For only two people/objects
	D) into	Preposition for direction (moving into somewhere)

Q10. Absolute Pattern 15: Prepositional Idiom

Passage keywords: not only ~

	A) and again	**"not only ~ but also"** cannot be replaced by any other combinations.
	B) but it	* In more complex question, it changes or drops the preposition within the correlative conjunction.
	C) as also	For example,
√	**D) but also**	(A) "not only to...but also"
		(B) "not only to...but also in"
		(C) "not only...but also to"
		All of the above options are incorrect.

Q11. Absolute Pattern 1: Adding, Revising, Deleting, Retaining Information

Passage keywords: successful leaders (positive)

	A) AS IT IS	Not stated in the passage
	B) overworked	Inconsistent with the question
	C) employee schedules	Inconsistent with the question
√	**D) embrace napping**	Positive

Q12. Absolute Pattern 18: Punctuation Error

Passage keywords: depends on, pollination, to increase	
	A) pollination—
	B) pollination: this is
√	**C) pollination,**
	D) pollination;

(C) The nonrestrictive modifier 'including...pollination' is properly offset by a pair of commas.

",including honeybee pollination" starts with a comma.

1> It should start with a comma because the phrase is nonrestrictive modifier (inessential information) that separates itself from the main clause.

2> Because it starts with a comma, it should end with another comma.

(A) A comma and a dash combination is incorrect punctuation.

(B) A comma and a colon combination is incorrect punctuation.

(D) A comma and a semicolon combination is incorrect punctuation.

Q13. Absolute Pattern 21: Subject-Verb, Noun, Pronoun Agreement + 6: Confusing Words

Passage keywords: importance (subject, singular)	
	A) highlights, affects
√	**B) highlights, effects**
	C) highlight, effects
	D) highlight, affects

"The **importance** of bees" (the singular subject) + effect vs. affect

(B) 'effect' is normally used as a noun

1> The main subject is "importance" (singular), not "bees" (plural)

2> Therefore, options (C) and (D) are incorrect because "highlight" is plural verb.

(A) 'affect' is normally used as a verb, a double-verb error.

Q14. Absolute Pattern 17: Pronoun Error

Passage keywords: 'They'

	A) AS IT IS	**A pronoun cannot start with the first sentence in the new paragraph.**
√	**B) known as**	(B) Starting with the modifier "known as ~" introduces the main clause with the subject 'this phenomenon' in the ideal location.
	C) **It is** known	(A) 1> Pronoun error + comma splice error.
	D) Colony	2> "They" starts with the new sentences in the new paragraph without having a precedent.
		3> The subject has no conjunction, comma splice error.
		(C) Wordiness. "It is" is not necessary and ambiguous.
		(D) The noun "Colony" automatically becomes the subject of the main clause, a double-subject error.

Q15. Absolute Pattern 9: Informational Graphs

Passage keywords: exceeded 25% *This question does not need a reference from the reading passage.

	A) exceeded 25%	2011, Incorrect value (less than)
√	**B) above, acceptable**	
	C) not changed	Antonym or opposite perception
	D) increased every year	Incorrect value (fluctuated every year)

Q16. Absolute Pattern 9: Informational Graphs

Passage keywords: fell   *This question does not need a reference from the reading passage.

	A) fell	Antonym or opposite perception
	B) double	Incorrect value (less than double)
	C) acceptable	Incorrect value (more than acceptable)
√	**D) rose**	

Q17. Absolute Pattern 1: Adding, Revising, Deleting, Retaining Information

Passage keywords: reasons that

√	A) reasons that	(A) This sentence functions as a topic sentence in this paragraph
	B) and, there are	(B) changes the original meaning by separating the original sentence using a conjunction 'and'
	C) reasons, why	(C) 1> Redundant error. 'reason' and 'why' are synonyms. 2> As used in the original sentence, 'reason that' is the correct syntax.
	D) delete	(D) loses the topic sentence.

Q18. Absolute Pattern 1: Adding, Revising, Deleting, Retaining Information

Passage keywords: neonicotinoids

√	A) support, previous sentence	Synonym or similar perception
	B) new idea	Not stated in the passage (New info.)
.	C) place elsewhere	Antonym or opposite perception
	D) contradict	Antonym or opposite perception

Q19. Absolute Pattern 3: Colloquialism (Nonstandard Language)

Passage keywords: Given the role

	A) scoffed	(A), (B), (C) use colloquial (nonstandard or spoken) language
	B) big deal	
	C) back burner	
√	D) ignored	

Q20. Absolute Pattern 18: Punctuation Error + Pattern 16: Precision, Concision, Style

Passage keywords: farmers, resorted (A complete sentence)

	A) crops; when, being	(C) 1> Always choose the most concise sentence from the options.
	B) crops, this is	2> The most concise sentence means having no conjunction or dependent clause without losing the original meaning.
√	**C) crops, an expensive**	3> This is called simplification rule"
	D) crops; an expensive	4> The option that usually starts with "an" is the answer under the simplification pattern.

(A) has several errors:

1> a semicolon should carry a dependent clause, which is not applied to this sentence.

2> the subordinating conjunction 'when' cannot be used together with the semicolon.

   (one simple exception exists)

3> the usage of 'being' suddenly changes the active voice into the passive within one sentence. (avoid an option that includes "being")

(B) 1> Comma splice 2> "this is" is ambiguous.   (D) Semicolon error

Q21. Absolute Pattern 14: Possessive Determiners and Possessive Noun Error

Passage keywords: farmers (plural), dependence

	A) they're	'they're' is the contraction of 'they are'
	B) there	'there' is an indicative pronoun to refer to a place
√	**C) their**	'their' is a plural possessive pronoun. 'their' indicates "other farmers" in the passage.
	D) its	'its' is a singular possessive pronoun

Q22. Absolute Pattern 1: Adding, Revising, Deleting, Retaining Information

Passage keywords: CCD, decrease, pesticides.

√	A) CCD, decrease, pesticides	The original sentence corresponds to the question's keyword 'future effort' **positively.** (A) 1> Positive 2> The question is seeking a positive prospect
	B) devastating	
	C) other aspects	(B) Negative
	D) Genetic	(C), (D) Not stated in the passage (New information)

Q23. Absolute Pattern 18: Punctuation Error

Passage keywords: Ferrua stood

	A) stood,	"hillside" should not separate from the verb 'stood' by a comma , semicolon, or dash—making an incomplete sentence.
	B) stood;	
	C) stood—	
√	**D) stood**	**stood on the hillside**

Q24. Absolute Pattern 15: Prepositional Idiom

Passage keywords: dotted with

√	A) with	'dotted with' is the correct idiom
	B) inside C) for D) on	

Q25. Absolute Pattern 23: Transition Words for Supporting Detail, Contrast, and Consequence

Passage keywords: this type of farming, farmers

√	**A) for example**	'for example' supports the preceding main sentence
	B) however,	'however,' and 'by contrast' are used for contrasting phrase or clause.
	C) by contrast,	
	D) thereafter,	'thereafter' is used for time sequence, meaning 'after that time'

Q26. Absolute Pattern 23: Transition Words for Supporting Detail, Contrast, and Consequence

	A) Although	'although' carries a contrasting clause
√	**B) Given that**	'Given that' carries the supporting clause
	C) So	'So' carries a consequence clause
	D) delete	You should delete this option from your selection (e.g., over 70%).

Q27. Absolute Pattern 1: Adding, Revising, Deleting, Retaining Information

Passage keywords: First-century

	A) Nature	The historical facts is used as an example
	B) all over the world	(C) "Farming" and "Moon" correspond properly with the topic sentence that introduces the following historical facts
√	**C) Farming, Moon, not new.**	(A), (B), (D) are all unrelated words and issues
	D) Talk of the Moon	

Q28. Absolute Pattern 1: Adding, Revising, Deleting, Retaining Information

Question keywords: specific info. calendar

	A) farm chores	(A), (B), (C) are too broad (vague).
	B) actions, farming	
	C) certain tasks	
√	**D) plant, weed, harvest**	Specific information

Q29. Absolute Pattern 14: Possessive Determiners and Possessive Noun Error

	A) almanacs	
	B) almanacs's	
√	**C) alamanac's**	To show a possessive determiner, add an apostrophe and the letter '*s*'
	D) almanacs'	

Q30. Absolute Pattern 19: Redundant Error

	A) skeptics, not sure	Choices A, B, and C literally write the definition of skeptics, which is not necessary at all.
	B) skeptics, yet convinced	
	C) skeptics—doubt	
√	**D) skeptics.**	

Q31. Absolute Pattern 17: Pronoun Error

Passage keywords: agriculture (subject, singular noun)

	A) their	Plural possessive pronoun. The sentence has no precedent with a plural noun.
	B) those	Indicative pronoun. To use it, "those" should have been mentioned earlier.
	C) it's	Contraction for 'it is'
√	**D) its**	<u>Singular possessive pronoun</u> for agriculture

Q32. Absolute Pattern 1: Adding, Revising, Deleting, Retaining Information

Question keywords: reinforcing, also skepticism.

	A) supporters, wait verified	(D) Negative
	B) no sound, data	1> The question is seeking a negative answer
	C) continue, farming	2> The preceding and the following sentences are also negative.
√	**D) not fact**	3> Therefore, the options containing a positive tone, however related and tempting, should not be the answer.
		(A) Positive
		(B) Insufficient Information by not mentioning lunar farming
		(C) Positive

Q33. Absolute Pattern 1: Adding, Revising, Deleting, Retaining Information

Question keywords: importance, senses

√	**A) smell, fragrant**	Two keywords in (A) suggest the importance of senses
	B) photographs	B), C), D) are unrelated to the question 'supporting senses'
	C) takes, notes	
	D) soil preparation	

Q34. Absolute Pattern 1: Adding, Revising, Deleting, Retaining Information

Passage keywords: manuscript (Informative)

	A) detracts	Negative
	B) No, previous sentence	It should not be deleted because it is informative
√	**C) defines term**	The underlined sentence further introduces the manuscript
	D) culinary artifact	Unrelated word or Issue

Q35. Absolute Pattern 23: Transition Words for Supporting Detail, Contrast, and Consequence

Passage keywords: astonishing size (cause), challenge (effect)

√	**A) because of**	'Because of' is used to relate cause and effect clauses
	B) regardless of	is used to contradict the previous text
	C) In contrast to	is used to contradict the previous text
	D) In addition to	is used to support the previous text

Q36. Absolute Pattern 19: Redundant Error

	A) donation, University of Iowa	The phrase 'Because of' emphasizes two elements: the size and the range of donation.
	B) donation, many culinary, artifacts	
	C) massive, donation, cookbooks	(A), (B), (C) not only repeat—redundant errors—the previously mentioned information but also dilute the phrase emphasized by 'because of', so that they all change the original meaning
√	**D) donations,**	

Q37. Absolute Pattern 7: Conjunction Error

Passage keywords: happy to show, too delicate.

	A) so	The conjunction for consequence
	B) for	The conjunction for cause-effect relations
	C) and	The conjunction for parallel structure
√	**D) but**	The conjunction for contrasting idea.

Q38. Absolute Pattern 14: Possessive Determiners and Possessive Noun Error

Passage keywords: volunteers (Third-person plural)

	A) our	First person plural (the possessive pronoun for 'we')
	B) his	Third-person singular (the possessive pronoun for 'he')
√	**C) their**	Third-person plural (the possessive pronoun for 'they or volunteers')
	D) one's	Third-person singular (the possessive pronoun for 'one')

Q39. Absolute Pattern 10: Logical Expression

The keyword in the passage: DIY

	A) prosaic	Negative. Prosaic means boring
√	**B) simple**	The sentence requires a positive word.
	C) bare-bones	Negative. Colloquial (nonstandard) language
	D) protocols	Jargon. Unnecessarily special language for the volunteers' simple tasks

Q40. Absolute Pattern 23: Transition Words for Supporting Detail, Contrast, and Consequence

Passage keywords: need, no expertise, puzzling

	A) moreover,	1> All the options are conjunctive adverbs.
	B) therefore,	2> Their purpose is to connect two clauses or phrases, by supporting details like (A), (D); by revealing the consequence like (B); or by contrasting the idea
√	**C) however,**	like the answer (C)
	D) in short,	

Q41. Absolute Pattern 6: Confusing Words

	A) access of	
√	**B) access to**	'access to' is the correct form of idiom
	C) excess of	excess means extra
	D) excess to	

Q42. Absolute Pattern 24: Verb Tense / Voice Error

Passage keywords: recipes, don't (present), while

	A) had worked	B) 1> conjunction 'while' requires the same time frames (the same tense) with the same comparison between the clauses in a sentence.
√	**B) work**	2> Because the main clause is present tense, the dependent clause should also use the present tense.
	C) worked	
	D) could have worked	(A) Past perfect tense
		(C) Past tense
		(D) is used to express possibility in the conditional clause

Q43. Absolute Pattern 13: Parallel Structure

Passage keywords: three categories

√	**A) cheesecake, pie, pie,**	1> It uses the compound nouns 2> Under the compound noun, all the nouns should be considered as a single word without any interruption by a comma.
	B) almond, summer, mince,	
	C) cheesecake summer, mince	
	D) almond, cheesecake, summer, mince,	

(B), (D) almond and cheesecake cannot be separated by comma

(C) almond cheesecake and summer mince pie should be separated by comma

Q44. Absolute Pattern Type 1: Adding, Revising, Deleting, Retaining Information

	A) after 1	The passage keywords: (A) library (B) cooking manuscript (C) 1800s (D) Fair, contestants
	B) after 2	The question keywords "the judges" and "delicious" match with the sentence sequence 1=> 2=> 3=> 4.
	C) after 3	
√	**D) after 4**	It is always essential step to read from the backward order 4>3>2>1 because finding the concluding sentence is a lot easier than finding the introduction sentence.

COLLEGE BOARD SAT PATTERN ANALYSIS

WRITING AND LANGUAGE PATTERNS

To download the test, please visit:
https://collegereadiness.collegeboard.org/pdf/sat-practice-test-1.pdf

SAT COLLEGE BOARD OFFICIAL GUIDE
WRITING AND LANGUAGE SECTION PATTERNS

Q1. Absolute Pattern 10: Logical Expression

Passage keywords: advantages, drawbacks

	A) outdo	1> The clause "The advantages outweigh drawbacks" is a sort of standardized expression.
	B) defeat	2> The other options are too extreme word usages to express drawbacks.
	C) outperform	
√	**D) outweigh**	

Q2. Absolute Pattern 1: Adding, Revising, Deleting, Retaining Information

Passage keywords: address/problem, a number of uses

	A) home, yogurt	1> The previous sentence states "acid whey" which is difficult to dispose of.
√	**B) convert, into gas**	2> "a number of uses (solutions)" is then presented starting with one example.
		3> Therefore, the following sentence should present another example.
	C) food additive	4> Only (B) contains the keywords relevant to another example of use.
	D) important diet	A), B), D) are all unrelated issues: the context should discuss "acid whey", not a yogurt as in (A), not desirable food additive as in (B), not an important diet element as in (D).

Q3. Absolute Pattern 24: Verb Tense / Voice Error

Passage keywords: If it is,

√	**A) can, waterways**	1> "If it is" is the present conditional clause.
	B) can, waterway's	2> Therefore, the main clause should follow the present tense.
		C) is incorrect because it uses the past tense "could have"
	C) could have	D) is incorrect because the conditional clause implies the possibility. "has polluted" implies it has been done already.
	D) waterway's	B) is incorrect because "waterway's" is a possessive form, which should host another noun after that.

Q4. Absolute Pattern 18: Punctuation Error

Passage keywords: and

	A) ; and	A semicolon in (A) or A colon in (B) can't be used amid a list of nouns.
	B) : and	D) a comma should not be placed after "and"
√	**C) , and**	
	D) , and ,	

Q5. Absolute Pattern 11: Logical Sequence

Passage keywords: difficult, dispose (Negative/the Main issue)=> If it is, pollute, deleting oxygen (Negative/ The supporting details)

	A) feed as supplement (sentence 4)	The Passage Sequence
	B) main problem (sentence 1)	[1] The main concern is explained => [2] The supporting details is introduced=> [3] The solution is
√	**C) produces larger, acid-whey (sentence 2)**	proposed=> [4] one of the example solutions is
	D) address the problem (sentence 3)	presented => **[5]The problem is presented.** Therefore, [5] should be relocated before [3]

Q6. Absolute Pattern 1: Adding, Revising, Deleting, Retaining Information

Passage keywords: Though, these, methods, well worth effort (Positive)

	A) Yes, not provide	The topic sentence should remain definitely.
	B) Yes, fails	Therefore, the answer should be either (C) or (D).
	C) No, how, can be disposed	(C) The description is based on the previous paragraph.
√	**D) No, benefits**	(D) The description is based on the paragraph where the topic sentence belongs to. Therefore, the answer should be (D)

Q7. Absolute Pattern 15: Prepositional Idiom

Passage keywords: it, digestive aid

	A) to be	"serving as" is the standardized form.
√	B) as	B) "as" is used to equalize two entities. (e.g., Tim serves as the captain of the team => Tim is the captain)
	C) like	A) is used for the future only.
	D) for	C) is used to compare, not equalize, two entities

Q8. Absolute Pattern 13: Parallel Structure

Passage keywords: "it is...serves, and (contains)

	A) it contains	The sentence is paralleling by using a list of the verbs in the simple present tense.
	B) containing	(A) "it" interferes the parallel structure. When the subject is identical, it shouldn't be used again in the same sentence after "and."
√	C) contains	
	D) will contain	

Q9. Absolute Pattern 23: Transitions (Supporting Detail, Contrast, and Consequence)

Passage keywords: healthy food, helping people stay

	A) also	A) It gives more information about Greek yogurt as a healthy food.
√	A) also	
	B) in other word	1> The previous sentence and the sentence in question deal with the different issues (low sugar vs. high protein). Therefore, (B) and (C) should be incorrect.
	C) therefore	2> The previous sentence is not the topic sentence of this paragraph.
	D) for instance	In fact, it is located in the middle of the paragraph, supporting its own topic sentence, Therefore, (D) is incorrect because an example sentence supporting another example sentence is a highly unlikely arrangement. B) is used to repeat the previous sentence in a different way. C) is used to draw a conclusion from the previous sentence. D) is used to give an added detail for the topic or main idea of the paragraph.

Q10. Absolute Pattern 10: Logical Expression

Passage keywords: per serving

√	A) satiated	A) is a physical concept. It means to supply food beyond desire.
	B) fulfilled	B), C), and D) are all mental concept that doesn't link to food as directly as (A).
	C) complacent	
	D) sufficient	

Q11. Absolute Pattern 7: Conjunction Error

Passage keywords: Because

	A) therefore farmers	B) Two clauses require only one conjunction.
√	B) ,farmers	1> "Because" is a subordinating conjunction or simply a conjunction. 2> "therefore" is a conjunctive adverb. or simply a conjunction.
	C) ,so farmers	3> Having two conjunctions (because, therefore) in two clauses, this sentence technically has no completely independent main clause but two subordinating clauses.
	D) :farmers	4> Therefore, the answer should be the one that has no conjunction. A) "therefore" and C) "so" are conjunctions (conjunctive adverbs) D) a colon also must be carried by an independent clause, which is disabled by placing the colon.

Q12. Absolute Pattern 9: Informational Graphs

The graph shows the average temperature can drop as low as (B) 12 degrees Fahrenheit.

Q13. Absolute Pattern 16: Precision, Concision, Style

Passage keywords: evidence, thawing

	A) following	1> The quintessential concept of precision and concision is eliminating unnecessary words and keep the sentence simple.
	B) thawing	2> For this type of question, (A) should be highly likely to be the answer even without reading or analyzing the reason for it.
	C) thawing	3> Simply because (A) doesn't use a conjunction "and" while all the other options are using "and" to create the subordinating clause.
√	**D) evidence**	A) chose to use the modifying phrase by not using "and" and the unnecessary subject and verb. By doing so, (A) avoids the redundant errors found in other options.
		B) and C) use "thawing" unnecessarily.
		D) uses "evidence" unnecessarily.

Q14. Absolute Pattern 23: Transitions (Supporting Detail, Contrast, and Consequence)

Passage keywords: typically, late summer, entire ice, underwent, earliest date

	A) for example	B)
√	**B) however**	1> "however" cancels out the previous sentence in order to emphasize the following clause.
	C) as such	2> Two clauses between the transition word show a clear contradiction.
	D) moreover	3> Therefore, it requires "however"

Q15. Absolute Pattern 22: Nonrestrictive Modifier (Inessential Information)

Passage keywords: an associate...

	A) Box, an associate...State	1> "an associate….State" is an inessential information.
	B) Box an associate...State,	2> That is, even without having this information, the sentence is completely understood.
√	**C) Box, an associate State,**	3> This is called the nonrestrictive modifier.
	D) Box, geology, State	4> The nonrestrictive modifier needs to be offset by a pair of commas.
		5> Therefore, C) is the answer.

Q16. Absolute Pattern 18: Punctuation Error

Passage keywords: another factor added, thaw

	A) thaw;	The function of colon is to introduce things
	B) thaw; and it was	C) The preceding sentence invites the colon at the end of the sentence and then introduces the name of the factor just like introducing a movie title.
√	**C) thaw:**	
	D) thaw: being	A) a semicolon doesn't have the same function as the colon does and they are not the same things. B) has two errors: (1) uses a semicolon (2) "and it was" is wordy. D) please don't choose "being"

Q17. Absolute Pattern 7: Conjunction Error

Passage keywords: , some of it

	A) of it	1> The subject "tundra fires" and the verb "produced" make it a complete independent sentence.
	B) soot	2> "Some of it" and "drifted" make it another complete independent sentence.
√	**C) of which**	3> However, these two sentences are connected with a comma.
	D) delete	4> This is called a comma splice error. 5> To avoid a comma splice error, the answer must contain a conjunction 6> Only (C) has it "which" C) uses "which" as a conjunction

Q18. Absolute Pattern 24: Verb Tense / Voice Error

Passage keywords: produced, drifted

√	**A) fell**	A) The verbs " within the sentence ("produced", "drifted") use the simple past
	B) falls	1> because of "2012", the time adverbial phrase, it requires the simple past tense. 2> Therefore, the following verb should also use the same tense.
	C) will fall	B) is present C) is future D) is past perfect
	D) had fallen	

Q19. Absolute Pattern 14: Possessive Determiners and Possessive Noun Error

Passage keywords: snow and ice

	A) it's	1> When there are more than two nouns in a given sentence,
	B) its	2> and the question asks which noun represents to the following pronoun, acting as a precedent,
	C) there	3> the answer noun is highly likely to be the one located closest to the pronoun.
√	D) their	4> In this case, "snow and ice", not "soot particles"

D) indicates snow and ice.

The sentence illustrates that soot particles are responsible for melting as they prevent snow and ice from reflecting the sun's rays.

Q20. Absolute Pattern 1: Adding, Revising, Deleting, Retaining Information

Passage keywords: absorbs, heat   Question keywords: self-reinforcing

	A) related, rising temp.	D) responds to the question keyword "self-reinforcing"
	B) raises, temperature	A) and B) are basically repeating the question, instead of answering the question "self-reinforcing cycle."
	C) cool	C) is opposite concept
√	D) melting	

Q21. Absolute Pattern 19: Redundant Error

Passage keywords: may, repeat, harmful

	A) again	A) "repeat" and "again" are redundant
√	B) itself	C) "with damage" and "harmful" are redundant
	C) damage	D) "may" and "possibly" arc redundant
	D) possibly	

Q22. Absolute Pattern 11: Logical Sequence

Key concept: For PATTERN 11. Logical Sequence, it is always easier to find the answer by reviewing the sentences from backward order.

	A) As it is	1> Sentence 6 describes the public will fund to help organize his team's expedition.
	B) after 1	2> Sentence 5 describes Box's team is to travel to Greenland for sampling. 3> **Sentence 4 describes Box is currently organizing an expedition.**
	C) after 2	4> Sentence 3 describes the harmful effect.
√	**D) after 5**	As seen above, sentence 4 should be located right before sentence 6 for two reasons: (1) to connect the idea concerning the expedition. (sentence 4 => sentence 6) (2) to connect the idea concerning the harmful effect and finding the evidence through sampling. (sentence 3 => sentence 5)

Q23. Absolute Pattern 19: Redundant Error

Passage keywords: quickly

	A) soon	A), B), and C) are all redundant errors.
	B) promptly	
	C) promptly	
√	**D) wore**	

Q24. Absolute Pattern 12: Modifier (Placement) Error

Passage keywords: Having, frustrated

	A) no colleagues	"Having frustrated" is what "I" experienced.
	B) colleagues	A), B), and C) all of which do not function as the main entity that was frustrated.
	C) ideas	
√	**D) I**	

Q25. Absolute Pattern 15: Prepositional Idiom

Passage keywords: read

	A) into	"Read about" is the correct idiom.
√	**B) about**	
	C) upon	
	D) for	

Q26. Absolute Pattern 18: Punctuation Error

Passage keywords: such as

√	**A) ,such as**	"such as" needs a comma to separate itself from the main clause.
	B) ,such as:	The comma should be placed before "such as", not after.
	C) such as:	No other punctuation goes along with "such as."
	D) ,such as,	

Q27. Absolute Pattern 23: Transitions (Supporting Detail, Contrast, and Consequence)

Passage keywords: office equipment

	A) however	1> The paragraph begins with the benefits of the coworking space.
√	**B) in addition to**	2> Generally, the following sentences support the topic sentence in forms of supporting details or example sentence.
	C) for these reasons	3> The second sentence describes the use of equipment as one benefit.
	D) likewise	4>The third sentence describes the space facilities as another benefit.
		5> "In addition to" is, therefore, the most ideal transitional word.

Q28. Absolute Pattern 1: Adding, Revising, Deleting, Retaining Information

Passage keywords: cost, co-working business

	A) kept, provides details	1> The topic sentence focuses on the advantages that individual users can enjoy.
	B) kept, main topic	2> Based on the context of the topic sentence, the sentence in question should be considered as new information
√	**C) deleted, blurs**	
	D) deleted, repeats	3> New information is always incorrect

Q29. Absolute Pattern 9: Informational Graphs

	A) prevented	A) Negative—The paragraph's overall tone is positive
√	**B) 71, creativity**	C) is a misinterpretation of the numbers. 74% is the figure that individual users favored, not related it.
	C) 74, giving ideas	
	D) 12	D) has switched the numbers.

Q30. Absolute Pattern 17: Pronoun Error

Passage keywords: are people

	A) whom use	D) a relative pronoun that carries a verb must be a subjective form "who."
	B) whom uses	A), B) "whom" is objective form, which can't carry a verb.
	C) who uses	C) 1> "who" is plural because it represents the people.
√	**D) who use**	2> Therefore, the verb "uses" should be "use."

Q31. Absolute Pattern 11: Logical Sequence

Question keywords: a quick tour, I took a seat

	A) before 1: try to use coworking	Reading from backwards: 1> It can be immediately noticed that sentence [4] and [3] are inseparable. 2> Topic sentence is always easy to identify. 3> Therefore, the sentence in question should be located between the topic and sentence [3].
	B) after 1:	
√	**C) after 2: I chose, open work area**	
	D) after 3: more people appeared	Sentence [2] and the added information matches the context. Sentence [1] is the topic sentence that doesn't link to the beginning phrase "After filing" Sentence [3] illustrates the narrator's observation after he took a seat.

Q32. Absolute Pattern 18: Punctuation Error

Passage keywords: I've gotten to know

√	**A) colleagues:**	1> A colon does one thing and one thing only: it introduces things or a brief information
	B) colleagues;	2> No other punctuation can do the exactly same function that a colon does.
	C) colleagues,	3> Therefore, the answer is (A)
	D) colleagues	

Q33. Absolute Pattern 10: Logical Expression

Passage keywords: help each other

√	**A) share advice**	Finding a logical expression is easy.
	B) wisdom	Defining an illogical expression is less easy. Illogical expressions are:
	C) proclaim	(1) too literal as in (B), (2) too strong as in (C)
	D) opine	(3) too formal as in (D)

Q34. Absolute Pattern 23: Transitions (Supporting Detail, Contrast, and Consequence)

Passage keywords: philosophy is the study

√	**A) in broad terms,**	"philosophy is the study of…." describes the term.
	B) for example,	
	C) in contrast,	
	D) nevertheless,	

Q35. Absolute Pattern 16: Precision, Concision, Style

√	**A) pragmatically,**	Compared to answer (A), all the other options are wordy, which, instead of adding a meaningful information, slows down the reading comprehension.
	B) programmatic way,	
	C) speaking in a way	
	D) speaking way	

Q36. Absolute Pattern 21: Subject-Verb, Pronoun, Noun Agreement

Passage keywords: philosophy (subject)

	A) teaching	B) is the only verb available among options.
√	**B) teaches**	
	C) to teach	
	D) and teaching	

Q37. Absolute Pattern 1: Adding, Revising, Deleting, Retaining Information

Passage keywords: philosophy, useful tools, only 18 percent

	A) consequently,	1> The answer for this question can be easily identified by simply looking at the transition word "however."
	B) therefore,	2> The tone between two sentences moves from positive to negative.
	C) notwithstanding...	3> "however" presents a clear contradiction.
√	**D) however,**	

Q38. Absolute Pattern 23: Transitions (Supporting Detail, Contrast, and Consequence)

Passage keywords: only 18 percent, 400, eliminated.

	A) Therefore,	1> The tone is consistently negative between two sentences
	B) Thus,	2> Therefore, (D) is incorrect 3> Two sentences function as an example of the paragraph.
√	**C) Moreover,**	4> Therefore, choice A and B are incorrect.
	D) However,	

Q39. Absolute Pattern 16: Precision, Concision, Style

√	**A) writing as**	A) is most concise and precise without changing the meaning.
	B) and these results can be	B) and D) are wordy by adding no meaningful words like "these results"
	C) which can also be	
	D) when the results are	C) uses the word "also" as if there's another reason. However, "also" is written in this sentence already, implying that this very sentence itself is another reason. It is illogical to have another reason inside another reason.

Q40. Absolute Pattern 21: Subject-Verb, Pronoun, Noun Agreement

Passage keywords: students (subject)

	A) has	B) The subject "students" is plural that requires a plural verb.
	B) have scored	Choice A, and C are singular.
	C) scores	Choice D is a participle.
√	**D) scoring**	

Q41. Absolute Pattern 12: Modifier (Placement) Error

Passage keywords: have no intention

	A) student's majoring	B) "students (who are) majoring" is the correct form of the adjective modifier.
√	**B) students majoring**	What is the adjective modifier? -It is a group of words that describes an immediate noun, normally starting with "~ing" form.
	C) students major	
	D) student's majors	For choices A and D, "many" must have "students." "student's" is a singular possessive form, not a plural. C) The sentence can't have another verb "major."

Q42. Absolute Pattern 1: Adding, Revising, Deleting, Retaining Information

Passage keywords: students majoring, these skills are transferable
Question keywords: ancient Greek philosopher Plato

	A) Yes,	1> The paragraph describes the practicality of philosophy in modern education. It has nothing to do with Plato.
	B) Yes,	2> Therefore, it should simply be removed; it's not about undermine (D)
√	**C) No, blurs**	
	D) No, undermine, passage claim	

Q43. Absolute Pattern 21: Subject-Verb, Pronoun, Noun Agreement

Passage keywords: That

	A) which	1> Here in this sentence that-clause acts as a subject. (e.g., **That I'm rich** is a lie.)
	B) that	2> That is, when a sentence begins with "That", finding a verb is the first step.
		3> a group of words that comes before the verb belongs to "that clause", which
	C) and	should be treated as a single subject with a long group of words.
√	**D) delete**	4> It can be understood as "The fact that…." which requires a verb.
		5> Therefore, the underlined portion should be deleted to make a verb.

Q44. Absolute Pattern 17: Pronoun Error

Passage keywords: today's students

	A) our	D) "their" refers to the subject "students"
	B) one's	
	C) his or her	
√	**D) their**	

WRITING AND LANGUAGE SECTION

70 Rules for the Sentence-Error Questions

70 Rules for the Sentence Error Questions

To optimize your success in Writing & Language Test and minimize surprise by making all the questions predictable, following 70 rules for the sentence error questions will change the way you react to each sentence error question.

*Please look at the "Hint" first before look at the answer.

Question 1
Down the road from the <u>school, my brother attend</u>, Seven Eleven convenient store is always open, and some customers are always there.

A) NO CHANGE
B) school, my brother attends
C) school my brother attends
D) school, which is my brother attends,

RULE #1 Hint: Quick Interjection	Restrictive Modifier The correct answer is C. "the school" is not any school in general but the only one where "my brother attends" Therefore, it is an essential part of the sentence and needs to be considered as a part of the sentence without offset by a pair of commas.

Question 2
It is comforting to see that the <u>Seven Eleven store. And its customers</u> are always there.

A) NO CHANGE
B) Seven Eleven store and that its customers
C) Seven Eleven store and its customers
D) Seven Eleven store with the customers

RULE #2 Hint: That	That-Clause as a Direct Subject The correct answer is C. Choice A is incorrect because that clause has no verb. Choice B is wrong because of fragment error. "and that its customers" makes the previous sentence "that the Seven Twelve store" without a verb. Choice D is wrong because possessive determiner "its (customers)" should be used instead of an ambiguous "the customers".

Question 3

The police's reasoning implied that, even if the robber was wearing a mask, it had enough knowledge to collect the <u>evidence: such as the robber's height matching the suspect, weight, and foot size.</u>

A) NO CHANGE
B) evidence; the height, weight, and foot size.
C) evidence, the height, weight, and foot size.
D) evidence: the height, weight, and foot size.

RULE #3 Hint: Colon	The Usage of Colon
	The correct answer is D.
	The single most important purpose of colon is to introduce things. It can introduce just about anything: a list of words, a list of phrases, a list of clauses.
	Option A is incorrect because colon means "such as." That is, they deliver basically the same function to the sentence and therefore one of which should be removed.
	Option B uses a semi-colon instead of colon. The colon and semicolon are very different in their usage.
	The primal purpose of the semicolon is to connect the following clause, not a list of words or phrase.
	Option C changes the original meaning by putting a comma.
	More examples and explanations Colon can describe almost any form of language. -Monkey has only one desire on its mind: <u>banana.</u> -Monkey has only one desire on its mind: <u>a pile of banana.</u> -Monkey has only one desire on its mind: <u>it wants to have a pile of banana.</u> -Monkey has three desires on its mind: <u>finding banana trees, piling banana, eating a banana.</u>
	Now compare the following two sentences -Apple corporation's cellphone beats its competitors specifically in the core area of waterproof functionality.

RULE #3 Hint: Colon	-Apple corporation's cellphone beats its competitors specifically in the core area: waterproof functionality.

As seen in the above comparisons, the main function of the colon is not only to introduce things but also to emphasize what the writer wishes to embolden.

If you are not sure whether to use a colon or not, just imagine a word "that is." In other word, colon means "that is." You can write "that is" in place of a colon.

-Monkey has only one desire on its mind <that is> banana.

-Monkey has only one desire on its mind <that is> a pile of banana.

-Monkey has only one desire on its mind <that is> it wants to have a pile of banana.

-Monkey has three desires on its mind <that is:> finding banana trees, piling banana, eating a banana.

Colon, however, cannot be used in the middle of an incomplete sentence that obstructs the flow of the sentence.

Correct: Apple specializes in high-tech gadgets: cellphone, iPad, and computer.

Incorrect: Apple specializes in: high-tech gadgets such as cellphone, iPad, and computer.

Question 4

However they choose their dormitory, college students at St. Johns are not entirely allowed to make their own decisions in choosing their <u>roommates: as a result,</u> many students choose an off-campus apartment.

A) NO CHANGE

B) roommates, as a result,

C) roommates; as a result,

D) roommates; and as a result,

RULE #4
 	
Hint:
 	
Semicolon
	The correct answer is C.
	
	The semicolon is used between two independent clauses. Semicolon functions as a conjunction. Therefore, it cannot be used together with other conjunctions such as *for, and, nor, but, or, yet, so.*
	
	Transitional words/phrase such as *"accordingly", "consequently," "for example, " "nevertheless," "so," "thus" etc. are all conjunctive adverbs that act like conjunctions. Because they are not genuinely conjunction, a semicolon must be carried along with them to actually connect the following clause.*
	
	More example
	Ex) Only the authorized Apple service center can replace the original Apple parts; unauthorized
	    service center can provide a repair service using generic parts.
	
	   -Only the authorized Apple service centre can replace the original Apple parts, but unauthorized
	    service center can provide a repair service using generic parts.
	
	As seen in the above examples, the semi-colon can be used when two opposite opinions are presented in both sentences.
	
	Ex) The number of drunken drivers continues to fall; consequently, the police focus
	    more on parking violations or speeding.
	
	Ex) Some physicians' handwriting makes it extremely difficult to read; accordingly,
	    all doctors' prescriptions for drugs are required to be recorded on the internet
	    website that links between medical doctors and pharmacies in the country.

Question 5

As New York Times reported last year, Honda's airbag scandals have gone so far as to set up something of the comprehensive <u>double-dealing; an intentional inspection report forgery and</u> fraud from the board members—to inflate the sales, while avoiding critical industry standards test.

A) NO CHANGE

B) double-dealing, an intentional inspection report forgery and

C) double-dealing: with an intentional inspection report forgery and

D) double-dealing—an intentional inspection report forgery and

RULE #5 Hint: Dash	DASHES (—) + Guessing based on the meaning of the keyword
	The correct answer is D The meaning "double-dealing" implies that two incidents will follow, not one, not three. The original sentence uses a semicolon and a dash (—) combination, which is an impossible cocktail. Option B is correct and very tricky. It maintains a well-constructed parallelism. The problem, however, is the change of original meaning. As introduced earlier, the word "double dealing's innate meaning", the overall sentence, and the already presented this cute "dash" prove that this sentence is made of a double dash, refusing to be a simple parallelism question. Option C also uses a colon and semicolon combination. Moreover, the elements after the colon are not paralleling. It starts with the preposition "with", and connects it with a conjunction "and" and then ends up with a dash. For the answer D, dashes are used to set off the interjection phrase to call more attention to what lies in between.

Question 6

The secretary of internal affairs picked the house speaker Paul Ryan as a next candidate for the position—a dynamic colleague in Washington.

A) position—a dynamic colleague in Washington.
B) position; a dynamic colleague in Washington.
C) position, who is a dynamic colleague in Washington.
D) position with a dynamic colleague in Washington.

RULE #6 Hint: Dash	Dash The correct answer is A. One dash functions just the same way as the colon. Therefore, they are interchangeable. Choice B is wrong because semicolon cannot be linked with a phrase. Choice C is wrong because of the misplaced modifier error. "who" is linked with the position, making ambiguous whether it refers to the secretary of internal affairs or the house speaker Paul Ryan. Choice D is wrong for the same reason as C.

Question 7

That nickel-and-dime store where I used to buy stationery when I was only five-year-old kid was abandoned, leaving only a faded signage on the roof of the building.

A) NO CHANGE

B) That nickel and dime store where I used to buy stationery when I was only a five year old kid

C) When I was only a five year old kid, I used to buy stationary at that nickel-and-dime store

D) I used to buy stationery at that nickel-and-dime store when I was only five year old kid

RULE #7 Hint: Hyphen	HYPHEN The correct answer is A. The hyphen is mainly used as an adjective by joining two or more words together. The "nickel-and-dime" and "five-year-old" are the correct forms. Option B, contrary to A. has no hyphens. Options C and D are run-ons. Example sentences using the hyphen as a compound adjective -The employer is fed up with his do-nothing secretary. -That thirteen-year-old girl got pregnant is not big news in some parts of Africa. -We cannot give you with a money-back guarantee under this discount term. -The newly introduced iPhone is not quite a state-of-the-art technology.

Question 8

The present interreligious conflicts in <u>France which was ignited by the extreme Jihadist turned the entire Europe in turmoil.</u>

A) NO CHANGE
B) France, that ignited by the extreme Jihadist, turned
C) France, which was ignited by the extreme Jihadist turned
D) France, which were ignited by the extreme Jihadist, turned

RULE #8	Double Commas for Non-restrictive Modifier (Inessential Information).
Hint:	
Punctuation	The correct answer is D.

Non-restrictive modifier means that some modifier is an inessential Information to understand the entire sentence.
It can be a short or long phrase or clause.
When placed in the middle of the independent sentence, it should be offset by a double commas acting as a parenthesis.

Option A is direct opposite to D and is called restrictive modifier. That is, essential information should not be offset by a pair of commas.
Option B is incorrect because "that" is normally used for a restrictive modifier only. In other words, "that" should not be followed by comma

Option C has only one comma, creating a sentence fragment.

Options A and C are also subject-verb agreement error. The subject is conflicts" ;therefore, the verb should be "were."

The following examples illustrate appositive elements (a noun or noun phrase that describes the noun right besides it using double commas)

Ex1) The heart of Europe, ***Paris,*** is invaded by another terrorism.

Ex2) The heart of Europe, ***Paris with more than 10% of Islam population,*** is invaded by another terrorism.

RULE #8 Hint: Punctuation	Ex3) The heart of Europe, ***Paris that has proclaimed the war against terrorism,*** is invaded by another terrorism. Other Non-restrictive Modifier Examples that require double commas. Ex4) Chad's dream, ***to become a national hockey player,*** is on the brink of a fiasco. Ex5) Lynn, ***the husband of the former Chairman in a big company,*** decided to buy an oil refinery company.

Question 9

The actor Tom Cruise established his own film company.

A) The actor Tom Cruise established

B) The actor, Tom Cruise, established

C) The acting film star, Tom Cruise, established

D) The actor who is Tom Cruise established

RULE #9 Hint: Punctuation	Omitting Double Commas The correct answer is A. If the appositive and the word it modifies are so closely related (essential information), double commas should be omitted. Without "Tom Cruise" the sentence will lose its original meaning and become very ambiguous because there are simply so many actors. Choice B is wrong because a double comma should not be used. Choice C changes the meaning Choice D is wordy.

Question 10

The doctor recommended his patient take three pills a day.

A) his patient taking

B) his patient take

C) his patient takes

D) that his patient to take

RULE #10 Hint: Verb	Imperative Verb in Subjective Mood

The correct answer is B.

Choice A is wrong because "taking" is gerund for going-concern.

Choice C is wrong because, in an imperative situation, the verb must use the base verb, pretending that there is "should" before the base verb.

Choice D is wrong because "to take" is not a verb.

The imperative verbs are used to give orders or instructions.

When the imperative verb is used in subjunctive mood—that you desire or imagine something to be done or someone to do something, the model verb "should" can be dropped, and the base verb is used.

Some typical imperative verbs are as follow: "ask", "demand", "determine", "insist", "move", "order", "pray", "prefer", "recommend", "regret", "request", "require", "suggest", and "wish".

The verb for the third person singular (he/she) drops the -s or -es so that it sounds like the present tense.

Question 11
After I graduated high school, I have never been in a serious relationship with anyone.

A) NO ERROR
B) With my graduation from high school
C) Since I graduated high school
D) When I graduated high school

RULE #11 Hint: Verb	Since + The Present Perfect Tense

The correct answer is C.

"Since" always comes along with the present perfect tense in the main sentence.

"After" can't replace "since"

Options B and D are illogical sentences.

Question 12
While reading a detective novel, <u>my cat was sleeping inside my arms</u>.

A) my cat is sleeping inside my arms
B) I held my sleeping cat inside my arms
C) I fell asleep with my cat inside my arms
D) a sleeping cat was inside my arms

RULE #12 Hint: Modifier	MODIFIER
	The correct answer is B.
	A typical question in dangling modifier is switching the rightful subject with our common sense.
	The original sentence—although it appears to be correct and clearly understood—is defective in that "my cat" can't read.
	The subject has to be a human, who can read.
	Dangling Modifier means a descriptive clause that must have noun or pronoun that it describes the after the comma.
	Harder Example Incorrect: Completely exhausted, <u>the marathoner's uniform</u> felt like wearing armor. Correct: Completely exhausted, <u>the marathoner</u> in uniform felt as if he was wearing armor.

Question 13: The correct placement for the underlined portion of the sentence should be Jenkins, the professor, invited his international students on Thanksgiving day to serve a traditional turkey, <u>wearing an old pilgrim costume.</u>

A) NO CHANGE
B) after "Jenkins"
C) after "students"
D) after "Thanksgiving day"

RULE #13 Hint: Modifier	Misplaced Modifier The correct answer is B. Misplaced Modifier means that a descriptive phrase must be located immediately after or before the thing or person it supposes to describe. The correct answer is B as the modifier "wearing an old pilgrim costumes" must be logically located after the person. Option C is incorrect because "costume" is singular, but "students" are plural, an impossible situation unless they all are wearing one clothes at the same time.

Question 14

Whatever the majority of the board <u>decides does not reflect the employees' pay increase.</u>

A) decides, reflect no pay increase of the employees.
B) decides, do not reflect the employees' pay increase.
C) makes on their decision do not reflect the employees' pay increase.
D) decides does not reflect the employees' pay increase.

RULE #14 Hint: Subject	A Whole Package of Dependent Clause as a Subject The correct answer is D. When an entire dependent clause is used as a subject, it should be treated as a single noun. The subject then should be " Whatever the majority of the board decides" The verb then should also be a singular "does not reflect" For this reason, all the other options are incorrect

Question 15

For the past year, every effort by Republican senators to topple Obama <u>care considering embarrassing failure.</u>

A) NO CHANGE
B) care considered embarrassing
C) care was considered embarrassingly
D) care was considering embarrassingly

RULE #15 Hint: Verb	Sentence Fragment The correct answer is C. Sentence fragment means a sentence that either subject or verb or both are not in place; therefore, not functioning as an independent clause. The sentence—based upon the meaning—requires a passive verb. Active voice options like B, D are wrong.

Question 16

Cancun was not my first destination for <u>vacation I found</u> it too hot temperature there was unappealing at that time.

A) NO CHANGE
B) vacation; because I found
C) vacation because I found
D) vacation, found

RULE #16 Hint: Conjunction	RUN-ON SENTENCES
	The correct answer is C.
	The original sentence is a run-on. A run-on sentence contains multiple independent clauses without having a proper conjunction. Options A and D are run-on,
	Option B has semicolon and "because" at the same time, one of which has to be dropped.

Question 17

<u>The house that belongs to my tenant</u> next to the backyard needs an additional repair.

A) NO CHANGE
B) The house that belongs to my tenant
C) The house of my tenant
D) My tenant's house

RULE #17 Hint: Wordiness	Possessive Noun The correct answer is D.
	A singular noun + apostrophe + s is the way to make a singular possessive noun The original sentence and options B, C are unnecessarily wordy.

Question 18

The recent data sent by Voyager II further confirms Dr. Ray's theory <u>whom</u> argued about water molecules in the Mar's atmosphere.

A) NO CHANGE
B) further confirms Dr. Ray's theory, in which he
C) further confirms Dr. Ray's theory, which
D) further confirms Dr. Ray's theory, who

RULE #18 Hint: Pronoun	Antecedent for Pronoun The correct answer is B. The object in this sentence is 'theory', not Dr. Ray. Therefore, both A) and D) are incorrect as "who" or "whom" refers to a human antecedent. There's no human in the sentence, only "Dr. Ray's theory" is. Option C can't be correct because "which" ("theory") can't argue.

Question 19

The passenger, who I saw yesterday, crippling and begging on the Mall, is standing right next to me, flirting with a much younger girl.

A) NO CHANGE
B) The passenger that I saw yesterday
C) The passenger whom I saw yesterday
D) The passenger, what I saw yesterday,

RULE #19 Hint: Pronoun	Who or Whom? The correct answer is C. If a noun (subject) follows right after either "whom" or "who" in the question, the answer should be "whom." If a verb follows right after either "whom" or "who" in the question, the answer should be "who."

Question 20

The other side of the calculus that keeps the dark business humming is the crooked police. They are paid handsome sums of the profits.

A) NO CHANGE
B) police paying handsome sums of the profits.
C) police, who are paid handsome sums of the profits.
D) police, and they are paid handsome sums of the profits.

RULE #20 Hint: Wordiness	Simplification The correct answer is C. The original sentence employs two independent sentences unnecessarily. Option B changes the original meaning by saying that police are paying the profits. Option D) uses an ambiguous "they"

Question 21

American athletes win most medals in the Olympics, <u>whereby America has such great systems</u> for preparing athletes.

A) NO CHANGE
B) because America has such great systems
C) moreover, America has such great systems
D) consequently, America has such great systems

RULE #21 Hint: Conjunc- tion	The Conjunction for Cause-Effect The correct answer is B. Option A "whereby" means "by which" to refer to means and method Option C "moreover" supports the preceding information Option D "consequently" refers to the effects.

Question 22

In a war against the Islamic State, women can be found <u>in the ranks</u> but also in command of guerrilla units.

A) NO CHANGE
B) not only in the ranks
C) by the ranks
D) more in the ranks

RULE #22 Hint: Conjunction	Correlative Conjunction The correct answer is B. Following conjunctions represent similarity and emphasis -Moreover / - just as / - likewise / - not only ...but also Correlative conjunction cannot be used separately or replaced with other form.

Question 23
Some European industries have declined, <u>and others are rising.</u>

A) NO CHANGE
B) however, others are rising.
C) since others are rising.
D) but others are rising.

RULE #23 Hint: Conjunction	The Conjunction for Contrast
	The correct answer is D.
	Following conjunctions (and conjunctive adverbs) represent contradiction
	-However /-on the other hand / -but /-nevertheless /-aside from / -while or whereas Choice B is wrong because "however" requires semi-colon."

Question 24
The car <u>making a squeaking noise as it veered to the right</u> finally ran into the bakery.

A) NO CHANGE
B) made a squeaking noise, veering to the right, and
C) ,which was making a squeaking noise as it veered to the right,
D) , making a squeaking noise as it veered to the right,

RULE #24 Hint: modifier	Restrictive Modifier
	The correct answer is A.
	The modifier should not be offset by a pair of commas if the clause requires it as a part of the essential information to understand the situation.
	Option B not only changes the original meaning but also makes a parallelism error. ("made", "veering" and "ran")
	Option C and D are non-restrictive modifiers, contrary to the original sentence.
	Option C is wordy as well as uses a pair of commas mistakenly believing the modifier is inessential information.

Question 25

Some of the survivors in the refugee camps of <u>Iraqi Kurdistan dominated by the heavily patriarchal system shows</u> how strong the tradition influenced the war.

A) NO CHANGE
B) Iraqi Kurdistan; dominated by the heavily patriarchal system, shows
C) Iraqi Kurdistan, dominated by the heavily patriarchal system, show
D) Iraqi Kurdistan, dominated by the heavily patriarchal system show

RULE #25 Hint: Modifier	Non-Restrictive Modifier
	The correct answer is C
	If the modifier merely putting an additional information, it should be offset by a pair of commas.

Question 26

For decades the paleontologists had assumed that the Ice Age killed the dinosaurs, <u>and their views changed</u> quickly when the most massive meteorite crater was found in Yucatan.

A) NO CHANGE

B) but their views had changed

C) however, their views changed

D) but their views changed

Rule #26 Hint: Conjunction	"But" should be used to contrast idea. "And" should be used to Paralleling idea.
	The correct answer is D.
	Use the conjunction 'but' to cancel out the previous sentence when two contrasting ideas are presented.
	Option A): 1> The keywords "views changed quickly" 2> Two clauses between "and" are conflicting each other. 3> This is called "Misused AND"
	Option B) is incorrect because "had changed" (the past perfect)" means that their views had changed before the crater was found, an impossible situation.
	Option C) is incorrect because 'however' requires a semicolon (; however,)

Question 27

Although the new discoveries suggest otherwise, <u>they</u> claim that there are other versions of the Old Testaments.

A) NO CHANGE
B) the discoveries
C) theologists
D) it

Rule #27 Hint: Pronoun	No Pronoun Can Be Used Independently Without Having Its Antecedent.
	This rule is called "The unknown antecedent for pronoun "

The correct answer is C.

In this sentence, the subject "they" in the main clause refers to "the new discoveries because there should be an antecedent for every pronoun,"

Because it is illogical to say "the new discoveries claim", we should make (find) one. A human concept option that can claim.

Theologists are the experts in Bible.

* Please remember that it's colloquial error to write "they" out of the blue in a written sentence. |

Question28

The guest was entertained <u>extravagant</u> by the mayor of the city of North Vancouver, whose city has a strong tie to the guest's company.

A) NO CHANGE
B) with extravagance
C) extravagantly
D) extravagance

RULE #28 Hint: Adverbs	Adjective Cannot Modify Verb, But Adverb Can. The correct answer is C. By simply adding "-ly" at the end of the adjective, it will switch to adverb that

Question 29

The New York Times chief editor has decided <u>requiring</u> all articles to be submitted at least one hour before the deadline.

A) NO CHANGE
B) to require
C) requesting
D) to requiring

RULE #29 Hint: Idiom	Prepositional Idioms that Imply the Future Action The correct answer is B. Any verb that implies "the future action" must use the preposition "to." (e.g., "wish to," "hope to," "expect to," "want to," "like to," 'plan to," "supposed to,")

Question 30

Forty-two years after the Apollo astronauts landed on the moon, new technology <u>was not developed</u> to initiate the same task easier.

A) NO CHANGE
B) has not been developed
C) has not developed
D) had not been developed

RULE #30 Hint: Verb	Guessing the Verb Tense The correct answer is B. "Forty-two years" indicates the things happened in the past. "after" also implies that the main clause describes the on-going event. Therefore, it should be present tense. B) is the present perfect tense. Option D) is the past perfect, an event that occurred before the past. Option C) is an active. It should be the passive because the subject is "technology."

Please refer to the following tense chart

Present Tense	Simple present	Jason works.
	Present continuous	Jason is working.
	Present perfect	Jason has worked.
Past Tense	Simple past	Jason worked.
	Past continuous	Jason was working.
	Past perfect	Jason had worked.
Future Tense	Future	Jason will work.
	Future continuous	Jason will be working.
	Future perfect	Jason will have worked.

HARDER EXAMPLE

Incorrect: I suspect the Olympic Council has a two-tiered vision for the future games: first, it had tried to replace the current exclusive sponsorship; second, it is wanting to add as much capacity to its operation as possible to have more multiple partners.

Correct: I **suspect** the Olympic Council **has** a two-tiered vision for the future games: first, it ***tries*** to replace the current exclusive sponsorship; second, it ***wants*** to add as much capacity to its operation as possible to have more multiple partners.

Question 31

Recent research has shown that Artificial Intelligence learns a natural algorithm as if <u>a human being</u> at a surprisingly fast speed.

A) NO CHANGE
B) a humankind
C) a human being does
D) as fast as human being learns

| RULE #31
Hint:
If-clause | "If' is a Conjunction that Requires a Subject and a Verb.

The correct answer is C

Choice D is wrong because "as fast as" can't link to "as if" |

Question 32

In a utopian socialism labeled by Henri de Saint-Simon, both rulers and subjects define themselves <u>as the leader of the society</u>.

A) NO CHANGE
B) like the leaders of the society
C) as the leading people of the society
D) as the leaders of the society

RULE #32 Hint: Agreement	The Antecedent Agreement The correct answer is D. 'leader' has to be plural 'leaders' to modify "the rulers and subjects." C) is wordy error "leading people" => "leaders"

Question 33

Meticulous analysis as well as the clinical researches of Parkinson's disease <u>reveal that the parts of the symptoms are markedly similar to Down syndrome.</u>

A) reveal that parts of the symptoms are markedly similar to that of Down syndrome
B) have revealed that the parts of the symptoms are markedly similar to Down syndrome.
C) has revealed that the parts of the symptoms are markedly similar to Down syndrome.
D) reveals that the parts of the symptoms are markedly similar to those of Down syndrome.

RULE #33 Hint: Agreement	As well as/ Together with / Along with Are Not A Conjunction The correct answer is D. The subject is "analysis, not "analysis as well as the clinical researches." Since "analysis" is a singular, the verb has to be a singular "reveals." Choice C is wrong because "the parts of the symptoms" should be compared to those of (the parts of) "Down syndrome." The original sentence compares "the parts" with the "Down syndrome."

Question 34

Of the two pictures, neither the main underground reservoir in the upper valley nor the five auxiliary reservoirs on the ground level <u>are built completely satisfactory.</u>

A) are built completely satisfactorily.
B) is built completely satisfactorily.
C) are built completely with satisfaction.
D) is built completely with satisfaction.

RULE #34 Hint: Correlative Conjunction	In "Neither ~ Nor," The Subject Is Placed After "Nor." The correct answer is C. If a subject after nor is singular, the verb has to be singular. Do not concern about a noun after "neither." "the main underground reservoir" is not the subject, but <u>"the five auxiliary reservoirs"</u> is. Choice A is wrong because adverb "completely" cannot modify another adverb "satisfactorily"

Question 35

Cindy cherished the moment of the day when <u>her and her mother Caroline met</u> the president of Walmart in recognition of the best employees of the year ceremony.

A) she and her mother Caroline met
B) her and her mother Caroline had met
C) she and her mother Caroline have met
D) her and her mother Caroline will meet

RULE #35 Hint: Pronoun	"When" is Conjunction and should be Connected to a Subject. The correct answer is A. Option B) and D) are incorrect because "her" is objective pronoun. Choice C is wrong because the tense in both clauses between "when" should be the same. "cherished" is the past tense, so is "met."

Question 36

The disgruntled shopper had a <u>tendency to claiming</u> a refund for the goods he fully used, perhaps out of expectation at having to receive courtesy gift cards in the past.

A) NO CHANGE
B) tendency to claim
C) intention of claiming
D) intention to claim

| RULE #36

Hint: Idiom | Noun that Must Use To-Infinitive Clause
The correct answer is B.
As introduced in Rule #4, the word "tendency" has the future concept. So the proper idiomatic preposition must be "to," which indicates the future action.' Choice A is wrong because "to+ base verb" is the right form, not "to+Verb~ing (gerund)."
Choice D is wrong because it changes the meaning. |

Question 37

Korean filmmaker Kim Sun Tak is similar to Alysia Syndayun in his use of ethnic backgrounds, <u>but unlike his film</u>, she dwells on the religious aspects of her film characters

A) NO CHANGE
B) but unlike him,
C) ; however, unlike his film,
D) but unlike the film he directed,

| RULE #37
Hint:
Comparison | The Usage of Unlike for Comparison

The correct Answer is B
In the original sentence, "unlike his film" is compared with "she.
"The sentence has two options to fix the issue: "unlike his film, her film" or "unlike him, she" |

Question 38

Donald Trump has received many complaints about his recent Republican presidential nomination speech, which some audience condemn <u>to be extreme</u>.

A) to have been extreme
B) to be extremely
C) as extreme
D) as to have been extreme

| RULE #38
Tense | The Past Tense for To-Infinitive Clause

The correct answer is A.

The main sentence indicates that Donald Trump has already received complaints. "to be" is used for a future action, which creates an impossible situation. The audience can only condemn to react to what happened already in the past, not the other way around. |

Question 39
The mutual relationship between the 2016 Brazil Olympic organizer and its sponsors <u>are</u> truly symbiotic, for neither can promote activities without each other.

A) is truly symbiotic
B) is based on a true symbiotic relation
C) are in true symbiotic relations
D) are nothing but truly symbiotic

RULE #39	Finding Subject
Hint:	The correct answer is A
Agreement	The "relationship" is the only subject, which is singular. Any word (s) that comes after the preposition—"between" in this sentence—is not a subject.
	Choice B is wordy and redundant.

Question 40
As the challenger throbbed in, the UFC heavyweight champion cringed, <u>the challenger's blowing-out-punch more strong,</u> and winding up the champ's last-ditch effort.

A) the challenger's blowing-out-punch more stronger
B) the challenger's blowing-out-punch more strongly
C) the challenger blew out punch stronger
D) the challenger blew out punch stronger

RULE #40	Modifier + Adverb
Hint:	The correct answer is B
Modifier	With a one-syllable word or a word ending in -y or –ly, add the suffix -'er' to form a comparative phrase (e.g., cheap to cheaper). For more than one syllable, use 'more' to create the comparative phrase (e.g., expensive to more expensive).
	In this sentence, however, all the options contain comparative "more," which should have been "stronger," instead of "more stronger," leading us to think of something else.
	The only option available is to convert the adjective "strong" to the adverb "strongly." Choice C, D are incorrect because the preceding clause "the UFC heavyweight champion cringed" does not have a conjunction. To avoid the comma splice error, it should remain as a phrase like A or B.

Question 41
Clearly, the products <u>will have been less appealing</u> if the head designer had not tried to disperse the design concept in YouTube.

A) will be less appealing
B) would be less appealing
C) would have been less appealing
D) might be less appealing

RULE #41 Hint: Tense	Past Perfect Tense for Conditional "If-Clause"
	The correct answer C.
	Because If-clause contains "had not tried", the past perfect tense, the main clause should also contain the past perfect "would have"

If clause (conditional clause)	Main clause (consequence)
If + past perfect (had + p.p)	Perfect conditional (would have/could have/ should have/must have/might have/ may have)
ex) If Jason had seen the accident,	He would have been fainted

Question 42

The amiable relation <u>between Jason and I ended</u> as soon as we each moved out on our own.

A) between Jason and me ended
B) between Jason and myself ended
C) between Jason and I end
D) between Jason and me would end

RULE #42 Hint: Pronoun	Use Objective Pronoun after Preposition
	The correct answer is A
	The pronoun after the preposition must be objective ("me" in this sentence), "Not Subjective "I".
	Choice D is wrong because the model verb "would," implies the repeated action in the past.

Question 43

<u>Being canceled</u> the job interview appointment that the company mailed to participate, Jason never canceled another job interview again.

A) Canceled
B) Canceling
C) Having canceled
D) After he made a cancellation on

RULE #43 Hint: Tense	The correct answer is C
	The verb in the main sentence is past tense "canceled," and the subordinating clause indicates that Jason canceled some job interview before this job interview, showing a clear time shifting. In that case, the past perfect tense "Having + P.P" should be applied. "Having canceled" means "After Jason had canceled."
	Option D) "made cancellation" is wordiness error.

Question 44

In a world _that the government has less and less control_ to terrorism, cold comfort has become a normal trend now.

A) in which the government has control less

B) where the government has less and less control

C) that the government has no control

D) that the government has significantly less and less control

RULE #44	Where vs. That
Hint:	
Place	The correct answer is B
Adverbial	
	"where" and "that" should not be used interchangeably.
	For option A, "in which" and "where" are interchangeable, which makes both of them correct. However, option A changes the original meaning by focusing on "controlling less to terrorism" than "less control."
	For options C and D, "that" can be used only when "a world" requires a modifier as a subject or object in the main clause.
	In a situation when a context indicates a clear place adverbial phrase like "in a world" "where" should be used.

Question 45

Because airplane travels allow people to reach around the world drastically faster and more convenient, some have claimed the concept of borderline _is radically different from earlier times._

A) NO CHANGE

B) is radically different from that of earlier times

C) is drastically and radically different than that of earlier times

D) is drastically different than that in earlier times

RULE #45 Hint: Comparison	In Comparison, Even a Tiny Insignificant Preposition should be Equally Compared
	The correct answer is B. "the concept of borderline" is compared with "the earlier times". Choice C is wrong because drastically and radically are redundant. Choice D is wrong because the preposition "in" instead of "of" is used. Also, "different from" is the correct idiom. HARDER EXAMPLES Incorrect: Some experts I spoke with said that a self-driving car population is closer at hand than one populated with trucks. Correct: Some experts I spoke with said that the ***future populated with self-driving cars*** is closer at hand than ***one populated with trucks***. Incorrect: Sometimes, the mysteries about Elvis Presley is more cryptic than Shakespeare. Correct: Sometimes, the mysteries about Elvis Presley is more cryptic than ***those about*** Shakespeare.

Question 46

Ford's first vehicle Model A, which was first owned by Ernest Pfennig, a Chicago dentist, <u>and capable of</u> a top speed of five miles per hour.

A) and capability of
B) and capable to
C) was capable of
D) was able to provide a capability of

RULE #46 Hint: Verb	Missing Verb The correct answer is C
	The original sentence does not contain the main verb. Choice D is wordy. In a complex form of statement like above, by simply covering up the non-restrictive modifier (inessential information offset by a pair of commas) you can drastically reduce the sentence complexity. That is, you can forget about ", which was first owned by Ernest Pfennig, a Chicago dentist," and try to find the subject and the verb.

Question 47

When Clarence Anglin escaped the Alcatraz prison on a handcrafted rubber boat in June 11, 1962, with two other inmates, John Anglin and Frank Morris, _he had realized that he_ _had left_ a note for a destination under his mattress.

A) NO CHANGE
B) Clarence had realized that Frank had left
C) he realized that John had left
D) Frank realized that John left

RULE #47 Hint Pronoun + Tense	Ambiguous Pronoun + Tense
	The correct answer is C.
	When two or more people with the same gender are in one sentence, it is necessary to identify who the second person is.
	In this sentence, choice C is correct because "he" in the main clause obviously indicates Clarence, which implies options D won't work. For options A and B, "had realized" is the past perfect, which means Clarence had realized even before the escape (the past tense "realized"), making an impossible situation.

Question 48

That women and black people _have to be given the enfranchisement were_ considered a radical idea in the eighteenth-century America.

A) have to be given the enfranchisement were
B) has to be given the enfranchisement were
C) have to be given the enfranchisement was
D) has to be given the enfranchisement was

RULE #48 Hint: Verb	A Package Information "That-Clause."
	The correct answer is C.
	A package information using a That clause is considered as a singular subject. Therefore, the verb has to be singular.

Question 49

The concerned parents were anxious to see if their teenage children _had drove_ the parents' vehicles recklessly.

A) had driven
B) had driven
C) have drove
D) drive

| RULE #49
Hint:
Verb | Irregular Verb
The correct answer is B.
Drive -> drove -> driven.
Please refer to the Appendix at the end of the last chapter. |

Question 50

Though the board members' criteria to select a new CEO for the company <u>were both</u> systemic <u>as well as</u> meticulous, the majority stockholders followed their own preference, thereby stifling the upcoming election.

A) NO CHANGE
B) was both systemic and
C) were both systemic as well as
D) were both systemic and

| RULE #50
Hint:
Conjunction | Correlative Conjunction
The correct answer is D.
The idiom "both ~ and" cannot be replaced with any other form.
"Criteria" is plural of criterion. |

Question 51

Concerned that recruiting students was challenging last year, the university announced several scholarship plans in order to <u>international students to be increased</u>.

A) NO CHANGE
B) to increase international students.
C) for the international students to be increased.
D) to increase international students and remove their concern.

| RULE #51
Hint:
Simplification | Choose an Active Voice instead of Passive.
The correct answer is B.
Options A, C are unnecessarily passive.
Compared to the answer B, option D is wordy. |

Question 52

Although the professor's promise " a completely open book test" suggested the final would be easy, students found it <u>not that simple</u> as they had expected.

A) not that simple
B) to be not that simple
C) not as simple
D) find it that simple

RULE #52 Hint: Comparison	As~As The correct answer is C. "As...As"is an idiom and can't be replaced with "that...as" Choice B is future tense, which should be the past. .

Question 53
The staff favored the new stock option plan, a scheme <u>the company's local divisions, rather than the reluctant head office, to decide</u> how best to allocate profit equally.

A) NO CHANGE
B) that the company's local divisions, rather than the reluctant head office, decides
C) in which the company's local divisions, rather than the reluctant head office, decides
D) in which the company's local divisions, rather than the reluctant head office, decide

RULE #53 Hint: Agreement	Subject-Verb Agreement In a complex form of statement like above, by simply covering up the non-restrictive modifier (inessential information offset by a pair of commas) you can drastically reduce the sentence complexity. That is, you can forget about <u>",rather than the reluctant head office, "</u> and try to find the subject and the verb The correct answer is D. "local divisions" (plural) cancels out options B and C, leaving A and D. Choice A becomes a verbless sentence.

Question 54
<u>Results of</u> the gloomy economic forecast in the upcoming fourth quarter sales, the CEO decided to sacrifice his perk, salary increase, and his merger plan.

A) NO CHANGE
B) Results by
C) Resulted by
D) Resulting in

RULE #54 Hint: Tense	Tense in Modifier The correct answer is C. The main sentence uses the past tense "decided." Therefore, the modifier must follow the same tense "resulted by"

Question 55
Without unanimity or no muted return, the UN security council in the meeting is entirely dependent upon the chairperson's final decision to send the UN peace corps to the conflicted region in Syria.

A) NO CHANGE
B) Neither unanimity or no,
C) Neither unanimity or,
D) Without unanimity or any,

RULE #55 Hint: Negative	Double Negative The correct answer is D. The preposition "without" is already negative. Having another negative "no" will cause a double negative error. Therefore, the option A is incorrect. Choice B and C are both idiomatic error. "Neither ….nor" is the correct idiom.

Question 56
Working with new people along with re-organizing the old employees to a new branch, are always a daunting task, especially when there is little consensus about the products it carries.

A) NO CHANGE
B) is always
C) always
D) always have been

RULE #56 Hint: Verb	Gerund as a Subject The correct answer is B. The gerund phrase is treated as a singular subject. *"along with" is not a conjunction. Therefore, whatever comes after "along with" is neither a subject affects the subject-verb agreement

Question 57
Those buyers who bought houses just before the subprime mortgage crisis in 2008 were either lucky or exceptional astute.

A) NO CHANGE
B) are neither lucky nor exceptionally astute
C) were not either lucky or exceptionally astute
D) were neither lucky nor exceptionally astute

RULE #57 Hint: Idiom	Guessing Tone (Positive-Negative) The correct answer is D. The sentence must be negative tone because those buyers who bought houses before the crisis were far from lucky. Therefore, choice A is incorrect. Choice B is using "are". It should be "were". Choice C is wordy. "not either" can be reduced to "neither"

Question 58

Some of the glacial sediment deposits support the evidence that the Ice Age <u>effected</u> every continent except South America.

A) effected
B) was affected
C) affected
D) inflicted

RULE #58 Hint: verb	Confusing word The correct answer is C. "affect" is commonly used as a verb, while "effect" is used as a noun. *please review the appendix after this chapter.

Question 59

The radiation emitted by high-intensity-discharge microwave oven is very effective in activating molecules; foods inside the oven, much like the way of electromagnetic waves that zap through the air from TV or radio <u>transmitters, are cooked or boiled safer and faster</u>.

A) NO CHANGE
B) transmits, and cook or boil safer and faster.
C) is transmitted as cooked or boiled safely and fastly.
D) transmitters, cook or boil safer and faster.

RULE #59 Hint: Agreement	Run-on The correct answer is A. Run-on sentence means a sentence that contains multiple independent clauses without having a proper conjunction Option A properly connects the subject "foods" and the verb "are cooked" Option B and C use transmitter as a verb. Option D uses active verb "cooked," making "foods cooked"

Question 60

The <u>Vancouver's Indian Reserves</u> was located in the University of British Columbia.
A) NO CHANGE
B) Indian Reserves in Vancouver were
C) Vancouver Indian Reserves was
D) Indian Reserve's Vancouver was

RULE #60 Hint: possessive	The Possessive Form Can't be used If the Noun Indicates the Title The correct answer is C. The noun used as a title is considered as a singular and can't be used as a possessive determiner.

Question 61

The initial estimation of safely disposing of the toxic wastes is roughly ten times what the Du Pont spent <u>to purchase it</u> in its factory

A) for purchasing it
B) for the purchase of it
C) to purchase its own system
D) to purchase them

RULE #61 Hint: Pronoun	Pronoun Without Antecedent The correct answer is C. The pronoun "It" or "them" cannot be used without a preceding antecedent.

Question 62

Michael Jorden, Shaquille O'Neal, and Charles Barkley, <u>each of these basketball players was awarded MVP more than once at the time they were playing.</u>

A) NO CHANGE
B) each of which basketball players were awarded MVP more than once at the time they were playing
C) each of these basketball players was awarded MVP more than once at the time each was playing
D) each of which basketball players was awarded MVP more than once at the time each was playing

RULE #62 Hint: Pronoun	Pronoun and Verb for "Each" and "Every" The correct answer is D. Each or Every is singular; therefore, the proper pronoun should be "she/he" and should use a singular verb "was." Therefore, options A, B are incorrect. Option C is a comma splice error. The answer D "which" functions as a conjunction and properly uses a singular verb "was" a singular pronoun "each".

Question 63

The theory of quantum mechanics that applies quantum correction <u>compliments classic physics.</u>

A) compliments classic physics
B) compliment that of classic physics
C) complements classic physics
D) complement that of classic physics

| RULE #63 | Confusing Word: Complement vs. Compliment |
| Hint: Words | The correct answer is C. |

Complement = fill the gap   Compliment = praise

Choice D is incorrect for two reasons: first, the subject "the theory" is singular; however, the verb "complement" is plural; second, "that of" is not comparing anything in the sentence. It is ambiguous and unnecessary.

Question 64

Some of the hypotheses that Charles Darwin established to explain the origin of species were <u>later rejected as inconsistent to</u> convergent and divergent evolution theories.

A) lately rejected as inconsistent for
B) lately rejected as inconsistent with
C) later rejected as inconsistent with
D) later rejected as inconsistent to

| RULE #64 | Confusing Word: Later vs. Lately |
| Hint: Words | The correct answer is C. |

"Lately" means recently.
The past tense "were" indicates the past occurrence, not the present. Therefore, options A and B are incorrect.

The correct idiom for the word "inconsistent" is "inconsistent with," which eliminates option D)

Question 65

<u>For we VIP customers receiving</u> extensive client care services seemed to be eagerly anticipating the courtesy programs at the mall.

A) NO CHANGE
B) For us, VIP customers receiving
C) For we VIP customers receiving
D) For us, VIP customers who have received

Question 66
Fully automated vehicles are a work in progress, an autonomous vehicle that drives without any human interaction, parks parallel along a narrow girder, and they will even send an emergency signal to the driver when it is required.

A) NO CHANGE
B) is capable of sending an emergency signal to the driver
C) even sending an emergency signal to the driver will be accomplished
D) sends an emergency signal to the driver

RULE #66 Hint: Parallelism	Parallelism The correct answer is D. "that drives, parks, and sends" are the correct form of parallelism. Options A and C break the parallel structure by including an independent clause. Option B is not only using the unnecessary word "is capable of" but also breaks the paralleling structure "that drives, parks, and is capable of"

Question 67
In the final exam, three identical questions appeared that had been miscalculated in the midterm test.

A) NO CHANGE
B) three questions appeared
C) three identical questions had appeared
D) three identical questions were appeared

RULE #67 Hint: Tense	Tense The correct answer is B. The midterm test should have been taken before the final. Therefore, the correct tense for "the final" should be past tense. .

Question 68
Novelist George Orwell's accounts of all animals are equal, but some animals are more equal than others begin with the author's allegory of the Russian Revolution and culminated with his reminiscence of his past.

A) NO CHANGE
B) and culminates
C) , culminating
D) and culminate

RULE #68   Parallel Present Tense in Descriptive (Narrative) Statement
Hint: Verb
            The correct answer is D.

            A descriptive statement such as a natural phenomenon or announcement uses the
            simple present tense.

            The original sentence is a narrative or descriptive statement that requires the simple
            present tense.

            The verb "begin" in non-underlined portion of the sentence indicates how the parallel
            structure should be maintained.

            Option A is past tense.
            Option B is incorrect because the subject "Orwell's accounts" is plural, while
            "culminates" is singular.
            Option C changes the parallel structure.

Question 69
The maid at the hotel asked, "is the room temperature right <u>for yourself and your family?"</u>

A) for yours and your family?"
B) for you and your family?"
C) for yourselves ?"
D) for your and your family?"

RULE #69   Reflective Pronoun "~SELF" Should Not Be Used Independently.
  Hint:
  Pronoun   The correct answer is B.
            Reflective pronoun (self) cannot be used alone and must have its antecedent.

Question 70
Every summer my parents invite their relatives, <u>those people come</u> for a family reunion.

A) who come
B) the people came
C) they come
D) which are invited over and come

RULE #70   Conjunction "Who"
  Hint: The correct answer is A.
  Redundancy Options B) and C) are comma splice error.
            Option D) Use "who" for people and also it is wordy.

APPENDIX:

Irregular Verbs
Subordinate Conjunctions That Requires Dependent Clause
Confusing Words

IRREGULAR VERBS

Stride	**strode**	**stridden**
strike	struck	struck / stricken
String	strung	strung
Strive	strove / strived	striven / strived
Sweep	swept	swept
Swim	swam	swum
Swing	swung	swung
T		
Tear	tore	torn
Throw	threw	thrown
U		
Undergo	underwent	undergone
Undertake	undertook	undertaken
Uphold	upheld	upheld
W		
Wake	woke / waked	woken / waked
Wear	wore	worn
Weep	wept	wept
win	won	won
Wind	wound	wound
Withdraw	withdrew	withdrawn
Withhold	withheld	withheld
Withstand	withstood	withstood
Write	wrote	Written

IRREGULAR VERBS

Reset	reset	reset
Rid	rid	rid
Ride	rode	ridden
Ring	rang	rung
Rise	rose	risen
Run	ran	run
S		
See	saw	seen
Seek	sought	sought
Sell	sold	sold
Send	sent	sent
Shake	shook	shaken
Shoot	shot	shot
Show	showed	shown / showed
Shrink	shrank / shrunk	shrunk
Sing	sang	sung
Sink	sank / sunk	sunk
Sit	sat	sat
Spin	spun	spun
Spring	sprang / sprung	sprung
Stand	stood	stood
Steal	stole	stolen
Stick	stuck	stuck
Sting	Stung	stung

Subordinate Conjunctions That Requires Dependent Clause

After	When	Whereas
Although	Whenever	Wherever
as	Because	Whether
Once	before	While
Provided that	Since	Why
Rather than	So that	Unless
Until	Whenever	Though
when	where	that
than	In order that	if

Confusing Words

Accept vs. Except	Accept (verb) - to receive Except (conjunction) - apart from
Affect vs. Effect	Affect (verb) - to influence Effect (noun) - result
Any vs Some	some - for positive statements any - for questions and negative statements,
Allusion vs. Illusion	Allusion (noun) - an indirect reference Illusion (noun) - a false idea
Beside vs Besides	Beside (preposition) - next to Besides (preposition) – additionally
Captivate vs Capture	Captivate (verb) –to attract something or someone. Capture (verb) - to take control of
Complement vs. Compliment	Complement (noun) - that brings to perfection Compliment (noun) – admiration
Career vs Carrier	Career (noun) – a job Carrier (noun) - person or thing that carries something
Elicit vs. Illicit	Elicit (verb) - to draw forth; evoke Illicit (adjective) - unlawful; illegal
Good vs Well	Good (adjective) Well (adverb)
Its vs. It's	Its (possessive pronoun) - belonging to It's (abbreviate form of it + is)
Fewer vs Less	Fewer – for a countable noun Less - for a measurable thing examples: Fewer students registered for the class. Less coffee means less caffeine

Confusing Words

Raise vs Rise	**Raise (verb) - to move upwards by someone or something**
	Rise (verb) - Something rises by itself
He's vs His	He's (abbreviate form of he is or he has.)
	His (possessive pronoun)
Most vs Mostly	Most (adjective) - almost all
	Mostly (adverb) – generally
Most vs The Most	Most (adjective) - almost all
Loose vs Lose	Loose (adjective) – something not firmly fixed
	Lose (verb) – to be unable to find
Your vs. You're	Your (adjective) - belonging to you
	You're (abbreviation of you + are)
Who vs. Whom	Who (subject pronoun)
	Whom (object pronoun)
Advice vs Advise	Advice (noun) - an opinion that someone offers. an uncountable noun, and always singular.
	Advise (verb) - to suggest something
Lay vs Lie	Lay (verb) - to put something down
	Lie(verb) - be in a resting position
Later vs Latter	Later (adverb) – a time in the future
	Latter (adjective) – the second one from two of something
Hard vs Hardly	Hard (adjective) – difficult
	Hardly (adverb) – almost not
For vs Since (Time)	For - a period of time.
	Ex) I have been living in Canada for 10 years.
	Since - a point in time (always followed by present perfect)
	Ex) since I graduated, I have never been to movies.
Except vs Expect	Except (preposition) - not including.
	Expect (verb) - something is likely to happen

I Could Of vs. I Could Have	I Could Of (incorrect form of I Could Have) Other incorrect forms: should of / would of
Precede vs. Proceed	Precede (verb) - to be before in time Proceed (verb) - to advance or go on
Principal vs. Principle	Principal (noun) - a governing officer at school Principle (noun) - a fundamental truth,
Site vs. Sight	Sight (noun) -a view, field of vision Site (noun) - a piece of land
Stationary vs. Stationery	Stationary (adjective) - not moving Stationery (noun) - writing materials
Than vs. Then	Than (conjunction) - the second element in a comparison Then (adverb) - of that time
Their vs. There vs. They're	Their (possessive pronoun) – of belonging to, made by, or done by them There (noun) - that place
Either ~ Or vs Neither ~ Nor	Either … or (for a positive statement) Neither ... nor (for a negative statement)
Discreet vs Discrete	Discreet (adjective) – careful Discrete (adjective) - separate
Decent Vs Descent	decent (adjective) – socially acceptable descent (noun) – going downwards
Data vs Datum	Data – plural Datum – singular
Council vs Counsel	Council (noun) - a group of people who make decisions Counsel (verb) - to give advice

About the author

San, for over 20 years of his career, worked in various educational industries. From college entrance consulting to teaching standardized tests such as SAT / ACT / IELTS / TOEFL / LSAT/ GRE, he has been helping numerous students to enter their top choice universities.

In fact, favoritism of College Board to high-level vocabularies and reading passages makes many high school students fearful and frustrated to SAT. But, despite of this fact, College Board most often than not follows unsurprising patterns—the patterns appear to be problematic and indeed are and will be an albatross around many, may students' necks—when they create SAT questions.

To create the questions and at the same time break the logics and patterns of SAT questions based on CollegeBoard's set-guidelines, San researched hundreds of Actual SAT tests released in the past 30 years.

Here, in this book, students can find how CollegeBoard exploits (?) SAT students by depending on a scenario remarkably similar to that of many questions for several decades.

San is currently living in North Vancouver, B.C. Canada, where he teaches—to further students' needs and realize their ambitions—and write books.

For enrollment through Skype lesson, please contact the author using his email: satvancouver@gmail.com

Dedicated to my wife, Eun Ju and my dog, Okong

23493524R00273

Made in the USA
San Bernardino, CA
26 January 2019